Lenny, Lefty, and the Chancellor

Lenny, Lefty, and the Chancellor

by

C. Fraser Smith

The Len Bias Tragedy and The

Search for Reform in Big-time College Basketball

The Bancroft Press ■ Baltimore, MD

ISBN 0-9631246-0-9
Library of Congress Catalogue Number 91-076815
Printed in the United States of America

For Eileen

And for
Alexandra, Anna, Emily, Jake, and Jennifer

Acknowledgements

For thoughtful reading, observations and suggestions, I have been reliant upon a number of friends and colleagues. I especially wish to thank my wife, Eileen, for her patience, sorely tested; Dr. David M. Brown for precious time stolen from titrations; Leslie Walker for proving the goal could be reached; Helen Winternitz for encouragement in the task she accomplishes herself so gracefully yet refers to as "shoveling cinder blocks;" Mark Hyman for his critical acuity and insistence on high standards; Marguerite and Joe Gallup for reliability and love where we need it most; Tim Phelps for consistent solicitude and generosity; Ann Sjoerdsma for countless deft improvements; Abe Bortz for being the reader I was hoping for; Patricia Meisol for her thoughts; Bill Salganik for suggested final touches that were fortuitous; and Bruce Bortz for, among many other things, a new definition of the publishing marketplace.

I am indebted also to those who afforded me time, observations and advance comments on the manuscript. Whatever errors of judgment and precision survive in this book are mine alone.

Contents

Introduction

When I was a kid in North Carolina, my father took me every year to the Dixie Classic basketball tournament at William Neal Reynolds Coliseum in Raleigh. The tickets were a Christmas present. The games were bigger and more exciting than the holiday itself. Everett Case, the man who brought showmanship and glitz to basketball in the Carolinas, was the coach of the host team, N.C. State. I remember Ernie Terrell's crew cut and two handed set shot. I remember the teams' discipline and control.

I wanted to play high school basketball in the worst way. When the gym at Pinehurst High School was closed on the weekends, which was always, I would let myself in by grabbing the front door handle with both hands and shaking hard until it opened. Many important championships were won in that gym -- by me, of course -- with shots taken from the corner with only seconds remaining. I was definitely a decent high school basketball player. With the help of a coach who spent time feeding me the ball, I revolutionized the sport in central North Carolina, no doubt scandalizing Ernie Terrell. I shot with one hand.

Football was important to me, too. Charlie Justice was then "the man" at Carolina. Every kid who played football in the south then, I suppose, wanted to be just like the shifty scatback the sportswriters called Choo Choo. I certainly did.

In one game for Pinehurst High School against arch rival Southern Pines, our team was on the verge of an upset. On the last play of the game, I slipped into the flat near the goal line. I was wide open.

The tailback, my good friend, Monk Gilliland, lofted me a pass. At the last minute, the ball was tipped by a lunging defender. The ball spun upward. My feet moved me toward it, I think, but not fast enough. Or did I freeze? The ball fell to the ground.

In my memory, though, it's still up there with the hang time of eternity, tantalizing in the cool evening air. I should have had it . . . the guy made a great play . . . I should have had it . . . what a great game . . , too bad somebody had to lose . . . I should have had it. In the remainder of my illustrious career, I made tipped balls a specialty. In fact, I can't remember ever missing another one. I knew they were a possibility and I was ready. Still, none of the later chances ever seemed quite as momentous.

Because of Charlie Justice (and low tuition), I went to the University of North Carolina. I was a freshman when Lenny Rosenbluth, Tommy Kearns, Joe Quigg and the others won the NCAA basketball championship in 1957 against Wilt Chamberlain's University of Kansas team. I still remember students jamming Cameron Street outside the Rathskeller during the celebration. (I think I was there. I know I *should* have been there.)

I tried playing college football at UNC. Didn't make it. Not fast or strong enough. Maybe I should have played basketball. I was a good basketball player. Shot with one hand.

In a nation of Walter Mittys, all of us imprisoned by the conviction we could have been star athletes given a few breaks, the spectacle of intercollegiate sports in turmoil is disturbing. At the University of Virginia, an NCAA faculty representative observed that many young men and women -- even many of those who do not harbor aspirations for the professional ranks -- allow athletics to divert them in ways that are damaging. So much time is spent practicing and competing that players reduce their chances of getting into graduate school, he said.

Peter Wolfe, a professor of mathematics at the University of Maryland, said a baseball player of average talent missed his final calculus examination last year because he was a shortstop on the university baseball team and had to be away at a game. On the makeup test, he scored an A. But it was a C he got for the course; in pursuit of groundballs and base hits, he had missed too much class work. "Apparently," Wolfe said, "this is a kid with some ability in math. Does it matter that he got a C instead of an A in this course? You tell me."

The University of Maryland's former athletic director, Dick Dull, said of the best athletes he knew at College Park: "They don't look at their alternatives because they have this great athletic ability that is only showcased at Division I basketball and football schools. So they look past an area where they should be [academics] and go into an environment where they should not be [sports]. It would be like me going to medical school."

And Wayne Curry, a Prince George's County lawyer who represented a few college basketball players in trouble, offered this observation: "You think you're going to be Magic Johnson, but you're more likely to be unloading a truck someplace, particularly if you don't get educated."

The record will show many college athletes not getting educated. It will also show that, while the financial justification for big time intercollegiate sports is fading -- more and more schools finding it harder and harder to break even -- the big games are here to stay.

A faculty committee at the University of North Carolina wrote recently, "The American system of competitive intercollegiate sports is driven by motivations that are deeply rooted in the society and the culture, and very difficult for universities to resist . . . Recommendations to rescind the Louisiana Purchase would be less controversial than the proposal that any major university renounce intercollegiate athletics."

Nothing demonstrates that culture more poignantly than the events at College Park, Maryland, beginning five years ago with the death of Leonard K. Bias. The scandal touched off by that tragedy provides the clearest possible illustration of how money and emotion keep the big games going and largely unchanged in spite of every damaging disclosure. The Maryland story bound together the lives of a star athlete, a legendary coach, and a committed educator/scientist -- all three of them exemplary in their way, all three shaped by sports and the surrounding society.

When the news of Len Bias's death was first reported, I thought surely WAMU-FM in Washington had made a mistake. The initial reports were without detail, consisting only of the fact that Bias was dead. I thought Bias's father had died and been mistaken for his famous son. I told my wife that the radio was making a big mistake -- or a tragedy had occurred.

In the beginning, I thought this death was something of a payback for the unreality of money and fame conferred by sports. The big salaries and the signing bonuses and all the rest of it had always struck me as something akin to a free lunch. As hard as I had worked to be an athlete as a kid, I had no idea how hard a player like Bias had worked to get to the NBA draft. To some extent, I guess, my view of all this was trapped in the '50s. There was nothing free about what athletes got, even if the money they were paid had grown grotesquely large.

Watching the Bias story unfold at College Park, I was struck almost from the beginning by the image of John Slaughter. He seemed calm and in control, a measured presence in a maelstrom of media competition, of general curiosity and of a growing academic scandal. Slaughter seemed like a decent man, a man committed to the right values, a man concerned about kids -- the kind of man you want running your university. In the fall of 1986, I began work on an article about him for *Regardie's* magazine. While doing research for it, I decided to write this book.

The story of College Park and its major characters -- Len Bias, Lefty Driesell, John Slaughter -- seemed to embody much of what sports in America has become in the '80s and '90s. All of the money and showmanship were there on the surface; the frequently unmet promise of athletics was there as well. I wanted to write a book about a common American dream, a dream too often shattered. My general sense was that fans knew of such problems in a somewhat abstract way, without really understanding what was happening and why they didn't get fixed. I wanted to write a book that showed more concretely how all the participants are captured and kept in a runaway locomotive powered by money and emotion. I thought people might want to help find solutions if they knew more clearly what the problems were.

I also thought there might be a solution. And there *may* be one: somehow taking college games out of the marketplace. But I suspect that no solution will be complete, that balance will not be achieved, unless there is constant care and hard work on each university campus. Some universities, including the University of Maryland, have learned they *can* prevail over the thoughtless forces leading them to embarrassment and worse. Others have yet to learn. All should think about what happened at College Park since June 19, 1986.

A final thought: Just as I was completing this manuscript came news that NBA player Magic Johnson had contracted the virus causing AIDS. The nation's reaction illustrates again the degree to which this country looks to athletes for inspiration. Johnson's encounter with AIDS has led many to hope for an expanded effort at finding a cure, educating the public to the threat, and developing greater tolerance for the victims. Shock and sadness alone will not sustain us in those goals. The death of Len Bias and the record of reform efforts thereafter have taught us this: in both drug abuse and the academic life of college athletes, important objectives can be undermined, chiefly by the cost of reform and by the unspoken idea that the victims themselves are to blame. As the shock and sadness of the Johnson news inevitably wear off, and as the Bias tragedy recedes further into history, we ought to be asking ourselves this question: why does it take the death or the mortal affliction of basketball superstars to get us focused on problems that affect us all?

C. FRASER SMITH
Baltimore, Maryland
November 17, 1991

Chapter 1

Dreams

Len Bias felt a rush of panic as he opened his eyes. The time flashed at him like an accusation.

An event he had dreamed of most of his life was starting without him. He was due at Madison Square Garden's Felt Forum. The 1986 National Basketball Association draft, his draft, was beginning, and he wasn't there.

"Oh, no," he must have thought. "I'll never make it."

He tore out of the sheets, scrambled into his clothes and ran into the street. No cabs. He started to run, turning down one street and then another and another. But he seemed to be running in place. He ran faster. He ran until he was gasping for air.

Then he woke up.

It was 6 a.m. Still early. Plenty of time to make it. Plenty of time for the dream to come true.

Bias and his father, James, had checked into the Grand Hyatt Hotel in New York City the night before. The young man was excited and apprehensive. Though his basketball future had been carefully scripted down to the finest detail, he could hardly believe how fortunate he was.

The star basketball forward knew he would be taken by the Boston Celtics. He was the personal choice of Celtics General Manager Arnold "Red" Auerbach, the patriarch of professional basketball, builder of the National Basketball Association's most storied franchise and one of its best evaluators of talent and character. Auerbach didn't pick losers. The legendary coach had been watching Bias from the time he was in junior high school. He had been available, and clearly anxious, to advise Bias's parents and Bias's coach at the University of Maryland, Charles G. "Lefty" Driesell. And he had plotted to be sure Boston could draft Bias, the University of Maryland forward. The Cleveland Cavaliers had traded for the first choice and they would take the University of North Carolina's center, Brad Daugherty. Auerbach, whose Celtics had won the No. 2 pick in the NBA's lottery, would take Bias. All the moves had been planned.

A few hours after his nightmare, which he mentioned to several reporters, Bias walked into the arena with his father. The star wore a light gray suit with dark stripes and a dark tie loosely knotted. Fathers and sons sat in rows of chairs in front of a small stage. They were a most exclusive group. Not many of America's basketball dreamers have this moment: Only one in 10,000 high school players makes it to college and into the pros. The odds of going first or second in the draft, of being chosen by Auerbach, of being in Len Bias's shoes, were hardly calculable.

Cleveland followed its part of the script, taking Daugherty. Then it was Boston's turn. With excitement barely suppressed in his voice and a smile flickering over his round face, Auerbach said, "The Boston Celtics, after five seconds of deliberation, draft from the University of Maryland, Len Bias." Auerbach was laying the cornerstone of yet another disciplined Boston powerhouse, finding and signing another key player for another generation of haughty, intimidating and talented Celtics.

"We feel like Len Bias can make us a better team than we were this year, and that's saying something," Boston assistant coach Jimmy Rodgers told reporters. A few weeks earlier, Larry Bird, Dennis Johnson, Kevin McHale, Robert Parrish, Bill Walton, and their teammates had taken Boston to its 16th NBA championship.

After Auerbach spoke for Boston, NBA Commissioner David Stern beckoned Bias to the stage, and before he got there, someone handed him a bright, Kelly green baseball cap with Celtics splashed across the front in white script. He carried it onto the stage in his left hand. Later, for the photographers, he put it on the back of his head and turned at a kid-like angle. The picture ran in papers throughout the country. As the audience applauded, Stern congratulated him. Bias turned his head away slightly as if the words were too flattering. Stern found him poised and gracious.

Bias was living a modern American dream. He was the latest in basketball's series of Horatio Alger stories: A black kid of modest means who works hard and makes millions in the NBA. His name was being added to a list of stylish players that included Walt Frazier, Julius Irving, Magic Johnson, Michael Jordan, great players with bankable images. There were enough of these success stories, and the stories were so well-known, so widely communicated by games and by television commercials, that even fans may have assumed that good basketball players usually got jobs in the pros.

But only about 150 of the thousands of eligible collegiate players are drafted each year and no more than 50 are signed by NBA teams. Those who want young men to know these odds are in conflict as they preach the lesson of overcoming odds, of "making it," of turning big dreams into goals. The players that make it are young, elegant and often well-spoken. They buy houses and expensive cars for their mothers, and mansions for themselves. They wear championship rings, floor-length fur coats, gold chains and suits from the pages of *Gentleman's Quarterly*. Life is good. They are in control. No one was more in control than Len Bias.

By the time he was a 22-year-old senior at the University of Maryland, Bias had sculpted himself into a striking physical presence. Even among basketball players, athletes with superb bodies, he was extraordinary, a David of hoops. He was 6'8". He weighed 205 pounds. He had hard-muscled arms and shoulders as wide as a door. He could bench press 300 pounds. His vertical leap from a standing position was 38 inches, higher than a kitchen table, and almost half his own height. With a running start, he seemed to neutralize gravity.

Len Bias had fancied himself an NBA star for some time. He called his '77 Cutlass "my Porsche." For an official UM team photograph, he wore a gold choker as thick as a garden hose and he gave expensive jewelry to his girlfriend, including a necklace featuring his Maryland number, 34, and his last name spelled out in gold letters. He had borrowed $15,000 that summer on the strength of his impending pro contract. And he had leased a Datsun 300 ZX sports car, cobalt blue, with a T-top. On the wall of his dormitory room, he had hung pictures of a Porsche, a Lamborghini, and a full-sized photograph of himself in a Maryland Terrapins uniform -- three high-powered machines, Sally Jenkins, a *Washington Post* sportswriter, had observed. There was a sense of omnipotence about him, a growing self-image that, occasionally, must have made him feel invincible, indestructible.

When opponents or hecklers in the stands tried to distract him, he would smile at them, unaffected. He was above it.

"Too good," he would say, sinking shot after shot. "Nothing but cake and ice cream."

He was the best. He was going to be rich. He was going to be a champion. He was a driven worker, thoroughly committed to playing better than people thought he could. By the end of his last year at Maryland, most of the basketball world was convinced of his ability. He was unstoppable. Fortune and acclaim were flowing to him as smoothly as the free throws he flicked toward the basket in smooth, unerring lines.

Basketball Times editor Larry Donald, analyzing the basketball class of 1986, said Bias was the kind of solid citizen and hard worker Boston always recruited. Auerbach thought he had the attitude and temperament a young professional needed. He was not going to whine about playing time or about not starting. He knew he had a lot to learn. With all his accomplishments, his game was still improving.

He had finished his college career as Maryland's all-time leading scorer with 2,149 points. As a senior, he was named Atlantic Coast Conference player of the year for the second time. In the ACC, one of the most competitive and talent-rich leagues in the country, he had been the leading scorer his last two seasons, hitting double figures in 85 of his last 86 games. He was on virtually every All-American team.

Between his junior and senior years, he considered putting himself into the so-called hardship draft under which the NBA can ignore NCAA rules and take college players who have not used all their collegiate eligibility. But in the shaping, grooming, and regulating of talent in the NBA, such decisions are not made quickly. And Bias's progress was being watched from the highest vantage point. One evening during his junior year, he and his parents discussed their options over dinner with Auerbach. Driesell was there, too.

"I told them that if he came out in the draft then, he would not be drafted in the top 10," Auerbach told a reporter later. "I thought he would be around 15th. I told him, on the other hand, if he stayed in school for another year, he would be one of the top choices, certainly in the top seven, putting him in the lottery, and that we might have a chance to get him. He told me he would love that. He would love to play for the Celtics." Had he entered the hardship draft after his junior year, Boston most likely could not have gotten him. Its 1985 picks were just not as high as for the year after.

So, that was that. Bias went to Auerbach's basketball camp in Marshfield, Massachusetts, that summer and the Celtics' coaches, K.C. Jones, Jimmy Rodgers and Chris Ford, were as impressed as Auerbach.

Still, when the 1986 draft finally came around, the Celtics might have gone for Daugherty or William Bedford, a 7-foot center from Memphis State University. The Celtics were going to need a center soon. But Bedford had been involved in various rules infractions at Memphis State. He had what editor Larry Donald called a citizenship problem. Bias had no blemishes. He could be combative on the court, but coaches liked that. He was a family-oriented kid, a born-again Christian, a young man whose work habits impressed every coach who looked into his career. Just the kind of player Boston prided itself in finding, the Celtics coaches said. "I think the Celtics went for the sure thing," said Donald.

As they left the Forum on their way to the airport and a flight to Boston, reporters crowded around Bias and his father. "I'm happy. I'm in the NBA. What else can I say? At Maryland we had a great team, but we were always the dark horse. I think I could get accustomed to winning," he said with a smile. "To be able to play for Boston . . . that was a dream within a dream . . . What do I think of Larry Bird? What do *you* think of him?"

He was elated. He was also exhausted.

The pre-draft weeks had been as difficult as they had been thrilling. Immediately after the season, Bias had played in a round of barnstorming all-star games. Promoters sent limousines for him. He negotiated with an agent. He was examined by the New York Knicks and the Golden State Warriors.

The all-star games, the traveling, the interviewing, the one-on-one games with the coaches, the medical exams -- all were almost a needless exercise, given Boston's interests and his own. His mother noticed that the travel left him fatigued and annoyed. One day he wandered into the Columbia Park Recreation Center two blocks from his home looking for his friends. Bias often went back to the boxy gym to see his old coach, Lee Madkins, and his friend Brian Waller, who had played college basketball at Providence College. On this day, as they sat in the glassed-in office with the posters of NBA stars in their Nikes or Reeboks, Bias told Madkins it was humiliating to be picked over and examined by so many people he did not know.

"Even your fingernails," he told Madkins. It was not the first time he had been treated like a commodity. College coaches had gone over him with almost the same intensity four years earlier. There was simply less pretense now. He was an investment, a high-powered machine more expensive than a Lamborghini, no longer just a star. Money was involved, and people wanted to inspect the goods. He was expected to get through it on the promise of a big contract. But sometimes the promise was not enough. Madkins knew it was a tough time for him and he knew it was going to get worse. He hoped the young man would adjust.

On June 17, 1986, he became Boston's property. The Celtics had scheduled a press conference at the Blades and Boards Club, a restaurant at Boston Garden, named for the Bruins ice hockey team and for the Celtics.

"Every kid wants to play for the Celtics or the Lakers," Bias said. Of his relationship with Auerbach, he said, "I feel like I have another family up here." He had virtually pleaded with the Celtics to take him. Jan Volk, the club president, remembered meeting him a few months before the draft. They shook hands and Bias held on for long seconds while he made his pitch. Volk had never seen a player do that. The image of that moment stayed with him.

After the reporters were finished with him, Bias and his father kept an appointment with officials of Reebok International, the shoe and sports clothing company. Nike's basketball star was Michael Jordan of the Chicago Bulls. Larry Bird was with Converse. Bias would be the leaping billboard and shoe salesman for Reebok.

He and his father had flown to Boston with the young man's agent, Lee Fentress, a Washington lawyer and partner in Advantage International, a management firm specializing in the promotion of athletes. Over several years, Fentress expected to make as much as $500,000 in fees for the contracts he negotiated for Bias. The first of these endorsement deals meant $325,000 per year for Bias. Fentress also represented the player's coach. Driesell, too, was about to sign an endorsement deal with Reebok. He would receive as much as $500,000 over four years, about $400,000 for putting his Terrapins in the company's line, and another $100,000 if the Maryland team took their Reeboks into the Final Four, the pinnacle of each year's basketball competition among colleges, the semifinals of the 64-team tournament for the National Collegiate Athletic Association championship.

Fantasy and reality were coming together in front of them all, coach and agent and player. Bias's lifetime financial needs would be taken care of even before he signed a contract with the Celtics, even before he took his first shot in the NBA. Fentress thought the Celtics would pay him as much as $700,000 a year. Altogether, he would be wealthy before he was 23.

Reporters approached the young man as if he had just won the lottery, which in a way he had. What would he do with all the money? He would buy two Mercedes Benzes, he told them.

"Anyone who has seen the way Len dresses knows he doesn't need any help picking out a car," said his father. He had promised to buy a Mercedes for his mother. Every first-round draftee wants to buy a house or a fine car for his mother.

Basketball's latest salesman-athlete walked into Reebok's suburban Boston offices, past reception area walls covered with huge action photographs of its endorsers. The men and women of Reebok said Bias instantly seemed like a member of the family, as if he'd been with them for years. They were struck by what they called his charisma. During a reception later at the Royal Sonesta Hotel, James Bias noticed that children crowded around his son, peering up at him, with something akin to reverence.

For lunch that day, Bias had a burger and fries. The food got cold as the young star answered questions. Reporters smiled at his teenage tastes as if, suddenly, he should have been ordering steak tartar. He lingered at the "Star Trek" game in the company cafeteria. At home in Maryland, he liked to go to the malls to shop and to play the video games.

As the day wore on, the new millionaire told Fentress and a Reebok official that he was tired and wanted to call his mother. He was 22, a basketball prodigy in an Italian suit. Revered by children, he was little more than a child himself. His open face seemed locked in a sheepish smile. He walked in an up-on-your-toes, big-kid gait.

The walk was so free and childlike it made people smile. As macho as he took care to be on the basketball court, he could be studiously courteous and self-effacing away from it. He was called a role model, though, sometimes, his friends thought he had just become adept at playing *roles*. He was the charismatic consumer, the matinee idol, and he was hailed as the true student athlete.

With their promotional work finally done, the young star, his father and his agent flew out of Logan Airport in Boston at about 8:30 p.m. Bias left Boston with an armload of shoes and shirts and caps from Reebok and the Celtics for his brothers, Jay and Eric, and his sister, Michelle, and enough to share with his teammates.

They landed in Washington around 10. He drove his father home from the airport in his rented "Z." Then he headed for College Park, the university campus.

He had been close enough to home that his parents frequently drove to the campus with crock pots of stew and spaghetti for their son and his dormitory friends. Ballplayers were always hungry and, besides, Bias always wanted to see his family. They went to all the games. His friend, Adrian Branch, another Terrapin player, was envious of how often his friend's parents visited.

During summer school that year, he shared a suite in Washington Hall with five of his teammates. He was the unchallenged team leader. Freshman David Gregg, who had come up behind Bias at Northwestern High School, not far from College Park, was in awe of the older player. Now they were roommates. On occasion, Bias treated players of lesser ability as if they were pledges in a fraternity. Jeff Baxter, another of his roommates, was proud of his license to criticize the superstar without fear of rejection. They had a kinship. Baxter was one of the better players and, like Bias, he was a sharp dresser, two of the clear qualifications for leadership. Bias called him Jazzy Jeff and GQ, short for *Gentleman's Quarterly*. And there they were in summer school as usual, even the seniors, making up credits missed or failed during the season.

Bias was protective of his friends, Baxter said. He was alert to the outside world's willingness to lionize Len Bias while treating his relatively anonymous teammates as if they were not there. He always introduced them to reporters, or store clerks, or fans.

Bias and another of his roommates, Keith Gatlin, had been a team within the Terrapin team: Gatlin was the point guard who fed long looping passes to Bias, who turned them into crashing dunks. The other roommates were Terry Long, a mediocre player whose basketball talents seemed to lapse at Maryland, and Phil Nevin, an awkward freshman center who stood nearly 7 feet tall, the only white player in the suite.

Bias strode into the dorm room from Boston like a young Caesar home from the Gallic Wars. He found some of his roommates and a few football players eating steamed crabs. He sat on his bed, Long and Gatlin said, describing his day, a day they had all imagined for themselves.

"He was talking about going to rookie camp and going one-on-one with Larry Bird. He was the happiest guy in the world," Gatlin said later.

Bias had called his girlfriend, Madelyne Woods, from Boston. She worked as a summer intern at WUSA-TV in Washington. That night she finished work at 10:30 and drove to College Park, where she was a student in the journalism department. Over the previous few months, she and Bias had gone out frequently, and he had shared his good fortune with her, giving her presents like the necklace with his number. They talked for about 15 minutes, and Bias walked with her to the parking lot.

He returned to the room but left again quickly, announcing, "I've got to drain my lizard." His friends thought he had a date.

But an hour later, he came back to the suite with Brian Tribble, a close friend and former student at the university who had once played junior varsity basketball there. A decent athlete, Tribble, too, had dreamed of the NBA until he injured his knee in a motorcycle accident. Like Bias, he had a trophy case full of basketball mementoes.

In a lawsuit he brought as a result of his motorcycle injuries, Tribble asked for, but did not receive, $1 million in compensation for lost income, the equivalent of a career in professional basketball. Tribble was not even a varsity player at Maryland. But the NBA dream is intense and deeply internalized by young men of modest ability who see themselves becoming Magic or Michael. Tribble had worked as a warehouse laborer, a mail handler, and a clerk at Howard University Hospital in Washington.

He had become one of Bias's closest friends. They worked out together, jogged and, occasionally, went to nearby nightclubs, Chapter II and Classics.

At 6 feet, Tribble was shorter than most of his basketball playing friends, but he had the build of the weight-lifter he was. He owned a Mercedes and three pit bulls he named Assassin, Lady Devour and Tan Man. He lived in a $600-a-month apartment.

He and Bias left quickly on a beer run. They drove to Town Hall Liquors, a small, gray-shingled bar and package store on the northern fringes of the campus. Stacked floor to ceiling with cases of beer, it was located just across the street from a McDonalds on Route 1. McDonalds provided bus service back and forth to the nearby campus on what it called McBus. Students got to the liquor store and its adjoining lounge on their own.

It was just after 1 a.m. when Bias walked into the store. Tribble waited in the car. Bias was still wearing the Italian suit and the same white shirt he had worn for the draft. He had removed his tie. Michael Cogburn, the manager, noticed his gold necklace and a gold bracelet with diamonds and LEN, in gold letters. Everyone noticed his clothes and his jewelry.

"He smelled so good," one of the young women clerks remembered.

Bias bought two six-packs of Private Stock Malt Liquor and headed back toward Washington Hall. As they got back onto the campus, Bias and Tribble passed a campus policeman they knew. The three of them talked about Bias's contract with the Celtics and the draft.

It was party time, they told the policeman, who volunteered that when he celebrated, he liked a good Cognac like Hennessey. So the star and his friend turned their car around and went back to the liquor store. Again, Bias went in alone and asked for a small bottle of Hennessey.

This time, Michael Cogburn spoke to his famous customer.

"You're big money now," Cogburn said. "You might as well buy the big bottle. You don't have to worry about money do you?"

"No, I guess not," Bias said. From a handful of bills, he pulled off a twenty for the $18 bottle.

Cogburn hadn't meant to push the brandy. It was just a way of recognizing the player's new status. Everything was moving faster now.

Cogburn had seen Bias in the store about once a week for months and had purposely treated him like any other customer. The first time Bias came in that night, Cogburn had said nothing. A second opportunity, though, he couldn't resist, not on the day that Bias had been drafted by the Boston Celtics.

"I'm a Celtics fan," he said. "Could I get your autograph?"

Bias smiled and obliged.

"I've got my new number, 30," he said. He wrote "Len Bias" in a strong, clean hand as strong and graceful as his game. He added "30" underneath the name. Cogburn walked him to the door.

"Take care," the store manager said.

"You bet," Bias answered.

He and Tribble got back to Washington Hall at about 2:30 in the morning. Bias swung through the door, commanding his sleeping roommates to join him.

"Wake the fuck up," he shouted, banging on Long's bedroom door. "We're going to celebrate." Long put on a pair of shorts, went to Gregg's room and woke him. He did not disturb Gatlin. Nevin and Baxter were out.

Celebration time in the past had meant cocaine time. The foursome, Bias, Long, Tribble, and Gregg, had had cocaine parties several times earlier that year in the dormitory room and in Tribble's apartment. Long said he had first used the drug when Bias walked into his room, tossed a folded dollar bill on the bed, and, according to Long, said, "Try this." Inside the bill was $50 worth of cocaine. Long thought Bias approached him because he knew Long had smoked marijuana. Away from the demanding glare of his celebrity, away from teachers and parents and coaches, the team captain, the can't-miss millionaire, took the kind of chances some other students took.

That Len Bias had tried cocaine was not an unreasonable idea to his friends and coaches. They knew the temptations would be there for him, perhaps even more intensely than for other students. Driesell and others warned him repeatedly. Still, the thought that he would succumb to drugs ran counter to the heroic, All-American folklore that had developed around him: He was so concerned about physical conditioning, people said, that if he downed even a single beer, he would promptly run it off, even if it was in the middle of the night. His coaches warned him to stay away from drugs and he, in turn, was credited with preaching that same gospel to younger kids. What he said and what he did were different.

Maryland's athletic department recognized these contradictions in its players. The university was aware that some players had used drugs. A drug testing program was instituted. The strategy was surveillance and education about the effects of drugs. The university proudly announced that it was doing this, doing it before the NCAA ordered such programs, doing it before many other schools had a plan. But the testing system had gaps: Tests were infrequent and there was no visual observation of the athlete providing a urine sample; the gaps, according to Tim Gilmour, university vice chancellor, stemmed partly from the university's fear of an American Civil Liberties Union legal challenge. The players, some of whom reportedly got around the tests in various ways, called the program a joke.

Long went to the refrigerator to get a beer. As he walked back into his bedroom, he saw a mound of white powder on a small mirror that had been taken from the wall. What he saw could have filled a coffee cup. It was an unheard of quantity for one party, more than sufficient to celebrate even this fabulous moment in a young man's life.

"Where'd this come from?" Gregg asked.

"From the bottom of a stash," one of them said.

Long kept soda straws -- from McDonalds -- in a yellow cup on his desk. His girlfriend liked to use straws when she had a soda. Straws from the All-American burger joint would serve well enough for cocaine.

Bias and his friends passed the mirror among themselves as if it were a polished serving tray. After about an hour, someone entered the apartment, walked down the hall and knocked on the door. It was Jeff Baxter. He had been out when Bias returned from Boston. When he walked into the dormitory room later, Baxter said his friend's monumental good fortune, his attainment of what Baxter and every ballplayer wished for, became real to him: he saw the Reebok shoes and shirts and hats on his teammate's bed. Coaches had told Baxter four years earlier that he would be a No. 1 NBA draft choice. He had known for some time it would not happen. At least it was happening for Len.

"Boston Celtics," he said to himself. He stood for a moment, trying to absorb the wonder of it.

Before letting him in, Tribble slipped the mirror and its contents into a drawer. Baxter could not understand why anyone would use drugs. Even if you were living in South Africa, he said, even under that kind of pressure, he couldn't see using drugs. So his friends hid their cocaine from him.

Gregg, Long and Tribble left the room. Baxter and Bias talked for about 45 minutes.

The young men talked about the draft, the Celtics, Larry Bird and what life would be like in the NBA. Baxter saw stress and change in his friend. Throughout their careers at Maryland, people who could hardly be described as friends had clutched at them. "Can you get me some shoes? Some shorts?" they would say. They wanted a piece of the big time, some shorts or shirts with the Maryland logo. Bias would try to oblige. He didn't want anyone to think he was leaving them behind. And now again it was all moving to a new level.

"The life he was going to lead was going to be so crazy. He needed somebody who didn't want anything from him," Baxter said. "He had all these agents, people trying to be his friend."

Baxter's whole family was close to Bias. The two friends liked to ride over to the Baxter home in southeast Washington to cook breakfast. On occasion, Bias would nag Baxter until he agreed to call his mother so Bias and Mrs. Baxter could talk.

Around 3:15, Baxter went to bed. He had a class the next day. And the four young men again bent over the mirror, seeing nothing in their reflected revelry to slow their pace.

Eventually, though, Tribble got up to walk to the bathroom. He wobbled.

"We're all fucked up," one of the four said.

And someone warned Bias. Wasn't he overdoing it?

"I'm all right," he said. "I'm strong. I'm a horse."

Only a few people, people like Baxter, could make him listen. Even Baxter had called him horse. He had carried his team. Horse became a way of flattering and needling him at the same time.

"No one has to tell me when to feed the horse," Keith Gatlin, the Terrapin point guard, had told a reporter.

"Hey, horse," they'd shout at him for no reason, "Get over here." They were recognizing his strength and talent without doing it directly. Sometimes Baxter would whinny at him.

At times, Bias seemed to buy it. He displayed a haughtiness that elbowed his shyness aside. His high school coach, Bob Wagner, wondered if the adulation heaped upon him, the speed of his life, the impending fortune had allowed him to believe that nothing could touch him.

When Bias got up to go to the bathroom, he stumbled, and one of his friends suggested he sit down for a moment. He did. He put his head back on the bed. And then, his body began to shake in hard, quick, lurching arcs.

Long, who had taken a course in cardiopulmonary resuscitation, thought Bias was having a seizure. Long was right, Tribble was sure.

Long took his scissors, the same ones he had used to shorten the straws, and put the wide end in Bias's mouth so he wouldn't swallow or bite his tongue. The seizures stopped. They eased him onto the floor. But then the convulsions started again. Long started mouth-to-mouth resuscitation. Gregg held his idol's legs as if that might stop the seizure.

Tribble called his mother. His sister, Priscilla, had epilepsy, so Loretta Tribble had some experience with seizures. She told her son to call the paramedics.

At 6:33 a.m., as Long continued to work over his stricken friend, Tribble dialed 911 and spoke to an emergency operator.

"I'd like to have an ambulance come," Tribble said when the emergency operator answered.

The operator asked him for the room number.

"It's 1103 Washington Hall," he said, his voice slow and sluggish. "It's an emergency. It's Len Bias and he just went to Boston and needs some assistance."

"What are you talking about?" the operator asked.

"I'm talking about, someone needs, Len Bias, needs help," Tribble said.

"Well, it doesn't matter what his name is," the operator said. "What's the problem?"

Suddenly, the door-opening power of the star's name seemed to be a liability. People were always calling in false reports about famous people. Tribble wondered if the operator thought the call was a hoax.

"He's not breathing right," Tribble said. He may not have been breathing at all. Long was trying to revive him.

"What's the address?"

"1103 Washington Hall on Maryland University's campus."

"Washington Hall?" the operator asked.

"Yes, sir."

"What's your name?" the operator asked.

"My name is Brian."

"Brian what?"

"Tribble."

"Tribble?"

"Yes, sir."

"What's your phone number, Brian?"

"I, I'm in Len Bias's room. I don't know the phone number here."

"What's the room number?"

"1103."

"1103?"

"Yes, sir."

"Okay. What's . . . It's just Washington Hall. What's the address of Washington Hall?"

"It's, I don't know, it's no address," Tribble said. "It's just Washington Hall. Come up by Hungry Herman's and go straight up there and it's on the right-hand side, sir. Please come as soon as you can. It's not a joke."

"Okay, Washington Hall, apartment number 1103."

"Yes, they're giving him mouth to mouth. You can hear it now," Tribble said, his voice higher in tone and more urgent.

"Hear 'em? This is Len Bias. You have to get him back to life. There's no way he can die. Seriously, sir. Please come quick."

"Okay, Washington Hall and apartment, um, room number 1103, right?"

Tribble said it was right.

The operator checked again: "That's one thousand one hundred and three?"

"Uh-huh. Eleven-o-three, one thousand one hundred and three."

"All right, we'll have an ambulance out, all right?"

"Excuse me?"

"We'll have an ambulance out."

With the rescue squad on the way, Gregg took the mirror and the remaining cocaine into another room of the suite. He searched through the trash for something to put the cocaine into. He found a cookie bag. As he poured, about half of what remained of the cocaine missed the bag. Gregg got cleaning powder like Carpet Fresh and rubbed the spilled cocaine into the carpet. He then returned to Long's room and handed the cookie bag to Tribble.

At the College Park fire station two-tenths of a mile away, volunteer fireman David Purcell's rescue team was dispatched to deal with "one not breathing" at Washington Hall. They got there in three minutes.

With the paramedics on the way, Gregg woke Baxter.

"Lenny's in the other room dying," Gregg said. He gave the news in a flat tone. He might have said, "Lenny's in the bathroom brushing his teeth."

"If he had been talking about me," Baxter said, "I'd have said, 'Well, maybe.' I'm kind of small. But Lenny was a horse. I thought I was dreaming. Sometimes in the morning I have trouble distinguishing between dreaming and reality.

"Then I looked in the room. I saw him, and I believed it."

Purcell walked in and saw Long bent over the still figure of Bias. The fireman recognized them both. In fact, he recognized everyone in the room but Tribble. It was the usual emergency scene atmosphere, he thought, except that he knew everyone and everyone was 6-feet-8-inches tall. The medics' routine was slower than normal because the patient was so big and the bedroom so small that they could not get their equipment in place for a few moments. They finally moved Bias into the living room.

"Did he take any drugs?" Purcell asked.

"Beer," Long said.

No one mentioned cocaine. Long and Gregg said later they withheld the information because they wanted to protect Bias's reputation. They weren't protecting themselves, they said. They knew they were in trouble. They didn't want to be in more trouble. It was a gamble that may have risked their friend's life to save his image. But they were sure he wouldn't die. He was a horse.

Gatlin, awake now, stood in a corner, a hand over his mouth as the emergency team worked. Purcell and the other emergency team members found no pulse, no electrical activity in the heart, no sign of life.

With their procedures completed, the medics put Bias on a stretcher and wheeled him to the rescue wagon. He was taken to Leland Memorial Hospital, in Hyattsville a few miles south of the campus on Route 1. Fireman Purcell, who returned to the room for a jacket he left behind, found Long putting beer cans, a pizza box and other trash in a garbage bag. He and Baxter, Nevin, Long and Tribble drove to the hospital. Several other players who lived in adjacent dormitories followed them.

A nurse at the hospital called Driesell, who was just back from the walk he took every morning with his wife, Joyce. At first, the nurse refused to tell the coach which of his players was stricken. He called back, demanding information. He was told then that it was Bias and that the player's parents, who had been called by Gatlin, were at the hospital and wanted him to join them. He and his wife left immediately. They found the Biases and waited with them as doctors worked to revive their son.

Driesell also called Lee Fentress. A former assistant U.S. attorney and campaign aide to Robert F. Kennedy, Fentress made a call to the Senate office of Edward M. Kennedy. He wanted Kennedy to help him arrange for a helicopter to transport a physician to Leland or to remove Bias to another hospital. A heart transplant was considered.

But it was too late.

Leonard Kevin Bias, All-American, magnificent horse, stylish dude, kid next door, was declared dead at 8:55 a.m. on June 19, 1986. He had proved you can make it beyond all imagining and still not have it made. The dream of a life in the NBA was just a dream after all.

Chapter 2

Crisis

On June 19, 1986, Candy DiPietro headed for work in a daze. When she saw her brother's car coming from the other direction, she stopped and waited for him for him to pull alongside, rolling down her window.

The two of them shared a $700 membership in the Terrapin Club, Maryland's athletic booster organization. They went to all the games and took turns wearing the small terrapin lapel pin. They often stopped for a moment in the morning near their homes in Laurel to exchange family news or to hash over the previous night's game.

"Mike," Candy said, "Lenny Bias is dead." A heart attack was the reported cause.

"No way," her brother thought. "A kid like that doesn't die of a heart attack."

Has to be drugs, he thought.

University of Maryland Chancellor John Slaughter was in Bethesda that morning for a meeting of the Sovran Bank board of directors. As he stepped off the elevator, a secretary hurried over to him with a pink while-you-were-out telephone message slip. She had printed URGENT across its top and bottom. Bud Edwards, the university's public affairs director, was trying to reach him. Slaughter dialed the number.

"I hope you're sitting down," Edwards said. "Len Bias has been taken to the hospital. He's in pretty serious shape." The hospital official to whom Edwards had spoken thought he had suffered a heart attack.

"They don't think he's going to make it," Edwards said.

"Oh, my God," Slaughter said.

He looked at his watch. It was 8:55 a.m., the precise moment, he learned later, that Bias was declared dead. It was a coincidence that offered a fixed point of reference in a world that seemed suddenly to be veering out of control.

An electrical engineer, a former director of the National Science Foundation, and one of the nation's highest ranking black university administrators, John Slaughter was College Park's chief executive officer and its No. 1 basketball fan. He saw himself as a mentor to Bias and several other players. On the campus, he had talked with them frequently, and a few had called at his house.

Slaughter walked down the hall to a room where he and the other bank directors chatted and had coffee before their meetings. He told his friend Peter O'Malley, a former member of the university's Board of Regents and an influential Maryland lawyer, what had happened.

"I have to get back to the campus," he said.

One of the other directors asked immediately if drugs were involved.

"A heart attack," Slaughter said, though the words made no sense to him as he uttered them. Slaughter's own children, John Jr. and Jacqueline, were college students of Bias's age. Children don't have heart attacks, he thought. No one who had ever seen Bias playing basketball, Slaughter thought, could believe the young man had been a heart attack candidate. But drugs still did not occur to him.

"It was antithetical to what I knew of him," he said later.

Slaughter left immediately for College Park. Climbing into his green Chevrolet station wagon, he switched on his radio. As he reached the corner of New Hampshire Avenue and University

Boulevard just west of the campus, WMAL radio personality and Terps play-by-play announcer Johnny Holliday interrupted "Hardin and Weaver," the morning drive-time show. Len Bias, stricken that morning at the University of Maryland's Washington Hall, had died of an apparent heart attack, Holliday said. The chancellor pulled to the side of the road and stopped for a moment to focus his thoughts. At that very moment, newspaper reporters and television news teams from Washington and Baltimore were heading for Cole Field House, the university's basketball arena. Bias's death instantly activated one of the heaviest concentrations of political, investigative and sports reporters anywhere in the world. Already, they were ahead of Slaughter and other university officials on the story. Some reporters were told by their sources as early as 7:30 that morning that Bias had been rushed to the hospital in critical condition and that drugs were suspected.

As soon as Slaughter arrived at his College Park office, he called the Bias home in nearby Landover. He did not really know Mr. and Mrs. Bias, but he had met them at basketball games. Len's 18-year-old sister, Michelle, answered and put her mother on the phone. It was about 10 a.m. None too confident of his own emotions at that moment, he said he would like to come by to see her later. The chancellor thought Lonise Bias's composure was remarkable. "She said she'd be very pleased to see me. A very calm individual. I had not expected that," he said.

Then he called Driesell.

Slaughter had to worry immediately about his basketball coach. A towering figure in a consuming sport, Driesell had turned Maryland into a national basketball power. With one of the best won-lost records of any coach in the history of the game, he was still one of basketball's truly unrestrained characters, even more intense and recklessly outspoken than most of his driven colleagues. Over the years, he had become as famous for inflammatory remarks as he had for winning basketball games. He was always a threat to make difficult situations worse. The annals of Lefty included the day he allegedly told a persistent reporter for the *Diamondback* (the College Park student newspaper) that snooping around was a good way to find yourself in a ditch with a bullet in your head; Driesell denies having made the statement. Still, in his 17 years at College Park, Driesell had lived through and in some cases provoked crises involving ballplayers and drugs, ballplayers and grades, ballplayers and sex, even ballplayers and sudden death. Two former players had died of a congenital heart abnormality called Marfan's Syndrome.

But none of his earlier troubles involved a player of such celebrity and talent. Certainly none had occurred under circumstances even remotely similar. Slaughter heard the raspy edges of fear and barely controlled panic in the voice of this supremely confident and commanding coach.

With so many reporters rushing to the field house, with so many questions to answer, with horror-stricken and frightened young men on his hands, Driesell needed time. He did not want a free-for-all. He said he was taking the team to his house, which was near the campus in Silver Spring, Maryland. Slaughter asked if the coach needed him, if he should join them at Driesell's house. Driesell said it wouldn't be necessary.

Then Driesell drove home. It was a house with a basketball court in the backyard. The Maryland state seal was painted in the middle of the court. It was the where he had talked these young men and their parents into signing with Maryland.

When everyone had arrived, Driesell and one of his assistant coaches, Oliver Purnell, went into the basement with Long and Gregg.

"Terry, you tell him what happened," Gregg said. "Tell coach what happened. You've got to tell him." Long told the story.

Again, Driesell called Fentress. At Fentress's suggestion, Driesell said, he sent Purnell to clean Room 1103 at Washington Hall.

The coach cautioned the players to be careful in their comments to anyone. He then sent Long and Gregg to spend the night with his friend, Bob Wagner, the coach at Northwestern High. He had remained particularly close to Bias, advising him in various matters.

Driesell then returned to Cole Field House.

By now, with news of Bias's death spreading, a few Maryland students began moving across the campus toward the gym. They sat in the red, gray and yellow seats by themselves and in small groups.

Most of them did not know Bias personally, but many felt close to him, the way some people feel close to movie stars they have not met. They had seen him play and they knew about him and his life from the newspaper sports pages. They had taken courses with him or they knew people who had. The Athletic Department used him for its pinup basketball poster during his senior year. Students hung the striking life-sized picture in their dorm rooms.

How could such a person be dead at 22? How could he be dead so soon after his day of glory in New York and Boston? Some of the students had come in disbelief, but when they saw the television microwave transmission towers and the reporters milling about, when they sensed the mood inside Cole -- some had seen Driesell sobbing as he talked on the telephone -- they knew.

Other friends of Maryland basketball arrived at the same time.

Retired drug company executive Cooper Curtice and his basketball buddy, Ivan Roop, had planned a drive to Cole Field House that day. Members of the Terrapin Club, the booster group that pays the university's athletic scholarship bill (about $2.7 million that year), they had planned to drop off their 1986-87 contributions, $2,500 each. In spite of the news and a certain apprehension, they went ahead.

Curtice counted 40 or more television trucks and vans and cars outside the gym.

"Ivan didn't see it at first, but I told him this is a major disaster. This is national . . . international. We're talking about a whole program that's going down in disaster right in front of us," Curtice said.

He and Roop, a retired banker, walked into the field house through a group of reporters "waiting like buzzards," Curtice thought. Immediately, they ran into Dick Dull, the school's athletic director.

"This is one day," Dull said, "when we really need you."

Dull took them around the top level of the below-ground arena to the Terrapin Club offices. They looked out over 14,500 red, gray and yellow seats, so often a scene of excitement, now dark and still. They walked under the red and white banners marking the teams' years of high national ranking: eighth in '73; fourth in '74; fifth in '75; eighth in '80; 10th in '84. Curtice wondered if his team would ever contend for a national title again.

Several hours later, after Cooper and Roop had gone, a press conference was held. A low platform was erected in the center of the small lobby, a room where the woodwork was painted bright Maryland red. Trophy cases bearing the university's athletic treasure lined the walls. The won-lost records and the scores of games played during undefeated, national championship football seasons were engraved on the plaques or printed by hand on the nubbly surface of game balls. Several shelves were devoted to the plaques awarded to Maryland stars who had been chosen as Chevrolet's Most Valuable Player.

One of them was football player Charlie Wysocki, a marvelous college-level running back who had been shattered when he was not picked in the 1980 National Football League draft. From that day on, he suffered from severe chronic manic depression, moving in and out of mental hospitals. Whatever the origin of his disease, Wysocki had been at the opposite end of the spectrum from Len Bias on draft day. No one wanted Wysocki. Most players who were not drafted suffered quietly and then went on with their lives. The trophy cases featured other stars who had gone on from their athletic glory to solid careers in business and the public life of Maryland. Silver trays, plaques, and loving cups in their honor sat on every shelf.

Driesell, Athletic Director Dull and Chancellor Slaughter stepped onto the platform before a struggling crush of cameramen and reporters. Driesell had difficulty beginning. He looked toward the ceiling, his left hand wiping at his eyes. He appealed for understanding. Maybe people could understand how difficult it was for him to speak, he said. He had thought of Bias as a son, he said. Like Bias's mother, Driesell always called him Leonard, a formality that seemed to carry a dimension of respect not there for all the players. Tears streamed down his contorted, ashen face as he struggled for control.

"He's in a better position than we are," Driesell said. "He's at home with the Lord. I'm sad but not even worried because I know where Leonard is. I know he's in heaven. We'll miss him. I love you, Leonard, and I miss you. I'll see you in heaven one day."

Were drugs involved? a reporter asked.

"I really don't think so," said the coach. He had just heard the players' version of the fatal cocaine party. But their account was neither conclusive nor helpful.

"Whatever it is," Driesell said, "it's not going to bring him back. That's all I was praying for."

Slaughter spoke briefly. He said Bias had been a generous and loving person. He had given freely of his talents to his teammates and his university. His death, Slaughter said, was a profoundly sad event, surely one of the most sorrowful College Park had ever known.

By now, Slaughter had talked with Maggie Bridwell, head of the campus health service that ran drug tests for athletes. Bridwell said she thought it very unlikely that Bias had died of a heart attack. There was nothing of heart disease in his medical history, she thought. Rumors of cocaine involvement were rife, and within a day reporters were told that cocaine had been found in tests on Bias's urine at the hospital.

Tim Gilmour, a university vice chancellor and one of Slaughter's closest assistants, thought the pieces of the picture they had were ominous. He wondered if they should be talking about what an exemplary young man Bias had been.

As soon as the medical examiner reported, he thought, the university would be in the eye of a firestorm.

"John, I think this thing is going to explode," he said.

Immediately, though, there were the logistics of a celebrity funeral and of dealing with the media, already inflamed by the volatile chemistry of sports, money, drugs, and the basketball equivalent of a rock star dying young. When the university's press aide, Roz Heibert, reached her office that morning, she found messages from more than 100 reporters. There were calls from all over the country.

As close as it was to sophisticated and worldly Washington, College Park was a most parochial place. The campus sprawled across Route 1, classrooms on one side, fraternity houses on the other. The face it showed the passing world had little sparkle. It was surrounded and nearly submerged by fast food joints, villages of student housing, pocket-sized shopping centers, car dealerships, bike shops, pizza joints, and banks.

Counting the 38,000 students, the professors and support personnel, the university community numbered 50,000.

"A city of 30,000 20-year-olds," Slaughter had observed. It was a subtle statement of the chancellor's burden. In 1986, Maryland was the sixth largest public university in the nation, a commuter school where 31,000 of its 38,000 students lived off-campus and commuted to classes. Bias, as a write-in candidate, had been elected president of the commuter students, though he was not a commuter. At College Park, there was a sense of overcrowding and hyper-mobility, as if the university offered education at a drive-up window.

Town Liquors and the 'Vous, a beery haunt more formally known as The Rendezvous Lounge, were part of this melange. The 'Vous was paired with R.J. Bentley's, a friendly den of hanging plants and framed copies of famous athletes' jerseys, including Bias's 34. Bentley's offered a rathskeller-style basement and a solarium. At its outdoor tables, one sat almost close enough to touch the fenders of the trucks and cars that roared by, leaving clouds of exhaust to filter through the pasta salad.

The campus was not blessed by setting in the way Harvard, Stanford, or the University of North Carolina were. Its chapel, resting on the highest point of land, was the most striking piece of architecture. At about the center of the College Park complex was the university dairy store, not a 7-Eleven, but an outlet for the produce of university cows. Maryland had big-time basketball. But there were vestiges of its Ag-school, cow-college identity even there in the middle of suburban sprawl. It was a place not quite grounded in its vaguely Georgian buildings.

Beyond all that, the campus still bore the imprint of its most defining experience, the end of World War II and the return of veterans in search of places to use their GI benefits. Between June and September of 1946, enrollment zoomed from 6,080 to 11,050. Seven hundred male students lived in double-decker bunks in the school armory. In the 1980s, campus signs were still made in a stenciled style reminiscent of army bases.

Size, if not still cows, defined College Park into the 1980s. Its chancellors declared periodically that quality was not incompatible with quantity. But the claim was not widely accepted even in Maryland. The university lagged in part because it lacked the financial support it needed from Annapolis, the state capital. Maryland was one of the wealthiest states in the union, measured by per capita income. But its legislature provided only 30 percent of the university's budget, far below the contributions of poorer states more committed to higher education.

Evidence of a precarious financial condition was everywhere. Paint was peeling from the building fronts and their grand columns. Some professors conducted classes in long, narrow rooms that resembled hallways. Labs and other facilities looked as if they were last painted before World War I. Computer facilities were inadequate. The library had been neglected for years. Even the athletic facilities, Cole Field House and Byrd Stadium, needed substantial repair or modernization.

Yet, the university's potential as a provider of scientific talent for Maryland industry was beginning to be recognized, particularly by the parade of high-tech firms burrowing in around the campus to be near it and the government agencies they served: defense, space, census, health, and communications.

The National Academy of Sciences found in a 1982 study that Maryland's engineering and computer science departments were among the nation's best. Its Center for Renaissance and Baroque Studies was headed by Sam Schoenbaum, one of the world's leading Shakespearean scholars. Schoenbaum had been drawn to College Park by its proximity to Washington, home of the Folger Museum and Theater, a majestic Renaissance playhouse and one of the world's richest storehouses of Shakespearean materials. Schoenbaum joined a growing number of students and faculty who were, finally, beginning to see that Maryland was well located for study of the arts and government.

But even in the best of academic times, the university's pockets of excellence had seemed shallow in the public mind. Its growing excellence was overlooked or uncredited. The university's image had been left, consciously at times, to powerful and often eccentric sports figures such as Driesell, who argued that competitive football and basketball teams would give the university the national prominence it needed for recognition as a superior academic institution. Every coach and booster in the NCAA made a similar defense of high-intensity athletic programs: Sports could raise a university's profile, give it prominence beyond its borders. But often, big-time sports programs actually worked against a university's academic aspirations, imparting an image of a school where sports were more important than academic accomplishment. This was the case at College Park.

The Athletic Department and the rest of the campus were, to some extent, estranged. Faculty suspected the coaches of using resources that might have paid for library books or improved laboratory facilities. The Athletic Department, in turn, suspected faculty of victimizing athletes in the classroom.

Considerable tension characterized the relationship between the university's central administration and athletics; in the 1980s, the administration pushed harder to bring coaches and athletes closer to the rest of the campus. One day in the 1960s, according to one account of the schism, then university president Wilson Elkins was driving around the campus when he spotted a building under construction.

"What is that?" he asked.

Someone in the car told him it was a new building for the football team. Elkins was the university president. Here, without his knowledge, a major building was going up a few blocks from his office. It was not so big, Elkins said later, and besides, the Athletic Department had a right to pursue its own interests.

A Rhodes Scholar who had played football at the University of Texas, Elkins had been a solid proponent of athletics, as well as a reformer during his early days on the campus. When he arrived, "Sunny Jim" Tatum was the football coach. Under Tatum, Maryland had won two national championships in quick succession. But Elkins discovered that the university was granting more athletic scholarships than academic ones. The new president corrected that imbalance, and Tatum left College Park for Chapel Hill and UNC.

The athletic enterprise had been woven deeply into the fabric of university life during the autocratic reign of Harry C. "Curley" Byrd. Byrd was a true son of College Park. He had been an undergraduate there. He returned after graduation to coach the football team, and in 1935, he was made president of the university. Byrd became the university's master builder. In Annapolis, where he alone among lobbyists was allowed to roam the House and Senate floors, he was a power center. He drove ever increasing budget demands to passage year after year, extracting more and more dollars for new buildings and programs. Admirers called him "an irresistible seducer of public funds." Less taken with him and not then a fan of public higher education, *The [Baltimore] Sun* said he was "a scheming empire builder." In time, he pushed too far and the legislators withdrew his extraordinary lobbying privileges, and the university's budget power waned. The aftertaste of Byrd's aggrandizing style stayed with legislators for years.

Byrd left another legacy.

In 1954, he ran for governor. The race began just six months after the historic *Brown v. Board of Education of Topeka* lawsuit, the U.S. Supreme Court ruling against separate but equal school systems. While campaigning in a conservative farming area, candidate Byrd faced this question:

"What are you going to do about Negroes trying to get into white schools?"

"I'm going to keep them out," he said, not knowing a reporter was present.

Byrd had urged legislators to authorize higher spending for the black college (now University of Maryland Eastern Shore) at Princess Anne, a small town east of the Chesapeake Bay on Maryland's Eastern Shore.

"If we don't do something about it, we're going to have to accept Negroes at College Park, where our girls are," Byrd said. He had also said, "I am unqualifiedly in favor of a continuation of the state's policy of maintaining educational facilities for Negroes and whites in separate institutions. The fine qualities of both races can thus be best preserved."

Notwithstanding his election language, Byrd's record on race was not as dismal as his politically motivated comments suggested, according to Prof. George H. Callcott, a historian who has written a careful history of the university. But in the state's black community he was remembered bitterly as the George Wallace of Maryland, a man who stood in the schoolhouse doorway. That was 30 years ago, of course. College Park had a black chancellor now. But it was still one of those places where one could see a Confederate flag hanging across the back window of a pickup truck. One of John Slaughter's first actions as chancellor was to end the half-time ritual of having a student run the length of the field with the Stars and Bars.

A studious, thoughtful man who believed in collegial decision-making, Slaughter frequently found himself in conflict with the enduring presence of Byrd, a man whose driving personality remained the standard by which successors were measured. Maryland was still undergoing a change in leadership style when Bias died. That shift deepened the crisis. Slaughter brought change with him. He _was_ change.

Slaughter's picture had been in the newspapers occasionally, and people began to recognize him as the university's chief executive officer. He wore wide-rimmed glasses and was seldom without one of his pipes. When he arrived in 1982, he was photographed for a feature story in _The Washington Post_ wearing a three-piece checked suit with the vest fully buttoned. He struck a jaunty pose, offering a stylish as well as scholarly presence. He had graying temples and a thick beard with broad white streaks. Some thought he looked a bit like the actor James Earl Jones. He generally spoke without academic mannerism, though on occasion he dipped into the over-wrought thickets of eduspeak to find words like "antithetical" or "foci" or "interface." More often, he spoke directly and with passion. Furrows gathered on his forehead as he talked and creases fanned out from the corners of his eyes.

His was a thoughtful, almost courtly presence; he was as modest and methodical as Lefty Driesell was impetuous and arch.

Slaughter's profile as chancellor may have been somewhat higher than his immediate predecessors, academic men whose names would have been known to few. He was black and he was involved in various community activities. He had headed a panel studying teenage pregnancy in Maryland. Still, he remained anonymous compared with Byrd and with the basketball and football celebrities. People felt they knew Lefty personally. They knew Lenny. And they knew Boomer Esiason, the former Terps quarterback who played for Cincinnati in the National Football League. They knew Bobby Ross, the football coach. In the style of sports and Southern good ole boys, they knew these men by their first names: Lefty and Lenny and Bobby and Boomer. Sports was family. Slaughter was an academic, a scientist, and a bit remote.

He was also more devoted to Maryland basketball than any previous chancellor, including Byrd. But he was not thought of as the jock chancellor. He had become a leader among university presidents who thought big-time college sports had lost their way. Soon after he arrived at Maryland, he was named by the other ACC schools to represent the conference on the Presidents Commission, a group of 44 chancellors and presidents from National Collegiate Athletic Association schools.

His ACC colleagues thought the commission would be time-consuming and essentially worthless, not something prestigious, Slaughter imagined. So they picked the new kid on the block to represent them. The commission actually started out as if it would be a force, pushing to NCAA enactment the so-called death penalty, a sanction that stripped a school of the right to play football or basketball, and the money each earned if it repeatedly violated NCAA rules. In the winter of 1986, Slaughter was elected chairman of the commission.

He particularly wanted the NCAA to rule freshmen ineligible for varsity competition. College sports were so big and demanded so much time that calling players "student athletes" was or should have been an embarrassment. People talked endlessly about putting the student back into the idea of "student athlete." They talked about it, knowing that there was little room for study in an athlete's life. To have new university students practicing and playing games before they bought their books, Slaughter thought, was all the proof anyone needed that college sports were out of control.

Yet, like Terrapin Club members who proudly asserted that Maryland had never been investigated for cheating or for any other infraction of the NCAA rules, Slaughter thought he was presiding over a clean program at Maryland. A study completed a year earlier gave the College Park athletic program good marks.

His concerns as a member of the Presidents Commission were directed mostly at other schools. But he knew his campus was vulnerable. Sports-related catastrophes such as recruiting violations, altered grades, gambling, and low graduation rates had shamed many universities. Something similar could occur at Maryland easily enough, he had said in an interview published on June 5, 1985, just over a year before Bias's death.

"Anything can happen anywhere," he told the *Baltimore News-American*. "I'm serious about that. Athletics are so big and have so many aspects, there's no way anyone can be sure he's on top of it all . . . Not anywhere. Athletics is big money. Unless you manage your athletic program, it can sink you."

Chapter 3

A Rose

For the funeral service, Maryland's political leaders, along with some of the most noteworthy members of the state sporting community, led 1,300 mourners up six flights of wide concrete steps, past the television cameras and into the university's Memorial Chapel. The brick church with its slate-capped white steeple and arched wooden windows stood on a knoll near the center of the campus, a vantage point commanding an expanse of university playing fields, dormitories, fraternity houses, and the traffic along Route 1.

Maryland's first Rhodes scholar, Tom McMillen, was there with his former teammate Moses Malone. McMillen had just ended his professional basketball career as a forward with the Washington Bullets and was running that summer for Congress in Maryland's 4th Congressional District. Malone, a player who had not attended Maryland but whose near-enrollment there was part of a might-have-been myth at the school, was the first high school player to go directly to the pros, bypassing college in general and Driesell in particular. Still, Malone had remained close to the coach and was a part of Maryland basketball history.

McMillen and Malone were followed by Thurl Bailey and Bennie Bolton, both of whom had played at N.C. State. They knew Bias from Washington area playgrounds. Basketball players Johnny Dawkins of Duke University and Olden Polynice of the University of Virginia were there. The cameras found Georgetown University Coach John Thompson; Steny Hoyer, who represented College Park in Congress; state Comptroller Louis Goldstein; Maryland's former U.S. Senator, now a prominent lawyer, Joe Tydings; Chancellor Slaughter; Driesell; Auerbach; and presidential candidate, the Rev. Jesse L. Jackson, who had been lecturing to schoolchildren about the evils of drug abuse. Jackson's sense of the dramatic might well have brought him to such a tragic scene on his own, but he had been invited by James Bias to speak that evening at the memorial service.

James and Lonise Bias asked if the funeral could be held at the university chapel rather than their family church, Pilgrim African Methodist Episcopal in Washington. It seated more people and it seemed the appropriate place.

Terps play-by-play announcer Johnny Holliday sang the "Lord's Prayer." The A.E. Housman poem, "To An Athlete Dying Young," had been quoted often in the newspapers. The verses echoed through the well-lighted sanctuary.

> " . . . Today, the road all runners come
> Shoulder-high we bring you home
> And set you at your threshold down
> Townsman of a stiller town.
>
> "Smart lad to slip betimes away
> From fields where glory does not stay
> And early though the laurel grows
> It withers quicker than the rose . . ."

Some of Bias's friends had not fully acknowledged their loss until they entered the church and saw his bier at the end of the main aisle, near the gently curving altar rail with its rose-colored kneeling cushion. The casket was open.

Baxter had been clinging to anger as a refuge. He imagined that Lenny had gone off to take a nap without telling anyone.

"I'm going to smack him for making us so crazy," he told himself.

In the church, the last shred of hope fell away. "I knew how he looked when he was sleeping in the dorm. He curled up just like a baby," Baxter said.

Slaughter wrote in his journal: "I had a bad time when I saw Len dead. I really wasn't prepared for that."

At the family's request, booster Jack Heise, one of the university's most active alumni, was the chief eulogist. Heise had advised Bias on how to handle the coming storm of NBA pressure. A Maryland graduate who practiced law in Silver Spring (just one town over from College Park), he also had given Bias and other players summer jobs with his firm. If a Maryland athlete got into trouble on the campus or with the police, Heise or one of his associates would handle the case. He was a Terrapin Club member and a member of the Fastbreakers, an even more devoted group of basketball lovers organized at Driesell's request to provide a Maryland presence at games on the road.

"Whether the site be on Tobacco Road, South Bend, Hawaii, Alaska, Atlanta or wherever," Heise said from the modest, floor-level pulpit, "the Fastbreakers were there to see Lenny perform his magic. The bus ride back to College Park, sometimes ending at 4 a.m., was always so much shorter after No. 34 carried the Maryland team on his back to victory."

Heise called Bias, "Our man for all seasons, the epitome of a student-athlete -- a solid citizen whose burning desire for achievement led him to the top." He was a loyal friend, an earnest young athlete. Heise recalled Bias's smile and "modest tilt of the head as he accepted praise and award after award." It was the smile he had given only days before, a lifetime before, to David Stern of the NBA.

Bias's "refreshing humility and words of credit for his teammates" set him apart as a superstar, Heise said, adding that Bias always appeared at Fastbreakers' functions.

James and Lonise Bias, their daughter, Michelle, and sons, Eric and Jay, sat at the front of the sanctuary. On the day his brother died, Jay had gone on to play in a summer basketball league game. The code of brothers and of athletes carried him. He seemed as strong then as his mother. It was what Lenny would have wanted, he told reporters. And, of course, it was something he could control, something to do when there was too much grief and confusion to handle.

Jay, who at 15 was almost as tall though not as well-developed as his brother, now simply cried as he walked slowly out of the church, past the glistening cherry trees, three on each side of the wide steps. Jesse Jackson held him for a moment before he got into one of the limousines. The chapel bells tolled softly as Bias's teammates and his friends from Columbia Park -- Brian Waller, Johnnie Walker, Terrence Lewis -- lifted the polished coffin into the hearse. For the first time in history, Maryland State Police closed the nearby Capitol Beltway around Washington; the unprecedented action eased passage of an athlete's cortege to Lincoln Memorial Cemetery in Riverdale, east of the campus. At the grave site, Driesell stood to the left of James Bias, holding his shoulders, supporting him.

That scene hid some of the day's underlying tension. The night before, a wake had been held at the Biases' church in northeast Washington. James Bias had thrown Driesell out, angrily accusing him and the university of neglecting his son. University officials watched nervously the next day, wondering if another encounter would erupt.

At the interment at Lincoln Memorial, Gatlin kissed the casket. The mourners sang "We Shall Overcome."

Television reporters stopped Driesell right after the interment. The light green canvas canopies covering the grave were the backdrop for an interview.

"We believe in the Lord. Whatever happens is in the Lord's plan," said Driesell, as if to forestall any suggestion that human failings were involved.

After the service, the university's press office, still struggling to answer phone calls from all over the country, was told that one University of Maryland player, either Long or Gregg, had committed suicide. An athletic department official quickly located both young men.

That night, a memorial service was held at Cole Field House. Though many students were away from the campus during the summer, 11,000 people came. Bias's teammates walked into the arena in single file and took seats on the front row of bleachers that extended down to the court. Gatlin sagged forward, his head cradled in his long fingers. A copy of the program with Bias's picture on the cover dangled from his right hand. The hulking old building seemed too brightly lit. Up in the stands, someone held up the requisite commemorative T-shirt, "Len Bias, 1964-1986."

The Biases came. Roz Hiebert, the university's spokeswoman, was not certain they would or, if so, what they might say if they spoke. Knowing of the incident at the wake, she wondered if they might be critical. The service would be carried on national television.

Jesse Jackson presided. He hailed the life of Len Bias and asked the crowd to give him one final standing ovation. With applause lifting and supporting them, Mr. and Mrs. Bias walked to the podium. Jackson embraced them. The clapping echoed through the building for minutes as if, somehow, it could call him back, bring him charging through the wide underground corridor from the Terps locker room, leading his teammates out to the floor in long, commanding strides, dunking and throwing fists in the air. Instead, there were only the words of a coach, a preacher and a stoic mother.

Driesell recalled a "picture perfect jump shot" and a ritual encounter with Bias before every game.

"Are you ready, Leonard?" Driesell would demand.

Bias would reply, "Coach, I was born ready."

His voice rising, Driesell whispered, "Leonard . . . he died ready. . . . He's on a team with the Lord that he'll be on forever." Bias's number 34 would never be worn again at Maryland, he promised. Auerbach gave Mr. and Mrs. Bias a Celtics jersey bearing the number 30. That gesture, the gift of a uniform never worn, was like a stifled cry of pain for what could have been. The city of Boston had not been so shaken, Auerbach told the crowd, since the assassination of President John F. Kennedy.

"I schemed for three years to get Lenny Bias," he said. The crowd cheered.

Jackson elevated the 22-year-old basketball player into the company of martyrs.

"God sometimes uses our best people to get our attention. Jesus, God's only son, a good man, a young man, was crucified. Dr. Martin Luther King, Jr., a good man, a young man, shot down in cold blood in the prime of his life. Mozart, Ghandi . . . and others, young, gifted, strong, and militant, all taken in the prime of their lives to the drastic intervention of death . . . ."

"If we had lost another plant, a lesser flower, we would not be here," Jackson said, "but God chose a rose . . . a rose of our generation."

Several weeks earlier, after a night of drinking, a coed had fallen to her death from a dormitory window. Alcohol was the real drug problem at College Park. But few noticed. There was no memorial service. No one knew the young woman's name.

When Jackson spoke, the cause of Len Bias's death had not been officially determined. But on the morning of his death, a television crew had filmed a campus policeman removing a plastic bag of what everyone assumed was cocaine from behind the dashboard of Bias's sports car.

Jackson proceeded as if there were no doubt about what had happened.

Drugs, he said, were a shadow of death over American society and a particular threat to black America. They threatened more savagely and effectively than the Ku Klux Klan, he said. Ropes and sheets were benign in comparison to the lethal potential of heroin and cocaine.

Presidential candidate Jackson had begun to confront students on drugs in classrooms across the country. When he spoke, he often asked for a show of hands: How many had a friend who was using drugs? How many had a friend who was addicted, jailed or killed as a result of using or selling drugs? At some schools, everyone raised a hand. Now he had Len Bias, famous basketball star, as a teaching tool.

"Tonight the children mourn," Jackson said. "I hope they learn." Few who knew anything of a cocaine user's thinking expected the death of a basketball star to have much curative impact. A more likely outcome was that the young man would become some sort of hero and that users would want to try the high-potency drug Bias had been using. Jackson was talking to the non-user kids and to what he hoped would become a community of more informed adults. It was clear, of course, that even the best kids, kids with the most to live for, were taking chances and losing.

Jackson also served as attentive minister. He tried to help his audience find its way through the conflicting images: the perfect body, the casket, the committed athlete, the born-again Christian, the loving son, the polite young man, possibly the cocaine user.

The candidate did not forget his spiritual duties.

"We cannot assume that he lingers here for he has gone to be with God," he said. But he offered hope.

"Tragedy will be transformed into triumph, the storm will be rolled away, the resurrection will be the treasure, and many lives will be saved because his life was sacrificed. . . . Lenny was vulnerable because all of us are vulnerable. He is being used by God to save a generation." The mourners could find comfort, he said, by accepting the tragedy as part of a plan.

"Suffering," he said, "is redemptive."

Lonise Bias spoke for her husband and their children. She wore a dress of white, red and black, not mourning clothes. By now, most of the community had seen on television the tranquility Slaughter heard when talking with her the morning of her son's death.

When Len returned from Boston, Mrs. Bias said she had been at a Bible study class. He had managed to get her on the telephone. It was their last conversation.

"Love you, Mom," he said as he hung up.

"Love you, son," she said. She was confident of one thing. She had loved him as much as a mother could love a son -- and she was sure he knew it.

Her strength came from something else as well. Months before, she had dreamed that someone in her family would die. It was the first of several premonitions. Her son's future in the NBA was assured. But one day as she walked through the living room, she paused to look at his portrait on the wall. She had been reading her Bible.

A voice said: "He'll never play pro ball."

"He can't be talking about Len," she thought.

She heard the warning again several times later, she thought, when she talked with her son on the telephone. "He'll never play." She told herself it was something she was imagining. But, in a sense, she was under control after his death because she felt prepared and, given her faith, the event seemed less cruel, a part of something almost rational or planned.

At the memorial service, she tried to ease the pain she saw in her son's friends.

"The Lord has assured me that Leonard's mission was accomplished here and that he is at home with Him. If you want to see him again, try to live the life he lived with humility and love. If you live your life with humility and love, we'll never have to cry again," she said.

Jackson sent the people home.

"For those who remain, let us work," he said. "Let Lenny rest as he slamdunks with the angels."

Here on earth, Bias's university and its chancellor were being slammed and dunked by almost every imaginable drug-related rumor and bit of speculation. The All-American had been free-basing. He and his friends had been using crack, a report more frightening then because crack was largely unavailable outside New York City. The basketball team was riddled with drugs. Illegal drug use was epidemic throughout the College Park campus. Manipulation of scores to favor gambling interests was being investigated.

At a meeting the day after Bias's death, the University of Maryland Board of Regents gave Slaughter complete authority to speak for the university in the unfolding story. An obscure board of directors in calm times, the Regents became even less visible in this crisis by deferring to Slaughter.

Like Bias's family and friends, Slaughter hoped that a cause of death other than drugs would emerge, or, at least, that the young man had made one and only one mistake during a foolish moment of celebration.

Anxious for any answers about what had happened, James Bias had tried to speak with Driesell soon after his son died, but the coach was talking to no one then, not even to the dead super star's father, who he all but threw out of his office, Mr. Bias said. Days before that ouster, Mr. Bias had thrown Driesell out of the wake for his son.

"He said he wasn't telling me anything. He told me to go and talk with his lawyer," Mr. Bias said.

Driesell said he was doing what his lawyers instructed him to do.

"I said, 'Talk to Lon Babby. Talk to Ed Williams.' I really didn't have anything to tell him. I had already told the police everything I knew," Driesell said.

Two days after the funeral, the state medical examiner, Dr. John E. Smialek, called Slaughter at his office. Smialek had scheduled a press conference and wanted the chancellor to know in advance what the autopsy showed. The cause of death was "cocaine intoxication." With its connotations of alcohol use, still less odious than illegal drug use, the term seemed less harsh and condemning than a "cocaine overdose." It was a term of art few had heard before. Thereafter, though, the phrases "cocaine intoxication" and "cocaine-induced death" would be repeated like a mantra of condemnation in hundreds of news stories about the University of Maryland.

Bias had consumed a prodigious quantity of the drug -- probably five grams. That was about three times a fatal amount, and at least *five* times what could have sufficed for an evening of "recreational" use. There was some confusion about how he had ingested the cocaine, leaving his parents uncertain about how he had died. One team of pathologists concluded that he had taken the drug orally -- an unusual but not unheard of method. That report led the family to wonder if somehow their son had been poisoned -- if he had been given the drug without his knowledge. Long and Gregg, however, said they had snorted the drug through the straws Long cut at the start of the party. Dr. Dennis Smyth, an assistant state medical examiner, said the route of ingestion could not be determined from the autopsy findings alone. Cocaine shows up in many parts of the body after it is used, including the stomach.

There was no controversy about the drug's potency. More than eight grams had been recovered in the cookie bag Gregg filled, even after he dropped half on the carpet. Laboratory tests showed the cocaine was 89 percent pure, or perhaps twice the purity of the drug then sold illegally on the street. In the months ahead, drug sellers on the streets of Washington hyped the strength of their product by offering something they called "Len Bias."

"Got that Len Bias," they would whisper to customers. The role model's name became a temporary alias for high-purity cocaine.

Before Bias's death, the drug had been losing its reputation as a killer. Some work-hard, play-hard Americans, some journalists, and others referred to it as "recreational," as if it could be used without consequences. Several professional basketball players had become addicted. Their devotion to cocaine diverted them from practices and games and interfered with their travel schedules. They would disappear unaccountably and eventually be suspended. Some admitted their problems or were caught in the urine screening begun by the NBA. One of the recovering users was University of Maryland graduate John Lucas, a kid like Bias, a kid from a good family with a lot going for him. People wondered why his difficulties, so well known to Maryland players, would not have been an effective object lesson for his successors at College Park.

Lucas was lucky. He did not die. He was merely tormented by his addiction. He survived prolonged use, but lost his high-paying basketball job. He recovered and became a player again. He relapsed. He recovered. He opened a chain of fitness clinics geared to the needs of drug users and made another comeback with the Milwaukee Bucks. He understood what was happening to him, but he knew, too, that understanding might not be enough. He began to acknowledge that he was living day to day.

Too often money seemed to get in the way of recovery. Athletes like Lucas, Bias, and Lawrence Taylor (the New York Giants linebacker), were revenue producers. The value of their presence at games apparently led owners and coaches to believe quick cures were possible. A "lifetime" drug-induced suspension from the NBA could end after two years. Football players who turned up "dirty" on tests were suspended for 30 days -- a mere second in the usual recovery time of committed drug users. Addicts were recognized by treatment authorities as the most manipulative of personalities. Addicted athletes had lawyers who wanted their clients to play. The professional leagues seemed willing to be manipulated if they could get their stars.

At his press conference, Dr. Smialek explained how cocaine alters the normal electrical activity in the brain, causing nerve cells to misfire. When the disturbed electrical currents reached the heart, they produce a chaotic rhythm, leaving the heart unable to pump well enough to provide sufficient oxygen, and sending the brain and body into seizures.

Dr. Smialek supported the belief that even if this had not been the first time Bias had used drugs, he was not an habitual drug user. The autopsy gave no indication of previous use, he said. It was a finding of some solace to the university, which might well have been asked how a longtime user could have escaped detection by its athletic testing program, or why Driesell had not known of his star's off-court activities.

Long and Gregg said Bias had been a user for months, but Dr. Smialek suggested he may have been "drug naive." The term suggested not only that the user had little knowledge of the drug he was using, but that, in medical terms, the body was unused to the drug as well. Like others who buy drugs on the street, Bias may have known little, if anything, about the strength of the cocaine he was using. Among the hazards of buying drugs illegally was the inability to measure strength accurately -- to know what one was taking.

For the world at large, however, the medical examiner's finding of "cocaine intoxication" was blunt and clear: All-American Len Bias died of a drug overdose. His death became a watershed in the history of drug overdose deaths in America. Instead of rewriting the NBA record books, Bias would now be the standard against which overdoses would be compared.

If Jesse Jackson and Mrs. Bias were right, if God had taken him as part of a plan, the timing was divine.

Bias's fans around College Park included the most powerful politicians in America, many of whom were in the middle of campaigns for reelection. The Reagan Administration was trying to regain control of the U.S. Senate. Democrats were trying to hold onto it. Most of the incumbents and their challengers were at home campaigning on June 19, 1986. They might have been excused had they been preoccupied with their own political doings.

As it happened, though, members of the U.S. Congress, along with the rest of the country, were transfixed by the unfolding story of Len Bias's drug-induced death. Congressmen had often seen Bias on television and in the sports pages of *The Washington Post*. To them, he was the athlete next door. With John Slaughter, they had watched him develop from the day he arrived at Cole Field House as a green and almost clumsy freshman. As a basketball player, he grew up on stage. After the Celtics drafted him, people started thinking about how to get tickets for Celtics vs. Washington Bullets games at the Capital Centre, an arena almost within sight of the Capitol and Bias's own house.

Boston's most famous political leaders, Massachusetts Senator Ted Kennedy and House Speaker Tip O'Neill, had invited Red Auerbach to lunch on Capitol Hill and asked him to bring Bias. Now their intended guest was dead and their cherished Celtics touched by scandal. They and the other Celtics fans were saddened, and some felt he had betrayed them. Len Bias had seemed a model of the right values. If he could become a victim, if he could succumb with so much to lose, every kid was at risk. The political leaders saw it, and so did their frightened constituents.

Anxious parents deluged the officeholders with questions. "What are you doing to protect my family and neighborhood?" they asked. House members put in frantic calls to the special subcommittee on drug abuse chaired by Representative Charles Rangel of New York. Usually, committee staff members catch up when Congress is away on recess. Not during the summer of 1986. They were too busy briefing representatives and their staff people on the various pieces of anti-drug legislation either introduced or in the pipeline.

Speaker O'Neill convened an extraordinary drug committee comprised of all the chairmen of standing committees. From the White House, where First Lady Nancy Reagan was pushing her "Just Say No" campaign, came signals that the conservative president was prepared to say yes to massive federal spending. Washington was answering the voters' questions by promising a war on the drug that killed Bias.

At College Park, parents and flamboyant Prince George's County prosecutor Arthur C. "Bud" Marshall hammered Slaughter with a different set of questions.

Marshall had raced home from the beach to take control of the investigation, immediately convening a press conference in Upper Marlboro, the county seat 10 miles southeast of College Park.

"I don't think the university is able to handle its own affairs," Marshall said.

Marshall stood on the courthouse steps, speaking into a clutch of microphones, his thick white hair and angular nose profiled against the old brick building with its white pillars. He said he would conduct an investigation of drug abuse, not only among the Bias case suspects, not only among members of the men's basketball team, but throughout the campus at College Park.

Marshall, too, was running for reelection. His opponent, a young black attorney named Alexander Williams, represented the aspirations of an increasingly active black electorate anxious to break into the strong and exclusive Democratic Party in Prince George's County. Marshall, the incumbent organization's candidate, had never faced so serious a threat in his 24-year career. Two years earlier, he had been defeated in his attempt to become a Circuit Court (trial) judge, so he was more than vulnerable. But now, he had what he thought was a public relations windfall: potentially widespread drug abuse and the death of a basketball star on a university campus within his county.

Marshall's flair for law-and-order drama was well known in Maryland. He had prosecuted Arthur Bremer, the busboy from Milwaukee who had tried to assassinate George Wallace during a 1972 presidential campaign visit to nearby Laurel. Marshall insisted on trying the case himself, though he had not been active as a trial lawyer for some years. He always wanted to be the tough prosecutor. In cases where the death penalty was possible, Marshall almost always requested it. He was so inflexible that even his longtime political backers questioned his judgment.

In the Bias matter, he faced a situation that needed no theatrics, but he provided some anyway. He held his press conference on the day of Bias's funeral, not the most respectful timing.

Marshall's investigative targets included the university itself, as well as Gregg, Long and Tribble, who were suspected of obstructing justice and committing other drug violations. But the major quarry was Driesell. Marshall wanted to slap him with obstruction of justice charges for sending Assistant Coach Purnell to sanitize Suite 1103. Fentress, too, was in the prosecutor's sights. Driesell and his agent insisted that they had no intention of thwarting the police. Fentress said he had been upset when he made his suggestion to Driesell. And Driesell, as if he had no judgment of his own, said he only did what his lawyer told him to do.

Marshall's and Driesell's public comments and actions were immediately threatening to Slaughter as the defender of College Park. He felt himself and the university defined not only by Bias's drug-abuse death, but by the remarks and reputations of two extraordinary public figures, both of them always eager to speak with the press, both of them concerned that their careers were in jeopardy.

The chancellor could not allow Marshall's characterizations of the university to go unchallenged. He wanted the community to know College Park was open to investigators. He said he would cooperate with the State's Attorney in every way. But he also wanted fair treatment, a trial at least, before a conviction. Slaughter had never met Marshall, so, through friends, he arranged a meeting for July 3, two weeks after Bias died. He hoped Marshall would moderate his tone if he saw that John Slaughter, not Driesell, was in charge at College Park.

When they met, Marshall told Slaughter of police investigator reports that Bias's drug use had begun eight months before his death, and that campus police turned away from drug offenses if they thought athletes were involved. Slaughter listened and promised to cooperate. He appealed for a more measured approach, and found Marshall cordial. But the prosecutor's inflammatory public comments continued. During his investigation, the State's Attorney imparted to reporters his personal view of what the grand jury should do, matters that demanded private and sensitive handling under procedure and law.

The chancellor had better luck with Driesell, who accepted his gag order. In his dealings with the usually irrepressible coach, Slaughter had a powerful ally: Edward Bennett Williams. The famous Washington trial lawyer, now deceased, had taken over from Fentress as Driesell's lawyer. Big-time college coaches could have many different lawyers at the same time -- lawyers for criminal matters and lawyers for financial matters, for example. In this instance, because Fentress might be implicated in the cleanup of Suite 1103, he could not represent the coach before the grand jury. So, at Driesell's request, Williams stepped in. At least as intimidating a figure as Driesell, he was one of the few men capable of making the coach listen. His effort to keep Driesell quiet would have been futile except for Williams, Slaughter concluded.

Driesell himself declined to speak about any of the issues that arose in the immediate aftermath of Bias's death.

Other forces affecting public perceptions of the university were even further beyond the chancellor's control. Bias's death reminded the public of earlier connections between drugs and Maryland athletes. Former basketball players Steve Rivers and Adrian Branch had been convicted of marijuana violations. The women's basketball team had been investigated for marijuana use. From these earlier infractions, some directly connected Bias's death with the university's failure to take effective action. Bonnie Shields, a teacher in Prince George's County, a graduate of College Park, and a Terrapin sports fan, was as embarrassed and angry as she was saddened.

"You have a major university athletic program with incidents of drug abuse over several years. How can you possibly sit back and say, 'We didn't know?' It's a little too naive. I don't think they used the opportunities, faced the issue they must have known was there," she said. If they had acted, she thought, maybe Bias would still be alive.

Shields was not alone in wondering if the university had ignored evidence of drug use among athletes, if it was more concerned with its image, with winning, and with money than with the athletes' well-being. After June 19, 1986, parents and students called the university to withdraw applications for admission. About 5 percent of the freshman class, including some students whose qualifications made them welcome even as late arrivals, enrolled elsewhere.

"People were jumping to the assumption that this was a place that was full of drugs, that everybody was snorting cocaine," Slaughter said later. That conclusion and the reaction to it wounded an aspiring university, one that liked to measure its emergence as a good school by the steady increase in its average combined SAT scores (they had risen from 950 to 1,025 in four years).

Slaughter appealed for perspective. College Park had a drug problem, he said, because society had a drug problem. He recalled the National Institute of Drug Abuse report of 1985 that the United States had 6 million regular cocaine users and 22 million others who had used the drug at least once during their lives. Some of these people, of course, lived on college campuses, Slaughter said.

The University of Maryland was as accessible to drugs as any other university, if not more so. It was located in an urban area where drugs were readily available, and the atmosphere on campus was sometimes conducive to illegal drug use. As a carryover from the more liberal rules adopted in the 1960s and 1970s, universities seldom intervened in the lives of students.

The idea that Bias had died in a dormitory at a cocaine party suggested that drugs had suddenly surged into safe havens of college life -- where only beer and Jack Daniel's had been before. This was not so, of course. Maryland students were known to sit in dormitory hallways, publicly smoking marijuana with water pipes. No one did much to stop these displays. Beer and bourbon encountered even less opposition. Dormitories were often more like condominiums than they were like dormitories of old, and the change had happened without much parental notice.

Before June 19, 1986, Slaughter himself was not particularly attuned to the pervasiveness of drugs, being far more "drug naive" than Bias. He had been around marijuana only once in his life -- that he knew of. His son and daughter told him he had walked near smokers without knowing it. The only time he was certain that marijuana was present was one evening, years ago, when he lived in San Diego. The son of a minister, a young man Slaughter knew well, took a joint from his pocket and started to light it in the chancellor's house. Slaughter threw him out.

A week after Bias's death, a Cleveland Browns defensive back named Don Rogers died of cocaine intoxication. A rush of stories about Rogers, all of them recounting the events at College Park, gave the Maryland story another shot of momentum. In those days, there seemed little likelihood that Reverend Jackson was right -- that Bias's death would have a truly sobering impact on the nation.

As stunning and horrific as it was, Bias's death was only the beginning of Chancellor Slaughter's problems. At the funeral, Fastbreaker Heise referred to Bias as the "epitome of the student athlete." Jesse Jackson said he was "a model student about to graduate."

But, during his final semester at College Park, Len Bias was hardly a student at all. Even as he was making All-American and All-ACC, and heading for the NBA big time, he withdrew from or failed all of his spring classes. The failures left him without enough courses to graduate and lowered his grade point average to 1.90, below the 2.0 or C average that was required.

Immediately after his death, campus authorities said Bias was nine credits short of a degree. He would have been able to finish his course work that summer, they said. Then, they revised the figure: He was actually 21 credits short. No one should have been surprised. It was not unusual for a collegiate basketball player to need more than four years to graduate. Of the first 18 players drafted by the NBA in 1986, only seven had enough credits to graduate.

But the confusion over Bias's status suggested that the university administration was unaware of his poor performance or attempting to conceal it. People were prepared to accept the fact that a university and its coaches could not police students 24 hours a day. But if College Park had ignored Bias's academic well-being to preserve his eligibility, perhaps it had turned away from his drug use as well, leading, however indirectly, to his death. Slaughter could argue persuasively that his university was part of a drugged society. But the classroom was his responsibility. Why was Bias allowed to play basketball when he was not a student?

"I didn't know it," Slaughter said. "I should have, but I didn't." Driesell did not apologize. He said his program was "solid" and "beautiful."

Teams of reporters from *The New York Times*, *The Washington Post*, *The [Baltimore] Sun*, and dozens of other newspapers moved in to learn what else Slaughter and Driesell had not known. A punishing wave of revelations broke over the already devastated campus. Each day in July seemed to bring another disclosure of academic failure and neglect. Hiebert later called those crushing July days a "rolling human tragedy," constantly growing more threatening to the university's stability.

The millionaire athlete had been failing and so had four other members of the 1986 basketball team, none with Bias's basketball talent or earning power.

In the spring of 1986, the basketball team's combined grade point average was 1.82 out of a possible 4.0 -- well below the 2.0 needed for graduation. And they were taking the easiest courses in the university. In the preceding six years, only about a third of the basketball players had graduated, but they all had remained eligible for basketball.

In most universities then, a player had to attain a certain grade point average to remain eligible. Maryland had almost no eligibility standards. Tim Gilmour, one of Slaughter's vice chancellors, tried to calculate it once and decided a 0.43 average out of 4.0 was nominally required. Players were "academically dismissed" with regularity, but this was a term of art that had no real consequence for eligibility. Players usually got back into school and seldom lost their eligibility even when, on at least one occasion, a player failed every course he took. They were clearly in distress as students, but never so severely that basketball was to be set aside.

The performance record of Bias and his teammates should not have shocked College Park authorities, including Slaughter. Three-quarters of the football players and most of the basketball players that the school admitted between 1980 and 1986 did not meet the university's usual requirements for admission. The average combined SAT score for basketball players over the previous six years had been 670 -- 355 points below the average score of other University of Maryland students. In one year, the two scholarship basketball players had an average SAT score of 560, out of a possible 1,600. One had scored 510, the other 610.

An athletic department official suggested to *The Washington Post* that some athletes had trouble reading the course catalogues -- and, therefore, had to be registered for their classes by athletic department officials. When *Post* reporters quizzed Driesell, he said he really didn't know how some of his players had gotten into school. He wanted his players to concentrate on reading and writing, he said.

Academic counselors steered players into safe courses, trying to keep them "on track to graduate." The players figured out ways to take the least challenging courses -- and, even then, often did no work.

Athletic Director Dull conceded that unqualified students were admitted to Maryland because they could keep the school competitive, keep the fans coming through the turnstiles and the cash register jingling. It was difficult, he said, to make academic decisions in a business context. To be competitive, you had to have good players. Many of the best high school players, it was widely assumed, were not adequate students. Although Dull had implicated his university in a system of exploitation, there was no particular reaction to his observation: The rest of the world assumed he was right.

While all of this was pouring out in the newspapers, Tony Massenburg, a freshman basketball player, was suspended from the team for cheating on a speech examination. Slaughter's crisis team learned later of another cheating incident involving an athlete. They met for one entire day in the middle of July to decide what action was appropriate -- a kind of pre-emptive disclosure or a hide-it-and-ride-it-out approach, hoping the reporters would not learn of it.

Spokeswoman Hiebert spent the day preparing versions of a press release. Slaughter finally approved a draft explaining the matter completely -- what happened and how the university was dealing with it.

At 6 o'clock, though, he changed his mind.

"Let's don't do this," he told her. "Let's take the chance it won't come out." It never did. Amid the incessant battering, Hiebert said later, it was a small, unsatisfying victory.

As the disclosures of academic failure continued after Bias's death, Marshall's grand jury began to hear witnesses in Upper Marlboro. Camera crews were permanently assigned. Every day another episode in the story's criminal justice side was written. Suspects or witnesses were led, sometimes in chains, into the courthouse. There were reports of a "mystery" woman friend of Brian Tribble and a mystery safe thought to be owned by him. There also were reports that Bias and Tribble had been seen in a section of Washington widely known as an outdoor drug market. All of this resonated in College Park.

"There was just one body blow after another," Assistant Chancellor Gilmour recalled. "Marshall would dump the trash out every afternoon and the reporters would rake through it. It was just too good to resist."

The prosecutor's charges were chilling. They gave official sanction to the perception, readily conjured in the public mind, that College Park had become a drug-infested swamp. Marshall's comments were followed almost immediately by recommendations from Sheldon Knorr, Maryland's commissioner of higher education, for an independent commission to investigate the Bias death. Slaughter and the Regents felt control of the university slipping through their hands.

Slaughter's small team of vice chancellors fought to keep their equilibrium. Ray Gillian, vice chancellor for special programs, thought it was like being in a war. "Battles are going on all over the map. You don't know what the hell is going on," he said.

Every morning, Gillian raced downstairs to get _The Washington Post_. Then he drove to the local 7-Eleven to buy all the other newspapers. "I had to see what we were facing, what was being said about us. We had fires everywhere. I never felt so out of control in my life," he said.

Athletic scandal, of course, had not been invented at College Park. The University of Virginia football team had been wracked by a drug investigation. And there had been stories about athletes who had gone through four years of college unable to read. Typically, the forlorn player was discovered in some small town or city long after he had graduated or left school, his professional aspirations withered, his prospects in the marketplace nil, another tall kid with a mop and pail. The basketball establishment survived these stories by acting as if they came from some alien and unaffiliated place. They were isolated tragedies to be identified with a single school -- not evidence of a system in crisis.

But John Slaughter made the Maryland crisis different.

During an interview after most of the revelations were out, he offered a startling acknowledgement. The university had failed its athletes. They had been exploited. "It was my fault," he said.

The brief, candid admission marked a rare moment in the history of big-time college athletics. Usually, chancellors and presidents had been the first defense against the charge of exploitation. Most often, university chancellors and presidents had talked about the spirit engendered by sports and the opportunities given to disadvantaged student athletes, notwithstanding lamentable exceptions to the rule.

But Slaughter talked of exploitation. He and the Board of Regents admitted the university's record -- publicly exposed after Bias's death by investigative reporters.

"We didn't know how high a price we were paying," said Regents Chairman Allen Schwait.

Slaughter's concession, however, did nothing to ease the onslaught. In his journal on the day he acknowledged exploitation, Slaughter wrote, "*Sun* reporters [Mark Hyman and Amy Goldstein] are being hard-nosed. They wanted to know if the university was responsible for Len's death. I said no. They are clearly after someone: Driesell, Dull, Slaughter."

What Hyman was after was a more candid and thorough expression of what was wrong at College Park and who was responsible for it. He wanted more detail on the infractions. Slaughter's acknowledgement of responsibility, he thought, was notable for its generality. The chancellor appropriately and sincerely accepted blame for the conditions that existed, Hyman thought, but he should have gone further.

And there was no support for Slaughter's frank assessment of the athletic program -- no backing in the debate then forming over what was wrong, if anything, and what should be done about it. Boosters grumbled. University President John Toll, who ran all five of the university's campuses, scolded Slaughter for his remarks. Even if what the chancellor had said about exploitation was true, and Toll didn't think it was, the chancellor shouldn't have said it.

Slaughter persisted. He appeared on the "Today" show with Digger Phelps, the basketball coach at Notre Dame. Phelps had been a severe critic of cheating in the basketball recruiting wars. During the program, he applauded Slaughter's honesty.

At one point in the interview, host Bryant Gumbel -- perhaps partially as a compliment -- said, "Dr. Slaughter has admitted that Maryland exploited athletes." Slaughter winced. His journal entry for that day observed that his confession "is beginning to haunt me."

The Regents had given Slaughter full crisis-period authority to speak for the university. They knew Toll would defend Maryland so fiercely that Bias's death would seem like little more than a distraction. They also knew that, absent their order, Toll would be unable to stay on the sidelines. A politically hyperactive bureaucrat, Toll had often tried to make day-to-day decisions for College Park that should have been the chancellor's. There was constant friction between the two.

As it turned out, Toll was well served by the crisis. Prior to it, sentiment among the Regents had been growing that he should be forced to retire. Though he had been a devoted manager of the university's affairs, the Regents did not regard him as the kind of leader who could boost College Park out of its historic doldrums. They wanted a first-rate university. Toll was committed to his own agenda, a statewide educational empire. He diffused limited state support as widely as he could. He always seemed to be on his way to an emergency, keeping "my Regents" happy, and embracing everything in a thick fog of obsequiousness. A dervish of activity, he was responsive to everyone and to no one.

Bias's death insulated Toll. There was no time to fire the president and get on with building a first-rate flagship university at College Park. The Regents were too busy trying to decide what should happen to the basketball coach.

Regents Chairman Schwait wanted Slaughter to be the sole spokesman during the crisis. He hoped to convey the picture of a university in complete control of itself -- to refute Marshall's conclusion that College Park could not handle its own affairs. Nothing would have undermined that objective faster than having three or four spokesmen, particularly Driesell and Toll, talking about what an exemplary program they had at College Park.

"Either they gave Slaughter the authority that was appropriate under the circumstances," said Ralph Bennett, president of the university's Faculty Senate, "or they hung him out to dry." Both of Bennett's assessments came true: Slaughter was given much of the authority he needed -- and he was hung out to dry.

"For me," says Schwait, "giving John complete control was a matter of personal integrity: We knew we needed someone who was committed to change. John was the person we needed."

Schwait says the pressure reached its peak when former Gov. Harry R. Hughes, then a candidate for the U.S. Senate, called with a chilling message. Hughes was going to conduct an investigation.

"I pleaded with him not to do that," Schwait says. "I told him we needed to build our own recovery. We had to be able to show the world we *could* run our campus." Hughes, though under great political pressure, relented.

Tim Gilmour says the campus and its administrators were fearful of "a real witch hunt" -- an investigation conducted by politicians running for office and looking for grandstands. "It could very well have been a sinking ship. We knew it could sink."

Over the next few months, the university would be criticized for its failure to move more quickly to escape the crisis. In a sense, though, it did not want to escape. Schwait and Slaughter wanted to address the problems they knew were there and they thought they might never have a better chance. The great churning enterprise of big-time sports would never be diverted in normal times.

As a result of these decisions, Chancellor Slaughter became an almost solitary flak catcher. He responded to every revelation. He made every decision, set every policy, took responsibility for every mistake. The Regents, to whom he was accountable, backed him silently by assuring him he was their man, but the decisions were to be his. He would take the risks.

Many critics of athletics at modern American universities want university presidents and chancellors to lead the reform movement. They assume that presidents can simply step into the athletic department and issue a few sharp, clear orders. If only the presidents had the gumption, the conscience and the will, they could put the system right, the critics say.

But the assumption goes further. It includes the apparent belief that university presidents like John Slaughter created the system operating on their campuses. Yet, few of the presidents were in office when it was decided that a campus could use sports to elevate its academic profile, or when the big TV money arrived, or when booster donations became so essential, not just for the player who was unable to pay his tuition, but for a program that grew larger and larger with ever more sophisticated equipment and wide-ranging travel. Everyone and no one was responsible for the system evolving from mere games to big business. And, yet, the idea persisted that a quick fix was possible.

The problem actually was rooted in policy set by state legislatures, which ordered university athletic programs to be profit centers. The policy of self support, operating at most state universities, had begun as a way of insulating political figures from the charge that state money was subsidizing big-time athletics at the expense of research and teaching. In time, though, the revenue stream itself became the governing reality. The reform impulse of a public university president was tempered by this financial reality. Clean the system up, but make money, was the unspoken order. A policy of state government had become a dark force sustaining the corruption of the big-time system.

Those who thought presidents could exert an iron hand of control also failed to account for the turnover rate among university chief executives. The job of university president had become one of the most fluid of occupations. Turnover reduced the institution's power to impose discipline on revenue-producing programs or on famous coaches who stayed for long stretches and who had tremendous clout among boosters and legislators. Historically, coaches had been vulnerable to firing because of unhappy, victory-starved alumni. Perhaps, as a result, some had been inclined to cheat to save their jobs. Now, though, coaches were far more institutionalized than the presidents and chancellors for whom they worked. Now they were cheating for the university, which needed to make money.

Presidential power over sports drained away in proportion to the success of teams and the flow of money. When revenue fell, the president was in deeper trouble: Pressure on the sports program rose and the president was loath to relieve it by diverting any other campus resources. College Park was relatively poor. By the 1980s, its pursuit of academic respect competed on an even footing with the need for nationally ranked basketball teams. At College Park, the idea of putting general campus funds into the sports program was not thinkable. The legislature, the Board of Regents, the faculty would not permit it.

In Slaughter's complex mission as a crisis manager *and* reformer, there was rich irony. Although he had lacked complete campus authority before the crisis, struggling as he was with President John Toll, he was delegated all the authority he wanted when disaster struck.

Here was one of the nation's highest ranking black educators in the midst of a grinding controversy over the proper care and nurturing of students and athletes, many of whom were black. Slaughter would now be asked to protect a system that had been compared to the plantation system, a system run by whites on the backs of blacks.

And the complications did not stop there: Slaughter knew that despite its on-the-court employment of blacks, basketball had a poor record in employing black head coaches, assistant coaches, athletic directors, and the like. He also knew that higher academic standards, if not managed properly, could deny educational access to minority students whose preparation for college had been inadequate and neglected. Slaughter had been asked to make his university more exclusive and more inclusive at the same time. He wanted a university of distinction, an open community in which black students would feel welcome, and a strong sports program.

And now he had a raging crisis on his hands. Gilmour says the chancellor seemed to be giving at least an interview an hour -- and not about the university's high ranking as an engineering school, its recruitment of black students, or the Renaissance center. Photographs of him appeared constantly in newspapers. He showed up as a guest on television interview programs, addressing the problems of drug abuse and academic failure among college athletes. He was on "Nightline," the ABC interview program, which later held a town meeting on drugs at College Park.

"I became a recognized figure," Slaughter recalled with discomfort. His bearded face translated into a visual leitmotif for the College Park story. He had a soothing presence that projected well.

Less than two weeks after Bias died, Slaughter took the first major step in the recovery. He appointed two task forces, one to investigate drug use, the other to look into the status of the student athlete at College Park. Former U.S. Attorney General Benjamin L. Civiletti headed a group of distinguished Marylanders who would study the campus's policies for dealing with drug abuse. Civiletti had been intrigued with the task. He had been convinced to do it by Schwait, also a lawyer, who cornered him at a bar association retreat in West Virginia.

Civiletti was a name partner in a Washington firm, Venable, Baetjer, Howard & Civiletti, itself an offshoot of Venable, Baetjer & Howard, one of Baltimore's largest law firms. He brought an air of businesslike authority and independence to his work at College Park. He was joined by Representative Steny Hoyer, the local congressman. A smooth political presence, and a rising and respected member of the House Democratic Caucus, Hoyer had once served as president of the Maryland State Senate, and had been one of the leaders of the Democratic Party in Prince George's County.

Other task force members were Benjamin L. Cardin of Baltimore, then the speaker of the Maryland House of Delegates (now a

Congressman), and former Maryland Court of Special Appeals Judge Solomon Liss (now deceased). All these lawyer-politicians were recruited for their judgment -- and for their collective ability to outflank and overpower Arthur Marshall or, at least, to deflate charges that the university had no leadership. Toll, the perfect staff man, stayed on the telephone until he had gotten all of them to agree to serve.

The idea was to reach some well-considered long-term policy judgments and, in the short run, to buy time. There were moments before the task forces were named when Gilmour thought neither the university nor Slaughter could withstand the imploding forces of disclosure and recrimination. He wondered if his boss and longtime friend might have to resign.

At first, drugs were the most volatile and fearsome of the issues. But Slaughter's second task force, one devoted to academic issues, almost immediately became the focus of the press. It was Slaughter's focus as well. The chancellor named physics department Dean Bob Dorfman to the panel's chairmanship. His group would inquire into the academic and student life of athletes.

A scientist who seemed born to be a dean, Dorfman wore a sleepy half-smile behind his gray mustache and goatee. The Athletic Department was suspicious of him in the same way it was suspicious of the faculty in general: He would never understand the department's problems. But Dorfman thought athletics had a legitimate role in campus life, and he brought an understated perspective to the events unfolding around him. His panel was to make an inquiry into "the integrity of academic programs and the support available to student athletes" at College Park.

Dorfman's good humor and obvious concern for students made him a stabilizing force in a time of uncertainty. The professor found that he enjoyed the interplay with reporters, who proved to be his constant companions as the task force began to hear testimony. He was not an athlete or a fan, but as a member of the university community, he had been concerned about what he called "a hermetic seal" between the athletic department and the rest of the campus. It offended his idea of a university.

Like many faculty members, Dorfman wanted his university to be seen unequivocally as an institution of higher learning. Dorfman was not anxious to have academics like himself compete with college athletes for the limelight, nor did he imagine that the stars of his discipline could ever be as popular as athletic idols such as Bias. He accepted Slaughter's charge with the conviction that neither the athletes nor the university had benefitted from their past uneasy alliance.

To reassure the athletic community, Dorfman and Slaughter made sure the panel had the insights of both athletes and academics. The membership included several athletes then enrolled at College Park, as well as former Maryland basketball player Len Elmore, then a law student at Harvard. Both sides were about to gain new and important knowledge about the other.

After he set the formal elements of his crisis management plan in motion, Slaughter found himself dealing with broken hearts and bad dreams among Bias's teammates. They were overcome by sadness, pursued by the police, humiliated by publication of their grades, and frightened by the overall atmosphere. Reporters were after their personal stories. Some were testifying before a grand jury.

Long and Gregg had grave, immediate problems. Along with Brian Tribble, they were suspected of drug violations and obstruction of justice. Needing a lawyer, they were directed to the campus legal aid office. But Bill Salmon, the attorney there, had no criminal law experience. He called his friend, Alan Goldstein, a well respected criminal lawyer who was very familiar with the courthouse at Upper Marlboro.

Goldstein met immediately with Long, Gregg, and their families. They were all terrified, Goldstein thought. Looking for a way to put them at ease, he decided his diminutive size might serve him. "I'm sure you've noticed that I'm only 5'2"," he said. "I just want to assure you I play 5'4"." Gregg, 6'9", and Long, 6'8", smiled at the lawyer's joke. The man could laugh at himself and he knew a little basketball.

One day, as the two young men were about to testify before the grand jury, Goldstein received a chilling phone call informing him that drug dealers had dispatched someone to find his clients, and that someone was, at that very moment, on his way to the campus to kill them. Goldstein instantly phoned Gregg and Long at their dormitory room. No answer. He ran out of his high-rise office building in nearby Laurel, climbed into his car and raced to College Park about five miles south. By chance, the first people he saw on the sprawling campus were Gregg and Long, who were walking together toward a class. He shoved them into his car, drove to a Chinese restaurant, took a seat where he could see the door and arranged for them to spend a few days in Richmond, where Long's parents lived. The threat later appeared to be a hoax.

Slaughter dealt with other fears. Several of the players had been in the dormitory room with Bias the night he died. At least two of them knew their teammate had used cocaine. No one had told the rescue squad. If there had been a chance to save him, they had chosen instead to protect his All-American image or themselves. The gamble had been lost. Were they responsible for their friend's death? They could all think of ways he might have been saved.

"I should have said, 'Come on, let's go to bed,'" Baxter told himself. "I would tell him that sometimes when we'd be out. He'd listen. I wish like hell I had told him, 'Come on, let's go to sleep. You can see all these guys tomorrow.' He may have done it. He may have said, 'I'll see all y'all later.'"

John Johnson, a freshman player from Tennessee who idolized Bias, went to the grave two or three times a week. Working out at Cole Field House, looking for a way to escape the loss, he found he couldn't go up for a shot -- some apparition of Bias would be there blocking it.

"That was the environment we were dealing with. We had to get help for these kids. We had to put something around them," Slaughter said.

So Slaughter, whose friends said he had a nursing instinct, put himself around them. He grieved with them, and they took advantage of it. He gave sympathetic attention to the players, meeting with them in his office and at his home after work. He arranged for counselors and psychologists to talk with them and their families.

Immediately, there was a suggestion that Slaughter, because he was black, was too concerned with the problems of a few black basketball players. There were only 15 kids on the team, after all. A chancellor had wider responsibilities: protecting the good name of the university, and talking about all the good things it did. The critics worried about "The Program" (basketball and football) and the university.

On July 7, Slaughter received an unsigned letter questioning his approach and the value of the young men he was ministering to:

"I do not see why the death of Mr. Bias is such a big deal. He wasn't forced to take it. And no one else is responsible for what he did. Who the hell cares?

"Other men die every day from dope but no one takes it to court or has an investigation. Why do it for this black? He blew it. It sounds like you are preparing a case for the family to sue the school for some of the millions Bias was to have made for them."

The letter concluded with these observations: "Lefty Driesell is a good coach. Let him alone. To me it is just another dead nigger."

At the same time, the university's sporting community worried about Lefty and grimly predicted he would be made a scapegoat. A week later, the defense of Driesell began in earnest and at a high level. Slaughter and Schwait received a six-page letter from Fastbreaker Heise. He urged the Regents to recognize the contributions Driesell had made to the university. And he took no chances. Heise sent the letter to Schwait even though it was Slaughter who would make the decision on Driesell.

Heise wanted everyone to know that a great deal of money was at stake in the Driesell question. "Many of the alumni and friends who first became interested in a program of giving through the [Terrapin] Club have also directed their financial interests to the greater university's other activities," Heise wrote. "The result has been a steady increase in funding . . . especially for the President's Club, a fundraising unit whose members gave a minimum of $10,000 to the university; some gave millions. Endowed chairs, special capital projects, scholarship support and the President's discretionary fund have all been the beneficiaries of the interest initially kindled by Coach Driesell's efforts." This was a variation on the theme of greatness through basketball, Driesell as chancellor, basketball as university.

If Slaughter needed a reminder of the sport's importance in the financial life of College Park, here it was in a single paragraph. Not that it was a surprise to find Heise playing pivot in the Driesell defense. It was Heise who made the first recruiting visit to Driesell 17 years earlier when Lefty was at Davidson College in North Carolina. Heise had gone as an informal emissary of the athletic department to see if Driesell, immensely successful at Davidson, was interested in the Maryland job. Heise had been at the old Lefthander's side ever since. Now, he wanted to tell Slaughter that Maryland's basketball coach was exemplary, and a key to the vault of private university fundraising. It was an assertion of questionable validity about any coach or any sport, yet widely accepted.

"If he has any fault," Heise wrote, "it may be that he has done too much for his players."

Chapter 4

Role Model

Soon after Slaughter arrived at College Park in November 1982, Driesell invited him over to Cole Field House to meet the basketball team. The new chancellor was well aware of the game's exalted status at Maryland. Someone had warned him, unnecessarily, that if he didn't like basketball he was in the wrong job. It was not enough for a university chancellor to have a doctorate in electrical engineering, to have been the provost at a major university, or to have held the top national government post in scientific education. A university president's or chancellor's resume had to include this entry: Basketball Fan -- Youth to Present. Slaughter's did. No Terrapin Club member loved the game more.

He headed over to Cole that day along the cement and brick pathways that run gradually uphill from his office on the campus's south side. He walked beside the broad central quadrangle that extends more than the length of a football field between the Theodore E. McKeldin graduate library and the main administration building. Bleak and barren in winter, a baked-out plain in summer, the quadrangle at springtime had a dazzling border of pink, white and purple trees and shrubs, and overflowed with Frisbee players and sunbathers. At Cole that day, Slaughter said his hellos and made a few standard presidential remarks. He reminded the players of their responsibilities as students and as representatives of the university. No one listened, he thought; kids heard responsibility speeches all the time.

These early weeks and months were exhilarating for Slaughter. It was a time to take control, to lead, to set goals, and to offer a vision of the ideal university. It was a time to enjoy the spirit and energy of campus life, including its sporting life.

A scientist and administrator with White House-level experience and connections, Slaughter imagined College Park would transform under his direction into a highly respected university, where teaching was done by caring and accomplished scholars like Dean Bob Dorfman. Slaughter knew also that College Park could help fuel an economic engine similar to the Research Triangle in North Carolina, where Duke University, the University of North Carolina, and North Carolina State University had all been connected. This was the Board of Regents' objective, but it was not Slaughter's priority. With him, teaching ranked higher than research and economic development. But he thought all the objectives could be reached.

And he made progress. Nearly every major engineering school in the country competed for a contract, supported by National Science Foundation money, to develop a computer-driven robotic hand. Harvard, also chosen, became partners with Maryland's $16 million Systems Engineering Center, one of the first of its kind in the nation. Slaughter had come to put College Park on the map, and he was doing it.

Slaughter also brought immediate, albeit symbolic change to the basketball program. The Athletic Department traditionally reserved a place for the chancellor high in the stands at Cole Field House, but Slaughter picked a spot on the floor, only three feet from the north end line. Long trestle tables, set aside for the press, were extended at a right angle around that end of the court; Slaughter's seat was almost directly under the basket. At games, the slapdash, street-clothed band, their horns glistening in the arena lights, would play behind him. When waiting for games to begin, the chancellor would talk to students and alumni, then at tip-off, pull himself up to his conspicuous spot, a table draped in red felt. At the end line, the word

"MARYLAND" was painted on the court floor, in large white letters on a red background. Slaughter sat just behind the letter "R."

Warmups began with the Terps streaming out of the locker room behind a cheerleader who carried the state flag on a 20-foot pole. The on-court progression brushed past the chancellor's left elbow. The band played Maryland's fight song and the acrobatic cheerleaders gave an exhibition of gymnastics. The fans needed no prompting.

During the games, Slaughter heard what the competitors said to each other, and on occasion fended off the sweat-slick body of a player who had launched himself out of bounds to keep a ball in play. From the corner of his eye he could see, a moment before the people in the stands could, Len Bias circling and accelerating toward the basket. Bias soared across the painted foul lane, took a looping pass at the apex of his leap, and hammered the ball home in one surging, declaratory statement. Slaughter felt the orange rim vibrate as Bias landed, turned and raced back on defense with 14,500 people chanting "LEN-NEE, LEN-NEE, LEN-NEE." No one had a better view than the chancellor.

Slaughter occasionally accompanied Driesell on recruiting trips and gave dinner parties at the chancellor's residence for recruits like J.R. Reid, the top high school player of 1986. Around the dinner table, the chancellor's guests tempted themselves with visions of Terrapin championships to come, of new scoring combinations: Alabama's Fess Irvin, a guard from Louisiana, passing to Reid, just as Gatlin had passed to Bias. Slaughter enjoyed the colorful Lefty and he grew close to some of the players, particularly Bias.

In fact, the chancellor put a heavy burden on the young man.

Bias could be just what the academically unmotivated and poorly performing team needed. He could be, the chancellor thought, the nucleus of a team whose members saw their opportunities and avoided a blundered pursuit of the basketball dream. He thought Bias's prominence and success as a player and student at Maryland could begin to change the atmosphere. If Len Bias were a No. 1 draft choice and a graduate of the university, he would leave something to build on. The goal seemed a modest one, yet so few players were managing to reach it. Slaughter told himself that Bias had a chance to be the ideal student athlete: friendly, polite, smart enough to succeed in the classroom, still a kid, but growing.

When Slaughter's friends teased him about the special seat he arranged for himself at Cole Field House, he looked at them somberly and said, "It's important to the team for me to be there." Then, with his reedy, lilting laugh, he acknowledged the self-indulgence. Boosters and students were happy to see such enthusiasm in the chancellor's office.

Slaughter was every fan with the best seat in the house. He was the chancellor of hoops, a man who loved inside basketball talk. If sports were a religion in America, Slaughter subscribed to the approach of total immersion. He wore his Maryland red sweater or his red blazer to the games. He wore his souvenir tournament wrist watch with "1984 NCAA" on its face. He attended the awards banquets. When provost at Washington State, he had written a poem of homage to the team, and read it at the annual basketball banquet there.

Slaughter kept a sheaf of yellowing newspaper clippings that chronicled his own exploits as a schoolboy athlete. He had not been in an athletic class approaching Bias's, but he had had his moments of glory. He had been the sixth man on Kansas State's 1951 championship cross country team, and a pitcher -- a wild lefthander, he said -- for Topeka High School in the 1940s. Playing in the Kansas YMCA league one summer, he had pitched against the future Hall of Famer, Bob Gibson of the St. Louis Cardinals. Slaughter lost, 3-2, but in one of his at-bats against Gibson, he doubled. Like every kid, he had dreamed of playing in the pros. But he had more than one dream, and in college, he gave up sports for engineering.

Now, 30 years later, Bias's success and the success of the Terps were especially thrilling for Slaughter. He saw basketball as an open-door opportunity for black players who might not be in college otherwise. At the same time, aspects of collegiate basketball at Maryland and elsewhere were troubling for him.

In April, after the 1986 basketball season ended, Slaughter met with the team. He was concerned about Bias and the other seniors. At the big-time schools like Maryland, the academic collapse of senior players in their final semester of eligibility had become an immutable law. The best players all over the country bailed out as soon as their collegiate eligibility was exhausted. Because they no longer needed to pass, players frequently dropped all pretense of being students. The basketball community shrugged it off as unavoidable. There was too much money. And wasn't that the point, getting these kids into the pros? Bias wasn't present for the chancellor's pep talk. He was on the circuit of all-star games, earning as much as $800 a night. He was beyond the chancellor's control and had been for some time.

After the meeting, Slaughter took Baxter aside.

"I want you to tell Lenny I'm really disappointed in him. He's not going to class. He's not doing the things he promised me he would do," the chancellor told Baxter, who, unbeknownst to Slaughter, had become a casualty, too, one of the four players who were academically dismissed at the end of the spring semester.

Slaughter made his displeasure known to others. He told Frank Pesci, then a member of the Maryland House of Delegates, that Bias was not attending class.

"He's got other fish to fry," the chancellor said. Pesci thought Slaughter did not excuse the practice, but had given up thinking he could change it. Indeed, the chancellor had *not* given up. He regretted the un-fried fish at College Park, but he could do little to counteract the power of the money that could be made.

A few weeks later, the chancellor and his wife, Bernice, went to a party held for the team by the Fastbreakers at Driesell's house. It was Bernice Slaughter who spoke to Bias that night. He needed to be serious about his work or he would lose contact with school altogether, she told him. People would know he hadn't graduated. *He* would know.

"You can still salvage your degree," she said. Bias smiled his smile. One thing these kids did learn, one of Slaughter's aides said, was what to say and when to say it. They became sophisticated in the art of pretending to be what people wanted them to be.

The idea of young men squandering their educational opportunities troubled John Slaughter deeply.

He had grown up in the 1940s in Topeka, whose public schools provided the setting for the U.S. Supreme Court's historic desegregation decision, *Brown v. The Board of Education of Topeka*. Slaughter graduated from Topeka High in 1951, three years before the high court ruled that a so-called "separate but equal" educational system for blacks was unconstitutional.

"I was a product but not a victim of that system," he said.

Slaughter's family was the only black one on his block. Every day he started off walking to school with white kids. But they stopped walking at the nearby, all-white neighborhood school while he continued 10 or 11 more blocks to all-black Buchanan Elementary.

He impressed people with his scholarship early. His second grade teacher, Althea McBride, still remembered years later how thrilled Slaughter had been on the day he learned to use the dictionary.

But on some days, resentment burned in the young Slaughter, resentment that he was forced to walk past the neighborhood school. Why? What was so good about that school? He sometimes had rock fights on the way home with his white friends. And when he played baseball near the whites-only school, Slaughter tried to hit the ball far enough to smash its windows.

The reaction of the segregated Topekan was often less confrontational. One of Slaughter's teachers in grammar school, the tall, straight-backed, and passionately dedicated Mamie Luella Williams, described the approach. Before the Supreme Court case, she observed, black parents in Topeka urged their children to persevere, and to ignore mistreatment and prejudice. Black people found another way to prevail, a way around the obstacles and around unthinking people who blocked them, sometimes just because they always had.

"One of the sayings you would hear a lot was that Lincoln lived in a dirt house, but he wasn't a dirt man," Mrs. Williams recalled. Before the *Brown* decision, black Topekans felt obliged to accept a school system that featured almost every possible combination of racial separation and racial integration. Four elementary schools were all-black. The junior high school was integrated. And at Topeka High, black and white students went to class together, but athletic activities and social events were strictly segregated. The white team was called the Trojans. The black team was the Ramblers. Slaughter kept his Ramblers jacket for years, a remembrance not only of his days as a baseball player and half-miler on the track team, but of the way life was then.

"It's a wonder," he said, "that we weren't completely schizoid. Segregation affected some kids in very negative ways. Some kids believed they were inferior. It became a self-fulfilling prophecy. But there were others of us who refused to believe it. I think it made us stronger."

His own stability, feelings of self-worth, and willingness to take risks were reinforced by his parents, particularly by his father, Reuben Brooks Slaughter, whom he remembers as an independent man of many enterprises. In his twenties, the elder Slaughter, who had attended school only until the third grade, worked in the coal mines of southeastern Kansas. His job was setting shot, a technique for blasting coal from the seams so it could be shoveled into rail cars and hauled out of the shaft. One day a charge exploded prematurely. Part of the mine collapsed around him and he was badly burned. After crawling more than a mile to the mine entrance, his face and arm bleeding, he was taken home and eased onto the front porch to await a doctor's visit.

"He'll be dead by morning," the doctor predicted after his arrival. The family did not take him to a hospital. Slaughter does not know why -- perhaps there was none close by, or perhaps no nearby hospital accepted black patients. But when morning came, Reuben Slaughter was still alive. He lost his left eye, but he survived.

Sometime after the accident, Slaughter's father became a Baptist minister. But in time he concluded that the doctrine he was asked to preach was in error.

"He just couldn't accept the hellfire-and-damnation theory," Slaughter says. "The idea was, of course, that if a believer did not follow the dictates of the church without deviation, he was condemned to a fiery hell. My father saw God as more loving. He thought redemption was possible."

So, rather than teach lessons he did not believe, Reuben Slaughter left the pulpit. He went to work cleaning apartment buildings. He also gathered cardboard boxes from the local supermarket, folded them and sold them to the local paper mill. He collected and refurbished old furniture, and sold that, too.

Over time, the barn in back of Reuben Slaughter's house filled up with beds, dressers, chairs, and a few broken radios. His son, who had taken a class in radio repair, started tinkering with the broken Zeniths and Sylvanias he found in the barn. He made them work.

"My dad saw he had a gold mine on his hands," he said.

One day his father came home with a truck full of lumber. He built a small shop and bought some used radio test equipment. The younger Slaughter fixed any radio in town for $2 plus parts. His sisters called the shop their father had built "the radio shack."

"When I got good," Slaughter said, "I raised the price to $4."

His father could have had no idea what would flow from this small enterprise. Fascinated by electricity, Slaughter took his parents and his high school teachers aside and suddenly announced his life's work. "I'm going to be an electrical engineer," he told them. He was riding a moment of pure discovery and he wanted to share it. People either laughed at him or looked at him with a fear and anxiety he did not completely understand.

"I vividly remember writing this theme about what I wanted to do when I graduated," Slaughter recalled. "I said I wanted to go to Kansas State. I said this to advisers and counselors, but the next thing I knew I was in vocational school. Absolutely nobody took me seriously." That included even his baseball coach, a mentor whom he trusted. "Nobody in my family knew what an engineer was. I didn't either," he said. All he knew was that he was going to be one.

His teachers and coaches were not only questioning his ambition, they also were failing to tell him what preparatory courses he needed for a college engineering program. Guidance counselors enforced tradition and were to be overcome. Slaughter walked out of the trade school classes they recommended and into some of the courses he needed: chemistry, physics, and calculus.

"When he was going to take algebra, we thought it was a foreign language. And calculus, that was the one that bothered us," his sister Marilyn told a Topeka newspaper.

They might well have been stunned. No black electrical engineers were counted in Topeka's 1940 census. Of 197 plumbers and pipe-fitters in the city, only four were black. There was only one black among the city's 215 electricians, and just a single black physician, who cared for black patients only.

A black attorney in Topeka at that time offered this picture of the labor force: "You'd look up and down Kansas Avenue early in the morning and all you could see were blacks washing windows . . . At least it was work." The few blacks who worked at manufacturing plants in the city almost never were promoted; they retired after working the same jobs for 25 years.

Although Slaughter had few professional role models, he found examples of dignity and courage at home. He was the son of a man who did not succumb to a serious accident, to the pressures of religious superiors who demanded loyalty to what he thought was false doctrine, or to an economic system that forced him to scramble a livelihood from the discards of others. Like his father, Slaughter would not accept a future imposed on him by someone else. "I was bull-headed even then," he said.

With the money he earned as a radio repairman, the young man bought fishing tackle and asked his father if they could try it out together at Lake Shawnee, about 15 miles outside of Topeka. His father said no, he was too busy with work that never seemed to end. So Slaughter got on his bicycle -- his father called it a wheel -- and started for the lake. On the way, he bought a bucket of minnows, hung it over the handlebars and pedaled on.

About three miles from the lake, he heard a vehicle of some sort coming up behind him. Turning around, he saw his father, sitting behind the wheel of his old blue truck, shaking his head. He was a busy man, a man of many occupations. He had no time for fishing. Young Slaughter put his bike and his fishing gear in the back of the truck and climbed into the cab beside his dad. If they caught anything that day, Slaughter cannot remember.

During World War II, when bike tires were made with unreliable synthetic rubber, young Slaughter was constantly patching holes. One day, after fixing another flat, he walked up to the neighborhood gas station to use the air pump.

"Get the hell out of here," the owner yelled.

Slaughter walked home. Noticing that he was not riding, his father asked, "What's the matter with your wheel?" The youth reported what had happened.

"Come on," his father said, and they walked back to the station. When they got there, his father went directly to the station owner and said, "You bastard, don't you ever speak to my son like that again." They put air in the tire and went home. It was the only time Slaughter heard the former minister swear.

Like most fathers, R.B. Slaughter was inclined to lecture his son. He had several favorite messages he repeated when seemingly appropriate. He was partial to bromides: "Always put it away when you get it and you'll have it when you need it. . . . Everybody wants to go to heaven, but nobody wants to die. . . . If you want to make anything of yourself, son, you've got to learn to sacrifice." Slaughter thought there was wisdom in these words and he was impressed with his father's own careful adherence to what he said.

Slaughter went first to Washburn College in Topeka, then to Kansas State University, on a Whiting Scholarship, an annual stipend of $150, which was a substantial sum in those days. The money was especially important; he had to take extra courses to make up for those he did not get at Topeka High School. Slaughter found he was not gifted in mathematics, so he needed even more time to catch up. Knowing his limitations and remembering what his father had said about sacrifice, Slaughter gave up track and baseball in college.

Slaughter had learned lessons from his father that modern basketball players and their parents had not.

One year, the mother of a young Maryland player called Slaughter to complain that her son could not register for classes because of hundreds of dollars in parking fines that had gone unpaid. The athlete apparently thought basketball players could park wherever they pleased; his mother thought the university was punishing her son unfairly because, she argued, the car was actually hers.

"If I had done anything like that," Slaughter said, "my dad would have walked all the way to Manhattan, Kansas, to take that car home with him."

As a frequent public speaker, Slaughter shared many of his father's guidelines with Bible study classes, commencement assemblies, and various other audiences, while advancing several of his own principles. His father would have smiled upon hearing his son advising audiences: "Attend to what you believe in and care about; remember your personal commitments. . . . Opportunities are often missed because they come disguised as hard work. . . . God asks each of us, whether we are rich or poor, to accept the condition we find ourselves in and put our trust in him."

He used speeches as opportunities to educate. One dealt with changes in the nation's labor market. In 1865, at the start of the Civil War, there were 150,000 tradesmen in the South. Only about 5,000 of them were white. Whites didn't work with their hands then. They didn't have to. They had slave labor. But within 50 years of Emancipation, as the economy of the South changed, the numbers reversed. Southern tradesmen were almost all white. Only 5,000 of the region's 150,000 carpenters and electricians and pipe-fitters were black. In his many speeches as Maryland's chancellor, Slaughter invariably mentioned this historic shift, offering it as proof of social engineering that had removed a tier of economic status and achievement for an entire people.

In the decades after the Civil War, the practice of stifling talent was discussed by almost every successful black man (entertainers excepted). One story that Slaughter liked to retell was that of Percy Lavon Julian, a chemist who first synthesized cortisone into a substance that could ease the pain of arthritis. Julian also did important work with a substance used in treating glaucoma.

As he was leaving his Jackson, Mississippi home for DePauw University, Julian's grandmother and grandfather stood at the train station to wave goodbye. Julian's departing gaze was fixed on his grandfather's maimed right hand. Two of the old man's fingers had been chopped off by his owner to punish him for learning to write. His grandson would face similar, though less physical brutalities, in his own life.

Like Slaughter, who did not have the math background he needed for engineering, Julian's high school training had been poor. To catch up, he carried high school courses, along with a full program of freshman and sophomore work. He waited on tables at a white fraternity house and slept in the attic. By the time he graduated in 1920, Julian was a member of Phi Beta Kappa and valedictorian of his class.

Slaughter saw himself in a web of connection reaching back at least to Julian and extending forward to today's black students, including athletes. He wondered if the athletes fully understood the sacrifices others had made to create opportunities for them. He recognized that, while fingers were left intact in the 1980s, there were other ways in which black youngsters were severed from educational opportunity: through poverty, poor inner-city schools, over-emphasis on SAT scores, continuing job discrimination, and dreams of the NBA.

Black students of the 1980s had a better chance at exploring and developing their talents than Percy Julian or John Slaughter had had in Topeka. At the University of Maryland in 1986, only 5 percent of the students in the College of Engineering were black. This was considerably better than the nation as a whole. Of the 12 million engineers in the United States then, only 1 percent were black. The overall number of black students at Maryland was rising quickly, from about 9 percent when Slaughter arrived in 1982, to more than 12 percent in 1988; and, while the number of black faculty members was higher than at most public universities, that admirable figure was, in Slaughter's view, disturbingly stable.

Because legal barriers to opportunity had been removed and blacks were prominent on television sitcoms and in athletics, Americans had a false sense that black progress was widespread. Such public progress was almost an impediment, Slaughter thought, because it suggested more gain than the black population at large enjoyed. Slaughter was a part of that same illusion. Blacks were falling further behind, particularly in scientific fields. Though blacks accounted for 12 percent of the population in 1986, only 4 percent of U.S. scientists and engineers were black. Black enrollment in universities was dropping nationwide, though, under Slaughter, the decline at Maryland had slowed and been reversed. The university felt it was becoming more effective at keeping black students enrolled. But the national progress begun in the 1960s and 1970s had slowed markedly, and Slaughter pointed it out constantly.

"American science and engineering today are where baseball was before Jackie Robinson, Larry Doby and Roy Campanella, where basketball was before Bill Russell, where football was before Deacon Dan Towler, where tennis was before Arthur Ashe, where literature was before Paul Lawrence Dunbar, and where the law was before Thurgood Marshall."

In 1983, a year after he took over at Maryland, Slaughter gave the George Washington Carver Memorial Address at Simpson College in Iowa. Once again, he said, the American ideal of equal opportunity was being ignored. At its peril, the nation was ignoring another generation of black children.

"How they spend their time now -- the amount and quality of the education they receive -- is going to determine not only their personal development and role in society, but also the future of the country. To ignore poor and black students is to perpetuate the obstacles that stood in George Washington Carver's way. There are many talented and bright youngsters being lost for lack of attention and training," he said.

And, surely, he thought this same thing was happening to athletes caught up in the big time. They were getting an opportunity denied to many others, but they were so starstruck that they often didn't see it. If they were poorly prepared academically, they were not inclined to remedy their deficiencies, as Slaughter and Julian had done. They were working on the left hand, the quick first step, and all the other skills that made a player unstoppable on the basketball court. If or when they were stopped, though, they had nothing else. They were, in one sense, victims of opportunity.

Somehow, Slaughter himself had not been lost. He had overcome not just authority and evil tradition, but the fears of people who loved him and worried that his seemingly overreaching ambition would bring him pain. His mother had thought it would be nice if he got a job in the post office. Even black people believed that there were certain jobs -- engineering, of course, even coaching -- that whites could do and blacks could not. Habit became a prison. But Slaughter escaped.

Though somewhat unsettled by the direction their son had chosen, Slaughter's parents made their own sacrifices. After his father died, Slaughter found an old Internal Revenue Service W-2 form. It showed that R.B. Slaughter had been making about $3,000 a year at his apartment cleaning job. From that $50 a week paycheck, he sent his son $10.

Slaughter graduated from KSU in 1956. "I was the first black electrical engineer I had ever met," he said. It had taken him five years to finish college, so he was not shocked to see that Bias, constantly diverted from his studies, would need more than four years to earn his degree. Of course, Slaughter's and Bias's motivations and courses were not comparable. Slaughter had completed a rigorous engineering curriculum. Bias coasted through a hash of courses, some of which were selected just to maintain his eligibility.

After Kansas State, Slaughter moved to California in pursuit of work and graduate degrees. He knew that he would need a doctorate to advance in his field and he proceeded to get one. First, he got his master's degree in electrical engineering at the University of California at Los Angeles in 1961. As a student, he wrote papers on such matters as digital controls for tactical shipboard weapons. Others covered such obscure subjects as "Twin-t Compensation Using Root Locus Methods and the Application of Separable Programming to Optimal Control Problems with Quadratic Cost and Convex Constraints." (*Translation*: adjusting antennas from remote locations.) The University of California at San Diego awarded him a Ph.D. in 1971.

His life, though, was more than books and weapons systems. Slaughter served as a director of the San Diego Urban League in the early 1960s and as chairman of the 11th Naval District's Equal Opportunity Council. In 1967, the Women's Guild of Temple Emanu-el in San Diego named him its "Man of Distinction" in recognition of his work in human relations.

Once, during a job interview, an interviewer remarked, somewhat ominously, that Slaughter had a reputation as a promoter of educational opportunities and jobs for minorities. He hoped the reputation was deserved, Slaughter answered. In the aftermath of Bias's death, his effort to sustain that reputation as a crusading yet pragmatic university president would be opposed by the most intense, cross-cutting pressures. Sometimes, he would turn aside suggestions to take what he regarded as suicidal actions in pursuit of a saner, more decent athletic program: He refused, for example, to declare freshmen ineligible for varsity play at Maryland unless the ACC joined him.

In 1978, Slaughter accepted a post at the National Science Foundation in Washington, D.C., where he was deputy director for Astronomical, Atmospheric, Earth and Ocean Sciences. After a year, he returned to Washington State University, where he was named provost and vice president. He was moving up quickly.

Having become what he said he would become, having seen the applied and academic worlds of science, Slaughter found himself turning increasingly toward education and administration. The orderly habits of the engineer were useful in this pursuit, and he enjoyed pointing students, rather than antennas, in the right direction. With the same resolve that led him to contest the orders of high school guidance counselors, he decided he would become a university president.

But in late 1979, President Jimmy Carter's science adviser, Frank Press, asked him to come back to Washington and the National Science Foundation, this time as its director. A university-like federal agency, NSF was charged with nourishing scientific research and education throughout the country, with sharpening the cutting edge of higher education in engineering, physics, astronomy, chemistry, computer science and a range of other scientific disciplines.

The White House was insistent. Vice President Walter Mondale telephoned. Slaughter listened, unmoved.

The President came on the line next.

"You are my personal choice," Mr. Carter told him. Slaughter said nothing. After a moment, the President asked, "How do you feel right now?"

"Your call certainly heightens my interest," said Slaughter.

Slaughter's diffidence suggested he was waiting to hear from someone with real authority. But he was definitely not star struck. He had his own agenda. He liked Washington State and it liked him. He was on track to become the university's president. Beyond that, traveling across the country with household and family was expensive. He was still in debt from the last move, and he loved the

Pacific Northwest. He occasionally drove down along the Snake River for a little fishing.

Finally, though, he said yes. "It's tough to say no to the President of the United States," he recalled later.

His friends say there was another reason he accepted the job. Inevitably, Slaughter saw himself as a player in the struggle to remove racial barriers in American society. He would have opportunities to make history -- first black director of the National Science Foundation, for example. It was a job in which he could influence policy-making for the benefit of black kids at every university, not just Washington State. He felt obliged to surrender some of his own interests, some of his own comfort, to history and to the future.

"If you want to make something of yourself," his father had said, "you have to learn to sacrifice."

So, one of the nation's highest ranking administrators of scientific education -- who also happened to be broke -- rented a U-Haul truck and moved his family back to Washington. Comparing notes later with members of the Reagan Administration, he learned that Education Secretary Terrill Bell had handled moving in the same way. So much for the lavish life style of government service.

And for what? Slaughter wondered. There were moments over the next few years when he second-guessed his impulse to serve his country in the Washington bureaucracy. Carter lost the presidency to Ronald Reagan, and Slaughter found himself in service to an administration that seemed determined to end governmental support of scientific education -- an objective that ran directly counter to Slaughter's personal goals.

But the job took Slaughter to the pinnacle of scientific education and research in the United States. The young radio repairman who had been shunted into vocational training now led one of the most prestigious scientific enterprises in the world.

Slaughter's father died in 1977 at the age of 91. He had lived long enough to see his son and fishing partner become a Ph.D. and a high ranking official at a major U.S. university, but not long enough to know that he had been courted by presidents or that he had become the head of a major public university. Or, for that matter, to see the pain inflicted by success.

Slaughter feared he had arrived at the NSF just in time to have it dismantled with his unwilling assistance. Budget cuts were ordered by the Reagan Administration. Officially, Slaughter supported them.

He was obliged to appear before congressional committees to defend a budget that eviscerated NSF's reason for being: providing graduate fellowships. These grants fell from $80 million when Reagan took office to $20.9 million a few years later. Slaughter was accused of aiding and abetting the enemies of education.

After one unsettling year, Slaughter had a chance to leave NSF. John Toll, who had been a physicist before he became university president, and who maintained connections at the NSF, asked Slaughter if he would come to College Park to be its chancellor. The two had met during Slaughter's first assignment at the NSF in 1978. Toll thought Slaughter was just what Maryland needed. But Slaughter declined. He did not wish to leave the science foundation so quickly. And he did not want to suggest by leaving, less than two years into a six-year appointment, that he flitted so easily between jobs or that he found the Reagan Administration so thoroughly wanting in its approach to civil rights or its commitment to education and science.

Occasionally he paid a galling price for his loyalty. At a Senate hearing one day, Senator Edward Kennedy (D-Massachusetts) chastised him and the Reagan Administration for abandoning the development of young scientists. At the end of his discourse, Kennedy tried to soften his remarks, telling Slaughter, "I'm glad to have you here."

Utah Senator Orrin Hatch (R-Utah), moving to the administration's defense, said he imagined the day's experience was an honor Slaughter might well have skipped. "Not at all," the NSF director interrupted, "I'm not always taken to task by such distinguished critics."

Slaughter defended the budget cuts as best he could: The Administration was cutting the budget, but it was not abandoning the foundation's fundamental commitment to education, he insisted. After a year, he no longer believed that himself.

Several months after turning down John Toll, Slaughter accepted an invitation to make the spring graduation address at College Park. The ceremony was held in Cole Field House, the only campus building large enough for a Maryland graduating class, its families and friends. As the graduates filed into the building, Slaughter waited in a basement passageway with Peter O'Malley. A millionaire lawyer who had built Prince George's County's Democratic organization, O'Malley was an ambitious man who remained closely connected with the state legislature and various governors. And he was then president of the university's Board of Regents. As the gowned graduates streamed past, the two men leaned against the wall, Slaughter in academic robes, O'Malley in a business suit.

In the 1960s and 1970s, in the midst of a metropolitan area with an increasingly affluent and politically active black electorate, the university had been challenged repeatedly on its commitment to equal opportunity for both black students and black faculty. O'Malley had said often that he wanted a harmonious, multi-racial university. Now he wanted to act in a way that would symbolically and substantively meet that commitment. In Slaughter, there in the basement of Cole Field House, he had one of the most able candidates available as a captive audience.

Why, O'Malley wondered, had he declined to be interviewed for the job of chancellor? Slaughter explained. After almost two years in the job, though, he had no further illusions or hesitancy to leave, he told O'Malley. He would probably go back to Washington State University. O'Malley was impressed with the sense of responsibility he found in Slaughter. One of the most candid and thoughtful people he had ever met, he said later. And he saw an opportunity.

"If you go back, you'll probably be comfortable, but you'll be as far as you can be from the problems you should have an impact on," he said. O'Malley's instincts were acute. Slaughter was part of the non-marching, indoor contingent of the civil rights movement. He and countless other black Americans were anonymous Jackie Robinsons.

When they reached the Cole Field House stage, O'Malley whispered to Toll, "I think we have a chance with this man. Is he still your first choice? I think we can persuade him." If Slaughter were an athlete, O'Malley thought, no possible inducement or argument would be left unused. He spoke quickly to Clarence Mitchell, Jr., another regent, who was sitting on the stage.

"I think Slaughter will come here, but it's going to take some people showing him how much we want him," O'Malley said. Mitchell and Slaughter went to lunch that day at the student union, a short walk down the hill from the field house. In the discussion, Mitchell had strong cards to play.

Before his retirement, Clarence Mitchell had been Washington lobbyist for the National Association for the Advancement of Colored People. He also was a confidant of Lyndon Johnson when Johnson was Senate majority leader. Beyond Washington and Baltimore, where he lived, Mr. Mitchell was less well known than other civil rights leaders, but his relatively anonymous work on the U.S. Voting Rights Act of 1964 was regarded as critical to its passage. Some called him the 101st senator.

Slaughter knew of him and of his work. He knew that in the 1930s, Mitchell, then a young newspaper reporter, had seen a black man lynched on the Eastern Shore of Maryland. And, working for the *Afro-American* newspaper in Baltimore, Mitchell also had covered the 1937 court case in which Supreme Court Justice Thurgood Marshall, then an NAACP lawyer, fought to open the University of Maryland law school to blacks.

Because he was black, Clarence Mitchell had himself been barred from entering the University of Maryland as an undergraduate. Almost fifty years after the law school case, as a member of the university's Board of Regents, he would cast a vote when the Regents chose a new chief executive officer. He told Slaughter that history had borne them to a moment of fulfillment.

After listening to his appeal, Slaughter told Mitchell, "I'll let you know if I decide not to do it."

"You can't decide not to do it," Mitchell replied.

Slaughter recalled his temporizing as if it were obvious to himself and to Mitchell. Slaughter's inclination was always to take more time, but he knew Mitchell was right even as he was trying to delay his decision.

A few weeks after the graduation ceremony, the Regents made John Slaughter College Park's new chancellor.

Despite his initial reluctance, he was very pleased with his new post. He came to the university as a man who believed that on a college campus, a more perfect community could be approximated and should be pursued. Good universities nurtured idealism and commitment, he thought. In his inaugural speech, he said Maryland should strive to become "truly multi-cultural, multi-ethnic and multi-generational." Maryland attracted many foreign students; its tradition of providing adult education dated from its service to World War II veterans. Slaughter wanted to increase substantially the number of black students and faculty.

When O'Malley asked how he would attract more black students, he said, "We're going to send a bus into Washington, bring kids out here and have picnics." Something assertive, structural and public was needed. That was commitment, he said. The university had to be noticeably reaching outside its walls. It had to find ways to be more approachable, he believed.

Some alumni were stunned by Slaughter's presence and his statements. O'Malley got letters from residents of College Heights, the virtually all-white neighborhood where Slaughter lived, objecting to the university's hiring of a black chancellor. Ted Lewis, president of St. Mary's College in southern Maryland and one of Slaughter's colleagues, recalled a buffet dinner on his campus right after Slaughter arrived as chancellor. Waiting to serve himself, a local judge, who had graduated from the university with both undergraduate and law school degrees, trumpeted his view of the new black chancellor. "We're on our way down. It's a damn shame."

Slaughter could not have avoided arousing this kind of opposition. It was there. It had to be faced if his commitment was real. His colleagues, while admiring his determination, thought he was taking big risks. It was widely held that university chancellors should concentrate on academic concerns -- and that too much attention to equality inevitably hurt quality.

Slaughter met that suspicion head-on and dismissed it.

"I believe we must be willing to move away from the ordinary and be willing to take intelligent risks to accomplish many of the things we deem worthwhile," he said early in his chancellorship. Too often, he said, administrators talked about changing racial attitudes, and usually did nothing to promote that change.

As NSF director, Slaughter had not thought it prudent to contest the power of Budget Director David Stockman or the mandate of Ronald Reagan. But now he was in charge. He had the power and *he* was setting policy.

On his campus, by accepting criticism of a new governing structure he had proposed, Slaughter skillfully avoided controversy over the faculty's role in policy-making. The power-sharing that resulted and the openness of the process helped give Slaughter a strong base of support in the summer of 1986. Ralph Bennett, the professor of architecture, thought Slaughter's handling of the situation was the best example of shared, collegial governing he had seen on the campus.

The son of Reuben Slaughter liked to quote a proverb from Kenya: "Sticks in a bundle cannot be broken."

Slaughter's first years on the campus included almost every public and private problem a chancellor could encounter. Some were serious. He and Toll struggled almost from the beginning over the definition of College Park -- whether it should devote its resources to research or teaching. Toll was a presence that never faded and, unlike Slaughter, he lived on the campus. The president's house had always been there. Slaughter had a beautiful residence in a nearby neighborhood, but the symbolic presence of Toll dominating the university was a strong one.

Some of the chancellor's problems were zany: *Playboy* magazine wanted to use College Park settings to photograph a spread it was going to call "Beauties of the ACC." Slaughter said no. It was exploitation of young women, of the university, and of the ACC.

Sometimes the problems came in a different wrapping, but many had to do with sports. He issued a public reprimand to Driesell for his response to charges that a UM basketball player had molested a female student. The community was evenly divided on that issue. Half thought Slaughter had humiliated Driesell without cause. Half wanted the coach dismissed. As a man who had seen political power at work, Slaughter had no illusions about the scope and depth of protection available to his basketball coach. No one had a constituency as rich and powerful as Lefty's. He had worked on it for 17 years. He had his sticks well bundled.

During the press conference on the morning Bias died, Driesell said the young man had been like a son to him. Writing immediately thereafter, Carl Rowan, a syndicated columnist, said the coach's words were empty: How could a father have so thoroughly neglected his son's academic well-being? Slaughter expressed no doubt about Driesell's pain. And he did not hold the coach responsible for the fatal drug party. But if it was reasonable to expect a big-time basketball coach or a university chancellor to be a stand-in father, a father like his own, Slaughter thought they had all failed.

Chapter 5

All-World

During Bias's senior year at Northwestern High School in Landover, Maryland, the famous basketball coaches called frequently at his family's brown-shingled, white-trimmed rancher. Lime green outdoor carpet covered the front steps. The shrubs were carefully trimmed into squares. In the living room, James and Lonise Bias listened to the great men of basketball praise their work and the accomplishments of their son.

Among the recruiters was North Carolina State's flamboyant Jim Valvano, a smoother showman than Driesell and one of the more entrepreneurial of the college coaches. Jimmy V and Lefty were as important to the big-money game as any player, even the most extraordinarily talented. With their flair, coaches inspired booster loyalty, and gave their teams a permanent personality. They were controversial, so they could become the focus of perpetual arguments about games and philosophies.

Valvano had a good chance of successfully recruiting Bias, who was drawn to State because several of his friends had gone there.

But when James Bias asked Valvano to outline his approach to academics, Mr. Bias found the answers all wrong.

"He acted like he didn't give a damn about academics," James Bias recalled. "He said, 'I got people right here to take care of that. These guys take care of that.'" Valvano gestured at his entourage of aides and assistants.

The former N.C. State coach remembers the conversation somewhat differently.

"There isn't a coach in the country who doesn't go in the door and say academics are most important," he said. "Most of them mean it. Coaches want their kids to be models. It's good for the coach."

Valvano says he enjoyed recruiting Lenny Bias. "He was a nice kid, a very easy kid to recruit. Some of these kids are more articulate and verbal and fun to be with and some are a pain in the butt -- as I'm sure we are to them. But we had so many kids from the Washington area and so many of them had been successful here that I thought Lenny would come to N.C. State."

At the airport, following Bias's visit to the N.C. State campus in Raleigh, Valvano and his prospect ran into a group of students. One of them, from Maryland, recognized Bias, and asked him where he was thinking of going to school.

"N.C. State and Maryland," Bias said.

"Maryland?" said the student from College Park. "I go to Maryland. You don't want to go there."

Valvano had seen this phenomenon before. "Students are like soldiers -- always unhappy," he explained. He had seen the chronic complaining work against him as State students urged recruits to go elsewhere. Just another obstacle for Valvano, and not the biggest one.

James Bias wanted his son to play for a coach who not only said he valued education for his players but took personal responsibility for it. If the head man didn't show commitment, he thought, the players would see that immediately and act accordingly. The coach was the most powerful figure in a player's life. By helping him perfect his skills, by giving him plenty of playing time, by getting the team into the NCAA tournament's high-exposure Final Four, the coach was going to make the kid's dreams come true. Frequently, the coach was rich and had the power to make his players rich if they worked hard. What the coach wanted and did, the way he handled himself in victory and defeat -- his values -- were riveting influences.

"These are 17-year-old kids, half scared, the TV cameras are rolling, the reporters all around. They don't know what's going on," James Bias said.

So for Valvano, with all his charisma and money, to dish off the responsibility for education to assistants was a powerful statement. "That killed it for him," Bias's father said.

And the door swung open even wider for Driesell.

James Bias was impressed with Lefty's presentation. "He didn't sell himself as someone who just cared about shoe contracts and endorsements or how many Final Fours he would get into. He sold himself as a role model on grades. That was the key issue. He knew that's what we cared about. He guaranteed that Lenny would get a degree in four years," Mr. Bias said.

And Maryland was attractive to James and Lonise Bias for another reason. They wanted to keep their son close to home. As strong and confident as he seemed, Lenny was a private person, immature, even fragile, they thought. He would want and need their support. Kids got in trouble when they went away. The newspapers had stories every day about basketball players in trouble. No parent with a talented athlete on the way to college could ignore these stories. Jeff Baxter had wanted to attend Syracuse University, but his mother pushed him to nearby Maryland. Maybe if the young men were closer to home, their parents thought, problems could be detected sooner and dealt with more easily. There was more control if your son was only a 15-minute drive away.

When the last phone call was made, Valvano says, he learned that the decision had been a family one.

"Lenny told me his mom had finally said something. She had never verbalized her thinking until then. Lenny said she told him 'I'd rather you stayed close to home.' That was it," Valvano said.

Before he enrolled, James Bias tried to get his son to focus on what he would study at Maryland. It was not easy when the best coaches in America were telling him he was a certain All-American. As fathers do -- as John Slaughter's father had done -- James Bias told his son stories from his own experience. He had known many good athletes as a younger man.

"A lot of them went from All-American to All-Nothing," he would say. He had seen it happen. He had seen the heartbreak and the deadening realization that nobody in business cared if you were a playground legend. James Bias, telling the story, used the "all-nothing" line over and over.

His son played that summer in the Derby Classic in Louisville, Kentucky, and he was voted Most Valuable Player in the McDonald's Capital Classic at the Capital Centre near his home. All-Nothing did not seem possible.

Future Maryland Terrapin Lenny Bias had learned basketball at the Columbia Park Recreation Center from recreation director Lee Madkins. The square, brick building, an addition to the neighborhood elementary school, was two blocks from Len's home in a pleasant suburban neighborhood just about on the District of Columbia line in Prince George's County.

His mother was a customer service supervisor at Washington National Bank. A deeply religious woman, Lonise Bias had a faith that gave her confidence and charisma. She seemed ready to stand in as mother for many of the Terrapin players. One of her brothers was a lawyer, and one worked for IBM. The family had moved to Columbia Park from the District of Columbia, where they had lived in a public housing project.

James Bias was a private man whose bent for thoughtful analysis seemed wasted in his work as an equipment repairman. Reporters writing about his son wondered if the family had reached middle-class status. Mr. Bias said he was not sure. They were working at it, he said.

Len was their first child. His mother nicknamed him Frosty soon after he was born. Overnight, it seemed, he grew into a tall and lanky youngster. She remembered looking up one day to find him towering over her.

Recreation center director Madkins said Bias, at first, was like a lot of kids whose bodies outpaced their coordination. At first, he wanted to play football. He thought he could be a wide receiver. But there were no junior football pants long enough to fit him, which was just as well. He was not good at football, and he did not particularly like the physical contact. Bias hated the beating he took from older players on the basketball court, Madkins remembered, until he grew big enough and tough enough to handle himself. Until then, Madkins said, he pouted and threatened to go home to get his father.

When he tried out for a junior high school basketball team, he saw how far he had to go. He didn't find his name on the list of players who had made the team, Madkins and others were fond of remembering.

"I couldn't believe it," Bias recalled later. "Right then I was determined to show those people I could play the game."

He told Don Markus of *The Sun*: "I've always worked harder when people said I couldn't shoot. I worked on my shot. When they said I wasn't a ball handler, I worked on that. Most of the time the criticism is coming from Coach Driesell. He'll point out a million things I did wrong, but it's helped make me a better player."

The skills came slowly. Though he had the jumping ability and the strength from the beginning, and could dunk, he had "no shot," and had what players call "bad hands." No one could take the ball away from him, if he got the ball, Madkins said. For a time, he had trouble catching it in the first place.

Bias became a world champion gym rat. Madkins came down in the morning, unlocked the building to let him in, and much, much later, locked it behind him. Neighbors hearing the ball on the floor or seeing lights in the building called the coach to make sure the young man in the rec center was authorized to be there. Sometimes he took exercise mats off the wall where they hung under the baskets, spread them on the floor and napped.

After his disappointment at not making the junior high team, a certain over-the-edge quality crept into Bias's approach to basketball. Young men, growing and testing themselves, could be wild, but he was wilder than most. His taunting approach to opponents made Madkins laugh in embarrassment. The coach remembered a trip to Philadelphia, Bias's first time away from home. He was 15 and he was dunking at will over players two or three years older. Dunking was his game then, his distinctive signature. He liked to let opponents know he was dominating them.

"You're looking at an All-American," he loudly told the opposing team in Philadelphia. It was as if he had to erase any doubt he may have had in his own mind.

The doubts did fade. His ability surpassed those of other players his age. He grew impatient with team drills he had mastered. Coach Wagner suggested his father buy him a set of weights. His jump shot began to develop, his range expanded and his sense of the court began to seem more instinctive.

But his emotional maturity lagged.

"You could see that he was a good athlete," Wagner said. "But he was kind of a big baby. He liked to hang out with little kids and a lot of times he ended up acting just like them." That description recurs in the stories about Bias -- stories told before and after his death.

John L. Moylan, the principal at DeMatha High School in Hyattsville, Maryland, found Wagner's assessment accurate. Bias might well have gone to DeMatha, where he would have played for Morgan Wootten, perhaps the most successful high school coach in America and unquestionably the most noted one in Maryland. But DeMatha was wary of him.

"He was a wild kid -- talented, but out of control," Moylan said.

Wagner himself benched Bias for losing his temper. Once, Lenny threw the ball at an official, and not so lovingly.

"With his big hands and his strength, he threw it like a golf ball. The guy [the referee] almost lost his lungs," said Mike Burke, then a sportswriter for *The Prince George's Sentinel*.

For a long time, Bias could not avoid the urge to deliver retaliation fouls. As a high school senior, some thought, he had grown even less mature. Wagner told the young man he could achieve virtually anything -- if he could find self-control.

Driesell and others knew of his emotional lapses. But they came calling anyway.

In a way, the outcome of the recruiting battle was never in doubt. Bias was almost a Terp before he arrived as a student on the College Park campus. When he was in junior high school, he sold ice cream during games at Cole Field House. Northwestern was not far from College Park and Bias knew several Terrapin players, notably Adrian Branch, who had gone to DeMatha. He had worked out at the university with Branch and other Terps while still in high school. He and Branch became close friends. "I raised him," Branch told his friends. College Park was home.

When he walked into the massive field house, he must have scanned the red and white banners commemorating the years in which Maryland teams held national rankings. Next to them were the jerseys of Maryland's best players, their numbers retired in the ultimate sports tribute a school can pay its best players. He imagined his own number hanging there in the pantheon of uniforms with Tom McMillen's 54, John Lucas's 15, and Len Elmore's 41.

Because of his immaturity, there was no guarantee that Bias would make it at Maryland or anywhere else. But he seemed to settle down at Maryland. For one thing, Driesell scared him a bit. Bias thought the coach's tirades were, on occasion, more than motivating.

"Don't worry about it," his teammate Herman Veal would tell him. "He does that. He'll cool off." But Len told Coach Madkins at the end of his freshman year that he might transfer. According to Slaughter, Branch talked him out of it.

One place that Bias considered for a transfer was North Carolina State. Jim Valvano says Bias called him one afternoon at his office.

"I'm not starting," he told the coach. "I want to play for you."

"I told him I couldn't speak to him," Valvano insists. "It was against the rules, an NCAA violation." Under the NCAA rules, attempting to recruit a player who is attending another college is considered "tampering" and is regarded as one of the most heinous infractions.

"I told him to go and talk to Coach Driesell. I have a feeling he'll straighten it out with you," Valvano said with a laugh. "He worked it out well enough that Lenny beat my brains out for the next three years."

Driesell discounts any suggestion that Bias might have been unhappy at College Park. In any event, he says, under NCAA rules he couldn't have transferred to a team in his own conference. As if no other proof were needed, Driesell pointed to the splendid outcome of the young man's career at Maryland.

As much as he may have yelled at the young man, Driesell said he found Bias immediately impressive, particularly in his capacity for work and his passion for the game.

Slaughter saw him play his first college game, against Penn State at the Civic Center in Baltimore, and thought he was looking at the classic lost freshman.

"Green as he could be," Slaughter recalled. After several misses, Bias hit his first shot from the top of the key. A big smile took over his face. His career was under way. But he played hesitantly, was benched, and did not make the starting lineup until the end of the year. In the last game of his first season, Bias held his own against Clyde Drexler, the University of Houston star.

He worked to round off the rough edges of his game, filling in the blank spots, building on his strengths. Macho Lenny took ballet lessons. He blindfolded himself to get a better feel for the dribble, a learned basketball skill that often comes more slowly to taller players. And he kept growing, building and schooling his body. His physical development stunned even his teammates.

"The muscles were just exploding on him," Baxter said. More discipline would have made Bias an even more dominating player, he thought. His self-control had improved, Baxter conceded, but he remained a hothead who would pout, snarl and glare when he was unhappy about the way the game was going. He looked like a player who, if provoked, might self-destruct, by retaliating and getting tossed out of a game. He made it clear he didn't like the physical play, and so, perhaps, he was served up more and more of it.

Bias first earned national respect and attention in the 1984 Atlantic Coast Conference Tournament when his 26 points against Duke led the Terps to a conference title. Still a sophomore, he was named the tournament's Most Valuable Player.

As much as he strove to be intimidating on the floor, Bias impressed almost everyone with his manners off the court. Still, he remained immature. During the summer after his junior year -- after he had made the All-ACC team -- Madkins took him to a local recreation-league tournament. Before the game, to the delight of the schoolchildren, Bias put on a one-man dunking exhibition with all the frills. When he was finished, he sat on the bench with Madkins. Suddenly, the coach smelled something burning, looked to his left and saw that Bias, grinning as mischievously as one of the youngsters in the crowd, had set a whole book of matches on fire. Madkins grabbed them and put them out.

The next year, he was ACC Player of the Year and a member of second- and third-string All-American teams. He repeated as ACC Player of the Year in 1986 and made every All-American first team.

In a game against Notre Dame at South Bend, Indiana, during his senior year, Bias struggled with an Irish player whose defense owed a good deal to leaning and pushing. Bias leaned back -- and worse.

"I could tell when he had it about up to here," Slaughter remembered. "I thought the elbows were about to fly."

Bias threw the ball at Irish player Mark Stevenson and earned himself a technical foul, not what Maryland needed in a close game. The Terps lost, 66-62.

If there was anything in this retaliation that suggested a more serious deficiency in Bias's self-control, basketball and its demands camouflaged it.

"He's been getting the hell beat out of him all year and that night he let out all the frustrations," said Tom Newell, personnel director for the NBA's Indiana Pacers, after the game. "It would bother me if he didn't. Of course, he's a little nasty himself. It's as if there are five guys playing with knives, and he's packing a .357 magnum. He's just smart enough to pick his spots. That's what I like about him."

John Slaughter was not nearly so happy about the outburst.

After the team got home from South Bend, Slaughter saw Bias and John Johnson, a freshman guard from Knoxville, Tennessee, in the student union. He took Bias aside and told him what he had sensed during the game.

"I understand how you feel. But I hope you know how much you have going for you," the chancellor said. The young man smiled, embarrassed.

Lenny Bias was a tangle of conflicting characteristics: He was boastful and aggressive, but he could be self-effacing. He loved Pac-Man -- and Armani suits. He was generous -- and self-centered. He was a public person who cherished privacy. He coveted a Porsche or a Mercedes Benz, but said he would be happy if he could draw all day for the rest of his life. And there was no time to sort out the conflicts.

"He was a good kid, basically," said Randy Hoffman, the assistant athletic director. "He got caught up in the limelight in the last year. He went from being shy and unassuming to a kid with an ego."

As a student, his father said, Bias lost his way academically almost immediately. As soon as he signed the scholarship form, his father thought, the idea of education vanished from the agenda. Practice, travel, and a lack of class preparation put him permanently behind.

When he arrived at College Park, Bias thought college would be like high school: Professors would recognize that you were a ballplayer and give you time to catch up.

"He talked to his teachers," his father said. "He would say, 'I've been off playing ball. What can I do?' At first, they worked with him. But after awhile, after all the missed classes, they hardened on him. 'I've made all the concessions I can make,' they'd say."

The traveling was a killer.

"Basketball was good for you only if you wanted to be a travel agent," his father said. "They had a busier schedule and covered more miles than the Washington Bullets. How could they succeed?"

The better his son got as a player, the more recognition he earned, and the more people wanted something from him, the less time he himself had for being a student or sorting out his life. The more control he gained over his body and his game, the less he had over his life -- particularly his life as a student. James Bias, too, seems to have felt a loss of control over his son's fate at College Park. He was hesitant to question "the almighty University of Maryland."

"The school has so much clout, the senators, congressmen -- and the deity of the coach," said Wayne Curry, the Bias family's lawyer. And all of them, he said, are trading on the dream: "These guys are superior athletes. They've come through a system where they know they want to play ball. But they could be shown what it all means, the odds against them." And even if a player has the physical gifts, he may not have his head on sufficiently straight to endure the pressures and confusion those skills bring him.

On the surface, Len Bias handled the stress and challenge of his life reasonably well. Except with reporters, for whom he had contempt, he was generous with his time, as generous as Fastbreaker Heise had said in his eulogy -- too generous, perhaps.

"He was a very caring and understanding person. That may have been part of his problem. He was always helping people. He was a private person. So am I," said his father. James Bias seems more introspective than his son was, but the younger man was not without his insights.

"People made a mistake if they only wanted to talk to him about basketball," James Bias said. "He was a shy sort of person. When you're that way, it can be a problem for you. People don't understand. And then you see how they react to you. He thought they were looking past him at his athletic prowess, at the sweat."

"They don't see me," he told his father, who saw a bit of the tempestuous John McEnroe in his son. "Basketball is not my whole life. It's just a game."

James Bias said his son had written essays about racial stereotyping and about the life of athletes. Basketball players were all "running head over heels toward destruction," the young man thought at one point. These papers were lost in the files of teachers whose names Mr. Bias did not remember.

His mother thought he lost sight of his responsibility to himself. "Everyone who smiles in your face is not your friend," Lonise Bias advised young people after her son's death. It was fine to help others, to be accommodating, but ultimately you have to know yourself. "Many of our young people love the outside of themselves," she said. "They don't know the inside."

Wendy Whittemore, one of the basketball team's academic advisers, said sports stars in America were treated as if they were community property.

"You go from place to place on the campus and everybody wants just a little time. 'Can I talk to you about this?' someone says. What are you going to do? I don't think Lenny was ever able to get away from that," she said.

Everyone used the role-model athlete for something.

As a part of the campus's minority recruitment program strengthened by Slaughter, the admissions office periodically brought high school students to the campus for what it called a "Prep Day Program." These were the bus trips Chancellor Slaughter had promised. Ninth, 10th and 11th graders from Baltimore and other local high schools visited the campus. On occasion, an athlete gave personal testimony, an inspirational pep talk. The university's admissions director, Linda Clement, would leave a message with the athletic department, asking for a player. Bias would frequently designate himself, Clement thought. Always anxious to have a good relationship with the admissions department, Lefty may well have ordered his star to appear. (Slaughter doubted that: Driesell was jealous of anything that distracted a player from basketball.) Either way, Clements said, Bias came with purpose and was brutally honest in what he said about his own situation. There was sad irony here: He was the star who helped fill the field house and provided an endorsement of the university for students brought to the campus as part of Slaughter's outreach program. Yet, as a senior, he missed so many classes in service to the demands of television that he was getting precious little of the education he recommended to others.

The high school kids before whom he spoke saw only glory and grandeur.

"LEN-NEE, LEN-NEE, LEN-NEE," they would chant. He might have smiled a bit, Clements said, but he did not present himself as a big man on campus. Almost the opposite, in fact.

"If I had worked harder in high school, I wouldn't be having as much difficulty," he would say.

The confession made him unhappy, not just because he was behind, but because his academic goals -- his interest in a business degree, his interest in art and apparel design -- were out of reach by then, according to his father.

James Bias says the atmosphere Driesell created at Cole Field House was controlling and discouraging. Every course his son selected had to be approved by the academic counselors -- a precaution taken by the university to keep track of athletes who were not always up to the selection task themselves. Lenny would sign up for one set of classes, and the advisers would change his selections without telling him. "They think I'm stupid," Bias told his father.

"They said, 'Don't worry. You'll be on schedule for graduation,'" James Bias remembered. "And that was it. You're locked into a cattle pen with different guys with different ideas but they're all locked in together.

"In the beginning, while you're being recruited, life is like a blank sheet of typing paper," Mr. Bias said. "But as soon as you sign the scholarship form, life shrinks to the size of a pencil point."

"I didn't tell my players what course to take," Driesell said. "I didn't want to play God with them. I didn't even tell my own children what to take. My daughter's taking philosophy. That's not what I would have recommended, but it's her life."

James Bias insists his son complained to Driesell about the courses chosen for him by others, but received no support.

"Where else you going to play? Where else you going?" Driesell asked Bias, according to Mr. Bias's account. By then, though he considered doing so, it would not have been easy to transfer. Grades that were acceptable at Maryland might not be good enough elsewhere. Moreover, he was in the flow at Maryland, part of its momentum, and there were many aspects of it that gave him pleasure.

But it was not an easy life. The players faced a mountain of class work, and every day, every week, it grew larger. And they fell further and further behind, according to Wendy Whittemore, the academic adviser. She was anxious to attack the stereotype that they had no ability and no motivation. "They cared," she said.

And they suffered.

Bias felt pressure to be the classic student athlete, the ideal around whom intercollegiate athletics is built. He became something of a myth -- an icon of the game, useful for the games themselves and for sustaining basketball at Maryland and beyond.

Coaches, boosters, officials, reporters -- everyone, including Chancellor Slaughter defined him as they wanted him to be. For the boosters, he was "our man for all seasons"; for the admissions director, he was an earnest, inspirational speaker with the right message; and for Slaughter, he was an opportunity to reinforce the importance of academics on Maryland's basketball team. A professional coach who played him one-on-one during the pre-draft spring of 1986 offered this evaluation: "He had the best balance between ego, dignity and confidence that I'd seen in a college kid." People saw what they wanted to see.

Everything depended on these characterizations, none of which was wholly false, many of which were self-serving. They were images crafted, perhaps only subconsciously, to sustain public support for intercollegiate athletics, the coach's career, the coach's shoe contract, the university's TV revenue and gate receipts, the chancellor's dream for the student-athlete ideal, the agent's commissions, the boosters' thrills -- and Bias's own financial future. Not the development of his mind, his critical judgment, his sense of self.

Professor Joyce Ann Joyce met Bias on the first day of the 1983 fall semester, his second year at Maryland. He walked into her introductory class in Afro-American literature and, at 6'8", was more than conspicuous as he found a seat.

"It was a chaotic day, and he came late, this very tall young man. He came in and he was so tall. I said, 'Well, do you play basketball?'"

The question was met with stifled giggles. Bias was a campus figure. Who didn't know he was a basketball player?

Her greeting was one of those "How's-the-weather-up-there?" questions that put basketball players into straitjackets. Others who were not as open and honest as Professor Joyce fit him silently into the mold. Either way, it was limiting and he disliked it. When he was being recruited so heavily as a high school freshman, Coach Wagner says Bias showed up one day with tears in his eyes.

"No one wants to talk to me anymore," the young man said. "They just want to know what college I'm going to play for."

"He never knew who wanted to know Lenny Bias the basketball player, and Lenny Bias the person. That really upset him," his teammate Herman Veal said. "I'm not talking for him, but I know that's what he felt. You couldn't go anywhere without people saying 'There's Lenny Bias,' wanting to be his friend, wanting to buy him things without even knowing him. That was one hang-up he really did have.

"He used to say 'Let me put a mask over my head. If you'll be my friend with the mask on, maybe we can be friends with it off.'" He did not enjoy being an icon.

In her classroom at Taliaferro Hall and in other places on the campus, Professor Joyce got to know him better. She found him a "sweet and thoughtful person." The description could not have been more at odds with his public image, an image owing everything to his aggressive and powerful style of basketball and little to the sensitivity and complexity that Joyce and others saw in him. He was Len Bias, the cake-and-ice-cream superstar headed for the National Basketball Association.

In Professor Joyce's class, he performed like most other ballplayers: He was indifferent, frequently absent, and a distinct under-achiever, but he was polite. Whatever he may have thought about Professor Joyce's greeting during his first day in her class, he gave no hint of irritation.

"Yes, I play basketball," he said. He smiled and sat down. His appearance that day was the high point of his participation in her class.

Professor Joyce began her course in Afro-American literature with the slave narratives, then moved on to the Harlem Renaissance, Richard Wright's *Native Son*, the work of James Baldwin, and the black poets of the 1960s. She stopped keeping track of absences after Bias missed five classes. On the only two assignments he completed, she gave him Fs. She invited students to come in for a pre-review of tests and she gave double credit for class presentations, but Bias did not take advantage of either offer.

Professor Joyce passed him anyway. It was something she did for ballplayers. "I gave many a D. It was grace," she said. A passing mark, though he had made no passing grades on the way. She told herself then that it made little sense to have him repeat the course. Now she thinks she was contributing to a destructive atmosphere of unreality, undergirding a sense that whatever one did or didn't do, there was a safety net.

She knew that Bias and his teammates cared only about their professional aspirations -- "chasing the dream" is the way Slaughter thought of it. Academics did not match up well against the lure of the pros. Like others who knew them, Joyce thought of basketball players as special people with special burdens who needed and deserved special treatment. They were geniuses at basketball who were harried by travel schedules and academic demands.

"The A student can't make As on the road," she said.

Like James Bias, Joyce did not make a federal case of what she saw. She tried to accommodate herself to the reality, just as the players did.

Bias and Gatlin improvised a 10-second skit about their lives at Maryland. The two friends and co-workers pretended to be harried lawyers, bankers, or stockbrokers with no time to be friendly, passing each other on the street or in the train station on the way home after work.

"How's the wife?" Gatlin asked.

"Great, great," Bias replied.

"How're the kids?"

"Great, great."

"It's 5 o'clock."

"Yup."

"Gotta go."

"See ya."

It was gallows humor -- a tableau of "The Commuter Athlete" -- about the absence of time and the lack of real contact with the rest of the world.

The athlete's life was a series of skits in which most of the scripts were written by others. Bias had to be a slamdunk, machismo warrior on the court. If he won, he could be charming. If he lost, he was almost required to be miserable and distraught. If he was not surly, he must not care enough.

"It's as if he lives in two separate worlds," his mother said. "When he's playing ball, everyone can see his talent, his macho image. Off the floor, he loves the privateness and peacefulness." He was a role model and, perhaps, a role player, moving in and out of celebrity and the confusing world of a young man growing up.

Bias's teammates were in awe of games in which he played as if "possessed." There was a kind of double thrill in his play then, as if he was making it happen, but there was also a force operating within him, guiding and lifting him. Even when he seemingly was in control, performing at peak efficiency, he was not in control. In those moments, particularly, he was the instinctive basketball genius.

No game was a better showcase of Bias's development than the one on February 22, 1986, against North Carolina at Chapel Hill. He had scored 41 points against Duke a month earlier, but the Carolina game was the one that people would remember. Moments from that game endure as incandescent images suspended in memory, pages in a mental scrapbook kept by players on both teams.

The Dean Smith Student Activities Center at Chapel Hill had just opened when the Terps arrived. Fresh paint stung the nostrils. It was the new mecca of East Coast basketball, a shrine to the power and dominance of Smith and the Tar Heels, not to mention an unintended rebuke to Driesell, who had promised to make Maryland the UCLA of the East. What Lefty promised, Dean had delivered.

Maryland arrived in Chapel Hill with a record of 13-11, and only one victory in seven ACC games. The team was in danger of being left out when invitations to the NCAA tournament were sent.

Carolina was ranked No. 1 in the national polls, a circumstance that made it a game worthy of the teams' historic rivalry: The Tar Heels were always No. 1; Maryland was the upset artist.

As game time approached, Driesell, full of nervous energy, paced, just as he had earlier in the day outside the motel. He moved around the locker room as the players prepared for the game. It was the kind of game that could impart forgiveness to an entire season -- adding to the lore of upsets and reviving the hope of playing for a championship. Upsets had the quality of partial rebirth, even salvation.

Driesell stopped in front of his starting players with one more review of what he wanted. His talk brought all the tension and expectations to a hard boil. Finally, the coach was standing in front of Bias with the question everyone in the room was waiting for, knowing it was coming, anxious for it, knowing it would release them.

"Are you ready, Leonard?"

And Bias replied as always, "I was born ready, Coach."

The words seemed to blow the locker room door open, propelling the team through an opening between the stands and onto the court. But pulsing excitement hardly showed. The players moved smoothly through the pre-game drills -- the effortless, soaring layups and easy jumpers. They were a calm counterpoint to the excitement around them. Carolina coeds pressed their faces against the crowd-scanning TV camera lenses like children making faces through a window. They had tattooed their faces with the sole of a Carolina blue foot, the heel appropriately blackened. Students held up Carolina blue hands made of Styrofoam, the oversized index finger giving the No. 1 sign. Each of the 21,500 seats in the $32 million arena was filled.

The game began with Bias moving into the right forecourt with three Carolina players checking him. He broke free and took a waist-high pass. Faking left with the ball, whirling right, he went up for the jump shot. It was not the picture-perfect, classic jumper Driesell recalled during the memorial service at Cole. The shot had a kid-like, straddle-legged quality to it. But there was no doubt about the power. Bias seemed to reach mid-air stasis, a platform for launching the soft, arcing shot that painted a strong line to the basket. He missed, but was fouled and made both free throws.

A minute later, he drove straight toward·the basket, taking the ball up for a clean two off the glass. He went over Carolina's 7-footers, Brad Daugherty and Warren Martin, as if they were clumsy junior high kids. At 6'8", he was almost as tall as they, but had the agility of a much smaller player. Again, he was fouled and made the free throw, a three-point play.

Maryland stayed close in the first half with Bias's 17 points -- seven in the last minute, cutting a 10-point deficit to three. The passion and the determination were there in every minute. N.C. State's Valvano said Bias was a player who never "disappeared," never took a breather while he was in the game, never paced himself.

In the second half, his game moved up a level. Gatlin thought he could see it in Bias's eyes -- the burning desire to get the ball, the will to score, an irresistible magnetism in every move.

With 12 minutes to go in the game, Bias drove from the left corner along the end line. Swinging behind the basket and almost off the court, he planted his left foot and redirected all his momentum back and up. Twisting toward the court and gliding upward under the backboard, he flicked the ball up and back over his head and cleanly into the net, an improvisation available only to a player of his physical gifts. The other nine players became spectators. Bias seemed suddenly alone on the court.

With just under three minutes remaining, Carolina led by nine. The game was falling into the seasonal pattern. At Duke, where Bias had scored a career-high 41, Maryland had lost by 12.

He then hit another long jumper, was fouled, and made the free throw. Then, instead of heading back up the court, he whirled, stepping in front of Carolina point guard Kenny Smith. It was a move every playground player tries, and every experienced player is watching for, a play that should never work in the ACC. But Bias intercepted the in-bounds pass. He landed with his back to the basket, and, with a leap so strong it looked like a seamless continuation of the steal, he dunked the ball backward over his head. The Carolina crowd gasped.

Bias was laying out everything he had: the strength, the court sense, the intensity, the determination. He wiped away five points of the nine-point Maryland deficit in 10 seconds. Only barely did he miss a second straight steal on the next in-bounds pass.

With 58 seconds left in the game, he nailed another jump shot, a long one from beyond the free-throw circle. The score was 69-67. Down by two, Tar Heel guard Kenny Smith was fouled and went to the line.

"Now's the time to miss," Bias yelled. Smith missed.

Maryland got the rebound. Trailing by two with just 10 seconds left, the Terps rushed toward their basket. Point guard Gatlin brought the ball up court. Bias was surrounded by Carolina players. Gatlin passed to Baxter on the right side of the court.

Baxter watched for Bias to break free, but saw that he could not and heard his friend, directing, encouraging.

"Go Jeff. Go Jazzy Jeff," Bias was shouting.

Baxter had taken the last shot several times that year and missed. This time, he thought, "Let me get a little bit of redemption."

His 18-footer fell. It was 69-all. And Bias was shouting, "Yeah, Jazzy Jeff. Yeah, yeah, yeah."

Overtime.

As the five-minute extra period began, Jeff Lebo, the Carolina guard, shot and missed. A shot by Steve Hale, another guard, was blocked by Maryland's Derrick Lewis.

Bias missed a 20-foot jumper, but came back quickly with a jump hook from the lane to make the score 73-72, Maryland.

With 50 seconds left, Smith moved down the center for a shot to put Carolina ahead. Bias, who was in front of him, slapped the ball away. In a scramble for the ball, Gatlin was fouled. When he sank both foul shots, Maryland led by three with less than 20 seconds remaining. Carolina did not score again.

Maryland got another two, winning 77-72 and pinning Carolina with its first loss in the Dean Dome. Lefty strode off the floor with his head down, an embattled look frozen across his face until, at mid-court, he seemed to realize what his team had done and pumped his left hand into the Carolina blue atmosphere.

Bias walked off the floor with a wide grin. Lefty met him at the locker room door with a high-five. "If you're not all-world after tonight, you aren't ever going to make it," Driesell said.

"God was with us tonight," said Gatlin, "and God was Lenny Bias." Players were often careful to thank God when they won, never to blame Him when they lost.

"The NBA shouldn't wait to draft this guy," wrote Thomas Boswell of *The Washington Post* a few days later. "It should put guards around him until he can start filling up NBA arenas."

In the hot, crowded, visitors' locker room at Chapel Hill, Bias was at his antic best, spraying a two-liter jug of Coke on anyone who got near him. He sat on a bench, leaning back against his locker. It was a rare moment of harmony between the star and his least favorite people, reporters.

Bias had often felt they were harassing him. And now he had the power to retaliate. He was the best in the ACC, and there were, perhaps, a hundred reporters, like Molly Dunham of *The Evening Sun* in Baltimore and John Hawkins of *The [Baltimore] News American*, who were after him for an interview. He would allow interview appointments to be made and then fail to show. He would sneer at the questions. Hawkins looked forward to reading about Bias going one-on-one with the sharp elbows of Boston's sportswriters.

"He was a pain in the ass the whole year," said Dunham, who covered the team during Bias's senior year. "I didn't like him. I guess it was just a power play, but I could never come up with a rationale for it."

Dunham found Bias manipulative, a young man whose basketball talent gave him too much power over his teammates. Long before he was accused of arranging cocaine parties for them, she thought, he tended to put the team into castes defined by playing ability. The younger players were in awe of him and he enjoyed their adulation. He acted a little like Driesell, at times: He was intimidating and bombastic when he thought he could get away with it. People thought he enjoyed the on-rush of can't-miss fortune and fame.

Bias's macho image made his insecurities even more intense. He looked super-prepared. People didn't know when he was hurting -- or, as Madkins supposes, reaching out in a kind of code. He wasn't supposed to have that much sensitivity. Complaints were not manly.

"You had a job to do," Baxter said, "and if you had any sense about yourself, you did it. You didn't complain."

As he headed for the NBA, Bias had a growing sense of how he should look. He liked three-piece suits and tassel loafers. He showed up for practice one day in a floor-length leather coat with an ermine collar.

"Only a New Wave haircut gave him away as anything other than an investment counselor," wrote Sally Jenkins of *The Washington Post*.

"My mother always dressed me nicely as a kid," he told another reporter. "I got into it when I got older, and now I can't be going around looking slipshod, can I?"

When Driesell saw him in the fancy coat, he asked where the outfit had come from. Well he might have wondered, since a gift could raise questions under the NCAA rules and Bias's personal income did not seem to support such extravagances. An answer to the question was not really desirable, however.

Herman Veal says people were always giving Bias things -- deals on expensive clothing, for example. Veal said he was with him one day in Washington when Bias bought a pair of $400 shoes for $150. How he had even $150 to spend for shoes was another issue.

By the time he was a senior, according to Madkins, Bias was getting substantial fees for speeches. A member of the Terrapin Club said players made money for appearances in automobile showrooms, posing for snapshots by giddy salesmen who showed up with their Instamatics.

A survey of former NBA players found that 19 percent of the ACC players who responded said they had gotten money in post-game handshakes or from the sale of tournament tickets -- the latter practice having been institutionalized at Maryland despite its illegality under NCAA rules.

Athletic Director Dull told Slaughter that he was concerned about an alumnus who was giving players $50 from time to time. But an informal investigation disclosed nothing, Slaughter said. Asked if

Bias and other Maryland players ever got illegal money, Veal said he would prefer not to say. "It might reflect poorly on the program," he said. Then again, depending on your viewpoint, Veal said, it might reflect an appreciation of what the players did for their school.

Slaughter thought Bias labored under at least two disadvantages in his dealings with media. Reporters tended to approach basketball players with various prejudices, thinking they were not particularly smart, or were street kids or vain clothes horses. Slaughter thought they were trapped in the preconceptions of their inquisitors and uncertain how to escape.

"People drew corrals around them. It's too easy to think in one way about black kids," the chancellor said.

The reporters were more of a problem during Bias's senior year. Branch had handled most of the interviews the year before, but now Bias was on his own. Bias felt misunderstood and under-appreciated even as he tried to avoid the interviews that might have presented him more accurately. And he was uncomfortable with the role of spokesman -- particularly the spokesman for a losing team. That's what Maryland was in the beginning of his senior year.

The Terps were playing a difficult schedule and losing regularly. After every game, Bias was asked why the team had not played well, how he felt, what was going wrong. His own performances were superb, but often not good enough to bring victory. He took the losses as if they were reflections on his character and ability. He became even frostier. Get comfortable with losing and you'd become a loser, he thought. "If you don't win, you feel terrible," he told a reporter. "When we were losing, I was blaming it on myself. I thought maybe I wasn't doing the job."

UNC's Steve Hale, who played with and against Bias from the time they were high school stars, said athletes tend to base self-judgments on their team's win-loss records.

"You have to find a separate identity. You have to get centered in yourself. But it wasn't easy to make the separation. We would win a game and everybody would be my friend," said Hale. "When we'd lose, it'd be deserted in the locker room. It's tough when you're 15 years old. And there's the same insecurity in college. Most of the confidence of athletes is because they have succeeded as athletes. It's not who they are, but what they've done athletically. You have to figure out how to cope with failure. If you never fail, if you never had real adversity, it's tough to develop character."

Sally Jenkins of *The Washington Post* asked Bias why he was so combative. "People are always talking about my attitude, but they never put themselves in my place. And the publicity gets hard. It makes me uncomfortable. I feel bad for my teammates who are helping us win as much as I am," he said.

His effort to share the press attention was characteristic of him, according to Slaughter and Baxter. He saw his anonymous teammates being ignored. He wanted to share the interviews as well, but it was not a situation he could control.

In the benchmark 1929 report on American college athletics, the Carnegie Foundation for the Advancement of Education suggested that among the crimes of big-time intercollegiate sports was the "demoralizing publicity showered on the players." The publicity showers of 60 years ago, during the pre-television era, paled in comparison to those of Bias's years at College Park.

But why demoralizing? Don't athletes get a lot of perks? Isn't it fun to be a star? Often, it must be.

Len Bias was embarrassed occasionally by attention received at the expense of his teammates.

"My parents treat my brothers and sister and I all equally. There are no favorites. Nobody is spoiled. Everybody gets the same. And I take that attitude here, because my teammates and I are like a family. These guys are like my brothers, and things should be spread about more evenly," he said.

His generosity was discounted. Bias was a superstar in a big-money sport. There was a role for him, and he had no choice about filling it. The fittest players survived by accepting the smothering adulation as a price that comes with stardom. Bias never quite adjusted. It was one of the roles he never learned.

When John Hawkins finally cornered Bias one afternoon in the fall of 1985, the reporter almost wished he hadn't.

"He was one of the biggest jerks I ever dealt with. It's terrible to say. But he was the surliest, the most uncooperative of all the players. I don't think he was a very happy guy. I never thought of drugs at the time, but looking back it doesn't surprise me."

The interview fell on Bias's 22nd birthday. It was not a mellow occasion. Bias was defiantly mute.

"I'm going to trash this guy's attitude if he doesn't tell me something usable," Hawkins thought two minutes into the interview.

Reporters are not anxious to write negative stories about players because it makes their relationships with the team more difficult.

"No one was going to write that Len Bias was a real jerk, because he was an All-American," Hawkins said.

Like other sportswriters, Hawkins concedes that he helped to create Bias's image as a role model, though he did not particularly think of him as one.

In this interview, however, Hawkins asked Bias what he did when he wasn't playing basketball. Something clicked. Bias began to talk -- about modeling clothes, about his family, about drawing and about his life away from basketball. Hawkins had known that Bias was a decent artist. You could see the feel for line in his strong signature. With some excitement, he told Hawkins about a cartoon he had done in which massive hands, holding a basketball, reached down from the clouds to deliver a cosmic slam. He had done humorous renditions of Driesell that no one but his teammates had seen. As a gift, he had done a portrait of Bob Wagner lifting weights.

All at once, a reporter had the religious, artistic, athletic, and childlike Bias tumbling out all at once.

In a *Baltimore News-American* article with a headline referring to Bias as "Terp Superman," he was quoted as saying: "I'm more into design. I do cartoons and sketches and other things, but I think I'm best at design, an architectural type of thing. For instance, I could draw the insides of Cole, with the floor and seats and baskets and all, and keep it on scale and make it look pretty nice."

He never failed to say how much he appreciated his years at College Park. "I've pretty much fulfilled my dreams," he told Hawkins, "making the most of my ability and staying out of trouble."

Bias's picture appeared that year on a life-sized promotional poster produced by the athletic department. The campus bookstore distributed copies. His likeness was suddenly on walls in dormitory rooms across the College Park campus, up there with Madonna, Sting, James Dean, and the Beatles. He had one in his own room.

"I can wake up every morning and look at myself," he said.

Professor Joyce ran to the bookstore one afternoon and scooped up what turned out to be the last poster. She hung it on the cinder block wall between her desk and the window in her basement office at Taliaferro Hall. Like everyone else, she marveled at the racehorse grace and power in Bias's body.

He was wearing the bright gold uniform with red piping. "MARYLAND," in big white letters, was spelled out across his chest. He posed at center court with the scoreboard in the background. It read: "I'm Bias 34, Maryland No. 1." Bias gave a hint of his smile, but largely held himself in reserve.

In Columbia Park, people still called him Frosty. It was a name that marked off home as separate and distinct from the pressing world of basketball. College friends might even have thought that "Frosty" was a variation of "Iceman," a basketball name given to those who have good nerves when the game is on the line. At times, though, the nickname captured his moods. He could be arrogant, overly sure of himself, threatening. It was useful sometimes to be menacing if that would repel people who thought he was their property.

Once Driesell got a call from someone who had seen Bias walking across the campus with a six-pack. It was true: He was carrying a six-pack of root beer.

This type of unofficial surveillance drove athletes together and deeper underground. They understood each other. They all had the same interests, insecurities, restrictions, and dreams. Veal, Bias and Branch were particularly close. Branch, who was regarded as glib and sophisticated, invented a fraternity and a pledge for them: Terps Psi Phi 'Til the Day We Die. Another variation was the Killer Bees. No wonder people thought they were clannish.

At his worst, Bias operated behind a veneer of hostility. At his best, he was accommodating, lighthearted, completely unselfish, sensitive to his less celebrated friends, and fun. Veal occasionally called him "Mad Max."

"He'd make you feel like going to a party. He'd get up and start dancing and acting wild. He could get you in a mood where you felt that was the best thing to do," said Veal. After his death, Veal added sadly, "Never gonna see my man Max again."

This was the same Bias who asked his teammates to go with him one Sunday to his family's church, Pilgrim AME in Washington, where he walked down the aisle alone to declare himself a born-again believer. After he died, his mother found the names of his teammates written on the front page of his Bible. At the suggestion of Buck Williams, a former Terp who went on to a great professional career, the team had gone on a religious retreat every year. One year the theme was "Living The Christian Life." Mrs. Bias says she was not aware of any particular event that triggered Len's declaration of faith.

"Conversion comes," she said, "when you feel moved in your heart." But she was not surprised at all that her church-going son would make his witness. She had encouraged him to do so.

"I used to talk to him about spiritual things," she said. "I'd talk to him while he was standing right where you are standing, leaning against the refrigerator. I'd tell him, 'Don't forget that God has given you a beautiful gift. You're a great player. You're on TV. But always remember that it came from God.'"

Wagner thought Bias's behavior was like the behavior of many college kids: It changed to match the behavior of those around him. "When he was with good people, he was as good as any one of them. When he was with bums, he was a bum," Wagner told a reporter. It was a variation on Mrs. Bias's two-worlds idea.

Other coaches and people who knew Bias as a high school student credited Wagner with settling him down considerably. But on the issue of which friends might be good to avoid, they disagreed.

Wagner said he urged Bias to stay away from kids thought to be involved with drugs. Bias insisted it didn't matter whom he was friendly with because everyone knew he was clean. For some time, it appears, he traded on the clean image suggested by his manners and his shy smile and perhaps by the unwillingness of people to confront him more directly.

As early as late 1985, however, he had begun to use cocaine, according to later trial testimony by Long and Gregg. On four or five occasions during their senior year, Long said, he and Bias used cocaine. The surefire NBA star decided to ignore the drug advice he had received from Wagner, Lefty, and others -- and the advice he himself had given to his younger brothers, Jay and Eric.

After his death, there were reports that he had purchased $800 worth of cocaine in Northeast Washington the night before he died. By then, he had the money he had earned in the post-season all-star games and the $15,000 he had borrowed with the help of Fentress, his agent. Where he might have gotten money for cocaine earlier was a mystery to his father, and one reason James Bias could not believe his son was using cocaine.

After the 1986 game against North Carolina State at College Park, Long said, Bias phoned him in his dorm room around midnight.

"It's that time," Bias said.

"I knew it was time to drink beer and do some cocaine," Long said.

They partied all night two days before the Duke game, when Bias scored his career-high 41 points. His ability, then, to use cocaine and still perform at or above his usual level may have led him to conclude he was impervious to damage from drugs.

Brian Tribble's mother said Bias spent a lot of time in her kitchen. "Lenny liked to eat my brownies and German chocolate cake," she said. "He could eat 12 brownies in 10 minutes. Then he'd jump up and say, 'I've got to go home for dinner. My mother will kill me if I don't get home for dinner.'" Bias lived with one foot in the kitchen and the other in the fast lane.

After Bias died, Driesell and Dull denied knowledge of drug use by team members. But there were drug users on the team. And Driesell, at least once, may have suspected Bias was one of them, according to James Bias and Jeff Baxter. Bias was suspended for missing a curfew after the North Carolina State game in Raleigh. When he, Baxter, and John Johnson, the freshman guard, came back to their hotel just before dawn, they were met by several coaches.

Baxter says Driesell was furious. "What've y'all been doing? Drinking? Have y'all been doin' drugs?" the coach demanded.

Bias rushed him and had to be restrained, Baxter said. Any time black players stayed out late, Bias shouted, someone assumed they were using drugs. After the incident, Bias, Johnson and Baxter were suspended from the team.

Driesell might well have pushed further. According to Long, when the coach confronted his teammate that morning, Bias *was* a user. The coach might also have been suspicious because he knew about Long. A year earlier, one of the team's advisers had seen Long on campus, obviously high. Driesell hauled him in for a lecture. Bias had been tested once under the university's program -- Long about six times. The tests were negative. University officials said later that Driesell had used drug tests as motivators when his players did not play or practice as well as he wanted. At a time when hardly any school in the U.S. required drug tests, Maryland was a leader. But its system was porous and seems to have been used rather selectively.

In its examination of attitudes about drugs on the College Park campus, Chancellor Slaughter's drug policy task force found a high-level ambiguity about drugs -- on the campus, as well as on the basketball team.

"We received information that there was an awful lot of abuse on the basketball team, abuse that was known about and covered up," said task force member, Congressman Benjamin Cardin of Maryland's Third District. "It was covered up because they thought they could handle it internally. They didn't want to jeopardize the reputation of the program."

Cardin considered the attitude about drugs symptomatic of the general attitude in the athletic department: "They showed no respect at all for authority. Look how many students were carried academically. They thought it was a big joke. You have to instill respect for authority. And they didn't. The Len Bias episode was not surprising in that type of environment."

Baxter was not sure if Driesell really suspected that he and Bias had been using drugs that night in North Carolina.

"There were a lot of mind games with Driesell," Baxter said, "a lot of provocative comments made to keep you off-balance, to see how you would react."

James Bias wondered later why the coach did not press for a thorough investigation.

"I talked to Lenny and he said there were no drugs involved. But if the whole sanctified University of Maryland was so worried, why didn't they send them down to have a drug test?" he asked. "There was none of that. Driesell should have put things under a microscope . . ." A look back at those days suggests many times when an investigation might have been done and many participants, including James Bias himself, who might have initiated one.

But there were all sorts of pressure against pursuing suspicions. When Bias was suspended, boosters called to demand that Lefty reinstate him. How was the team going to win if it didn't have Bias? How was Maryland going to make the NCAA if Bias was on the bench? No one said, "We can't put this kid back in uniform until we find out if he's using drugs." Often, a coach's responsibility as a father figure, counselor, social worker and disciplinarian was in conflict with his desire to win. Suppose the kid was clean? Would his parents sue the university? Would reporters find out about the tests?

Lee Madkins, who continued to see Bias occasionally at the rec center, thinks the young man may have been reaching out for help and no one recognized it. He remembered the days when Bias came into his office, weary and distracted after the round of pre-draft physical examinations. Madkins listened. He didn't ask many questions, and he never asked what the young man would do if basketball didn't last. Maybe it wouldn't have made much difference for someone who thought he was a horse.

Madkins also was haunted by earlier suspicions that Bias was using drugs at least a year before he died. He says Bob Wagner called him one day at the center. "Lenny's over at DeMatha with a bunch of guys. I think they're doing drugs," Wagner said. "Can you get over there?"

Madkins closed the center and drove to DeMatha. "We're not using," Bias told them, as he would later tell Lefty. "Wagner's lying." The matter ended there. Madkins didn't know if Wagner ever told Lefty or Mr. and Mrs. Bias, but Madkins said nothing.

James Bias said he never had any hint his son was using drugs. "There was no indication that Len had anything to do with drugs at all. I know when people are using drugs. That gives me an advantage. I know what to look for. I know the signs," he said. But cocaine is one of the more difficult drugs to detect through user behavior. James Bias, who saw less and less of his celebrity son, may well have missed any changes.

Veal thought he understood something of his friend's thinking. Coaches are always urging their players to be in control of game situations -- "control the situation or the situation will control you," they'd say.

"Being around this place, being in the environment we're in, the situation is always in control," Veal said. "You are acting like a big-name athlete. You're acting the way people expect you to act, not like the person you want to be. So what is that? The situation being in control of you.

"Sometimes you do things you wouldn't do just because you can. There's nobody watching, so you say I'll do it now just to spite them." In search of control, Bias had given even more of it away.

Mrs. Bias thought her son had allowed others to lead and to use him.

Veal thought that no completely satisfying answer was possible or needed. "I believe what Mrs. Bias said," he said. "It was just that time. Lenny Bias lived in 22 years what most of us live in a lifetime.

He was the best known of the athletes. He was famous. He had lived a full life. It's not that I'm being cavalier. Three other people were in the room -- none of them died. It wasn't their time."

Veal continued: "I can't say what happened was out of Lenny's control because he was using drugs. Then again, things have a way of making you be the way they want you to be. The situation took control of him. He didn't take control of the situation."

Jeff Baxter continued to struggle with his friend's death.

"Cocaine has no pre-arrangements with you," Baxter said. "It doesn't say it's going to let you know when you've had enough."

"Why he would do it is the biggest question. I think it was bad choices as far as who he was funnin' around with, what you were funnin' around with."

Coach Wagner, a man who seemed to have the most thoughtful insights into Bias, wondered if he hadn't lost the ability to think of himself as merely mortal. "He probably asked himself, 'What's me and what's reality?' Where do you draw the line between 'I'm a 22-year-old kid just growing up,' and 'Here I am, I can handle anything. What can I not handle? I've been through it all.'"

Wagner had termed Bias's lack of self-control the only limit to his development as a basketball player. Clearly, he was more right than he could have imagined.

But maybe Wagner had it backwards. Could Bias's commitment to becoming a basketball player have been a limitation on his development as a person? Did the game take him too far beyond the critical observations of his father? Did his importance as a player at College Park take him beyond the sober assessments of university authorities?

Almost everyone saw the behavioral difficulties Bias was having. But there was no time to address them fully. If he threw elbows, failed courses, set fires or made intemperate remarks, his behavior was discussed as if it were hazardous only to his NBA draft status.

Chapter 6

Filling The Field House

Bias's play in the North Carolina game and in the ACC Tournament earned Maryland another invitation to the NCAA tournament. In the first round of the NCAA, the Terps defeated Pepperdine, then lost to the University of Nevada Las Vegas. Possessed one more time as a Terrapin, Bias scored 19 of his team's final 21 points against the Nevada juggernaut, but it wasn't enough.

After the game, his last for Maryland, he sat with a towel wrapped around his head for an hour, refusing to talk with anyone. From there he went on the senior all-star circuit. Games were often built around him and limousines were sent to fetch him at the airports. If he had begun to feel a step above the rest of the world -- a bit invincible -- once again, there were reasons for the feeling.

He had essentially dropped out of school for that semester, but one day when he was back on the College Park campus, he got a call from Professor Joyce. She was arranging a reading by the poet Gwendolyn Brooks, and asked if he would present a bouquet of flowers. She wanted Len Bias for two reasons: "It brought him into the realm of academia, and he was pleased that I respected him enough to ask. He was as excited by the idea as I was."

Joyce wanted to show a link between the excellence of black basketball players and black poets, to show the artistry of both. Though she knew well enough that Bias was not a serious student, she thought he might have been and that his participation could lend to poetry the heightened respect that students have for basketball players.

The reading was scheduled for the same night as the annual basketball awards banquet, but Bias assured Joyce he would be there. His role was scheduled for the end of the evening, but he arrived before the reading was half over. Professor Joyce saw him pacing in the lobby outside the auditorium. She went out to get him.

"You're early," she said.

"I can't stay. I have to get back," he said.

He was fidgeting and smiling, nervous about appearing before so many people outside of a gymnasium and about being absent from the awards banquet. But he had come just as he said he would.

Professor Joyce walked back into the hall with the star in tow and interrupted the reading. Bias presented the flowers to Ms. Brooks, gave her a kiss and quickly left. The reading resumed.

About a half-mile from LeFrak Hall, where poet Gwendolyn Brooks was doing her reading, the 1986 basketball awards dinner was being held in the Stamp Student Union. Len Elmore, one of the school's most successful athlete graduates, was the guest speaker. Elmore had been a leader, with Tom McMillen, of Maryland's basketball teams between 1970 and 1974. He had gone on to play 10 years in the NBA, and then graduated from Harvard Law School. He was the first NBA player to make such a transition.

Around Maryland and among basketball insiders, McMillen and Elmore were a legendary partnership, a perfect demonstration of the student-athlete ideal. Both were as good as any basketball players in the country, smart and well-motivated. McMillen is white; Elmore is black. They were the wholesome role models basketball yearns for and too often doesn't get. Basketball helped them launch spectacular outside careers. Other basketball programs across the country were hit by stories of players who had not graduated or who had graduated but could not read. Maryland had occasional lapses, too, but it also had McMillen and Elmore.

Their team won the National Invitational Tournament in 1972, and the Terps were ranked in the Top 10 in each of their four years at College Park. In 1974, they came very close to winning a national championship -- or so boosters like Cooper Curtice and Bob Novak insisted. In fact, they didn't even play in the NCAA tournament that year because they did not win the ACC Tournament and, in those days, only the tournament winner went to the national playoffs. In 1974, three ACC teams were among the top five nationally ranked teams. North Carolina State, led by David Thompson, ended up winning the NCAA national title. Later, the rule would be changed and any team with a good record could be invited to what players called "The Dance" -- and what university presidents might have called "The Big Pay Day."

The 1974 season and the hope of a McMillen-Elmore-Driesell championship ended in the ACC Tournament with a 103-100 defeat by N.C. State. Maryland finished the season ranked fourth in the nation. It should have been at least third, fans said. Such distinctions were important. A nagging injustice like that could keep Heise, Novak, and Curtice talking long into the night at ACC tournaments and wherever Terrapin Clubbers gathered.

Elmore had come to College Park from Power Memorial High School in Queens, N.Y. A young man with big-city seasoning, he had been a member of the National Honor Society and president of his class. At Maryland, he became a record-setting rebounder. He majored in English and was the host of a campus radio show.

As a pro, Elmore was an itinerant journeyman. He played for the Indiana Pacers, who gave him a $1.4 million contract fresh out of Maryland. Later, he spent time with the Kansas City Kings, the New Jersey Nets, and the New York Knicks. He managed to hang on about twice as long as most professional players, but his knees finally told him it was time to retire.

His acceptance at Harvard told him the same thing, less painfully. While he studied, he did color commentary for the Raycom Sports Network, which broadcasts ACC basketball games, and for a time he was a commentator for National Public Radio. He had solid careers under way in broadcasting and law.

Elmore's somewhat spectacular emergence from the hermetically sealed, hyper-concentrated world of basketball was exceptional. Even for Elmore, someone who thought about the future and planned for it, there was a price to pay for playing basketball.

"Usually," he said later, "you're sitting in that small world, and you think it's going to last forever. When you finally come out in the real world all your peers have 10 years' experience and you have none." Elmore liked to quote Herschel Walker, the National Football League running back from Georgia: "He said that when he left football, he wanted to be able to hold a conversation about who he is and what he does -- not who he *was* and what he *did*."

McMillen, too, had planned for his life after hoops. He had been one of the most ballyhooed high school players in the history of the sport. Maryland's first and only Rhodes Scholar, he was called "The Senator" by some of his teammates, though he had majored in chemistry and considered going to medical school. His goal was to have several career options. Many assumed he was on his way into politics, following "Dollar Bill" Bradley, first of Princeton, then of the NBA's New York Knicks, and now a U.S. Senator from New Jersey.

After 11 profitable years in the NBA, McMillen arranged to play his last few seasons with the Washington Bullets, where home games were convened in the Capital Centre in Landover, Md. The move reintroduced him to voters in Maryland's Fourth Congressional District, whom he hoped to represent in Congress. He was called a carpetbagger when he finally ran, but in the fall of 1986, he was elected by a margin of 444 votes over Robert R. Neall, a highly-regarded local officeholder and Maryland native, a man who had spent 12 years in the Maryland state legislature. Neall's record was not quite sufficient to offset the star quality of a Rhodes Scholar and one-time basketball player.

At College Park, though, the tradition faded. Within a few years after McMillen and Elmore graduated, they were no more typical of Maryland players than they would have been of many other high-pressure, big-time programs. Driesell's Maryland team suffered a succession of nagging embarrassments: a newspaper disclosure of poor grades in 1977; the drug difficulties of alumnus John Lucas, one of Maryland's best players; a breaking and entering charge against one member of the team -- after which Driesell said, "Boys will be boys"; the marijuana arrests of Branch and Rivers; a sexual misconduct charge; and the dramatic suspension of Bias and Baxter in 1986.

Elmore thought basketball at Maryland was in more trouble than even these events suggested. So, at the awards banquet, instead of the usual patter of jokes and jock stories, he offered a critique.

"There was a period of time," he said, "when Maryland was renowned for basketball and for having quality people -- when the program had just gotten off the ground. Academic excellence and quality teams became synonymous with Maryland." But now, he said, the program was in steep decline. The slide had to be acknowledged so it could be stopped.

"Your stature as basketball players shouldn't be limited to the basketball court," he said. "A lot of young people look up to you. You should reach out to them for your own peace of mind, for repayment to the community." The player, too, could profit, he said. Once, when he was injured, the 6'9" Elmore tutored at an elementary school in Washington. The experience gave him an important perspective: "Those kids were so young they did not even understand I played basketball. They just related to me as somebody who was real, real tall."

To borrow another expression from Chancellor Slaughter, he was not "wrapping himself in satin." Like Bias, Elmore had wandered off into the excitement of senior all-star games, travel and NBA money without first graduating. But he returned almost immediately and finished.

"There's a time," he told his audience, "when all boys have to grow up. You can grow by disciplining yourself early or you can flounder. I floundered for awhile. But, finally, I just decided I wasn't going to leave and lose all contact with the school without getting a degree. My pride was at stake." He saw less pride in Maryland players now, he said.

For the boosters and the 1986 team, the message and the messenger could not have been more surprising. An honored son of the university was delivering a somber, sad lecture. James Bias, who attended the banquet with his son, had wondered when someone would tell the truth about Maryland basketball in the 1980s. Everyone was just hanging on, minimizing the difficulties, and hoping that nothing more serious would happen.

"I never heard anyone who had been through that program speak so honestly about it," James Bias said. "There were some red faces in that room. People were sitting there with their mouths hung open.

They must have been thinking: 'What's wrong with him?'" Mr. Bias went up to Elmore after the program to congratulate him.

Three months later, on June 19, 1986, the problems Elmore had worried about were projected onto the public agenda in a way that could no longer be ignored.

Until then, the difficulties of Maryland basketball had been willed into remission by Charles Grice "Lefty" Driesell.

Driesell personified the power of basketball in America. The game and its television coverage had made him the University of Maryland's most visible ambassador, its chancellor of public image, far better known than John Slaughter, John Toll or the even the governors who came and went during Lefty's reign. College Park's standing as a teaching and research university was uncertain, but almost certainly lower than it should have been. Its rank as a basketball school, however, was indisputably high. Driesell supplied the lift. He was colorful, provocative, and always competitive, even when his team was struggling. If there were occasional problems, they were submerged by financial success, and subordinated by the spectacle of major upsets and the potential for a national ranking. The field house was always full and the money from television contracts -- $2 million a year or more -- flowed ever more steadily into athletic department accounts. Basketball under Driesell was a bonanza far removed from the dismal program he inherited on coming to Maryland.

In the late 1960s, long after the Atlantic Coast Conference had made itself one of the best in the nation, Maryland's basketball teams were second- or third-rate. Every year, the university endured the embarrassment and financial loss of sending back part of its allotment of tickets to the ACC Tournament. Maryland fans had not been drawn in numbers to the thrill of that event, so bored and put off were they by the lack of excitement at Cole Field House. Often, only 3,000 or 4,000 fans came to the 14,500-seat College Park arena, then one of the largest and newest facilities in the conference.

In those days, gymnasium floors were swept from basket to basket at half time. Cole Field House had two sweepers. One wore a shirt with gold sleeves. The other man's sleeves were black. They would begin together, but one would move ahead, and part of the crowd would cheer for him as if he were a horse in a race. Others would back the other man. The lead would switch back and forth until the fans were in a frenzy of zany cheering. This was Maryland basketball pre-Lefty.

In the three years before Driesell arrived in 1969, Maryland's record was 27 wins, 48 losses. In Lefty's first year, the Terps went 13-13 -- and from then on challenged for ACC and national titles. And, as he liked to point out, they usually led the league in attendance.

In Driesell's 17 years at College Park, the Terps won 348 games and lost 159. In 10 of his 26 seasons as a college coach, first at Davidson College in North Carolina and then at Maryland, Driesell's teams were ranked among the Top 10. He averaged better than 20 victories per season.

"People loved him for taking a completely dead, defunct organism and changing it into a powerhouse," said Terrapin Club member Cooper Curtice. "It was something to go from empty one year to full houses the next year. It just caught you up in it."

Before a game started, Driesell would stride from the wide tunnel at the north end of the field house with his hands above his bald head, his fingers thrust upward in two Vs for Victory. The house would erupt.

During games in those early years, Lefty scandalized and delighted the crowds by throwing his sport jackets to the floor and stomping on them whenever referees displeased him. In later years, his coats stayed on but he kept stomping. His arms flew up and his feet clapped down. He was the hybrid of a rooster and a clog dancer. The Lefty Stomp was a barely controlled, country-style tantrum that brought fans back again and again to watch and wait like gawkers at an auto speedway waiting for the crash. In between these outbursts, he paced, hitched his trousers, and fondled the knot of his tie like Rodney Dangerfield, except Lefty got more respect than nuclear physicists.

He became one of America's showman coaches, a group of manic professionals who borrowed more from Alice Cooper and John McEnroe than from some idealized mentor. Like Bobby Knight at Indiana, Jerry Tarkanian at UNLV, and others who seemed to work at their public personas, Driesell operated constantly on the edge of proper decorum and even, it seemed, of sanity. He took his fans deliriously to the edge, and then back. Many people resented Lefty's antics, but just as many were charmed by them. Basketball fans remembered the lean years and honored Driesell for taking them to the excitement that came with being a threat to the best teams in the country.

Driesell quickly worked himself into the life of the community. Insiders would point with awe to the clothing store where he bought the jackets he abused. In the early years, he owned a restaurant near the campus. You could get a nice steak there -- and a necktie with Lefty's face painted on it. Terrapin Clubber Curtice wore his Lefty tie to ACC Tournament games to irritate the fans from Tobacco Road.

Students and even the odd university president at other ACC schools sat in the stands, wearing swim caps that mocked Driesell's bald head. Adrian Branch's mother, Carolyn, thought this was atrocious. He couldn't help it, she said, if God gave him a bald head. But it wasn't all ridicule. It was love. Driesell was both a laughingstock and a hero.

He survived by acting the part of a rollicking, dumb-sounding good ole boy. Like his players, he was not so much a role model as a role player. And he was shrewd. Molly Dunham, the Baltimore *Evening Sun* reporter, said the coach "wore cornpone as armor." If grits could talk, said sportswriter Bill Glauber of *The Sun*, they would sound like Lefty. A graduate of Duke University, where he had been a decent basketball player, Driesell had gone on to earn a master's degree in secondary education and physical education at the College of William and Mary. But his dumb jock shtick was more important to him than his degrees.

"I ain't never seen anyone put on an exhibition like that," he said of Bias's Chapel Hill performance against UNC during his senior year.

Driesell's most familiar assertion, made defensively and repeatedly throughout his career, ran to three words: "I can coach." This declaration came in response to those who said he was a better recruiter or who said simply, "Lefty can't coach."

"I can't do a lot of things," he told *The Post*'s Sally Jenkins. "I can't run a computer, and I can't do bookkeeping. I don't even know how much money I have. But I can coach.

"A lot of coaches go their whole life and never get in the Top 10. People write that I get great talent and make them mediocre teams. That irks me. It irks me when they say that. Sure, I've lost 10 games this season [1985-86]. A lot of teams have been playing bunnies [weak teams]. I could do that, too, but I have the nerve to play my schedule. It's amazing I've done as well as I have with all the negative publicity. I've been here 17 years and I've averaged 20 wins a season. So how is someone going to come in here and tell me I can't coach?"

According to Driesell's friends, a lot of what he said and did publicly ran counter to who he was. They said he was a decent man who spoke without thinking and could not concede error.

"He's got an aggressive personality," said his former assistant, Joe Harrington. "He speaks his mind. He's not a con. Sometimes you might not want to hear it, but he plays it straight. That irritates some people, so they criticize him, want to cut him down."

He could be charming, funny, and engaging. "You may think you don't like him, but sit with him for a while and I guarantee you're going to like him," says booster Hotsy Alperstein.

But he also could be a snarling, crass, street fighter. He loved to play Cornered Man. He made himself a prisoner and then struggled for freedom. Cornered or not, he acted as if he were. He was the author and hero in a basketball soap opera. He was the frustrated worker, the misunderstood husband, the neglected wife. Unlike them, he could hit back when he wanted. He was almost completely unrestrained. He screamed at game officials and university administrators as if they were the Fates. Such defiance got him into trouble, and out of it. Each episode enhanced his standing. When he was in trouble, his supporters were in trouble with him.

After a chair kicking incident during one game, Lefty was asked to pay for the damage. One of his fans, a restaurant owner in Raleigh, North Carolina, bought the chair and hung it on the wall in his office, a trophy from the old Lefthander. The wonderful and woeful perils of Lefty played out again and again, season after season. Players were at College Park for four years. Lefty was there for life.

He tapped a rich vein in modern American life: the tendency to invest psyche and soul in the home team, a dislike of boundaries and authority, a fascination for the outrageous. People wore the clothes of athletes; their figures of speech were often drawn from sports. Businessmen demanded a "level playing field." A company's sales force might put on a "full-court press." "Slamdunk" became synonymous with crushing defeat. An amazing spectrum of people was conversant in the arcane of professional sports drafts, of times for the 40-yard dash, of a player's weight-lifting abilities, of body fat percentages, and of who might be the best fifth-grade point guard in the country. (In 1986, that distinction went to Michael Irvin of Chicago, a good ball handler with good moves and, according to

Sports Illustrated, a great smile.) Driesell was a major part of the sports preoccupation in Maryland. A university chancellor had no similarly broad and passionate constituency. On the contrary, he was more likely to be regarded with suspicion, someone who would try to limit what the coach and his team were doing.

At his very first College Park press conference in 1969, Driesell put himself in a career-long corner. He promised that Maryland would become the UCLA of the East -- equivalent to Slaughter promising that College Park would become the Harvard of the Mid-Atlantic. When he was the coach at UCLA, the venerable John Wooden won 10 NCAA championships. Quickly, the Driesell promise appeared on bumper stickers. Just as quickly, Driesell recruited top talent, and his teams became competitive with the best in the nation.

Over 17 years at Maryland, Driesell's teams went to the NCAA tournament eight times, losing in the first round six of them. They reached the quarterfinals twice, in 1973 and 1975, but never made the Final Four, never won a UCLA-style championship, and never came close to backing up the famous boast.

When Lefty set his goal in 1969, he looked like a clean-cut innocent, flushed with his easy rise to the big time. He had started as a junior high school coach in his hometown of Norfolk, Virginia, where his father owned a jewelry store. He moved on to Davidson College, where his teams were spectacularly successful, winning 176 games and losing 65. Four of his 10 teams were ranked in the Top 10 in the nation. Davidson never had had a basketball team so highly ranked before -- and after 1969, when Driesell left, never did again.

While in the beginning, it might have been easy and fun to challenge the best in the country, over the years, the strain and pressure of doing so began to show in his face. He seemed to smile less easily, and when he did, less confidently. He had a grim and anxious look about him. To author John Feinstein, then a *Washington Post* basketball writer, he conceded that his zeal had flagged a bit in his recruiting. He didn't enjoy it as much, he said.

Driesell produced his best team at College Park almost immediately. In 1970, he out-recruited North Carolina's Coach Dean Smith to land Tom McMillen. McMillen had all but moved into a dormitory at Chapel Hill, North Carolina. Still pursued by Lefty and under pressure from his father, who loved Driesell, young McMillen changed his mind and enrolled at Maryland. Driesell's image was constructed upon such epic recruiting triumphs. Some critics said victories of this sort also led to trouble. Driesell, they said, spent too much time on players he probably could not woo away from North Carolina or Duke, and thus lost opportunities for less well known players.

A man who once sold encyclopedias door to door in Virginia, Driesell knew how to keep the pressure on. According to Lefty lore, Driesell told prospect Howard White that if he came to Maryland, the two of them would ride in parades down Pennsylvania Avenue with President Nixon, and people along the parade route would ask, "Who's that riding with Lefty and Howard White?"

McMillen remembered with precision the Driesell approach. The coach arrived at his home in Mansfield, Pennsylvania, with a carload of assistants and a well-rehearsed presentation.

"He had charts that would have made Caspar Weinberger [a former Secretary of Defense] happy," McMillen recalled. "The whole entourage came into my house. They tried to sell me on the importance of playing in front of the president of the United States. . . . Buy Maryland, a stock that is low now. Don't buy North Carolina. That stock has peaked." Given the continuing success of Carolina teams in the years since, a certain irony infused McMillen's story.

McMillen's older brother, Jay, who played at Maryland in the 1960s, first suggested the "UCLA of the East" idea to Driesell. But Tom was a hard sell and Lefty almost lost him -- because Maryland was not up to the young man's academic standards. Over the years, Driesell sometimes had trouble landing players he wanted because Maryland was denigrated, with some validity, by competitors with more academic respect. Other schools offered more in the classroom and in the way of facilities. Recruits were urged to believe that "you didn't go to Maryland if you cared about getting an education," said reporter John Hawkins. In the trade, it was called "negative recruiting."

McMillen recalled his own opening thrust: "Coach, truthfully, in my research I've learned that UNC and Virginia have three times as many books in their libraries as Maryland. How can you make this case about Maryland being a serious academic institution?"

His mother and father were horrified at the impertinence of a high school kid. "Not Lefty," McMillen said. "He looked me right in the eye and said, 'Son, if you can read all them books, then you go to them schools.'"

On occasion, Driesell delivered himself of the apparently proud assertion that he had never read a book in his life. At other times, he would say he never made as much as a B in his life. But, during his senior year at Duke, he had been on the Dean's List. Under pressure, he would speak of himself as an educator.

"Coach was proud of his Duke education," McMillen said. "But do you know something? He never used it." The line drew a tremendous laugh when McMillen delivered it at a party for Driesell.

The McMillen-Elmore years gave Driesell the foundation for a tradition -- good players, good scholars, good program. But the players Driesell recruited in the late '70s and '80s were inferior academically, and sometimes athletically, to the McMillen-Elmore standard. For a man who won good players by sheer hardscrabble hustle in his career's early years, recruiting had become increasingly difficult.

The recruiting rules, he said, tended to suffocate his best tool -- his persistence and ability to win over parents.

"I used to outwork people," he says today. Rules on limiting contacts with players, he says, are "good in a way, and bad in a way." Teams that need to improve need good players -- and the better programs always have an advantage over those still striving for status.

College coaches were not as well taken care of in the days before coaching became such a lucrative enterprise. Driesell had little money then. He slept in his car. But the old door-to-door salesman did well in the conversational clutch.

Later, thought Jack Heise and others, Driesell took a few players whose academic, athletic and personal failures left stains on the program's fabric, and drove better recruits to other schools. In the chemistry of recruiting, Heise said, the school was important, but the coach and the other players were the real selling points. Heise thought Driesell's program never really recovered from the poor choices he had made after recruiting became more difficult.

What was the Lefthander's approach? First, he had to sell the players on Maryland. And, often, he did it by selling the player's mother. Carolyn Branch says she was won over by the closeness of Driesell's own family and by his solicitude toward her. When she visited his house, he hovered over her nervously, saying, "Here, have this, have that, have the whole house," she recalled. She liked the atmosphere around the Driesells. She liked Lefty's deference to his wife and his obvious love for his children. "Anybody who says Lefty didn't care about his players just doesn't know what he's talking about," she said.

Others thought Lefty's commitment to a player off the basketball court was limited -- always there on the record, but undermined by the long practices, the away games, and Driesell's own comments about education. Education and educators, in a sense, became his enemies, or at least his adversaries, they said. The coach and the university became antagonists.

In any event, after he won the confidence of a player and his parents, Driesell had to sell that player to the university. Increasingly, his recruits were academically unacceptable. The coach was caught in a fundamental dilemma: The academic standards at the university were increasingly incompatible with its need to enroll high-quality ballplayers who could make the team competitive and financially productive. Lefty had no doubt about his way of resolving that dilemma. He wanted to win, to fill the field house, and he went after the players that could help him do that. If he was pushing too hard, he said, he was only attending to tasks assigned him by the university.

In the eyes of Maryland's boosters and others, Driesell was a recruiting wizard. But his recruiting intensity got him into trouble as well. He was all but banned from Baltimore's rich field of basketball talent, particularly Dunbar High School, because he had offended the principal and the basketball coach, Bob Wade, a former NFL player who put together several national championship basketball teams. When Driesell refused to abide by Wade's recruiting protocols, Wade put out the word to other Baltimore coaches: Don't talk to Driesell. Wade, the high school coach, was also angry that Ernest Graham, a Dunbar graduate, had not gotten his degree at Maryland.

Many of Wade's post-Graham graduates -- Reggie Williams and David Wingate, for example -- ended up at Georgetown University with John Thompson or at other ACC schools. Since he effectively barred Maryland from Baltimore talent, Wade became an enemy of the Maryland basketball family, the legitimacy of his gripe with Driesell notwithstanding.

The territory was shrinking and by alienating Wade, Driesell was helping to shrink it. Equally driven coaches were hitting the road against him. Sometimes, it took extraordinary effort and shrewdness for Driesell to succeed.

At one point, the coach would offer a scholarship, sign the player and then approach the admissions director, Linda Clements. If she said no, she recalled, he would start talking about morality and ethics. "This young man bypassed other university offers to sign with Maryland. We have an obligation to him. You have to let him in," he would say. Clements's staff, in offices down the hall, would hear Driesell ranting. In due time, the procedure was changed: Admissions officials had to say yes before a player could be offered a grant to attend Maryland.

So, Driesell looked for other ways to get the players he needed. He went to Ray Gillian, then in charge of an intensive educational assistance program for minority students not qualifying for admission under the usual guidelines. These students were not allowed to take more than 10 credit hours per semester while they worked to overcome deficiencies in math and English. Nor were they permitted to take part in any extracurricular activity, including basketball, or to have a job. They needed all their time to develop the skills they lacked. Athletes were barred from Gillian's program because, under one of the many NCAA rules, they were required to take *12* credit hours per semester. And, of course, they were involved in a consuming extracurricular activity. Basketball players frequently had academic profiles similar to those of the students in Gillian's program, and yet they played. It made Gillian angry to see this disrespect for a young person's best interests. He wondered how anyone could say "student athlete" without blushing.

The Athletic Department viewed the restrictions in Gillian's program as discriminatory. With some justification, they thought there should have been a program tailored to the needs of the athletes. But Gillian thought Driesell simply wanted to use his program as a back-door admission point.

Driesell's pushing and demanding finally resulted in a change in the rules at Maryland. An athlete could be admitted to the special program, but he would have to abide by the rules, including the ban on extracurricular activities, such as basketball. Predictably, Driesell pushed for further relaxation of the rules. One year, Gillian said, on the last day before admissions closed, Driesell came to see him with admission materials for a marginal recruit he wanted.

"You have to let him in. They're having a going-away party for him tomorrow," the coach said. When Gillian said no, Driesell said, "Well, you call and tell him."

"I had no difficulty with that," Gillian said. "I made the call. I told the kid we weren't going to admit him because we didn't want to put him in a situation where he couldn't succeed."

The pressure to find talented players who could survive in college was only one of the many problems Driesell encountered in later years. For a time, College Park's Cole Field House had been one of the biggest and best anywhere. But over time, other schools built bigger and brighter arenas. Driesell then faced the dome gap. Coaches needed something like UNC's Dean Dome or the Carrier Dome at Syracuse to compete for the favors of 17-year-old pivot men and power forwards. Driesell told associates he and Maryland were finished after a recruit saw the new arena at Chapel Hill. The recruits weren't comparing the number of volumes in the library. They were comparing domes.

To compensate, Driesell had to make extraordinary efforts. In 1983, he went after two players who appeared to be completely unprepared for college. One of them, Keith Gatlin, had scored 510 on his Scholastic Aptitude Test; the other, Terry Long, scored higher -- 640. The average score at Maryland that year was about 1,000 -- almost twice Gatlin's score. Students are given 200 points -- 100 on each half (math and verbal) of the tests -- simply for signing their names.

A weary Admissions Office, annoyed over the amount of time it had to spend analyzing athletes' applications, was rejecting both recruits, according to a story given wide circulation on campus. But Driesell insisted he had to have at least one of them. He kept hammering. Finally, he was told, okay, he could have one. He picked the best player. He was the one with the lower SAT score.

Having gotten his first pick, Driesell went back to force acceptance of the second. How could admission be denied to Long when his SAT scores were higher than a kid who had already been passed through? This story was told around the campus to illustrate the essence of Driesell and his street smarts.

Ray Gillian says Gatlin came through the usual university procedures, a set of standards that can be adjusted if a student has poor grades but a special talent, such as basketball and football prowess. Such an adjustment definitely had to be made in Gatlin's case. Long was admitted to Gillian's program with the usual restrictions -- no extracurricular activities. But he was immediately on the basketball team. Gillian says he received a note from Athletic

Director Dull saying Long could play. He thought Slaughter had decided to let him play. But Slaughter thought Gillian had relaxed his standards or found Long suddenly capable of handling the academic and athletic loads. Neither investigated further. Both Long and Gatlin flunked out, got readmitted, and got into trouble on the campus. Driesell's own account of this admissions saga was unavailable, though he insists he exercised care in selecting the players he would recruit.

"You have to be careful," he said, agreeing that the academic talent of today's players increases the pressure on coaches.

"The (U.S) education department says the schools are not doing the job, particularly in the inner city. That's been proven," he said.

Nevertheless, he said, some players with poor high school records turned out to be solid students. One of these was Steve Shepard, a forward on Driesell teams of the late 1970s who played on the Olympic team and made All-Academic in the ACC.

According to Dull, regardless of what produced the admission of Long and Gatlin to the University of Maryland, one thing is clear. "As long as you are required to run a self-supporting program, there are going to be times when you are tempted to compromise your integrity academically," he said. "I've been on record as saying we probably took kids who were not proper candidates for admission. Most institutions would take a more jaundiced eye toward admitting a marginal kid if they did not have these economic concerns. If you truly want to make academic decisions, then you have to be taken out of the atmosphere where you have to make economic decisions."

Eventually Long became a drug user. He flunked all of his courses twice but never lost his eligibility to play basketball, though his basketball skills seemed to lapse and his play became inconsistent.

In the short run, Long and Gatlin were great for the Maryland program. They helped Driesell accomplish the goals he thought he was hired to pursue: winning, filling the field house, pursuing championships, and hanging banners in the rafters. With these two players contributing, Driesell and the Terps won the ACC Tournament in 1984 for the first and only time. The coach was so thrilled he said he was going to strap the trophy to the front of his car, like a big hood ornament, and drive all over Tobacco Road with it.

To be sure, given the consuming pressure to win and to be profitable, a coach's responsibilities are often in conflict. What would a father do if his son were caught breaking into a building, using drugs, or failing in class? Would he ground him and ban him from extracurricular activities? Many would. But what should a coach do in similar circumstances? Maybe the offense would come at a time when the player was needed for a crucial game.

In some rule infraction cases, Driesell did act by benching players. He talked about the student-athlete ideal. But Slaughter thought the coach resented anything that distracted a player from his major occupation, playing basketball. He seemed jealous of Slaughter's relationships with the players, and, Slaughter thought, tried to limit them. McMillen says Driesell was a supporter of academic development when he was a player at Maryland, but in later years he would brook no conflict between the game and the classroom. Practice and game films came before everything, Slaughter and others concluded.

Driesell hired academic advisers for players, but then struggled with them over how much of a player's time could be given to school work. He said later he thought the counselors were brought in to "keep up with the Joneses." If your recruiting competitors had counselors, you better have them. He seemed to project his own cynicism on his players. Driesell told *The Washington Post*: "I'm not 100 percent sold on academic advisers. It's a crutch. I mean, if I was a great athlete and I knew my coach had hired an academic adviser, well why did he hire him? He hired him to keep me eligible, so maybe they're just going to do my work for me. I just know that I had an excellent success without academic advisers. I mean, I'd send my assistant coach over to the dorm in the morning to make sure people were going to class."

Advisers were not so much a crutch for the players as they were program cosmetics, prerequisites when you sat with a recruiting prospect's mother at the kitchen table.

"Everything Lefty does, every step Lefty takes, is geared to the benefit of Lefty Driesell," said John Hawkins, who claims Driesell as a friend. "That's just the way Lefty is. It's not mean. It's instinct."

The instinct and the cornpone persona simultaneously promoted *and* undermined the value of education. Driesell pointed out that his own son and daughters were smart, but he insisted they got their brains from his wife. If you played pro ball, you didn't need a degree, he said. He wrapped himself in the success of Elmore and McMillen -- and trashed it at the same time. It had gotten to where he couldn't understand what Elmore was talking about: "He goes to Harvard. I went to Duke," he would say. If he reduced the importance and value of education, maybe he didn't have to feel let down or like a failure when his players failed.

According to Elmore, Driesell thought of himself as a victim of societal permissiveness. "He saw it as an avalanche that couldn't be stopped," he said. "For a lot of those kids, it was too late. You just wanted to get through the four years without an incident. When the cycle of coddling ended, he thought he could recover what he had before, become the old Lefty."

As brash and controlling as Driesell sought to be, his friends thought he had given up or lost control. "He has a little trouble with discipline," said Sam Meloy, a retired circuit court judge and former president of the Terrapin Club. Driesell was not as tough as he seemed to be, particularly when it came to the prima donnas on his team. Some thought he, like other coaches, had to be careful that he did not drive his players to other schools by being too demanding. Others thought Driesell had simply quit.

"It used to be," Driesell said during a coaching seminar in Rhode Island, "that kids got in trouble for fighting or siphoning gas." Siphoning gas? Driesell critics said his problem was age -- he just didn't know much about what kids did in the 1980s.

Basketball players got into no more trouble than students as a whole, but they were "stars" and they paid a higher price if they slipped. Often, when a Maryland player was in trouble, Driesell occasionally made things worse. He made himself the issue -- perhaps, on purpose.

"He wore a target on his back," Elmore said. "No one knows if the style was calculated to deflect criticism from his players, or if he wasn't able to stay out of a fight."

If *he* was the target, he could shield and save his players. Like others in his profession, Driesell relied on intimidation. He used it with referees, with reporters, with faculty members, and with administrators. For a time, the outrageous remark was a part of his political strength: He put eggheads in their places. But the image that filled the field house in earlier times began to work against him as the university reached more eagerly for respect as a teaching and research institution.

In the spring of 1984, he and Slaughter found themselves embroiled in yet another battle over a ballplayer, Bias's friend,

Herman Veal. A strong rebounding forward from Jackson, Mississippi, Veal, then a junior, was suddenly benched just before the Virginia game. At first, no one would say why.

But university officials reported eventually that Veal was being disciplined for an incident involving a 21-year-old woman student. The disclosure was made at the same time a basketball player at the University of San Francisco, Quintin Dailey, had been charged with sexually assaulting a young woman there. Veal's alleged offense was far less serious, but the stories echoed in the public mind. At first, Driesell declined to say anything and, had he continued to follow that policy, life might have been considerably easier for him. But Driesell and silence were not compatible.

"They told me not to say anything so I'm just saying it [the suspension] was administrative, even though I don't know how to spell it. Before it's over," Driesell told reporters, "I'll have plenty to say."

The story was that Veal hoisted the young woman over his head, threw her onto his bed, and began to fondle her. "I don't like foreplay," he allegedly said. The young woman reported the incident to campus authorities. Several other players had been in the room with Veal and the young woman just before the alleged incident. They backed up Veal's account.

In the fall before the basketball season began, a campus disciplinary board reprimanded Veal. He appealed. Fastbreaker Heise's law firm represented him. The appeal bought time, at least. It took until the end of the season for the process to run its course. The appeal was disallowed. Veal was then suspended -- just before the important game with Virginia.

"If I've got anything to do with it," Driesell declared, "he'll play. I've got some pull around here, and we'll see how much."

Driesell was rushing for the corner. He had tried to be the admissions director. Now he would be the disciplinary board.

"It never occurred to him to watch what he was saying," said Hawkins. "He loves to talk and he's a captivating guy. He kept the good old boys coming to the field house." The daring, challenging, intimidating style of the sideline coach did not fade after the game for Lefty. He was not a bully or a male chauvinist, President John Toll insisted, but his performances sometimes beggared the terms.

Heise thought there had been a good chance to win the appeal. "But my good friend Lefty had to make his statement and the minute he did it, it was out of our hands." By that he meant that the board had to stand with its original decision or risk the appearance that it was in thrall to Driesell.

In addition to his public remarks, Driesell phoned the alleged victim. He says he called to counsel her as a father would. He wanted her to know, he said later, that if the matter became public and protracted, her reputation could suffer. He insisted he was trying to save her from that pain -- but his fatherly concern also included suggestions to reporters that they investigate her background. Players were whispering that she was a jock groupie; some went to reporters with suggestions that they check her reputation at another ACC school.

When his conversations with the young woman were made public, Driesell was blasted by the campus women's center. He blasted back.

"I don't care about the women's center," he said, "I'm the men's center. In my mind, Herman Veal's the victim." Driesell could have been right. Slaughter thought he was at least partly right about Herman Veal. But he was making that conclusion hard to believe.

The pattern was easily recognizable by Driesell analysts.

Judge Meloy said, "He's a bit positive. He tends to foreclose the other point of view." Driesell had always put it this way: "You're either with me or you're against me."

With his boasting about "pull" and the "men's center," Driesell seemed to put his team, the Virginia game, the ACC Tournament, and the NCAA tournament above the interests of civility and decency on the campus. Various newspapers suggested that he be fired. An inquiry was ordered by Chancellor Slaughter.

The investigators produced a 25-page report. Slaughter called a press conference to publicly chastise Driesell, calling his actions "contrary to my expectations." Lefty sat alongside the chancellor for his public scolding. Reading a scripted statement of apology, the role-model coach winked at his audience. Like a kid apologizing with his fingers crossed, he very nearly turned the tables and humiliated Chancellor Slaughter. Meantime, his players were elated. David Simon, then a reporter for the student newspaper, *The Diamondback*, watched the team members arrive for practice that day. They walked around laughing and slapping each other on the wrists -- suggesting that the penalty was not a penalty, really, and exulting in yet another win for their coach.

Among those who were accustomed to seeing Driesell punish his accusers, though, this was almost a victory for law and order.

Driesell had turned a bad situation into a disaster. He had cornered everyone: himself, of course, the university, the young woman, and Veal. The woman went into a campus bar one night, and the patrons booed her for interrupting the basketball team's concentration. She left school.

Veal suffered, too, for his own behavior and for his coach's defense. "I was initially outraged at what Herman did and was purported to have said," said Jan McKay, another of Slaughter's vice chancellors. "He operated out of a position of great naivete, a consequence of the isolated social environment he was living in. It was an outgrowth of the macho culture. He was not growing socially. In effect, he was being protected from social growth. He was publicly humiliated. Much of it he brought on himself. But someone else reacted for him, and that made it a lot worse than it was to begin with."

Nevertheless, McKay was reluctant to condemn Driesell: "I have learned some new sympathy for coaches. They are required to perform almost impossible roles. They have to be parents, guidance counselors, moral developers, and winners."

Veal was hit with a short suspension and a long-term image problem. At next year's Duke game in Durham, North Carolina, condoms, naked dolls, bras, and panties were hurled at him by the always imaginative Blue Devil fans. Veal pretended not to notice. Maryland beat Duke soundly that night largely on the strength of Veal's play.

Slaughter sympathized with Driesell and appreciated his protective impulses. At the same time, the chancellor wanted a new atmosphere in the basketball program. In the fall of 1985, the year after Veal graduated, Slaughter called Driesell and Athletic Director Dull to his office for a review of the basketball team's graduation record. At Slaughter's request, Dull had gathered the data and Slaughter confronted Driesell with it. Over the previous 10 years, only 56 percent of the players had gotten a degree -- and among the black players, only 29 percent had graduated.

"Where'd you get that stuff?" the coach wanted to know. Slaughter felt Driesell was more interested in the source of the information than in its significance. "It was clear to me that I was a lot more interested in some of the team's problems than he was," Slaughter said. Driesell could insist if he wanted to that the university was not enforcing any standards, but the chancellor concluded the session by insisting that the team would have to improve its classroom performance.

A few months later, in the spring of 1986, Slaughter began to review the transcripts of Maryland players. As chairman of the NCAA Presidents Commission, he was pushing to have freshmen made ineligible for varsity competition. He had studied transcripts of players at other schools. When he looked at courses taken by Maryland players, he was horrified.

"They were abominable," he said. The courses included the usual array of jock courses with questionable utility: racquetball, Jazz 1 (New Orleans) and Jazz II (St. Louis). More alarming, players appeared to be taking introductory courses aimlessly from a wide spectrum of fields. As introductions, these courses were purposely less demanding. Athletes, who waited much longer than other students to declare a major, tended never to take courses in a subject that they liked well enough to explore more deeply. They took the intro courses because they were easy. Slaughter brought this to the coach's attention, but Driesell, as always, said he didn't get involved in course selection.

During graduation ceremonies that spring, Slaughter looked up and was surprised to see Driesell, in cap and gown, sitting in the faculty section of the field house. Slaughter, who was constantly hammered by Driesell's detractors, needed some sign of change, so he made sure everyone knew Driesell was there.

"With us today," he said, "is a man who conducts his classes here, the dean of Maryland basketball, Charles Driesell." The thought of Lefty in cap and gown was ludicrous -- or encouraging. Here was the coach who talked about the value of street smarts displaying his skills at a commencement.

Whatever the downward turning point was for Driesell at Maryland, the point of no return came in the Veal affair. What the coach said and did in that set of developments became a lash for his detractors in the summer of 1986. By then, the Driesell archives made some people think, as he put it himself, that Lefty was "some kind of animal out of the sky."

He himself had helped to paint the picture. He had became a symbol of what Slaughter called "basketball uber alles." Driesell was an environment unto himself, a weather system, a stationary front. You could *talk* about him, but you couldn't do anything about him. You couldn't change him and he couldn't change himself. For almost a generation, Lefty's persona had worked well for him. He had good teams. He filled the field house. But when defiance and provocation started to bite back on him, he seemed unable to get out of the way. If he changed, the wins might not come, the people might not come. He could not change and still be Lefty.

After Bias's death, Driesell declared the Maryland program solid and beautiful. As Slaughter's task force on the student athlete worked its way through a long list of witnesses in late July 1986, Athletic Director Dull declared that, for its coaches, Maryland had no philosophy beyond winning.

According to almost everyone who knew him, Lefty had internalized that goal thoroughly. Depending on your point of view, his commitment was a vice or a virtue.

"He was absolutely eaten alive by the need to win," said reporter Molly Dunham.

Driesell did not disagree: "I hate to lose. I never get used to that. To me, losing's like failure. I'll do anything to win," he told a reporter. "If I think kicking a chair or intimidating officials will help me, I'll do it."

Jan McKay and others were struck by a change in the definition of winning in college sports. The sportsmanship ideal had been abandoned, replaced by the value of winning. Perhaps that ideal had never been honored as highly in reality as it had been in the abstract. But the change was observed in an open and proud rejection of the ideal. In order to win, Driesell once changed the numbers on his players' uniforms to confuse the opponents. Winning by playing within the rules -- the idea that cheating was not really winning -- seemed to be lost.

Well, maybe the idea that he would do "anything" to win had been an exaggeration.

"I don't want to win by cheating," he said years later. "What satisfaction would there be in it if you cheated? It'd be like playing golf and cheating on your score."

Dull was sure of one thing: If he graduated everyone but didn't win, he'd be fired. No one thought the rules were any different at other big-time athletic schools.

When Driesell came before the student-athlete task force, he insisted his program was in fine shape. He had his charts and graphs with him.

"Lefty is a remarkably strong-minded person," said Ralph Bennett of the architecture school and a member of the task force. "His first move was to say, 'What problem? We don't have a problem. There's no problem about academic performance.' He got all the records out. It took a whole meeting before we persuaded him that whether he liked it or not, there was a perception that his program was in big trouble."

Recognizing that it had the ultimate power, the task force decided not to have a confrontation with Driesell. They let him have the floor. But when he said the basketball players' grade point averages -- below the minimal 2.0 needed to graduate -- were "not too bad," Chairman Dorfman could not restrain himself.

"You think this record is not too bad?" he asked.

"Absolutely," responded Driesell. On the street, among those who watched the Maryland program and hoped their best players would go there, Driesell's assertion was accepted. Sterling Parker, a coach in the Amateur Athletic Union leagues of Washington, said he was elated to see that Bias was only 20 credits short of graduation. He knew Bias's limitations as a student and the pressures of big-time basketball. He could hardly have done better, Parker thought.

On the campus, though, the assessment was at the other end of the "solid and beautiful" spectrum.

Len Elmore, who had been appointed by Slaughter to the academic task force, sat in for Driesell's testimony. He had a high regard for his old coach, and he found it painful to see Driesell pretending he had no problems. The coach's considerable strength of mind was wasted in this transparent defense. For Elmore, who had previously seen Driesell almost entirely from the athletic side, the perspective was new and revealing.

"He argued that all his players were passing -- with minimal passing marks -- except for three who were failing. He thought that vindicated his program. The educators looked around and wondered how he could be proud of a program with that kind of record," said Elmore.

Chapter 7

Low Point

Slaughter saw more of reporters in the summer of 1986 than he did of his wife, Bernice. His days often began with TV cameras waiting for him as he backed out of his driveway, and his days usually ended with a round of calls to reporters who were looking for his comments on some development. University spokeswoman Roz Hiebert insists that Mark Hyman of *The Sun* very nearly strangled her once to impress her with his urgent need to see the chancellor.

Hiebert's occasional protectiveness of the usually accessible Slaughter sometimes spurred reporters to more aggressive pursuit of the news as they saw it, although they probably would not have done otherwise, no matter what Hiebert did. Critics of the university's public relations effort, including some university administrators, say the crisis plan was not thought out in advance. To them, no guidelines were apparent, no recognition of a public university's obligation to provide information. Others argued just the opposite. The university, they said, had made itself highly vulnerable to outside criticism by refusing to take a bunker-like approach to the press.

As vividly as Hiebert remembers the hectoring throng of reporters, Hyman remembers waiting: waiting for Hiebert, waiting for Slaughter, waiting for Lefty. He waited at Cole Field House. He waited outside the task force meetings at the comfortable and sprawling Adult Education Center on the campus's west side. And he waited for Slaughter outside the main administration building, sitting at a rickety, moss-covered picnic table under one of the tall evergreen trees that shade the windows of the chancellor's office.

Frequently, Hyman wished Slaughter goodnight -- after asking again what he was going to do about Lefty, Dull, or football coach Bobby Ross, or the academic collapse of the basketball team. At summer's end, Slaughter gave Dean Dorfman, chairman of his academic task force, a Terps football helmet as a kind of doleful protection against encounters with the press. It was a piece of equipment that Slaughter may have coveted himself.

Hyman and his partner, Amy Goldstein, covered all the Bias fronts on the College Park campus. At the top of the story list was Driesell. Would he stay or go? Only slightly less compelling for the reporters were football coach Bobby Ross and his insistent demand for a vote of confidence -- a clear statement for the record that he was unimplicated in the Bias crisis, and that his program was commendable. Ross periodically put out the call for this endorsement -- and Slaughter consistently declined to respond, observing that the entire Maryland program was under review. Had he accommodated Ross then, he would have been saying all over again that coaches could always overrule process, he thought. Reporters took up a Lefty watch and a Bobby watch, a feverish, daily reading of administration tea leaves for some clue to the fate of these men and their programs.

Hyman and Goldstein became students of Slaughter's press management style. "He fumbled at first," Goldstein said. "It was an art he didn't have. But he learned to trust himself more. He got slicker as he went along." He learned to say enough to satisfy without revealing too much. He was too good at it, Hyman thought.

Slaughter was absolutely certain that he had not "managed" any reporter or paper. He never felt he had control of anything written about the crisis or the way he handled it. Sometimes he groaned when he read in the newspaper what he had said the day before. On "Nightline," he felt he had embarrassed himself. When host Ted Koppel asked him why the university tolerated poor academic performances by athletes, Slaughter delayed his answer while he welcomed "Nightline" viewers to College Park. Koppel stopped him with a withering restatement of the question. For the rest of the night, Slaughter appeared tentative. He was despondent about his performance.

Hyman referred to Slaughter as Father John and stuck a picture of him on the wall next to his desk at *The Sun*. There was no doubt of the chancellor's sincerity, Hyman thought, but he was lacking in resolve. Put Slaughter and Driesell in the same room to argue about something, Hyman believed, and there was no question who would come out the winner. He saw Driesell as a man who had lost touch with the values he was so quick to talk about. Slaughter, on the other hand, seemed indecisive, unwilling to act on his instincts and, Hyman thought, unwilling to come completely clean. He saw Slaughter's acceptance of blame as essentially empty and pro forma.

What Hyman's analysis seemed to ignore, however, were the other pressures on the chancellor and his office. Boosters, for example, saw Slaughter as a turncoat, a man who not only had failed to defend his university, but had admitted exploitation of athletes, something they thought the university was not guilty of. There was a sense that summer that no one would be satisfied with the level of Slaughter's contrition until he opened a vein. Regents Chairman Allen Schwait said the critics forgot the momentum of sports history. A member of the Board of Regents for several years before Slaughter arrived at College Park, Schwait brought his own sensitivity to the problems of student athletes -- as much as he recognized those problems abstractly. But that sensitivity had been dulled by the money and the political realities. "It's not my university," Schwait would say, as if he might take a different position if it were. He thought there was no question that Marylanders demanded the kind of sports programs run by Lefty and Bobby.

News organizations thought Schwait's assumption of public support was perfectly accurate. They covered events at College Park the same way they covered the Baltimore Orioles or the Washington Redskins, daily and in detail. The Goldstein-Hyman team competed with reporters from local weeklies and *The New York Times, USA Today*, television and radio stations -- and particularly with Mark Asher, an intense and tireless digger for *The Washington Post*.

Just before Bias's death, Asher and his colleagues had been preparing a long series of articles on Maryland sports. In the scramble to advance the Bias story -- the daily demand for something fresh after the crisis turned from drugs to the classroom -- that work gave *The Post* a significant advantage. Asher and company already knew the Maryland athletic department.

At the beginning of each day, *The Sun* reporters went off to make their checks. At the end of the day, they met at Cole Field House to discuss what stories they might have for the next day's paper. Settled into seats a few rows down in the darkened arena, they would sometimes hear Asher's unmistakable footfall. The leg brace he wore made an ominous, purposeful click against the concrete floor.

"It was a scary sound," Goldstein remembered later. "He couldn't have been up to any good as far as we were concerned." The sound was a competitive spur, driving them to go over the same ground, talk to the same people, know everything Asher knew.

Among College Park administrators, this rivalry between ambitious reporters on competing newspapers was seen as the primary reason for the story's distorted longevity. The Spacecraft Challenger explosion, more than one university official observed, escaped Page One attention after two weeks. College Park remained there for five *months*.

Here was a university that was virtually ignored by the newspapers three years earlier, when its computer science and physics departments earned high rankings from the National Academy of Sciences. Now its step-by-step recovery from the depths of a sports scandal was a staple of the day's leading news stories.

Ben Holman, a black journalism professor at Maryland, thought the story had been hideously over-covered, and he blamed racism. The story was compelling for the white-dominated national media because it involved black athletes, black nightclubs, and a black chancellor. There would have been far less attention, he said, if the player who died had been white.

"The worst elements of the profession come to the surface whenever race is an issue," Holman said. For most reporters, race was not an issue at all -- and, to some extent, that was the problem, Holman thought.

"It has been my experience as a practitioner going back to the early 1950s that when the largely white press in this country has to deal with race, it gets blinders on and its professionalism seems to go out the window. There is a total lack of sensitivity in dealing with black athletes. They were made to appear drugged, dumb and in school only because of their brawn. It's far from true across the board," he said. The nightclubs -- Chapter II in Washington and Classics in Southern Maryland -- were written about as if they were illicit sinkholes where loose women and cocaine were measurable by the square foot. No one wrote about the feelings of isolation among black athletes and other College Park students that drove them off the campus to places where they were comfortable, he said.

What had happened in the Bias story was the subtle, instant and irreversible application of the black drug user stereotype. And, Holman thought, this had occurred long before there was evidence that Bias was not a newcomer to cocaine. In effect, a police mug shot was superimposed on the yearbook image of Leonard Kevin Bias, Class of '86.

Wayne Curry, the Bias family's lawyer after Bias's death, thought the transformation had been carefully engineered to protect the university. Bias had died under circumstances that were, at best, acutely embarrassing, and, at worst, immensely costly in reputation and money if a damage suit were brought by Bias's parents. But, Curry thought, if the young man were made to look like a thug, the responsibility would shift to him and his family and away from College Park. And there was a tendency to put distance between the dead athlete and the program he had supported so well when he was alive. Other unlucky college students, Curry thought, could die in a bout of foolishness and keep their reputations. Black athletes could not.

Slaughter, too, felt the momentum swing in the direction of the stereotype. "He was a nice kid, an intelligent kid," the chancellor said. "It would have been one thing if he was an outlaw. He wasn't. That was the hell of it."

Vice Chancellor McKay may have had the best take on it: She thought the story was driven by voyeurism. An English professor who was regarded as one of Slaughter's most able assistants, she agreed that the drug-induced death of a basketball player had built-in staying power. But she thought editors, reporters and readers were riveted to it, not by race or Establishment-saving conspiracies, but by the lurid appeal of a young millionaire dead in a bout of drug-taking and by the prospect of powerful victims still to come. When was Slaughter

going to roll Lefty's head? What about Dull? When would someone
dismiss the chancellor himself?

College Park was in a free fall. Slaughter wanted to stop it without
throwing bodies overboard.

"There aren't bad people involved here," he said. "They're people
of integrity. Maybe they didn't do all the things they should have, but
straightening it out wasn't a process of saying 'Aha! You're guilty,
you're bad, and therefore we're going to do something about you.'"

Looking at similar catastrophes in the world of college sports, the
writer Frank Deford said during a congressional hearing on the
turmoil in college athletics, "We in the press love to discover villains
and regularly we turn up administrators, coaches or players who
cheated. But there really are not any true villains here. It is just a case
of many good people being trapped in a very bad system."

As the crisis churned along, Slaughter realized more fully that he
was himself a target of the "fire somebody" frenzy. The intensity of
the drive to dump someone amazed him. He had his own vote of
confidence: The Regents had given it to him immediately, when they
muzzled Toll and made Slaughter the chief spokesman. But there was
a broader indictment brewing against him -- that he was incompetent
and protected because he was black.

He was attacked viciously by letter writers. "You were sitting in
that chair when all that drug shit was going down," one said. Slaughter
was inclined to dismiss this as understandable unhappiness in a
difficult time, but no one had ever questioned his motives before. He
was the kind of person whom people liked and admired. He had been
courted by a U.S. president. But the possibility that he might fire a
beloved basketball coach -- or fail to fire one -- made him a target of
intense criticism.

When Maryland professors left the campus in those days, they
were confronted with the clucking and head-shaking of critics. Some
faculty members thought the summer's calamitous events proved that
college sports and real universities were incompatible; if you tried to
preserve the competitive quality and economic value of the teams,
according to this theory, you inevitably sacrificed the best interests
of the students and the integrity of the university.

A major campus advocate of the radical reform thesis was
anthropology Professor Aubrey Williams, a thin, dour man who

occasionally wore boots and western shirts with epaulets and who
was an expert on American Indians. He saw sports in America as a
damaging cultural phenomenon at least as addicting and corrosive as
cocaine. Sports and money were the real drugs, Williams thought. He
wrote Slaughter early in the summer, urging him to take advantage
of the opportunity, arriving unhappily with the death of Bias, to regain
control of his university.

Professor Williams made his appeal public. Reform was an
illusion, he warned. The university should simply abolish its football
and basketball teams. A few times during these days he would arrive
at his office to find "Fuck You" and other messages tacked to his door.

Williams persisted. "Bias was the ultimate expression of the
athletic business. But if you look at it from an educational point of
view, it was a dismal failure. We failed him," he said.

Williams wanted Slaughter to debunk the fiction, widely
accepted by sports fans, that football and basketball were part of the
academic enterprise, vehicles for character building. Somehow
people didn't see through this, didn't care, or were certain that
opposing the sports juggernaut was fruitless. Even parents who
should have cared, Chancellor Slaughter said, were chasing dreams
of big money through their sons.

But Slaughter did not have the power to abolish football and
basketball -- even if he had thought that that was the right course of
action. He did not favor abolition. He thought basketball and football
could still enrich campus life, if they could be reconnected with the
values used to justify them. But the growing dependence on
sports-generated revenue made the condemnation of intercollegiate
sports at Maryland increasingly difficult to refute.

At the very least, Professor Williams suggested, Slaughter should
rid the campus of Driesell. He thought Lefty was a catch basin for
anti-intellectualism and an insult to everything a university should
represent.

"Driesell seemed quite ruthless. He presented himself as a person
who wanted his team to win almost at any cost," Williams said. "When
they didn't win there was something wrong. He was slamming chairs
around, spitting on the floor. There was something uncouth about
him." Even Jerry Tarkanian, the NCAA-sanctioned coach at UNLV,
had a concern for his players not discernible in Driesell, he said.

But Slaughter was inclined to keep Lefty and thought he might
have no choice. The pressure to win did not come from Driesell alone.

He was simply its unquestioning instrument. Driesell or someone like him, Slaughter thought, was an inevitable part of life at a school like Maryland. And the chancellor hoped he could rehabilitate Driesell -- not the least because he knew it would be pure hell to get rid of him. He could fire a coach for failing to win, but failing to educate had never been a firing offense. Coaches had been hired at Maryland to win games, not by Slaughter, but by his predecessors, and their writ still supported Driesell and his backers.

Like his other vice chancellors, Ray Gillian struggled with Slaughter to cut Driesell loose. Gillian thought of himself as one of the chancellor's confidants and one of his most outspoken critics. He thought the criticisms were the strength of their relationship, that Slaughter valued his passionate honesty.

"I thought Lefty was the biggest con man I ever met," Gillian said. "John thought there was good in everyone. He said you always had to see things from the other guy's viewpoint. He never wanted to give up on anyone." Arguing with the chancellor about ballplayers who were not performing as students, Gillian urged Slaughter at one point to dismiss the players.

"He wanted to make some hard decisions at one point, cut out the rotten core, suffer for a few years and get strong. Then you would have the environment you wanted," Gillian said. In the end, though, the radical act always seemed imprudent. How would the team continue? How would the university replace lost revenue?

Slaughter's personal and leadership styles did not include peremptory action or confrontation. "He tried to get people to buy into the system," said Gillian, who was occasionally frustrated by his boss's approach. "He was not the sort of hands-on guy who would step in and say, 'You have three openings in your department. I want one of them for a black candidate, one for a woman.'"

Gillian thought Slaughter's views were, in part, a function of the chancellor's preoccupation with administrative matters. One evening at a dinner for black graduates, the chancellor was startled to hear a black coed describe her years on the College Park campus. "She was in tears. She was very hurt by the racial isolation she felt. Her story brought student life to the foreground for him," Gillian said.

In the beginning, while prosecutor Marshall's grand jury was at work investigating the events leading to Bias's death and the use of drugs at College Park, the Maryland attorney general's staff warned Slaughter that he had no choice but to ride with Driesell. The university could not act until the grand jury acted -- indicted the coach or exonerated him -- without provoking a costly lawsuit. Slaughter was unwilling, in any event, to agree that Driesell should go until all the information on the coach's performance -- and all the possible termination scenarios -- had been analyzed. Those wanting immediate action did not appreciate the chancellor's determination to be fair, the efforts to avoid a lawsuit, or a dozen other powerful impediments to action.

In many ways, Slaughter was the embodiment of a university. Universities were places where process and procedure were honored, where instinct and impulse were suspect. Universities operated on monastic time, Ph.D. time -- the time of scholars and thinkers. Studies had to be done before action was taken on anything. Search committees were formed to find replacements for important job openings. Task forces were always at work somewhere. Committees labored over final reports. Months were like days in real time. Now, though, the two worlds were butting up against one another. The collision sent a rooster tail of sparks into the chancellor's lap.

During these days, Slaughter was criticized for his attempts to preserve university ideals and for his ways of doing business -- his concerns for people.

"Maybe things were worse than they needed to have been because of the delay in dealing with Driesell," said history Professor George H. Callcott. "People wish he [Slaughter] had shown a little more leadership." Slaughter had been "less than completely strong," he added.

Some of the unhappiness with Slaughter, Callcott said, was rooted in Slaughter's other campus objective, his drive for a multi-racial, multi-ethnic, multi-cultural community at College Park.

"They [critics] wish the concern of the university would be more in terms of quality than democracy," Callcott said. No one disagreed that the university should be reaching out to provide more opportunities, he said, but there was debate about the correct emphasis. Some, he said, felt that an "emphasis on opportunity diminishes the emphasis on excellence."

Through most of July and August 1986, Slaughter and his assistants met twice a day around the long conference table in his dark paneled office. Memorial Chapel was visible through the wood-shuttered windows. The chancellor's desk sat at the opposite end of the room, a triangular, walnut name-plate holder on its front, a vestige of Slaughter's career in government. A round coffee table, atop a muted rose and blue Oriental rug, commanded the middle of the room.

Slaughter met with reporters, friends, regents, alumni, basketball players, and other visitors in this room. They sat in armchairs of mint green upholstery tacked down by shiny brass brads. Other tables and desks, arranged against the walls, were covered with books, ring-binders packed with work papers, computer instruction manuals, correspondence, and business magazines. Slaughter would toss his tobacco on the coffee table next to a small bone-handled pocket knife, blade open and ready for bowl cleaning. A wooden humidor, its top etched with the grid of a terrapin's shell, was on an end table. A replica of Willie The Wildcat, the mascot of Kansas State University, Slaughter's alma mater, hovered on one of the bookshelves.

During the height of the crisis, these "war meetings" were run by Vice Chancellor Gilmour, who often began with a grim review of the latest disaster -- usually a newspaper story disclosing some further academic shortcoming. Slaughter was particularly distressed in late June and early July by publication of the basketball players' dismal grades, not only because their performances were embarrassing to him and the university, but because it was illegal for the university to release a student's personal records. He thought the stories invaded the privacy of fragile, traumatized young men whose feelings and welfare seemed to many to be the least important aspect of the crisis.

Slaughter's team was frequently embarrassed to find itself ratifying actions that already had been reported by Asher or Hyman. There was no leak chasing, but there was suspicion about leakers, and much of it attached, rightly or wrongly, to Athletic Director Dull. The group began to delay discussion of sensitive matters until Dull was out of the room.

Slaughter wanted to address the needs of the players, but he knew he needed to show he was in control of his program, and that he was purging it of unhealthy influences. Hoping to do something decisive quickly, he looked at three alternatives: 1) abandoning football and basketball altogether; 2) canceling the 1986-87 season to allow a period of emotional and academic recovery; and 3) shortening the 1986-87 season by canceling a holiday tournament and limiting first semester practice time to allow the players a brief period of healing.

A memo analyzing these alternatives was prepared by a committee headed by William E. "Brit" Kirwan, vice chancellor in charge of academic affairs. The committee findings starkly outlined the limitations within which the university had to operate -- unless it were willing to abandon intercollegiate sports altogether.

The memo set forth the several options, offering a prediction of how each would be received by various groups: Maryland politicians, Atlantic Coast Conference athletic directors, coaches, athletes, sportswriters, and Maryland's faculty. The chancellor and his advisers could not choose simply on the merits. It was not a matter of deciding what was right or what would be most beneficial to players in grave academic and emotional trouble. The university had to make sound financial and political judgments.

"There were so many constituencies to please, so many decisions every day," Vice Chancellor McKay recalled. "We had to remind ourselves that we were dealing with a personal tragedy. I often dealt with it in an abstract way: 'What about X or Y?' John, though, had the kids in focus."

But Slaughter's ability to initiate reform was limited. A semblance of standards needed to be established, but the basketball team's academic anemia was profound. "Most players would not survive long-term increases in academic standards," the Kirwan memo said. If the players did not survive, Maryland would have no team, no revenue and a political firestorm.

Pressure for change continued: "We run a great risk of appearing generally inept and appearing to have acted for the wrong reasons if we do not improve upon the academic progress of the basketball players," the memo concluded.

With that dismal forecast in hand, the chancellor's team necessarily left the long-term issue of academic standards while it groped for some immediate action.

Option 1, dropping football and basketball outright, got almost no consideration. The reasons were money, politics and Slaughter's belief that sports were still valuable elements of university life. Some universities ran good programs. Maryland could, too. Abolition was defensible only if one concluded that Maryland's basketball program was "totally corrupt," he said later. The University of San Francisco had dropped basketball when one of its players was accused of rape, and then was found to be the beneficiary of a no-show job given by a booster. Tulane University abolished basketball when some of its players were implicated in gambling activities.

The scandal at Maryland was even more compelling. A player had died. Two years earlier, two Maryland players had been convicted of drug violations. There was the Veal affair. Driesell, reprimanded for his actions during that episode, now was under investigation by a grand jury. Slaughter thought the athletic department pushed players toward meaningless degrees. The program was not "totally corrupt," but it had been badly damaged by corrupting forces.

Slaughter remained anguished about the stressful lives of basketball players, but he had no middle-of-the-night epiphany leading him to end a program that had victimized the players. A central conflict for him was between concern for the players and his view of basketball as an entree into university life for Americans with precious few avenues. The program, he thought, could be fixed. And he was determined not to preside over the dismantling of an American institution.

Only a bit more consideration was given to Option 2: canceling the entire 1986-87 season. The cost of a year away from the big time would have been $2 million in lost ticket sales and television revenue, and possibly more, if contributors (Terrapin Club members in particular), deprived of their ACC Tournament, walked away. Maryland would probably lose its membership in the conference.

Kirwan's memo said, "We believe that recruitment for next year's basketball players is dead in the water at present. We do not believe that any short-term solution will make much difference for next year's recruitment, but if we unilaterally, long-term, take action to shorten the season or in any way de-emphasize the program, we believe it will hurt recruitment significantly." So, within the academic councils of the university, the health of basketball at Maryland had a higher priority than the team's academic welfare. "We can't do stupid things," Slaughter said later with resignation. "We need the gate receipts."

Alone among the chancellor's advisers, Ray Gillian argued strenuously for a year off. He saw plenty of corruption. He had fought with Driesell to keep unqualified students out of the university because he knew they would be unhappy and disruptive. Long and Gregg and others were such obvious examples that it was criminal not to see it. People did see it, he thought. Universities pretended basketball players had a legitimate chance to be students. He resented the way just about everyone denied that fact.

Gillian was a passionate defender of the student-athlete ideal -- something, he thought, that did not exist at Maryland. He had been a defensive back on Ohio State's national championship football team in 1966. On the wall of his office, just down the hall from the chancellor, Gillian had framed Ohio State Coach Woody Hayes's motto: "Win With People." This admonition meant that character, honesty, and hard work win in sports and in life -- not strategy, new formations, or tantrums. (Not that Coach Hayes was beyond an occasional tantrum.)

"When I went to Ohio State as a freshman, I wouldn't say I was a good citizen," he said. "When I left, I think I was a very good citizen. I give Coach Hayes a lot of credit for that." At Maryland, Gillian thought, athletes were often like Bias, shaky citizens when they arrived and in serious trouble before they left.

He saw the basketball team as a particular problem. Basketball teams traveled so much and played so many games. "I can't imagine being a basketball player in a history class at 10 a.m., listening to a professor when you're going to be on TV that night against Duke. You only have so much emotional energy," Gillian said. "We all want to give 100 percent, but basketball means they can't give 100 percent to studying. You can't convince me it's possible. If they were all McMillens or Elmores, maybe. But they're not. So it's unreasonable to expect it, but we do."

The obvious demands of the program bred cynicism in players.

"They're reasonably smart. They know the goals are championships and money. Otherwise, why in hell do they schedule practice during the week of final exams? If they do practice and they do play games during that period, what message does it send?" The players begin to act on their belief that no one really cares if they study or not.

Gillian and Slaughter argued about what should be done to change this situation. "The thing that bothered John the most -- more than it did me -- was that kids weren't being educated in a classic sense. He felt they would be unable to function in the world if we didn't educate them. And we weren't educating them. They learned the slide-by games." Like Bias, Gillian said, "They all knew what to say and how to say it. But they weren't learning anything. John hated that. It was really unfair that he got caught in this thing. He wanted to do it right."

Gillian argued a pragmatic case: Most people, he said, learned their life's work on the job even when they did graduate from college. The degree was like a union card. Knowing the pressures he would face, it was grossly unfair, to bring a marginal student to College Park and then turn him out with nothing. If, at admission time, standards were dropped for the convenience of the university and its basketball program, how could those standards be snapped into full service when eligibility ran out? Gillian did not wish to hand out phony certificates, but he was not as concerned as Slaughter about the smorgasbord transcripts. And he was ready to take a radical step. He thought the basketball team was so lacking in discipline and ability to perform that its members should be excused from the team to become full-time students. They would be replaced by players who had a chance and a willingness to do well. In the meantime, everyone deserved a real breather. "I thought we ought to let go of damned football and basketball for a year or so," he said. But his view was rejected by Slaughter and the Regents.

Slaughter and his task force wanted to provide adequate breathing space for emotionally distressed young men, and they wanted to take stock. Doing both was too expensive. College Park was part of a conference television contract. It could not withdraw from the conference play without incurring major expenses. It could not dismiss players for academic shortcomings without losing the team and the gate receipts. Money dictated decision-making, even in the face of death and the most humiliating disclosures about academic failure. The chancellor was completely committed to change, anxious to intervene on behalf of the athletes, but constrained by financial realities.

What the task force finally decided to do was feeble and transparent: Option 3, a unilateral, one-time-only shortening of the season. That limited action, the memo said, would "likely be seen as positive by most constituencies -- except coaches, the athletic department, and student athletes."

And there would be a cost -- about $100,000 to compensate the teams on Maryland's schedule that would lose their share of television revenue and gate receipts. But Slaughter was ready to pay: "We have to give these kids a chance to reconnect with themselves," he said.

Slaughter had hoped the respite could be longer -- but the television schedulers had the rest of the season in place before he could act. What he seemed to be saying was that he had no control or only limited control over what would happen in his basketball program. He might well have overruled those decisions, but, in truth, he could not prudently do so. He needed the receipts.

The Slaughter work group was assured by the university's chief athletic department fund-raiser, Tom Fields, that the season-shortening action could be taken without a critical loss of support from the Terrapin Club.

The memo provided this additional insight: A shorter season was important, not just for the players, but "to get the attention of the athletic department, the coaches and the players." Len Bias was dead, the campus was engulfed in controversy, and something was still needed to get the attention of the athletic department. Aubrey Williams wanted Lefty fired. Slaughter was trying to get the man's attention.

At first, Driesell resisted the season-shortening proposal. "I ain't got any problems," he told Vice Chancellor Gilmour. "You gonna screw me up. I don't see why you're doing this to me."

Then, within a week, Driesell changed his mind. He became a fan of the shorter season. Gilmour was stunned. Here was Driesell capitulating, a remarkable event. "He was out there saying, 'Shortening the basketball season is the best thing we've ever done, and I'm proud to do it.'" Gilmour thought Edward Bennett Williams had persuaded Driesell to go along with the idea, just as he had managed to get Driesell to refrain from public comment.

On August 13, nearly two months after Bias died, Slaughter called a press conference to announce the season-shortening plan. Dog-day heat settled over the main administration building's front steps like another layer of concrete. Reporters, cameramen, coaches, and administrators crowded once again into the low-ceilinged foyer, covering the black-and-green flecked marble grid just down the hall from the chancellor's office. Driesell read a statement.

When the press conference ended, Slaughter headed down the hall toward his office. Reporters shouted after him. Did Lefty's presence at the press conference mean a decision had been made to keep him? Was his presence a tacit vote of confidence? Over his shoulder as he walked away, Slaughter gave them their answer:

"I'm not prepared to give anyone a vote of confidence," he shot back.

As long as Driesell was still the coach, Slaughter could not exclude him from matters involving the team. To leave him out was to suggest strongly that he *was* finished, not something Slaughter was ready to say. But he regretted his hurried answer right away. He had only Dull and Lefty in mind, but all of Maryland's coaches felt vulnerable during this period and all of them, particularly Bobby Ross, felt the chancellor had left them hanging out there with Driesell. Every remark was like a diplomatic communique, its language and tone carefully scrutinized.

Slaughter hoped his admittedly modest reform would bring some important support from his presidential colleagues. He thought his ACC opposite-numbers sympathized with him and would step forward to say so.

But his colleagues were silent -- or critical. "I don't think the people who made this decision were thinking about the other schools," said Wake Forest Athletic Director Gene Hooks. Dean Smith, widely credited with insisting on academic achievement from his players, criticized the action. The Maryland players would continue to practice on their own, he predicted. He doubted that they would profit much from the respite. He may have been right. But the alternative was to do nothing.

Within a few days, the ACC called Slaughter to account. For a special meeting with representatives of the other presidents, he drove around the Capitol Beltway to the Marriott Hotel in Crystal City, Virginia, located on Washington's south side. There he learned that the predictions of acceptance for Option 3 had been laughably optimistic.

The presidents demanded that Slaughter explain why he had taken what they called an arbitrary and capricious action. Slaughter was struck by the words -- "arbitrary and capricious." In Maryland, he was criticized for being cautious and deliberate.

He was informed that his action had cost the conference $80,000. One of the games Slaughter canceled was a televised conference match-up. Once in motion, the basketball enterprise was so large and complex that no adjustment could be made by a participant school for its strictly individual needs.

"Let me make it perfectly clear to you," he said. "If I were faced with the same decision at this moment, I would make it again. I don't care how much it would cost. I invite you to send us the bill." They did.

Slaughter had believed he would find university officials supporting an action taken to assist young men in trouble. But that subject, the well-being of the players, did not arise or did not match up well with the financial concerns. It did not occur to anyone that the league might have shown itself to be a compassionate community. "Lenny was vulnerable because we are all vulnerable," the Reverend Jackson had said at his memorial service. But there was no ACC inclination to share Maryland's pain.

Later, some of Slaughter's ACC judges praised his handling of Maryland's difficulties, but he rejected the compliments, saying, "They weren't there when I needed them."

Slaughter was pinned between the reformers and the championship seekers. In time, he concluded, any decision he made would antagonize half of the community. He could switch the halves around, but he could not reduce the opposition. There was no middle ground. If even a token step could not achieve some consensus, real change was a most dubious proposition.

Slaughter turned then to the question of Driesell's continued presence as coach, an issue of such significance that it almost amounted to Option 1. There were those at Maryland who could not conceive of Maryland basketball without Lefty. Lose him, lose the program. Unilateral disarmament. De-emphasis. It was that simple. At the Terrapin Club's annual cookout in August, Driesell received a vote of confidence from the constituency that mattered most to him. Club members had worried all summer about what Slaughter would do to their coach, expecting and half-hoping that Driesell would be made the scapegoat because that would affirm their view of a world run by crooked referees. And now they had a chance to cast their votes loudly in the summer air. Did they want Driesell to stay? Hell yes!, they screamed. Free Lefty!

Chapter 8

Joining The Lynch Mob

August 21, 1986, brought yet another parade of superstars to the courthouse in Upper Marlboro.

Lefty Driesell walked into court to face State's Attorney Arthur "Bud" Marshall and the Prince George's County grand jury. Beside him was Edward Bennett Williams, owner of the Baltimore Orioles and one of the nation's most prominent courtroom lawyers. Williams was a nexus for the power of law, politics and sports in Washington. When he was part-owner of the Washington Redskins, U.S. Supreme Court justices sat with him in his box at Robert F. Kennedy Stadium. His clients had included Teamsters boss Jimmy Hoffa, Mafia boss Sam Giancana, and others who needed Williams to preserve their freedom and fortunes. Republican President Richard Nixon wanted to put him in charge of the CIA. Democratic President Lyndon Johnson wanted to appoint him mayor of Washington. He declined both offers.

Driesell had been introduced to Williams by George Allen, the former Redskins coach. Williams had been there when Driesell worked himself into the Veal difficulties. The coach bragged then about his pull. Now, with Marshall sending a grand jury after him, he needed all the pull he could find.

"If you ever didn't do something like I didn't," he told his friends later with a grin, "get EBW for a lawyer."

Driesell and Williams, both physically impressive men, moved confidently through the metal detector into the courthouse, sending a charge of excitement through its busy corridors. They were the ultimate jock celebrities of a star-filled summer in Upper Marlboro, a rural but changing county seat, a place where the suburban condo developments built for government employees in Washington had begun to encroach on tobacco barns.

Marshall charged that Driesell had obstructed justice by attempting to have evidence removed from a crime scene. The prosecutor also thought Driesell had counseled his players not to speak with the police. Slaughter thought Driesell had acted properly in regard to the players who needed sheltering, and was more cooperative with police than Marshall's protests suggested, having given them, shortly after Bias's death, a full account of what he knew.

The target of a grand jury rarely testifies during an investigation unless granted immunity from prosecution. Driesell appeared without this grant. It was reported that Williams counseled the coach against appearing. But Driesell usually did what Williams suggested, so the attorney may not have objected strenuously. By appearing without immunity, Driesell was saying he had nothing to fear. The tactic was suitably audacious, a clever appeal for the jury's and the public's sympathy.

Driesell's story for the grand jury was this: The coach had acted upon a fatherly impulse to protect his players. Perhaps it had been rash to send someone to clean a room where someone had died, but it was the kind of thing parents would understand. He was just trying to protect his boys from the further consequences of their fatal party.

Marshall insisted that Driesell had been trying to protect himself and his basketball program from scandal. To make the charges stick, the prosecutor, under state law, had to show that the motive was "evil." Prosecutors usually have their way with grand juries, and Marshall, who grew to dislike Driesell as he learned more about the atmosphere surrounding the Maryland basketball team, wanted to nail the legendary coach. He assumed that the voters would be with him in that objective -- or, at least, in his pledge to go after illegal drug use on the campus.

Driesell's appearance before the grand jury came three weeks before Maryland's September 9 primary election, the one that would decide Marshall's political future. The timing could hardly have been better. The case gave him extraordinary media exposure and an opportunity to counter one of his political opponent's major charges: that he had been lax in prosecuting drug crime in the county. Now he was taking on users and pushers as well as a seemingly untouchable basketball coach.

Slaughter testified the same day Driesell and Williams appeared. With the veniremen, he engaged in a dialogue on the problems of high-intensity athletic programs. The day was long and demoralizing for Slaughter. When he was excused, Jeff Harding, one of Marshall's assistants, escorted him out of the courthouse. To avoid reporters, Harding advised using a rear exit. The two men walked down a stairway to the bottom of the old building. When they opened the door, Slaughter stepped into the teeth of the vigilant media which, he thought, knew exactly where he would be coming out. He was sure the reporters had been alerted by Marshall and Harding, so television could record that the university chancellor, too, had been brought to heel by the hard-driving prosecutor.

As the summer's proceedings wore on, members of Maryland's extended family continued to assure each other that a famous basketball player could have died of cocaine intoxication at any campus in the United States. College Park and Driesell had just been unlucky. Boosters complained that College Park had become a whipping boy for hypocritical newspapers whose writers covered college sports teams as if they were professional and went into shock when they discovered the players weren't going to class.

Among those who felt most sorely aggrieved by Bias's death and the furor it unleashed were members of the Terrapin Club, Maryland's 3,700-member booster group. Every university in the country has a similar organization of Tigers or Wildcats or Rams. No Kiwanis or Lions or Rotary club is more officially committed to doing good and having a good time doing it than an athletic booster club. According to the boosters' gospel, sports teach discipline, sacrifice, brotherhood, and ethical living -- while providing excitement for the boosters and other fans, and uplifting the less fortunate.

In 1953, the Terrapin Club's first president set forth what he hoped would be an enduring statement of purpose: "Nothing I have done in my life has given me more personal satisfaction than to help some of these boys get a college education. Some of their families are so impoverished that they would never see the inside of a university if it weren't for their ability to play football." On campuses like College Park, boosters clung desperately to the founding impulses.

Only about half of the Terrapin Club members were Maryland graduates, but the others were no less committed to the university's sports program, to Lefty and to Tom Fields, the energetic fund-raiser who had turned the club into a force.

In the beginning, Terrapin Club membership was limited, and demand for the club even more so. But when Fields arrived in 1970, a year after Driesell, he found ways to promote the flamboyant new coach and his increasingly competitive teams. Fields was meticulously attentive to his members. The club was almost as much a product of Field's cultivation as it was of Driesell's rowdy panache.

Between 1969 and 1986, booster contributions grew from about $30,000 to $2.7 million a year. The university became dependent on that money to pay the scholarship bill for intercollegiate athletics. Money became as important as the ideals upon which the club was founded, just more so.

Like former Athletic Director Jim Kehoe, who hired him, Fields had been a Marine. A captain in the Pacific theater, he had been a rifle company commander and battalion executive officer during the invasions of Iwo Jima, Guadalcanal and Bougainville. On Iwo Jima, his command suffered huge casualties. He buried a lot of his men, won the Bronze Star, and didn't look back. You couldn't hesitate the way Maryland was hesitating in the aftermath of Bias's death, he said. In general, the boosters wanted to think of Bias's death as an individual failing. They wanted to ignore the disclosures it triggered about the Maryland program.

Fields had been an All-American track star at Maryland in 1941. In the way of credentials, he had just about everything a fund-raiser needed. He put out a regular newsletter and filled it with inside news items about the teams, about prospects for the next season, and with inspirational messages in keeping with the founding principles. He gave club members small pins in the shape of the Maryland terrapin, a species of turtle indigenous to the state, its official amphibian, and the university's mascot.

A $250 contribution each year entitled the member to a silver terrapin pin, free home game tickets, and, most importantly, priority for the purchase of ACC Tournament tickets. Those who gave $750 received a gold pin. And then there were the big benefactors. A Diamondback Terrapin member contributed $1,500 annually; a Super Terrapin committed $2,500; and the Life Member was in for $10,000. Fields worked to keep the members moving up the ladder of giving. And well he might, since he received, above his salary, a percentage of all the money he raised.

The boosters' contributions, which went eventually toward athletic "scholarships," were officially deposited into the Maryland Educational Foundation, a somewhat misnamed repository of the club's largesse. The term "scholarship" dated to a time in the history of intercollegiate sports when a kid played football or basketball in order to get an education -- not to get into a professional football or basketball league. By the 1980s, these grants might well have been called "athleteships."

This booster club money essentially bought the athletes who made the programs go. Without those funds, the university might not be able to give athletic scholarships, since athletics at College Park are required by state policy to be self-supporting. The self-support system created a fundamental problem in big-time college sports: it inevitably put power or the appearance of power in the hands of people whose objectives were not necessarily academic.

By 1986, Maryland football and basketball brought in about $4.5 million a year in gate receipts, television payments, and other income. They were the major revenue sports. All the other programs were defined by what they were not: non-revenue. There was even a division of the athletic department called The Office of Non-Revenue Sports. Terrapin Club money, plus student fees and television money, paid for the 21 other sports. On its broad back, the Terrapin Club carried intercollegiate sports at Maryland.

The size of the club, 3,700 members, was regarded by university officials as a major advantage. It meant, they thought, that no fat-cat contributors would be able, singlehandedly, to corrupt the athletic department. But the club did have significant influence. A core of longtime contributors who made significant personal commitments to the program -- the $1,500 to $10,000 givers -- had a proprietary feeling about the university's athletic program. Reporters treated them as if they had veto power over the hiring of coaches and athletic directors. Slaughter's crisis team evaluated options for reform against its estimation of the Terrapin Club's likely reaction.

Over its 40-year history, the club grew proud of its record of avoiding play-for-pay recruiting or other booster-related scandals that erupted at other schools. And the university slowly learned to accept the pressure exerted by the increasingly large, and legal, sums of Terrapin Club money. Booster influence was a factor for every big-time college program. Nationally, the reform spotlight focused on the chronic renegades who were caught committing gross illegalities. But these embarrassing interludes were merely squalls on a great sea of influence that kept the programs large and swelling out of control.

In addition to booster control, state legislatures that required an athletic department to make a profit and television networks that scheduled games during exam periods were important forces in defining college sports and in contributing to their corruption. Even if one could eliminate cheating, the money given to universities by boosters who wanted championships created a barrier to the change critics of college sports were demanding.

Nowhere was the Terrapin Club's power more evident than in its support of Driesell. The coach's opponents had no similar lobby, no similar hold on public attention, university officials, or the state legislature. The club was a fierce and powerful constituency, a force akin to a special interest group like the National Rifle Association in its ability to fight off restrictions. Public opinion surveys showed that many Americans thought intercollegiate sports were out of control, but little changed. The general public's involvement was non-existent, while the boosters' concerns were focused with laser-like sharpness. A modern basketball coach had to have a constituency. Lefty had the Terrapin Club.

Having defended and supported the Maryland athletic program so loyally and generously, club members sometimes acted as if they owned the program. To some extent they did. They had purchased it, with the willingness of the university and the Maryland legislature. In a sense, the players were employees of the club because it paid their tuition. The university did not provide the scholarship money. The legislature did not provide it. The Terrapin Club did.

Booster money was held privately in a fund that was not audited or managed by the university. Few knew how much money the foundation had, how the money was invested, what it could be used for -- whether it was a totally flexible slush fund to be used for such things as enhancing contracts, buying houses for coaches and athletic directors. The Education Foundation money and givers' underlying attitudes helped to shape athletics at Maryland.

The club's zeal, carefully manipulated by Tom Fields, took it beyond its official philanthropic goals. Over time, the club became a business entity unto itself, as devoted to its athletic fund-raising prowess as any of its members were to their companies' sales.

Terrapin Club members came from almost every corner of the local community -- Maryland, Northern Virginia, and the District of Columbia. Most of them were white and male. A survey of member occupations showed the degree to which boosterism and sports intertwined to drive and protect the program. Hardly an occupational segment of society was unrepresented in the club. Its members included a national political columnist, a former U.S. senator, a congressman, the Maryland state comptroller, a former governor, a former mayor of College Park, the chief operating officer of the state's major public utility, a major department store executive, a Washington furniture dealer, an auto dealer, a retired pharmacist -- and thousands of anonymous others, including Candy DiPietro and her brother, Mike Anderson, who split the cost of their basic $750 annual gold membership and shared the club pin.

People like DiPietro and Anderson were the small-scale boosters the university hoped would insulate it from club pressure. Their father had gone to the university; they were basketball lovers, pure and simple. At Jack Heise's request, Candy and her husband, Bob, a former Laurel, MD. mayor, had taken Albert King under their wing when he was playing for Driesell. Heise and Bob DiPietro worked for the same bank.

Life Members of the Terrapin Club, boosters like Heise who contributed $10,000 or more, were automatically members of the President's Club, a new, 1,200-member organization of major university donors. Its promoters argued that sports had opened a gateway to university giving: One anonymous member of the President's Club had given $16 million. But others thought the value of sports-generated giving was vastly overstated, particularly in light of the exploitation committed in its name. Such donations might well have been made whether the university offered winning basketball or not.

Other universities found that boosters remained in the fold even under the worst stresses on their sports program. Similarly, the record at Maryland showed that something other than sports -- a commitment to the university as a university -- kept the supporters giving.

In 1986, after basketball had been dropped at Tulane, donations to the university increased by $5 million. (Some of this increase may be attributable to changes in federal income tax law that year.) During the years Irish football was struggling under Coach Gerry Faust (1981-85), Notre Dame raised more money than ever before in its history. Administrators at Notre Dame observed that while football created some spill-over contributions, the prominence of sports also impeded the university's effort to be taken seriously as a university.

Notre Dame's Richard Conklin said the idea of sports-generated giving "tempted people to stress athletics at the expense of other things that are much more important to the institution's academic mission because they have the misguided impression that it's going to be a solution to their financial problems."

Some schools were in a better position to experiment, however. In the summer of 1986, no one at the cash-starved College Park campus wanted to risk the loss of Terrapin Club givers. At the same time, however, Slaughter was doing things that pushed the boosters hard, defying them in almost every way.

As much as they might have resented the periodic reform impulses, many club members were well aware of basketball's problems at Maryland and beyond. Many of them thought Driesell had lost control of his teams.

"In the last few years," said Mike Anderson, "Lefty didn't have his finger on the pulse. Bobby Knight [the Indiana coach] knows what his kids are doing. I don't approve of the way Knight plays with kids' heads, but he knows if they're going to class. Maybe the times passed him [Driesell] by. Maybe the kids changed. But he just wasn't doing the job as far as kids were concerned. I think he thought he was so big, the program would take of itself. But you have to understand, these are 17- and 18-year-olds."

Some club members thought they were providing scholarships and opportunities for players who were insufficiently grateful and foolishly neglectful of academics. The boosters had no illusions: They knew they were helping to bankroll a minor league for the National Basketball Association. Some of them regretted this reality. But overall, they remained committed to the system as it was. If there were victims, they were not, by and large, the sons and daughters of club members.

Cooper Curtice felt he had been there at the creation.

Curtice became a Maryland fan after what he regarded as the decline of hoops at his own alma mater, George Washington University in the District of Columbia. When he was at GW, the school didn't have a gym. The Generals played in breweries, at a roller rink, and at high school gyms. One of Curtice's physical education teachers was Red Auerbach, then a graduate assistant at George Washington. Auerbach had played for the GW team and, after graduation, started a professional league that played in the old Uline Arena, now called the Washington Coliseum.

Curtice and his friend, Ivan Roop, a retired pharmacist and banker, became basketball vagabonds. Like Heise and Novak, they were highly evolved examples of the general species, Fan. They were up for a trip to any place that had 10 guys, a ball and a gym. Thrilled by the logistics -- getting to the games, getting tickets, getting home just in time for work -- they lived for basketball.

"It's my one excess," Curtice said. "I used to get sick if my team lost. I'd brood. I'd play the games over and over all night long. I suffered with every defeat. I just had a passion for basketball. I guess maybe I wasn't fully grown up. That's what my mother always said." When ESPN began to provide almost round-the-clock games, Curtice purposely declined to subscribe. He was afraid he would never leave his TV room.

Curtice met Tom Fields for the first time at an ACC Tournament. Not then a club member, he was, as always, looking for tickets. With a note placed on the hotel bulletin board, he asked if anyone had spares. Fields, spotting the query, seemed to drop everything to accommodate him.

"He didn't even know me. You have to respect a guy like that," Curtice said. As soon as he got back home, he became a Terrapin Club member.

A pleasant, white-haired gentleman with a Tidewater Virginia lilt in his voice, Curtice pronounced it "Maaland" and "Caalina." Like most Terrapin Clubbers, he loved the ACC Tournament more than anything on his basketball agenda, and he loved it at Greensboro most of all. Novak was right. It was more exciting in the other guy's gym, meeting and baiting your friends from the other ACC schools.

Curtice loved the tournament best in the early days. Because it was like real life, you didn't get second chances. Win or go home. Everything hinged on making it through Tobacco Road. Only the winner went to the NCAA tournament in those years. That stoked the excitement to a flash point. The old tournament structure, he thought, was built on the rule of survival of the fittest. Some of that ethic remained, however: Kids who were academically or emotionally unfit did not survive.

Now, Curtice said, the tournament was too forgiving. Only the worst teams were out of the running for the NCAA tournament. Schools needed to play in the big national tournament because they needed the money they would make there. The ACC Tournament, too, was driven by money: Tournament tickets were bait to land new boosters. Anyone who wanted to attend the sold-out tournament had to be a booster.

Tournament rules were not the only thing that had changed in basketball over the years, Curtice said.

"There weren't any black players in the beginning. If you played any blacks you played them when you went to Rhode Island. Maryland had the first black players in the ACC. Maryland's the Free State. So, it's fine," said Curtice, as if he were still getting used to the idea.

Black players raised the quality of basketball, he thought, but they also made the game more unstable because they were apt to get into trouble.

"They're a house of cards," he said, adding that the decline of Maryland basketball began when black players started to predominate. You just didn't know when something would happen, he said. Lefty was naive to think he could control these kids. Curtice was not the only Terrapin Club member to think of the team in racial terms.

As the task force on student athletes considered new standards of eligibility and admission at Maryland, Slaughter ran into a Terrapin Club member who told him, "Dr. Slaughter, you can't raise standards too high -- we won't be able to get the good black ballplayers."

When Driesell arrived at College Park in 1969, one of the first people he called was Terrapin Club member Hotsy Alperstein, a close friend and political supporter of Marvin Mandel, who was then governor of Maryland. Lefty wanted Governor Mandel to help him recruit ballplayers, Hotsy said. He understood what the coach wanted.

"When the governor calls and wants so-and-so, they're gonna get on the phone," Hotsy said. He wasn't sure he could do what Driesell requested, but he called, and Mandel agreed to do what he could. It was not unusual for politicians to recruit a player. Several legislators wrote to Bias, urging him to attend Maryland. Others tried unsuccessfully to persuade Baltimore players to choose Maryland.

During the mid-1970s, Driesell took the team to the Governor's Mansion in Annapolis. The tall coach had given a basketball to the considerably shorter but obviously thrilled Governor Mandel. When he and the coach were photographed together by a newspaper, the governor was holding the ball in the same hand as his trademark pipe. A trip to the Governor's Mansion was said to be broadening for the players, part of the experience basketball gave them. Governors got a kick out of it, too.

Club members like Hotsy saw their lives reflected in the basketball program and in Lefty. Driesell was a distillation of the traits they thought were needed to make an intercollegiate team successful in the marketplace. Driesell was a fighter, an entrepreneur like many of the Terrapins, a salesman who could make something out of nothing.

"You might not think you like him, but you sit down with him and I guarantee you'll get up liking him," Hotsy said.

Slaughter's deliberate style was smothering Maryland's athletic future and threatening to make a scapegoat of Driesell, thought Hotsy. What you had to do was fight back, and Slaughter was just standing there taking blow after blow.

Like Lefty, Hotsy was proud to be a fighter. People still introduced him by recalling his days as a Terrapin boxer. Short, bald, 65, and still near his best ring weight, Hotsy in 1986 asserted he and his brothers were fit enough to fight. Their parents had come from Russia and Poland. He was the youngest of seven brothers. As a child, he carried baskets home from Baltimore's public markets for tips and shined shoes. He also sold newspapers for two cents apiece and fought to keep the corner where he sold them.

In those days, university scholarships were rare and almost never given to more than one member of a family. Hotsy and his older brother, Benny, a three-time, All-American boxer at College Park, felt a huge debt to Maryland after both received grants. Hotsy became team captain and was undefeated as a college boxer. A picture of the college fighter in uniform, his gloved hands raised, his black hair wispy and already retreating from his forehead, hung on the wall of his office. Hotsy especially remembered his last fight at College Park. Until then, he was undefeated, but had never knocked anyone out. His coach urged him to correct that part of his record. In his last fight, he had a ready victim, but he thought his opponent was already beaten. He could feel his fear across the ring. He declined the glory. There was a limit.

After the war, Hotsy built a successful furniture business, moving from Baltimore to Washington as he prospered. He and his six brothers established close attachments to the university. They were part of the web of contributors and political backers that Jack Heise referred to in his letter defending Driesell.

Like some boosters, Hotsy took his support beyond the athletic department. In the early 1980s, he and Mandel convinced one of their classmates, New York developer and real estate baron Sam LeFrak, to contribute $500,000 for a new campus building. The building, called LeFrak Hall, was just behind the campus chapel. It was the building where Gwendolyn Brooks gave her reading; it opened a few months before Slaughter became chancellor. Slaughter learned quickly who Hotsy Alperstein was.

In the summer of 1986, club members served as defense counsel for Driesell, for the university, and for the club itself.

No one was more outraged by what was regarded as Slaughter's languid style than Terrapin Club member Bob Novak, the Washington-based syndicated political columnist. He became an unofficial spokesman for the club.

"If you had a university that stood up to people and not panicked, stood up to the media . . . Sure there would have been a downside after Bias died, but this . . . Slaughter was led by the yellow journalists in *The Post* and *The Sun* into a panic. I don't think he was a very strong person," Novak said in an interview. "He was sucked up in all the currents. When you have an administration joining the lynch mob, it's an outrage." He thought Maryland was being stampeded into a period of athletic mediocrity. "They want to be a part of the Ivy League -- and they're getting pretty close in football and basketball," he said.

Everyone wanted to get out of the crisis quickly. Ben Unkle, then the student representative on the Board of Regents, thought it was remarkable that so many counseled speed. Speed led to error. He admired Slaughter's determination to move at his own pace, to honor his own instincts.

"Could he have moved faster? Yes," answered Allen Schwait, the Regents chairman and a staunch advocate of Slaughter's policies. "Was it realistic to have him come in and buck a 50-year athletic tradition? No. It's a very political job."

Schwait recalled that, well before Bias's death, Slaughter was making it clear to Lefty and other coaches that he wanted athletes to progress toward degrees -- and he wanted athletes enrolled in meaningful courses.

But as Ray Gillian observed, administrative cajolery was unusual for Slaughter, whose administrative style was collegial. He preferred to delegate considerable authority to division heads such as the athletic director.

"John is not someone who sits on you, keeps constant watch over you. He gives you a lot of tether to work with," said Chuck Sturtz, a vice chancellor for administrative affairs who served as interim athletic director -- some said he was a budget-cutting hatchet man with no real love of athletics -- after Dick Dull resigned.

A tradition of weak central administration, successful revenue sports and a history of athletic department dominance helped the athletic department hang itself, Sturtz said. Fat television contracts for the revenue sports had created a strong cash flow in the early 1980s, but, Sturtz says, there was no planning, no careful analysis of what the department could afford.

The loose operation under Dull was illustrated by a story, which Sturtz confirmed: Local automobile dealers had loaned the athletic department cars in exchange for their advertising in game programs. An inventory of the fleet by Sturtz disclosed, however, that one department employee had given the courtesy car to his wife in a divorce settlement.

Sources familiar with the department alleged that some employees were getting $40,000 for "passing out jock straps." An exaggeration, said Sturtz, who reported that some personnel were carried in ill-defined tasks.

"By not being a hands-on person, I think he [Slaughter] is not as alert to what's going on in the various units, and trouble can come that way. You get people who carve out their own domain, enlarge their domain and think they are larger than the department," Sturtz said, alluding to Driesell. "It's clearly a risk associated with that kind of management." Slaughter's management style "put the premium on getting good people." And, in fairness, he had been in charge at College Park only long enough to begin asserting his own standards.

The plus side of collegiality, Sturtz said, is that you get a significant number of people involved in solving a problem.

"Slaughter was not paranoid," he said. "There are lots of bosses who can't stand to have someone taking a critical look and coming out with a report that says there are 64 problems associated with this program."

Slaughter impressed faculty members with his willingness to review and revise policies that drew criticism, but he didn't impress the Terrapin Club.

Novak had been a member for 17 years when Bias died, and he, like Cooper Curtice, was a $2,500-a-year man. A fierce interviewer, he approached basketball with at least as much ferocity as he did politics. Basketball sailed along on an All-American cushion of emotion, and Bob Novak was one of its most committed defenders.

In the summer of 1986, with his friend, Jack Heise, he moved quickly to Driesell's defense. Novak and his pals would have gone to Afghanistan if Lefty and the Terps were playing there, he declared. It was one thing to watch games at Cole Field House, Novak thought, but the atmosphere created by Driesell on the road was supercharged.

"I saw games when teams would go on the road, and the coach was kind of slinking onto the court. Not Lefty. Lefty was, figuratively, going out there and giving them the sign. He was daring 'em," the columnist said. "That was what the fun of it was. That was what made it so much fun for a Driesell team to win on Tobacco Road. . . . There was an air of defiance."

For Novak, the real thrill of Leftyball came in places like Duke's Cameron Indoor Stadium on Tobacco Road, those miles of North Carolina state road connecting N.C. State University, Wake Forest University in Winston-Salem, Duke University, and the University of North Carolina at Chapel Hill. Novak thought making these trips to enemy territory -- by car, on the Fastbreaker buses, or on small airplanes -- was the real test of Terrapin loyalty. "Everything was against you," he said. "All those people shaking their fingers at you, cursing at you. The whole impression of the world against you." That underdog feeling, that feeling of taking on the furies without backing off. That was Driesell's gift to the most devoted fans.

One year, Maryland made its tour of North Carolina's big four -- and won all of them. "Fastbreaker Sweeper," Novak called it. The day after the final victory, Novak liked to recall, one of his traveling friends went out, bought all of the Sunday papers, and read all the game stories "real slow."

Novak had a military image of road games with Lefty. "I thought it was something like the Polish cavalry charging the Nazi tanks and winning," he said. In the fall of 1986, Novak wrote to Slaughter, asking the chancellor if he planned to de-emphasize sports at Maryland and suggesting that he would stop sending his $2,500 if he didn't like the answer. Slaughter assured him that he thought sports would remain an important part of campus life, and Novak stayed in the club.

The boosters felt good when they gave. They were helping the less fortunate. Sometimes, though, the impact of the generosity grew in the retelling.

Former U.S. Senator Joe Tydings recalled an incident that, in his mind, proved the goodness of Lefty and Lefty's program at Maryland. When Len Elmore arrived at College Park in 1970, Tydings said, the young man needed help with diction, and Lefty asked Tydings to arrange some special classes. That bit of assistance, Tydings suggested, helped Elmore on to Harvard Law School.

Elmore remembered the story differently.

He had come to Maryland with a score of 1,100 on his SATs and an 87 average in his high school courses. He remembered talking with Tydings about enrolling in a pre-law program. But he needed no tutoring in diction, he said, and Tydings did not arrange any for him. Elmore was quite adept, actually, having won his confidence in combat with New York reporters. He majored in English and hosted a program on the University of Maryland radio station. Except for a senior year lapse when he succumbed to the lure of all-star games, he had a respectable grade point average.

Other players, no doubt, were given help by Tydings and others with speech and diction, but the players themselves were certain that

Driesell and the boosters cared more about their performance on the floor than anywhere else. Moreover, in the minds of some boosters, the helping instinct had been replaced by the belief that help was futile, that the players were too committed to basketball. Their academic deficits were clear. If reading proficiency stood in the way of eligibility or admission, some boosters thought the solution was to offer less demanding courses.

Former Governor Marvin Mandel was among the boosters who thought academic expectations for athletes were too lofty.

"This business of being critical of athletes as students is all wrong," he said. "Success should not have to be based on intellectual ability. Some of the greatest violinists never went to college, but they had an ability. Fifty or 60 percent of these athletes would never have gone to college if they didn't have an athletic talent. They should be trained to be sportscasters, coaches, athletic directors or agents. It's a whole new industry. The university has to recognize the importance of specialized training.

"Very few of them become pro athletes," continued Mandel. "But an awful lot of them find a niche for themselves. Look at Gene Upshaw, the NFL union guy. Instead of making them take botany, why not put them in a field where they excel? Professors resent this, but every one of us can't be an intellectual. The players' big problem is lack of interest. But make them a broadcaster or something, and they'd be fine."

Mandel offered his theory to Slaughter one day at a football game. The black chancellor listened without comment. The real problem, Slaughter thought, was that expectations were too low. If the players were challenged honestly, if their eligibility for basketball had been based on academic performance, he thought, they would perform in class as well as they did on the court. Experience with Proposition 48, with its pitifully low minimum standards, showed that players could improve their scores and their standing in class. The NCAA rule required players to have a C average in 11 core courses in high school or a combined score of at least 700 on the SATs.

Mandel and his colleagues were suggesting that the college game was too demanding to test higher expectations. To raise expectations was to lose on the field and at the bottom line. These attitudes, convictions, and fears kept the program careening along on its desperate, exploitative course.

In the past few years, Mandel thought, "You had a different type of kid, and that precipitated the problems." The character and ability of the teams had declined. Mandel remembered back in the 1970s when the Maryland players came to the mansion. "They were all dressed up. All gentlemen."

Mandel, Curtice, and others espousing the lowered expectation approach believed they were taking a generous and enlightened stance. Slaughter did not say so directly during the summer of 1986, but he saw a damaging lack of respect in this viewpoint. The corrosive, system-wide problem in big-time basketball, Slaughter thought, was low expectations. That thinking found its way into the assumptions people made, assumptions that lay at the bottom of jokes about athletes not being rocket scientists, assumptions that made it easier for boosters to tolerate classroom failure and to be critical of Slaughter's leadership style.

Even setting aside race, Slaughter thought Mandel's theory was nonsensical. No one whose intellectual development was abandoned could ever make it in the high-powered world of sports agents, athletic directors or broadcasters. The vocational objectives the former governor sketched out were admirable -- particularly compared with the courses that Maryland players were taking. But, as Ray Gillian observed, it was unrealistic to think players in big-time programs would ever reach those objectives.

"We all know it's impossible for these kids, but we pretend they can make it. I don't understand it," Gillian said.

Booster Fred Frederick didn't understand it either -- from a different point of view. He thought Slaughter's approach after Bias's death was ruining what the Terrapin Club had built. "It just tears your heart out when you spend as much time as we did putting it together," he said.

Round, gruff, and impatient, former Marine Frederick was president of the Terrapin Club when it went over the $1 million mark in annual contributions. He and other club leaders operated as team captains, staying in close touch with a daisy chain of 20 or 30 members. He kept them informed, excited, and ready to give.

Yet, what he saw at Maryland was a corrupt environment that "feeds on itself." No one could tell the truth about the program because they were all profiting from it, he said. "Nobody stepped up to the plate when they should have. Ten years ago," he said, "coaches and others knew there were problems with drugs and did nothing."

Discipline was lacking, he said. He blamed the NCAA -- which allowed cheats to go unpunished. He also blamed Lefty.

The problem, in Frederick's view, was not the consuming demands of the program, the number of games played, the yearlong seasons, or the toll that they took on a player's education. It was Lefty's lack of discipline and the players' lack of focus.

"I tried to help 'em out," he said. "I hired one guy, and he comes with his ghetto blaster. He's got a red sweat suit on and he's with his girlfriend. He says, 'She always stays with me.' I called Lefty and said, 'Come get this guy.' That was the kind of discipline Lefty had."

Frederick kept a small credenza next to his large desk at his Chrysler Plymouth dealership in Laurel. The top shelf was covered with military mementoes. Above the shelf hung a wooden plaque given to him by Lester Maddox, the segregationist former governor of Georgia, the man who gave out ax handles at his restaurant in Atlanta. The plaque bore a painting of Lee's celebrated surrender at Appomattox, rendered as a victory ceremony for the South in the Civil War. Frederick met Maddox in 1974 when Maryland played football in the Peach Bowl.

His sporting souvenirs included a basketball given him by former Maryland player Ben Coleman. Frederick kept the ball on the credenza. It was a trophy of his years as a booster and sports lover at College Park. He liked to point out to visitors that Coleman had misspelled both "Frederick" and "Terps."

"And he's a graduate of the University of Maryland!" Frederick said, laughing. His scorn for the university and ridicule of Coleman seemed to undercut the generosity that officially motivated his participation in the Terrapin Club. Or perhaps it was a way of having it both ways -- enjoying the camaraderie of the club and the excitement of the games, yet acknowledging the program's difficulties. The story of Fred Frederick and his basketball was known in Prince George's County, and he was seen by some as a redneck waving the Confederate flag.

Frederick's complaints had nothing to do with the academic performance of players, however, although he was indirectly critical of it when talking about Coleman. What he wanted was more pizzazz in the program on Saturday afternoons, a bigger and brighter marching band, more effective billboards. In the weeks and months after Len Bias died, what the program at Maryland lacked, he said, was the "zing" of a real leader determined to make a commercial comeback.

"There is emotion out there about your university. You've got to get it with you," he said. Slaughter was providing no leadership. "There's nothing there. If we were trying to pull ourselves together, fine. But there ain't nobody there," he said. "It's just laying there."

Of course, Slaughter was hardly concerned in those days with the sizzle of the athletic program. He wanted to graduate people who could spell "Terps" and "Frederick." "People with different goals," Slaughter later wrote in his journal, "ought not to plan for one another."

Judge Meloy thought basketball flourished because Americans loved such provocative, unrestrained characters as Driesell. Maryland basketball was a version of a cabaret or the Roman circus, flourishing in a live-for-today atmosphere that had a dizzying appeal for everyone. There was something in this out-of-control feeling that made it all the more intoxicating.

One of the most noted Terrapin Club leaders, Meloy had brokered as many as 200 season tickets for football and more than 100 for basketball. Ironically, it was his courtroom in Upper Marlboro that was now the scene of the grand jury proceedings against the university and its basketball program. The circuit court judge could walk through the dimly lit, polished, wood hallways of the courthouse in Upper Marlboro, buttonholing colleagues and lawyers, asking if they had their tickets. At first, there was no rabid following of the Terps. But, in time, the courthouse crowd spent the lunch hour at nearby restaurants engaged in a "Tastes great! Less filling!" debate about Driesell: Was he a good coach or just a good recruiter? Conversation on this nettling puzzle occupied Terrapin Clubbers for hours.

As a young man, Meloy drove Porsches and Corvettes. He played tennis with Bob Considine, the newspaper columnist. His wife was in the state legislature. He was part of the political and sporting network whose attitudes sustained and defended the sports program. He was part of the great river of emotion and money that transported athletics beyond the reach of reformers.

Meloy saw the players in the wider sporting arena as "oblivious" young men, caught in the undertow of wealth earned by a few players before them. They were mesmerized, he said, by the sight of their coach buying a beach house with money earned from putting his team in a particular brand of basketball shoe.

But Meloy did not buy the exploitation theory. "They've been given a great opportunity and some have not taken advantage of it," he said. "They've concentrated on their professional aspirations. The opportunities were there and the coaching leadership was there. But a lot of the players said, 'I'm a horse.' I don't think they've thought much about their future. I think they just want to perfect their skills so they can get to the NBA."

At the same time, Meloy, too, was critical of Driesell and the atmosphere at Cole Field House. Maryland basketball had been "loose and lackadaisical for years." Dick Dull was in thrall to Driesell, he said. Meloy was sympathetic to the players: "How can a 17-year-old kid -- called the greatest, wined and dined -- cope with his studies?" Driesell cared about his players, the judge thought, but he couldn't control them.

Meloy agreed, in part, with Slaughter. College sports were too big and too competitive. What was needed was a national playoff system and distribution of the proceeds to all schools, so the Penn States and Michigans wouldn't constantly reap the bonanzas and the others wouldn't wager their souls to claim the scraps. Some of the big-time coaches thought the playoff idea would bring a final end to any thought that players were students. The intensity of the drive to win and the time needed to be competitive would be even more defeating, they said.

Tommy Marcos had opened his restaurant, Ledo's, at a time when there weren't many restaurants in College Park. His business grew with Maryland and Maryland sports. Sometimes he fed the teams when they stayed on the campus during holiday breaks. On occasion, he bailed a football player out of jail.

"You didn't have to put up any money in those days. You knew all the policemen. You'd say, 'Help this boy out, he plays football for Maryland,'" he explained. The young man had gotten into a fight, perhaps. People were always trying to take on athletes to prove how tough they were. Or, maybe the player had gotten drunk. Once, a particularly strong football player was jailed for pulling a urinal off the wall. Marcos got him out.

Ledo's was the restaurant in which Lefty brought the house down with his V-for-victory gesture after games. On the wall near the front entrance, Marcos had a 1957 black-and-white, wide-angle photograph of a packed Byrd Stadium on the day when England's Queen Elizabeth attended. If you had been to what they called "the Queen's Game," Marcos and Meloy thought, you had been around long enough to have an opinion about sports at College Park.

A former club president, Marcos got involved with the university one day at lunch time when the former football coach, Jim Tatum, leaned backward too far in his chair and fell to the floor on his back. Marcos rushed from behind the bar to be sure his patron was not hurt -- and right into the life of Maryland football teams. He became one of the team's biggest supporters, sponsoring an award each year to the best Terrapin lineman.

Tatum gave Maryland its first taste of the big time. He brought national championships to College Park in the early 1950s. His teams went undefeated and won an Orange Bowl game in 1952.

On his 60th birthday, Tommy Marcos's wife bought him a $10,000 Life Membership in the club. He liked being a member, he said, because membership imparted a certain status and respect. "Terrapin Club members are involved in everything. Everyone knows the Terrapin Club members," he said.

Perhaps the best known Terrapin Club member was Heise, the man who gave one of the eulogies at Bias's funeral. Heise had served the university and particularly its sports program in a multitude of ways. There was virtually nothing he could not be called upon to do. When Bias's friend and teammate, Adrian Branch, was convicted of marijuana possession in 1984, Heise arranged a 30-hour community service placement for him. (The player was also sentenced to six months' probation and fined $200.)

Shortly thereafter, Branch spoke against drugs before the members of Kids Against Crime in Laurel. Brian Lee Tribble, the man charged with supplying the drug that killed Bias, was with Branch at the speech that evening. Branch introduced Tribble as his strength coach. Parents who took their kids to the Branch-Tribble anti-drug lecture took snapshots of the ballplayer and his friend. Athletes -- even those recently convicted of drug possession -- were regarded as suitable role models and vehicles for the anti-drug message. The photograph offered an engaging scene: happy youngsters looking up to their idols.

No Terrapin was more deeply devoted to the Maryland team than Jack Heise. He had watched Len Bias play at Northwestern High School. At Driesell's request, he had helped to organize the

Fastbreakers. He also had recruited Driesell and had helped Driesell get McMillen.

An undergraduate at College Park, he had four brass terrapin paper weights on his desk. From time to time, near the end of his career at Maryland, he had met with Bias, urging him to stay in school. He had seen the pressure on other Maryland players -- agents, reporters, and scouts.

"I can take care of it," Bias told him.

But the draw of the money in the senior all-star games was too much, Heise said later. Playing in those games, he said, amounted to dropping out of school. Driesell should have done more to enforce rules on studying, he said -- and he thought this lack of authority in the program was Slaughter's main concern about Driesell.

Heise conceded that Driesell's program had "dipped." He had not found a dominant big man since he lost Moses Malone to the pros in 1974. Worse, Driesell had taken chances on players who essentially poisoned the well, players who did not work out well for one reason or another. "You have one year like that," Heise said, "and it puts you behind the 8-ball for years. The coaches talk about the importance of stadiums when they go out to recruit. But the issues are the players a kid is going to play with and the coach himself." If a player could not imagine himself getting a lot of playing time on a team with a chance to win, Heise said, he would be hard to recruit. "One slip and you're building back." Driesell had never quite made it back, he thought.

Like Judge Meloy and Marvin Mandel, Heise had ideas about what needed to be done to reduce the pressure on the players.

"They should not play the NCAA championships or allow the all-star games until school is over," Heise said. "What's a young man supposed to do when he has a chance to make some big money?"

And he had another idea: "Don't load the players up with so many reading courses if that's not their forte."

Others thought the players would never prosper if they could not read well enough to take meaningful courses.

Dervey Lomax was among those club members who advocated reading and warned players how few of them would make it to the professional leagues. "Even if they did make it, what were they going to do after that? They couldn't play pro ball forever," he said.

Lomax, a retired government employee, says he was constantly after the players to get serious about school. He was particularly unhappy about the fact that most of them were enrolled in General Studies.

"You've got to take courses that will get you jobs," he told the players. "I was never satisfied with General Studies. There has to be a pattern. Businesses want guys who can produce for them. General Studies did not provide a job-producing background."

When he delivered his lectures, he sometimes ended by saying, "You've got to get it up here," pointing to his head, "before you get it down here," pointing to his wallet pocket.

Often, seniors would stay with him for months after their classes had graduated. He made room for Veal and Tom "Speedy" Jones while they finished their course work and looked for jobs.

The search was often a painful and unhappy experience. And almost every year, Lomax said, Driesell would plead with members of the Terrapin Club or the Fastbreakers to find jobs for former Maryland players. Usually, it was too late. By then, many of the boosters saw the players from the perspective of Fred Frederick -- undisciplined and unqualified products of Driesell's program.

When Lomax went to the ACC Tournament or to away games with the Fastbreakers, the people he met assumed he was the father of a player. He was black, and not many blacks belonged to the Terrapin Club. But, for the university and the players, Lomax was one of the club's most important members. In a sense, he was a father to them all. He made his house a refuge.

Lomax's mother had been a fraternity house cook on the Maryland campus for 25 years. Lomax was a frequent visitor to the campus. One day in 1975, during a stop at the student union, he spotted Chris Patton, a basketball player.

"I saw how he looked like he was lost," he said. "I wanted to give him a home-cooked meal." His mother started cooking that day for another kind of fraternity -- Maryland athletes, particularly the ones from other states.

A year later, when Lomax built a new house, he made it much bigger than his family needed. "I made space so I could encourage parents to come here," he said. "There was no affiliation with the university, but I wanted to give them a chance to feel comfortable and know that their sons had someone who was watching out for them. Before the rules changed, I wrote to players to help with recruiting. I would assure their parents that I would be their father away from home."

When he wrote or talked to a player's parents, Lomax says he always stressed his intention to push the young man toward the books.

"I really emphasized education," he said. Apparently he was a persuasive university representative. Keith Gatlin's mother gave him a written statement, designating him as her official representative in matters pertaining to her son at College Park. The 1983-84 team -- the one that won the ACC championship -- gave him a silver plate, inscribed, "To The Lomaxes From Your God Children." It hangs in Lomax's basement den.

By the 1980s, the historic link between the boosters and college sports had been lost to memory. But a tangible monument did exist on the College Park campus: A message on a water fountain touted the virtue of "unappropriated funds" -- money earned by the football team, not begged from the legislature.

Pressure to remain competitive in the entertainment marketplace stemmed in Maryland from legislative insistence that intercollegiate sports at College Park, and at all the state university's other campuses, be self-supporting. In service to the self-support philosophy, universities all over the country went into the entertainment business. Not because they wanted to, or because they thought entertaining made them better universities, but because legislators demanded the revenue. In a way, though, Maryland demanded more than self-support. It demanded that football and basketball support all 22 intercollegiate sports, when it knew that only two produced much money.

The university and the legislature averted their institutional eyes when these sports brought in the best players regardless of academic ability. The pressure could have been relieved if the legislature and the university really had seen sports as educational and had paid for them the way that they paid for biology, for example. Short of that commitment, a fund might have been provided for rainy day assistance, a safety net for seasons in which the fans were less supportive or the bowl invitations did not arrive. But faculty would have been enraged by such a policy. Regents Chairman Schwait and Chancellor Slaughter declined to ask for that kind of support -- even after the death of Bias and disclosure of the team's academic failures.

"As long as you are required to run a self-supporting program, there are going to be times when you are tempted to compromise your integrity academically," Athletic Director Dick Dull said. "I've been on record as saying we probably took kids who were not proper candidates for admission. Most institutions would take a more jaundiced eye toward admitting a marginal kid if they did not have these economic concerns."

Moreover, the money that the university got for sports might cost it library aid, aid to improve the computer system, or funds for constructing new buildings and painting old ones on a campus that already suffered from serious deficiencies in all these areas. In the year that Bias died, the university's library still ranked well behind the institutions that Tom McMillen had used as comparisons when he was a freshman recruit 14 years earlier. On all measures of a state's contribution to higher education, Maryland ranked in the bottom half of the nation -- though in the top 10 for per capita income.

Tim Maloney, an astute and perceptive legislator who sat on the Maryland House Appropriations Committee, said he could not imagine the legislature allowing the university to break free of the self-support policy. Legislators were not going to overlook a revenue stream, he said.

Maloney thought the university's concerns were too abstract to win a political struggle in Annapolis. Legislators had many interests to consider. If the program fell into the grip of scandal, no political leader wanted voters to think he had any power to control it. He wanted to be able to say, "That's the university's problem. We're not involved in that."

In exchange for self-support, Maloney said, the university won the right to decide what to do with much of the money it received from government. University administrators might well appreciate relief from self-support in athletics, but they would not trade it for control over their budget. Fred Frederick was right about one thing. There was no sting of accountability -- except in the office of the chancellor, and he had too little power.

There was little likelihood of change, though the circumstances were far different than in the 1950s when the self-support policy was set. Then, the idea was to insulate policy-makers from the charge that athletics were stealing scarce resources from libraries and teacher salaries. No one foresaw a negative impact on the players, or pressure on coaches to cheat, or pressure on universities to drop academic standards. Thirty years later, young men and women were asked to practice long and hard, to play well enough to make money for their university -- probably not what the legislature had in mind when it first set the policy. Game monies did not then raise questions about whether players should be paid -- paid not just in scholarships, but paid commensurate with the fortunes they earned for the schools. The question has yet to be honestly addressed, not only because the university's interests are at stake, but because the myth of amateurism and the relative purity of the earlier times still govern.

Terrapin Club members were not oblivious to the insulation they provided for the politicians. Cooper Curtice thought he knew exactly what he and the other club members were doing with their scholarship money: "Legislators don't want the stigma of being a high-pressure athletic factory, so they stay clear of it. They don't support it. But they don't mind when it's smiling on them. They don't mind the money coming in and they don't have to pay anything out of the state treasury," Curtice said.

Members of the legislature loved the games and governors liked having the players down for dinner and a photo session. University administrators thought they always did better with their budget requests in Annapolis if the teams were winning. A quiet bargain was struck without discussion of assumptions or consequences.

The policy might have protected the Establishment from the scandals that occasionally erupted in college sports. But it helped to create an environment in which scandal was almost inevitable. By forcing the sports program to compete in the marketplace, the legislature created the corrupting pressure. The policy of self-support and the ill-concealed interest in winning led directly to the recruiting of illiterates, to smorgasbord diplomas, and to the development of cynical and sometimes unhappy young men who were mistrustful, isolated and unsuccessful in college.

The damaging policy thrived in silence. The legislature ceded power over college sports programs to columnists, furniture dealers, and former senators. The university faculty, too, was implicated. Professors clearly would have opposed legislative relief, arguing that the money would be diverted from the classroom. Administrators who allowed ill-prepared athletes into the university argued that the state should not pay the scholarship bill for athletes who were not really qualified students.

In 1986, the Athletic Department was staring at a $1 million deficit -- the result of having received far less money than expected from the Cherry Bowl in 1984, and from failures of financial planning. Under those circumstances, it was a perilous move for an administrator such as Slaughter to risk the loss of Terrapin Club support. But Slaughter, whom Novak described as weak, took that risk by pointing his athletic department in a new direction.

In the school's graduate library, named after Theodore McKeldin, a former governor of the state, there is a room devoted to the late Katherine Anne Porter, author of "Pale Horse, Pale Rider" and "Ship of Fools." The novelist left the university much of her library and some memorabilia of her literary life. Framed and hung on the south wall of the Porter Room was a letter from Mark Twain. In one passage, Twain observed that the world is filled with liars. "Let persons devoid of principles lie wantonly, gratuitously, if they will," he wrote, "but let you and me make it the rule of our life to lie for revenue only."

Constrained as he was by financial issues, Slaughter wanted to stop "lying for revenue" -- pretending his university was doing something for the basketball players when its attentions were at least divided among the players, the championships and the money. He risked the club's anger in virtually everything he did -- including his refusal to act quickly in the matter of Driesell's future. Terrapin Club executives, equating the university with their businesses and Slaughter with a chief executive officer, couldn't understand why the chancellor didn't just act. Fire Driesell or keep him, they thought, but do something. A sportswriter suggested during this period that Slaughter was like a man who spent an hour every morning trying to decide whether to wear his brown or his black shoes. The supreme irony here was that Slaughter was doing exactly what the Terrapin Club wanted: protecting the university and trying to save its sports program.

Driesell kept after the chancellor as if he were a recruit or a recruit's parent. The stories of his charm with recruits and their mothers, with boosters, with governors and others led him to believe completely that he could prevail in any situation. So now he was going to take the ball directly to the basket. Driesell remained confident.

One day the coach asked the chancellor to visit him at his dark paneled office in Cole Field House. There were some things he wanted Slaughter to see.

Driesell took his boss through the inevitable series of charts showing his accomplishments, his won-lost record, the careers of his students, the number of players selected by the pros, and their rank in the draft. He had the record of his years at Davidson and for the years at Maryland. For 15 years, he told Slaughter, Maryland led the ACC -- in attendance. He had filled the field house. The recitation must have been soothing to him. Slaughter, too, was impressed with some of the figures, but the chancellor also knew quite well that most of the coach's sparkling academic successes had occurred in his earlier years at Maryland.

At the end of the presentation, Lefty asked, "Am I going to be your basketball coach?"

Slaughter demurred once again. His investigation, his interviews with the players, were still under way, he said. "I'm just not comfortable making that decision right now."

Driesell didn't hesitate.

"If you fire me," he said, according to Slaughter, "it'll be the biggest mistake you ever made. I've got a lot of powerful friends. When I meet them on the street, they say, 'Hang in there, Lefty.'" Slaughter should also know that a lot of his friends were black, he said. They wouldn't like it either if he got fired.

Driesell, who declined to comment on Slaughter's account of the meeting or on anything else regarding the chancellor, wanted more than a vote of confidence. Having tried to run the admissions office, having intervened in the Veal matter, where he asserted his "pull," now, he was telling Slaughter, in effect, "You don't decide who the basketball coach is. I do, and my friends do. Better get it straight." The Driesell question was no longer who would coach basketball; it had become who would run the university. Slaughter looked at Driesell for a moment, thanked him, and walked out of the office.

A few days later, a friend took the chancellor to lunch. The friend was concerned that Slaughter could not survive if he tried to fire Driesell. There were too many Hotsy Alpersteins, Marvin Mandels, and Sam LeFraks ready to back the coach over anyone, including the chancellor. Also, coming over the political horizon was the next governor of Maryland, William Donald Schaefer, a man who had many friends among the Terrapins -- including Mandel and Alperstein -- a man the Terrapin Club members supported with their campaign contributions.

"We were turning back into the campus when I told him [my friend] what Driesell had said," Slaughter said later. "He saw what I had to do."

Slaughter said nothing about Driesell's implied threat. Had he done otherwise, he knew the pressure for an immediate firing would become irresistible. As much as he might have wanted to fire Driesell, his own feelings, the pressure he felt personally, were only two of the factors in the decision he had to make. More of the process had to unfold on its own, more information was needed, to make a decision that would serve the university.

On August 28, the grand jury said no to the prosecutor's demand for an indictment of Driesell. The jurors concluded that Lefty had no "evil intent or desire to corrupt." Beyond that, he had ordered a cleanup, but it was not carried out. Oliver Purnell, the assistant coach, decided on his way to the dormitory that he would not follow Driesell's orders this time. Besides, by the time Purnell arrived, Terry Long had tidied up. What remained was the charge that Driesell kept the players away from the media and the police, a fatherly sheltering of young men who everyone agreed were not up to the grilling that awaited them. In general, people felt then that the coach could not be held responsible for a player's drug overdose.

Driesell had escaped the criminal justice corner. A furious Marshall bolted from the courthouse to tell reporters that Driesell should at least be fired by the university. The coach had failed miserably in his responsibilities to the players, the prosecutor said.

Reached at their beach house in Delaware, Mrs. Driesell told reporters simply, "We're happy."

Edward Bennett Williams called Slaughter immediately to say that he hoped Marshall's tirade would be ignored, as the university began to consider whether Driesell should continue as coach.

A week later, Marshall lost by about 5,000 votes in his re-election effort to Alex Williams, who became the first black elected public official to win a county-wide office in Prince George's County. Marshall was stunned. He had thought the drug crusade, with all its publicity, would be a winner.

But voters who loved Terrapin basketball and revered Driesell were a countervailing force. Marshall thought members of the Terrapin Club and their friends had made the difference at the polls.

Chapter 9

Outcasts

A promotional film prepared by the university's public relations office had referred to the 1986 Terrapins as "another crop of seasoned men." But after four years as chancellor at Maryland, Slaughter had concluded that the appearance of power and confidence in college athletes, exquisitely embodied in Len Bias, was misleading and pernicious.

He thought of them as outcasts. The demands of their sport pushed them out of campus life and deprived them of opportunities for personal growth. They became clannish and defensive.

"They aren't part of the student body," he said. "They don't have the opportunity to develop social skills. Even if they wanted to become part of the institution, they're not sure how to do it. Their whole experience is with another basketball player -- maybe a football player." Their seasoning was pretty one-dimensional.

Many of the things done to help athletes succeed, in recognition, officially, of the time they spent practicing and competing, were harmful to them as students. Unlike typical students, they were spared situations forcing them to pull themselves out of trouble, small victories that inspired confidence and the ability to prevail over an indifferent system. Athletes did not have to endure the insecurity of signing up for courses and failing to get the ones they wanted, of sorting out conflicts in schedules, of thinking through what they wanted to study. Athletic department advisers made these decisions for them, stood in line for them. They were protected.

After he met his basketball player clients, Gregg and Long, Alan Goldstein was struck by how forlorn the two seemed, how distant they were from the student body. By then, of course, they were the targets of a grand jury investigation. Still, the isolation was not related solely to their legal troubles. Among the other students, they were conspicuous by size and by the widely held suspicion that they weren't really students at all. Among fans and sportswriters, the idea of big-time athletes as students was a joke, a matter for considerable cynicism. The athletes did not think the joke funny, but some of them became cynical, too.

"Maryland has a pretty patriarchal attitude toward ballplayers," Goldstein said. "I suppose every big-time school does. But a lot of these kids have been shit on out of kindness. People treat them like babies and they become babies. If you made them responsible, they'd have been far better off. They get the idea that they'll be protected. Daddy, the sports structure, will make it right for them. It doesn't mature them."

As much as universities trumpeted the student-athlete ideal, they tolerated the pace of Division I basketball and, indirectly, relied on the view that athletes were incompetent students. "They're not exactly rocket scientists," people would say. It was a joke that, subconsciously, perhaps, lifted responsibility for failure. If expectation is low, failure is not so damning. Dumb jocks had always been laughed at the way people used to laugh at drunks, as if there were something funny about being an alcoholic or being unable to read. If they had been sent to libraries as enthusiastically as they were directed to the recreation centers of the world, Slaughter thought, they would have been good students. But that was not the way of the world. Sports were good. Sports were character-building. Perhaps sports were the yellow brick road.

In the short run, as long as their eligibility lasted, failure was painless. Driesell insisted that none of his players had ever flunked out of school. They might have been "dismissed academically," to use the university's phrase, but they were usually able to get re-admitted and they seldom lost their right to play. The system assumed failure, acknowledging in a sense that its demands and the athletes' deficiencies made failure likely. The system made provisions to overcome failures and to preserve eligibility. After the first decision to lower standards, a succession of others ratified that decision.

A college athlete was like the boy in the bubble: When he left the gymnasium or the football field, he might well have no vocational or social immune system. When Herman Veal went to testify before the campus disciplinary board, he showed up in a sweat suit, hardly the best way to express respect for authority or to recognize the seriousness of the alleged offense. As Goldstein observed, ballplayers were kept apart from the world beyond the basketball court, yet were expected to excel there when their playing days were over. If they had been held out of basketball practice, they surely would not have been expected to excel during games.

"What this campus has to offer is not there for them," Slaughter said. "Maybe it means something more to me because of who I am . . . They're in that constrained little area." For basketball players, the chancellor concluded, the advantage of college was an illusion. Young men whose parents and grandparents had been barred from campuses by discrimination were now diverted from education by the demands of a sport.

Herman Veal made the case vividly for Slaughter.

Unlike Bias, Veal had not been highly sought after by college coaches. One of Driesell's assistants discovered him at a tournament in Florida during the summer after his high school senior year.

When Veal arrived at College Park, the university did not embrace him, nor he it. A tough, well-muscled rebounder with an exuberant, mischievous smile, Veal became quickly devastated by loneliness.

"My first year here, I had to see a psychiatrist. I felt trapped. If you're on scholarship, you can't have a job. You can't fly home even if your grandmom died," he said, observing that he had no money for a plane ticket back to his hometown of Jackson, Mississippi, and the NCAA rules prohibited gifts to ballplayers who landed in university sites far removed from home and family.

"My family is not poor, not compared to some of the other guys I've seen come through here, but my mother had seven daughters and three sons. How," he asked, "could I justify calling home to ask for money? I got $125 in four years from my parents. It wasn't just me. Some guys didn't have coats. The NCAA says you can't give a guy a damn coat. We had guys walking around here in the middle of the winter in a windbreaker."

College basketball players made millions for their school. They played for a coach whose income approached a half-million dollars a year. But they couldn't afford coats. The reality of kids in windbreakers during winter clashed with the suspicion that ballplayers drove big cars and had charge accounts at chic clothing stores. Some did, maybe. But not all. In a sense, average players probably had the worst of two worlds: They couldn't always afford adequate clothing, yet people assumed they had carte blanche.

A 1988 survey of black athletes, prepared for Slaughter and the NCAA's Presidents Commission, found that 61 percent of black football and basketball players nationwide had less than $25 a month for personal expenses. The survey also found that many players, like Veal, felt isolated, racially and otherwise. They expressed difficulties in talking about their problems and in meeting other students. About 33 percent reported incidents of racial discrimination.

If college athletes were wanting in anything, though, their swagger tended to conceal it. Veal was a good example of the lost ballplayer syndrome. He had as much macho presence as any of his teammates, but was an emotionally fragile 18-year-old. For four years at College Park, he was enraged and hurt.

Basketball was a refuge and a trap for Veal. Every day began, he said, with an assistant coach hammering at his door. Wake-up calls were part of the mixed signals sent to the players by their protectors: Go to class, do well, stay "on track" to graduate. But the demands of practice and playing schedules took them away from classes and showed them where the priorities really were.

"All your time was *their* time," Veal said. "They want you to be responsible for your own actions, but they wake you up for breakfast."

Many basketball and football coaches insist upon the near-isolation of their players. Coaches' objectives demand intense player concentration. Outside distractions are the enemy. Such intrusions include classes and laboratories.

In the months after Bias's death, football coach Bobby Ross complained of an all-time high number of distractions for his players. Ross spoke as if a player's death, the near-indictment of Driesell, and a consuming academic scandal could be dismissed as distractions. What a college coach wanted from his players was the antithesis of university life, a life expected to open and flourish in a succession of new and diverting experiences. Certainly, there had to be discipline. Certainly, basketball and its attendant wonders were experiences of their own. But there was often no balance.

Slaughter thought certain courses were off-limits to athletes, not because they were unable to handle them, but because they took the player's mind and sometimes his body away from concentration on the next game. The result was an unofficial no-growth policy. Veal said he always wanted to be something more than "Herman the athlete, Herman the jock," but the kind of development he needed was not always in the program's best interest.

"If you're just a student, you can go to the bars, the Rendezvous or Bentley's, but those are places your coach would prefer you to stay away from," he said.

Veal thought the university had forgotten that ballplayers were people who needed a life beyond basketball and books. Even when universities were urging a player to study, they were doing it for selfish reasons, he thought.

"It's all a matter of frigging intellect. Give me something I can do," he said. "Every day, it's the same thing, the same thing. Your body's so wound up. After you eat, you don't feel like reading no book. That's the ideal thing to do, but who feels like reading a book after you've done all that running? You feel like lying down for 45 minutes and then having fun for two hours before curfew."

The idea of an education as life experience was not there for ballplayers. "You have guys who come through here who can't even sit down and hold a conversation," Veal said. "They all go places together. They hang with each other. They're not able to mingle socially."

And then people were always reminding him of how indebted he was to the university and its boosters.

"It always came back to that, the scholarship," Veal said. "They say half you kids can't afford college. I may not be able to afford college, but the university wouldn't be in the financial shape it's in without me. I'm getting an opportunity to have an education. But I'm out there every day busting my butt."

No one, he thought, really cared enough about Herman Veal, the human being.

"The university just wanted me to stay out of trouble. They don't care about you as a person. The system doesn't care. The system's just holding its breath. That's the adjustment program: holding your breath. At times," he said, "I just didn't give a damn."

The drug testing program, he thought, was a good example of the system's indifference.

"What's a drug test if you don't get educated? If you don't get educated, all you'll have is 25 athletes overdosing in the summertime. A testing program is not dealing with the social and academic failings of the players. You're just protecting the program."

Athletes who looked back after four or five years of playing ball often acknowledged a complete disregard of their educational opportunities. Veal thought he had more potential as a student than he had achieved.

"I can't blame that on anyone but myself. Just knowing I didn't have anything to do socially, I didn't care that much. Day after day, I was doing the same thing over and over," he said. "You get fed up with it. I'd get a low C, and know that if I had studied a day earlier, I would have had a B or an A. In that way, I failed myself. You're 17 years old, not handling the situation. The situation's handling you. You're not being the person you want to become. It's easy to say, 'I'm being my own person,' but you're not."

In his own case, of course, the observation had far more significance. The Herman Veal hauled before disciplinary authorities to account for his behavior was not the Veal he had in mind or the Veal known later to Slaughter and others on the campus. Veal did not blame Driesell.

"He's my man," he said. "I didn't put the effort into the books that I could have. We had all the support programs we needed. I didn't really care about it." But the experience also taught him this about universities: "They really didn't care anything about the athletes as people. All you are is a piece of meat, and everybody wants a whack."

After his senior year, Veal returned to complete his degree. A criminology major, he could not pass a required course in statistics. "I hadn't had math since high school. If I had taken algebra and calculus in high school, I might have been able to deal with it," he said. "In Mississippi, you didn't have to take any more math when you got to high school."

Veal was hitting on something important here: High schools' failure to provide the math courses he needed was only one example of how young male and female athletes were ill-prepared for university-level work.

Veal eventually transferred into General Studies and graduated.

After his playing days were over, he remained something of a notorious figure on campus. The old charges hung over him. He ignored the shunning, just as he had ignored the women's underwear and the taunting signs during the Duke game. He presented himself as a witness during public hearings held by both the academic and drug policy task forces. In the back of the room, an outcast still, Veal sat by himself until it was his turn to speak. For those who did not know his thoughtful side, he was still Herman the jock, Herman the athlete, the ballplayer who got in trouble with the girl.

Finally, though, he was a participant in campus life. He was doing things he had never done as a student. He was speaking in public, offering his views. He had a strong voice and no nervousness as he spoke. He was saying something important, as if he were looking for a way to redeem himself. He might have walked away. But he had acquired a confidence in his views and he offered them with urgency. Notwithstanding his notorious past, Slaughter thought Veal showed courage and character.

The real trade between universities and players was made in the currency of dreams. What drew many basketball players to college was not the opportunity for an education, but dreams of the NBA. The NCAA's 1988 survey of big-time schools found that a large percentage of athletes had had no intention of even going to college until coaches talked them into it. They hadn't planned or studied with college in mind. But the argument of the boosters and the coaches was always: "It beats pumping gas for a living." According to this theory, just passing through college was beneficial.

Slaughter recognized that he had not demanded enough of Driesell, of whom he admittedly had been awe-struck initially. Slaughter was a man of gentility who expected people to do as he said, as when he had strongly suggested to Driesell that something be done to improve the team's academic performance. The coach, his friends said, took anything less than whip-cracking orders as license to go on doing what he was doing. Judge Meloy and others observed that as long as Driesell was still standing, he felt he had won any argument.

In the late summer of 1986, as he completed his talks with the players, Slaughter began to be highly critical of himself. He had previously told newspaper reporters that the problems at College Park were "my fault." Now, after talking with the players, he used much stronger language. "I felt I was a co-conspirator," he said.

The stories of Bias, Veal, Johnson, and Baxter cast a pall over him. He had been part of an exploitative system. He had helped sustain Driesell's influence. For too long, he told himself he was providing a genuine opportunity for Lefty to change, and expected he would -- or could. He didn't want to order people to comply with his directions. He wanted to prevail by force of argument and principle. He wanted Driesell and others he supervised to "buy in" on their own.

"I knew there were problems," said Slaughter, "but I had just been scratching the surface. I didn't realize how deep they were. I hadn't invested myself enough to know what some of the real problems were." When he joked with his friends about his seat at Cole Field House, he had been right. The players *had* needed him. He discovered that, in his court-side seat, he had been too close -- too close and not close enough.

"I was as close to that group of kids as I've been to any group before or since," he said. "I had so much personal investment in Leonard Bias and the others."

In his speeches, the chancellor occasionally had observed that young black males were more likely to be victims of homicide than to enroll in college. They were more likely to become brain surgeons than they were to make it in the National Basketball Association.

Black males, he said, were losing ground at every level of education at U.S. universities. At the University of Maryland, black basketball players were very likely to leave school with no degree or no degree of value. In the summer of 1986, Slaughter began to wonder if there was much difference between the brutalities of the street and the deceit of the campus. He frequently quoted H.G. Wells: The quest for excellence, Wells had said, is a "race between education and catastrophe."

At College Park, catastrophe had won.

Driesell, of course, thought otherwise. He insisted that 80 percent or more of his players had graduated. The 80-percent figure was well above the university-wide graduation rate of 40-plus percent. And it was much higher than figures reported by sports think tanks such as Northeastern University's Center for the Study of Sport in Society in Boston; it held that nationwide only 20 percent to 25 percent of all football and basketball players graduated. The U.S. General Accounting Office, an investigative arm of Congress, found that some schools graduated less than 20 percent of their athletes.

Driesell's yearly figures were better because they were based on his definition of a graduation rate. He counted only those players who made it to their senior year. The university's rate made no such distinction. When it used Driesell's raw data for the period 1974 through 1979, it found 29 percent were graduating.

Driesell presented graduation figures for his years at Davidson as well as for those at Maryland. At Davidson, only one player who reached his senior year did not get a degree. His graduates included seven doctors, one dentist, 11 lawyers, 14 businessmen, a minister, a Rhodes Scholar, and several coaches. One or two of his players majored in physical education, but most were in rigorous academic disciplines: pre-med, pre-law, business, sociology, and the like. Driesell was proud to say later that he had coached young men who, in their professional lives, could handle any problem their old coach might encounter.

During Driesell's first six years at Maryland, his graduates were almost as productive. Judging by the variety of majors they chose, players worked hard and left College Park, not only with some idea of what they wanted to do in life, but some qualifications for doing it. But by 1976, the program had begun to slip. Maurice Howard became the first player who permanently entered the did-not-graduate category. From then on, not graduating was a common occurrence in the program.

Between 1976 and 1986, 10 of 31 basketball players left Maryland without degrees. Driesell said that six of those who did not graduate went on to play professional basketball. It was an excuse he did not need at Davidson, where all five players drafted by professional leagues also graduated. One became a doctor, one a lawyer, and two went into business. Had the demanding basketball environment of 1986 -- the number of games, the number of classes missed while traveling, the hours of practice -- existed at Davidson, Driesell might not have produced as many doctors and lawyers. Pre-med students would have run into academic difficulty had they missed 40 percent of their classes.

During an interview later, Driesell initially insisted the college game had not changed much, had not become more demanding or pressurized.

Any differences, he said, stemmed from television, which exerted pressure because university presidents and athletic directors "want you to make a lot of money."

The pressure was greater, he said, because the rules favor winners. Every other big athletic enterprise (the NBA and the NFL) give the most preferential draft picks the next year to the teams with the worst records, he said. "The NCAA is the only organization in sports that doesn't try to create parity," he said. "The rich get rich and the poor get poorer." And they feel more pressure. "How are we ever going to catch Duke and UNC?"

Other factors made basketball under Driesell at Maryland different from the Davidson years. Admission standards at Davidson, a private university, were considerably higher than at Maryland: Davidson students, including basketball players, had to have a "B" average and at least 1,000 on their SATs. His record at Davidson, he suggested, largely reflected the academic accomplishments of the players that were admitted.

At Maryland, between 1976 and 1986, 10 of 17 Driesell players drafted by the NBA did not graduate. Of the ten Maryland players chosen for the All-ACC team during these years of academic decline, only two graduated. These figures made James Bias's point that the better ballplayer you were, the more unlikely it was that you could be a decent student.

"If a player don't graduate," Driesell had told *The Post*, "that's on him." The successes were "on" Lefty. Those he was willing to take credit for. Driesell would have been better served had he acknowledged the pressures felt by an athlete wanting to be a student. The difficulty was apparent in his own carefully collected records, records that spanned the old basketball days at Davidson and the days of televised, big-travel and big-money basketball at Maryland.

Something was curious about Driesell's figures on their face: the players were arriving with extremely low SATs, and yet they graduated at twice the rate of the university proper where SATs were on average hundreds of points above that of athletes.

Slaughter dismissed the statistical debate. Anyone could make the numbers work in his favor. But no one could deny that for many basketball players at Maryland, the claim of real education was false. In many cases, the degrees had debatable value. The records kept by Driesell at Maryland included only one player who had gone on to become a doctor -- and none who had become a lawyer. Surely, medicine and law are not the only meritorious careers, but the professional degrees that Driesell had prized among his Davidson players were largely absent at Maryland.

In Driesell's later years at Maryland, those players who received professional training were heavily outnumbered by those who left College Park with no degree at all, or by those who graduated with a General Studies degree. General Studies saved the graduation rate: If you couldn't handle the major you had chosen, as Herman Veal found he could not, or if you never got around to picking a major, you could downshift into General Studies. These were the courses of study that appalled Slaughter when he made his inspection of transcripts.

Driesell, of course, disagrees with this assessment of the years at College Park. General Studies, he said, was "a legitimate major." His daughter, a magna cum laude graduate of Maryland, had been a General Studies major. Clearly, given her academic performance, the young woman was the sort of student for whom the program had been provided.

If the major had been abused, Driesell went on, "that was the university's fault. Was that my fault? It's not my fault."

The initial idea of General Studies was actually progressive. If a student could not find the major he wanted at College Park, he could construct one of his own. The flexibility was there, theoretically, for the university's best and most independent scholars, people who could negotiate the course catalogs on their own and build what they needed out of the university's offerings. This was not a description of high profile athletes at Maryland, whose academic lives were often directed by others, and whose performance in class put them at the opposite end of the student continuum. While only a small fraction of the student body majored in General Studies, a large percentage of athletes did. Driesell defended his program, as if it were largely unchanged from the one he had had at Davidson or during his first years at Maryland. He did say freshman eligibility had hurt his graduation rate. McMillen and Elmore, for example, had not been eligible as freshmen. Freshmen became eligible under a 1973 NCAA rule change because some recruits were good enough to attract fans immediately and could help to make a school a contender -- and because maintaining two programs, freshman and varsity, was expensive. Making freshmen eligible was a financial move.

Players without the celebrity of McMillen, Elmore, or Bias had varying views of Driesell's interest in their academic progress. Lawrence Boston, a member of the Maryland class of 1978, said in an interview with *The Sun* that he did not think it possible to play well and to be a good student, too. "It's only my opinion, but I don't believe many people can do both well," he said.

"You want to do well in the classroom," he explained, "but how can you? You're up all night studying for exams and then off to practice. There's no way to give it your all, your best." After a semester at Maryland, Boston essentially gave up on school and concentrated on his professional basketball aspirations.

A story still told among athletic insiders at College Park concerned the rapidity with which Boston left after the basketball season ended in his senior year. After the last game, he was never seen again on campus.

Athletic Director Dick Dull shrugged off such stories. Bias and Boston were part of a national phenomenon, he said. Seniors with no more eligibility and no further reason for being at the university simply left. Boston played briefly with the NBA's Washington Bullets. For 10 years, he hung onto his career, playing for the Rochester Zenith of the Continental Basketball Association and with teams in Spain, France and Yugoslavia. During the off-season, he worked in the States as a park ranger.

When he finally stopped playing, Boston, who settled in Cleveland, thought he would try to use the college credits he had earned at Maryland to qualify as a substitute teacher. He might also try to sell real estate, he thought. Instead, he continued with his job as a park ranger, enforcing park rules in wooded areas. "There's always some knucklehead somewhere drinking a beer," he said.

Some players sorted it out better than others. Wilson Washington, one of the nation's top high school players when recruited by Driesell, lasted one year at College Park. His feeling that he wasn't playing enough combined with homesickness to send him back to Old Dominion University in his hometown of Norfolk, Virginia. In

1974-75, he led that team to a National Invitational Tournament championship, but he did not earn his degree. Washington also had a few bouts of trouble with drugs, and tied the start of his drug use to John Lucas, the former Maryland player who became addicted to cocaine. Now a car salesman, Washington blames the basketball system, not Driesell, for the failure of players in the classroom.

"Be realistic. I tried to go to class. When we were playing at UCLA, it's kind of hard when you're 3,000 miles from campus," he said.

Veal's friend, Reggie Jackson, a starting guard on the Maryland team in the early 1980s, dropped out his senior year, but returned later to finish his degree. Jackson is now a salesman and fitness counselor for Holiday Spa in Hyattsville, Maryland, not far from College Park. Jackson thought Driesell might have done more, especially in his academic counseling. If players didn't work at school, they shouldn't have played, he said.

"On the exterior," Jackson said, "they always preached academics, but deep down, I don't think they're all that concerned. They're selfish like anyone would be. They wanted a Top 10 team and that was the priority." The NCAA survey found that many athletes thought their coaches did not really encourage them to study and to succeed in class.

Still, Jackson thought Driesell taught him how to be a man.

"I learned to deal with people. We traveled the world," he said. "You don't forget those experiences. I'm on my way. I have a degree. I'm confident. I have self-esteem. I'm very happy with my life."

There was no reason to believe, as some apparently did, that athletes were resigned to leaving the university without a degree. In the beginning, Bias had shown little commitment to the student side of his life at Maryland. By the time he was a senior, he said he regretted it.

"One thing I really want is a degree," he said as he approached the end of his career at College Park. "I didn't used to want it that much. But now I do badly. I'm not the greatest student, but I could be if I paid attention to it. I want people to know I went to Maryland and that I left with something. So they'll say that's where Len Bias graduated from. That's an accomplishment."

Given the amount of professorial grace that went into it, how valuable would a degree have been for Bias? In the end, at least, he was saying the words.

Though responsible for a $400-million budget and an academic community of 50,000, Slaughter was expected to know what was happening in every department of his university, particularly the athletic department. And, indeed, when it came to the academic problems of some athletes, Slaughter had detailed knowledge. He knew that some members of the football and basketball teams needed intense academic assistance. Wielding his authority as chancellor, he had overruled admissions officials to admit players previously rejected. At the request of Driesell and Ross, he had personally arranged enrollment or re-enrollment of about a half-dozen players. He had allowed himself to become a court of appeals when the coaches were unable to get a talented player they wanted through regular channels. He had done this, he said, because he felt some students had been poorly advised and deserved another chance. The outcomes of these decisions, he said, frequently justified his faith.

Slaughter intervened on the theory that, given an opportunity, in the right circumstances, and with careful guidance, some young men might discover unused capacity and succeed at College Park. In high school, he knew, little was asked of ballplayers. Filled with the dreams of glamour, fame, and money, they made little effort to succeed as students. Their test scores, he thought, were of little value in judging their academic potential.

Slaughter saw many students coming to Maryland -- not just ballplayers -- who were poorly prepared and who were enrolled as "special admits." There were those on the campus who disagreed with him, but he thought in the early part of his tenure that a public university should and could undertake the required remedial programs. He could not turn away young men with precious few opportunities beyond basketball, he felt.

"A university education was not something, often, that black ballplayers knew of through family members. Their heroes are the guys who can dunk the basketball. If anybody in their neighborhood has any money, they didn't get it by going to the Harvard Business School," he said.

For many black students in the United States, basketball and football were a far more critical path to education than some may have realized. The 1988 NCAA survey found that while blacks comprised 12 percent of the nation's population, they represented only 4 percent of the enrollment at predominantly white Division I universities. At those same institutions, 37 percent of the football players and 56 percent of the basketball players were black.

"Visitors to a campus would be correct about half the time if they identified any black student they saw on the campus as an intercollegiate athlete," the NCAA report observed. Without sports, the number of blacks on campuses would have been much lower. So, after all these years, sports remained a major force in creating access to college for black students. Black students were less in demand as students at many universities. Universities wanted black students -- if they were athletes.

Schools with official affirmative action policies could find basketball forwards across the country, but they had difficulty locating non-athlete black students in their own neighborhoods. Slaughter's record with athletes at Maryland, though, was consistent with his across-the-board commitment to getting more African-American students enrolled at College Park. He took risks with athletes *and* non-athletes, knowing that there were precious few opportunities for such youngsters otherwise.

At Maryland, Slaughter's administration raised the percentage of black undergraduate students from 8 percent to 12 percent, about three times the average black enrollment at other Division I schools. The chancellor thought poor students might learn to learn.

Slaughter's theory that players could learn to be students might have been valid if anyone in the athletic department had taken it seriously. Sister Mary Alan, athletic director at St. Anthony's High School in Jersey City, New Jersey, a school that graduated many premier athletes, said it was criminal to bar players from college because of their SATs. Players coming to her high school often had extremely poor preparation but they became adequate students, she said.

"Almost every one of them who is coming into our school is coming in below grade level, and I am not saying one level," she said. "We have students entering school coming in on the fourth-grade reading level. If we can get them in four years to have a 2.0 in the core curriculum, that means they have worked in high school." At many universities, including Maryland, the faculty was skeptical that remedial efforts could ever overcome the deficits seen on the basketball team. But Sister Mary Alan insisted that specialized programs and individual attention could work.

On paper, Maryland promised the Biases, Baxters, and Veals something like a graduate high school, complete with counselors, tutors and other advisers, a self-contained environment for players who needed extensive academic remediation. It was said to be a $250,000 enterprise. In fact, there was not much in place, Slaughter found.

"We didn't have a thing," Slaughter said. "If there was financial trouble in the department, the tutoring and support were the first things to be cut."

A year before Bias's death, one of the basketball team's advisers quit in a dispute with Driesell, a dispute that had at its core the matters that became so embarrassing to the College Park chancellor in the summer of 1986. In a letter to Driesell, academic adviser Larry Roper suggested that the athletic department was serving basketball, while working against the long-term best interests of the players.

"Do we keep players eligible and just build credits or do we deal with human development?" Roper asked. He and other advisers had grown uncomfortable knowing that their presence lent credence to the university's claim it really cared about athletes' academic progress. The academic support team too much resembled eligibility monitors, he said. Similar disputes broke out between advisers and university officials at other schools across the country.

Roper resigned. When the story of his unhappiness and departure was published in local newspapers, Driesell suggested he was a crank. Ben Unkle, a student member of the Regents and a friend of Roper, called him a man of principle. Slaughter knew Roper and agreed that he was a conscientious professional, not a malcontent. But he did not inquire further into Roper's complaints, missing an important opportunity to learn exactly what was happening or not happening in the athletic department.

No one at Maryland set out to create a dishonest, exploitative program. Under the pressure to win and make money, standards eroded slowly over Driesell's 17 years, and were replaced by a cynical rationalization: The administration is responsible for education; they let these kids in here; let them deal with the problems. They would bring in kids they knew were academically unqualified. When players flunked out, they felt a guilty commitment to them. Reluctant to send them home, they let them back in, again and again. A student could be sent home for failing, but failing was so likely, given the demands of basketball, that this punishment hardly seemed fair. Second chances tended to be given so long as the player had eligibility. There were casualties as well. Terry Long failed all his courses twice, and Slaughter allowed him back into school. Even more remarkable, university rules did not bar him from resuming his position on the basketball team. Some wondered how university history and the Len Bias story might have been altered had College Park sent Long home. But such questions blame one foolish young man for the faults of the system.

Ralph Bennett, then the Campus Senate president, called Long's approach "fleg neg," short for flagrant neglect. There was no excuse, Bennett thought, for failing courses twice. Players just didn't try, and no one required them to.

"There was a tremendously negative atmosphere on the basketball team. 'We don't study. We're in General Studies.' The old guys passed it on to the new ones," Gillian said.

Terrapin forward Derrick Lewis, who had exceptionally high math scores and was inclined toward engineering, fell under this influence, Gillian said. John Slaughter, the engineer, had hoped Lewis could handle the demands of engineering and basketball. He was discouraged anew when Lewis failed to meet his twin goals.

Driesell liked to talk about the success of his former players. He kept their addresses, inquired of them on occasion, and told stories of his life with them. He especially enjoyed the story of Darrell Brown, class of 1973. Brown, a member of the famous McMillen-Elmore team, had started in the big ACC Tournament game against N.C. State, the one that cost Maryland a chance to play for the national title. Lacking the talent of his more famous teammates, he often played very well, and moved in and out of Driesell's good graces.

One year, the coach recalled, there had been a fight at the South Carolina game. Brown rushed up to him afterward in the locker room, anxious to report that he had punched a couple of South Carolina guys. But a film of the game revealed Brown hiding under the bleachers. It was typical, the coach said, of a kid who "slicked" people. In addition, Driesell went on, Brown occasionally invented tear-jerker stories to win the use of a classmate's car. Once, the coach said, Brown said his mother's leg had just been amputated and he needed the car to drive home for the weekend. McMillen had fallen for that scam, Driesell said.

At one point, Brown decided to put braids in his hair, directly flouting Driesell's decree that any player with braids would be benched. Brown did the braids anyway, even though the team was playing in Pittsburgh, his hometown.

"This has a lot of meaning," Brown told reporters before the game. "It's the only time my friends will have been able to see me play. It's a great feeling." Before the game, someone came up to Driesell to report that Brown's brother was in the audience packing a 45.

"He's gonna shoot you if you don't let Darrell play," the messenger reported.

"He'll have to shoot away," Driesell said, fearlessly, "because he's not going to play." The coach was adamant. Brown did not play.

Darrell Brown was less focused than his teammates Elmore and McMillen. At 6'6," he was an attractive prospect, not only to basketball teams but to the Washington Redskins and the Dallas Cowboys. Football didn't work out for him; nor did basketball. He was cut by the Washington Bullets in September 1974.

Brown held a succession of jobs, including one as a correctional officer in Western Maryland. He had not graduated with his class, but he continued to take courses. And in the spring of 1986, 13 years after he was supposed to graduate, he had accumulated the credit hours he needed -- but could not get them accepted at College Park. He asked Slaughter for help.

"He showed up in my office about 11:30 one morning. We talked for a while. He was a marvelous guy. He told me, 'I'm a success story waiting to happen.' He had done a lot of things. But he knew he needed his degree."

Slaughter took him home for lunch. And, later that day, he wrote a letter to the campus authorities who review credits earned off campus, recommending that Brown's be accepted. They were. Slaughter thought Brown's problems with the campus bureaucracy were the kind that discouraged, rather than rewarded, enterprise. That spring, Darrell Brown came to College Park with his wife and daughter, put on his cap and gown, and went back to Cole Field House for his commencement.

In after-dinner speeches before booster groups or in conversations with reporters, Driesell told part of the Darrell Brown story: "Some people said I wasn't into academics. But I said, 'Darrell, if you ever graduate, I'll give you a hell of a present.'"

"I kept after him and after him," Driesell said in a later interview. When he graduated, I wrote him the check and told him to buy himself a TV. I forgot to sign it and he called me up and said, 'Hey, coach. You didn't sign the check!' I wrote him another one and sent it to him."

Brown was the first of Driesell's seniors to leave Maryland without a degree -- but he served his old coach ultimately by winning the sheepskin and boosting the old graduation rate. Driesell may have considered it too sentimental, during his speeches, to point out Brown's long academic labors, or to provide further details of his life.

Why had Brown persevered for so long? Had there been something at Maryland or in Driesell's approach that convinced the kid with the braided hair and the tight end's body to keep studying? For Driesell, the answers might well have been useful in the summer of 1986, but he seemed to prefer the memory of a slightly goofy hustler to the image of someone who had struggled for 13 years to get a degree missed the first time around.

Jeff Baxter, a graduate of Bishop Carroll High School in Washington, was recruited by coaches at the best basketball colleges and universities in the nation. Of those he met, Baxter most liked Jim Boeheim of Syracuse and Dean Smith at the University of North Carolina. But his family wanted him to stay close to home. His mother thought kids got into trouble when they went too far away. Baxter observed later that, while he was at Maryland, there was not a year in which someone, usually including Driesell, wasn't in some kind of trouble.

When he and Bias were suspended for missing curfew after the N.C. State game, the news reached Hawaii, where one of Baxter's aunts was vacationing. She called to be sure he was all right. It was the kind of thing that happened when you played for a Lefty team, he said.

"He's a limelight type of person," Baxter added, somewhat ruefully. The light was bearable if you had a $300,000-a-year job, but not so easy if you had none at all.

In the weeks after Bias's death, Baxter's brother came to see Slaughter with Jeff's transcript.

"This is a travesty," he said, handing the document to Slaughter, who also read it with anguish.

"It was abominable. There was nothing there that looked like a sequence of courses that led to a degree or to any useful skill," the chancellor said.

Under normal circumstances, Baxter would have been a successful student. Like Derrick Lewis, he arrived at Maryland with a decent high school record: respectable scores on the SATs and a decent high school grade point average. He had wanted to study accounting.

"Somebody over there at the athletic department told him, 'This isn't for you. This other thing is for you,'" Slaughter said. He ended up majoring in General Studies. With or without ability, it seemed, athletes ended up doing poorly scholastically and in General Studies.

"General Studies is a route when you're confused," Baxter said. "At Maryland, a lot of people are confused. You're confused because of the pressure academically and athletically. They wouldn't evaluate your needs. 'Do this, do that,' they said. There was no individualization. Instead of sitting down to talk with you, to find out what you wanted to do, they said 'Do this, and do that.'" All the black players, added Baxter, were directed into the same courses, into the corral James Bias saw at College Park. Baxter didn't complain, nor did his parents. It was, according to Ray Gillian, unheard of for a relative to appear in the chancellor's office.

After Bias's death and the revelations that followed it, Slaughter heard the players and their parents criticized for not complaining. He criticized them, too, but he knew the criticism was blaming the victim. Eighteen-year-old kids, as poorly prepared as these students knew they were, were unlikely to come forward with critiques of the athletic department's academic advising. How did they know if they were getting good or bad advice?

Their parents were equally unlikely to challenge what James Bias called "the sanctified university" and its powerful coach. It was not knowing how to plead their cases with white or even black authorities, Slaughter thought, that led parents to acquiesce in the abuse of their sons. He also blamed the NBA dream for blocking a parent's critical faculties.

Everything in the athlete's code and in the power relationship with his coach militated against an athlete's protest. The fact that players had hardly any other relationships of value or importance to them during their college years made their relationship with the coach even more important. Life with Driesell, Baxter said, was discouraging. "But if you had any sense of yourself, you just have to deal with the punches. You're there. You had to adjust," he said.

Baxter spoke as if getting screwed was to be expected. His job, he said, was to endure. Because death is too close and too common for them, Bias's demise did not shock many black ghetto kids. Baxter considered what happened to him part of the same drill. He watched with interest the struggles between Driesell and Wendy Whittemore, who succeeded Larry Roper as academic adviser to the basketball team.

"She was not going to give in. She was trying her best to get people graduated," he said. "There were problems because, on the coaching side, you want to win. You wanted your players to work out at certain times. The academic side wanted players to get their grades. Someone stepped over someone's boundaries. You probably know which one that was."

Lefty had no boundaries, he said, but Whittemore did. She resigned just before Bias died, citing the concerns voiced earlier by Roper.

"When you have power," Baxter said, "when you're up on that plateau, you can control situations like that. You can control it the way you want to control it, turn it on and turn it off. He [Driesell] wanted her to conform. She felt the system was not allowing people to do their work. You want to help someone, but you have someone breathing down your neck."

In the end, after four years, Baxter was less willing than Veal to credit Driesell with caring. He didn't know if the coach cared about him or his education. Surveys of college players would suggest later that many players were as doubtful as Baxter about the depth of support they were getting from the coaches.

So, in the summer of 1986, Baxter marched off into the job market. It was going to have to be a damn good, well-paying job, he thought, to earn him the kind of money he had earned for the university. When he was a player, Baxter had worked during summer vacations for area accounting firms. Athletic department personnel and boosters got him and his teammates good jobs with federal agencies, local stores, the post office, or law offices in Washington. Some worked for Prince George's County judges. Dream jobs these were: They paid well, and, sometimes, the athletes got course credits for them.

When his eligibility ran out, however, so did the job assistance.

"Nobody will come to the phone," said Baxter. At the Dean Dome in March 1986, he had made the winning shot against UNC. In August of the same year, no one with a job to offer remembered it.

"It was ridiculous. It's like, well, you're an alumnus now. Where are all your friends? Where are all the people who were helping you out in the summer? There was no contact except when you go to a basketball game. I couldn't touch base with them. They were totally unavailable. I got depressed, but you have to deal with situations in life," he said.

Baxter had no real hope of getting a job. "Even if he had made good grades," Slaughter said, "and he walked into an employer with that record, the man would have said, 'It doesn't make sense. It's a smorgasbord.'"

Slaughter arranged an interview for Baxter with another local businessman. But the prospective employer reported to Slaughter that Baxter did not have the necessary grades. Slaughter appealed. He knew the average wasn't there, but the young man had ability. He needed a chance. A second interview was arranged, but, again, Baxter was rejected.

"We just couldn't seem to get over the hump," the chancellor said. The difference between Slaughter's hopes and reality grabbed him "by the jugular." Though, of course, he would have liked more playing time, Baxter had played the big-time game at Maryland without complaining. He had finished his eligibility, and even with the university chancellor running interference for him, he was being shut out of the job market.

Baxter was learning the truth of booster Dervey Lomax's forecast: In the real world, General Studies didn't sell. But he and his brother had an idea. They suggested to Slaughter the formation of a university foundation that would instruct high school players and their families on how to select a college, and how to cut through the coaches' promises. The university would put up $50,000. Jeff Baxter would be the foundation director.

"Kids don't understand coming out of high school. Coaches tell you exactly what you want to hear," Jeff said. "They tell you, 'You're going to be a No. 1 draft choice. You're going to average 30 a game.'"

Slaughter liked their idea, but lacking the requisite $50,000, he offered instead to bring Jeff back to the campus and finance his re-education. "He could come back, pick a major, and turn his transcript into something that had meaning," he told Baxter's brother.

Baxter thought about it. He thought also about going to law school at Howard University in the District of Columbia. He thought about trying to hook on as a coach at Maryland. Nothing made much sense.

Other players had gone overseas to play in the European basketball leagues. With its threat of hi-jacking, drugs, war, and another delay in addressing the future, Baxter was wary of that option.

"When I came back, I would still have to start from scratch, negotiate myself a new reality of life," he said.

After four years at Maryland, four years as a student in the charge of Charles G. "Lefty" Driesell and John Brooks Slaughter, Jeff Baxter had to start over.

Chapter 10

A Good Contract

Slaughter and his vice chancellors met on August 28, the day the grand jury had vindicated him, to discuss the future of Charles G. Driesell. Slaughter listened without comment. According to Vice Chancellor Gilmour, the man who was regarded by the boosters as Driesell's chief executioner stayed out of the discussions about the coach, except to defend him.

"It really amazed me how much he defended Lefty," Gilmour said. "He and Driesell were such different people. I could never really understand it." Slaughter put the matter in baseball terms, assigning himself the role of manager. "He told me once that he tended to stay with his starting pitcher too long," Gilmour said.

In this case, Slaughter did not expect the pitcher to get stronger. But he wanted to do what would best serve the university -- and could not predict what that would be until more of the facts, from the various investigations, were in hand.

"That wasn't all of it either," Gilmour said. Slaughter thought no one was guilty of a heinous, deliberate crime, including Driesell. He was unwilling to savage anyone to make himself seem decisive.

"I think he was the kind of Christian that Christians always say they are and seldom turn out to be," the vice chancellor said.

Before Slaughter interviewed the players, the matter was far less clear-cut for him than his friends and enemies imagined. The chancellor knew the problems of basketball went beyond Driesell. In the end, however, the mouthy coach made Slaughter's task easier by refusing to assist in his own salvation. He confessed no sin, so he was a hard man to save. There had been many opportunities for Driesell to change. Slaughter had provided them to no avail. Now, he thought the man simply could not change.

The meeting of vice chancellors, Slaughter's own private task force, adjourned and reconvened immediately as a cabinet, a smaller group that did not include Dull.

Then, finally, Slaughter spoke. The contemplative and methodical engineer had made his decision. What College Park and Maryland basketball needed was what Jeff Baxter needed, a new reality. What the players said, what Driesell himself said, had convinced him that Maryland could not have a different program unless it had a different coach.

"I concluded that he did not have the respect for the players that would be needed if they were to succeed in life -- not at basketball, but in life," Slaughter said. "Lefty talks a lot about McMillen and Elmore, but I honestly believe he has lost the respect for players he had then. Maybe he thinks the players he's getting aren't what they used to be. It's no excuse."

To leave him in charge, Slaughter determined, would be to tolerate his lack of respect for, his indifference to, the intellectual and social development of his players.

One evening after deciding to force Driesell out, Slaughter and Gilmour dropped into their chairs in the chancellor's office for one of their stock-taking sessions. As the sun went down, narrow rectangles of light sculpted by the wooden window blinds moved slowly up the east wall.

The grand jury had proved of no use to them -- no cover for firing the coach. Had Driesell been indicted, they might have dismissed him.

Now, they needed their own inquiry, focused tightly on Driesell's job performance. Had he violated any provisions of his contract? Had he ignored university policy? Had he done things clearly contrary to the interests of the school or his players?

Slaughter did not have to find criminal intent to reject Driesell as a coach, but he had to know if the contract provided any avenue for dismissal. As always, the question became one of money: How big a settlement would have to be made? If there were clear violations of the contract, the amount could be smaller. If there were no violations, the sum could be prohibitive.

Slaughter arranged to have lunch with Edward Bennett Williams in early October at the university's Rossborough Hall, a colonial-style, brick building just a short walk from the chancellor's office. The two men met amid raging press speculation. A Baltimore *Sun* headline announced, "Driesell Reportedly Might Leave -- For a Price." The price, the paper reported, could be as high as $3 million.

Slaughter began by telling Williams of his internal investigation of Driesell's job performance -- and of his tentative decision that Driesell was finished. Slaughter wanted to give Williams an immediate and unambiguous signal. His investigators, he said, were looking to answer these three questions:

- What had Driesell done on the first day of the crisis, the day that Bias died?
- Had Bias hired Lee Fentress, the lawyer-agent, at Lefty's insistence -- and had Reebok paid the coach for delivering Bias?
- Had Driesell violated university policies regarding a coach's responsibilities?

Under pressure from boosters and sportswriters all summer to resolve the crisis one way or another, Slaughter was more in control now. But he was certain Driesell could drive the price higher or make it prohibitive. And he feared that Driesell would drag them all into the corner. To Gilmour, Lefty seemed "like a caged animal then."

Williams did nothing to ease the fear within the university's councils. "He's coming unglued," Williams told Slaughter. "Is it still important to keep Driesell muzzled?" he asked pointedly. Slaughter, who knew he needed time to work out the separation agreement, said yes.

The problem was Driesell's 10-year contract signed in 1984. Its terms were generous: six years of coaching and then the option of moving into a non-coaching position for the remaining four years; a

salary of $86,000 a year for nine years; a guarantee of $50,000 in
radio and television fees while he remained coach. Not part of the
contract, but still a consideration, was a separate shoe endorsement
deal with Reebok. It provided him $105,000 in the first year, $110,000
in the second, $115,000 in the third, and $120,000 in the fourth -- with
a $30,000 signing bonus and bonuses (up to $25,000 per year) to be
paid later if the Terps played in the NCAA tournament. In addition,
Driesell had a $10,000 endorsement deal with MacGregor, the
sporting goods company that provided Maryland's basketballs, *and*
the university gave him free use of Cole Field House during the
summer for his basketball camp, which reportedly earned the coach
another $100,000 per year. These non-salary aspects of Driesell's
compensation "package" were what Williams referred to as
"consequentials."

All the benefits were pretty standard for the modern basketball
coach -- the salary deal, the shoe deal, the ball deal, the media deal,
the camp deal. The package was worth about $390,000 a year, and all
of it was on the table when Slaughter's inquiry began in early
September.

The contract was remarkable, however, for its length and its
timing: Maryland had given Driesell a 10-year deal despite conduct
that had led to a public reprimand, behavior that had created chronic
PR problems for the university -- notably, in the Veal affair. In
retrospect, the contract seemed another example of Slaughter's
inattention to Driesell's demands, or a gross catering to them.

Regents Chairman Schwait called the 1984 contract, "One of the
dumbest things we ever did." Slaughter told reporters he should have
had "a great deal more insight at the time." Insight, though, was not
the issue. Driesell was, simply, beyond Slaughter's control. Various
newspapers had called for Driesell's head after the Veal affair -- and
so, coincidentally or not, the canny coach had gone out and cemented
himself into his Cole Field House lair. There was no challenge. He
made himself more untouchable. All the insight in the world would
have meant nothing to Slaughter then, though he might have cut back
on the terms. Dull argued that the contract merely granted Lefty tenure
-- a status he thought the coach had earned by filling the field house
and winning more than 20 games a year for 15 years.

In the summer of 1986, the contract severely undermined
Slaughter's political position. Terrapin Club members demanded to
know how the university could fire someone so soon after granting

him such a long and lavish contract. Slaughter also wondered how he could buy out a contract worth at least a $1 million when his athletic department was at least that much in debt.

Williams wanted to save his client's job, or, failing that, to make him financially whole. The secondary goal was a lever for the first. In his negotiations with the university, Williams used the famous Driesell persona, threatening to unleash him and his rhetoric. The contract-breaking talks began in an atmosphere of mutual deterrence, each side possessing power and leverage against the other.

James Mingle, an assistant attorney general assigned to the university, was Williams's legal opponent. He conducted the inquiry for Slaughter and, within two weeks, concluded that there was no violation of the contract, in part because there were no performance standards that might have been violated.

The sides met on October 8 in Williams's Washington office. According to meeting notes made by the university, Mingle opened the talks.

"We accept Mr. Driesell's word that he did not steer Bias to his own agent," Mingle said, answering the first question raised in his internal investigation. "We have no evidence otherwise."

Fentress had told reporters after Bias's death that he assumed Driesell was influential in the young man's decision to select him as his agent. If the coach was satisfied with Fentress as his agent, then one of his players might understandably find him attractive, too, he said.

As it happened, Slaughter had personal knowledge of how the nation's best player had shopped for representation. In the fall of Bias's senior year, the chancellor was a guest on a television interview program in Baltimore. The host was Ron Shapiro, a Baltimore lawyer who represents quite a few Major League Baseball players, including the Orioles' Hall of Famer, former third baseman Brooks Robinson. Shapiro had helped to bail Robinson out of some financial difficulties, and his reputation as an honest representative was strong.

As the crews were clipping microphones into place, Slaughter asked Shapiro if he represented basketball players. "I would," Shapiro said, "but you're not supposed to sign them until their college eligibility is exhausted." In practice, he said, following that rule meant he got no new basketball clients; despite the prohibition, most players committed to an agent before the eligibility deadline. Here was another example of how the players' well-being was being ignored and undermined -- and how the participants felt powerless to change the system.

"I wish you could handle Len Bias," Slaughter said. "He's a nice kid. He's got a great family. He deserves good representation."

Shapiro said he was interested. Slaughter suggested he write to Driesell, expressing his interest. Shapiro wrote. Sometime later, Driesell informed him that Bias was signing with Fentress because he wanted an agent closer to home.

Wayne Curry, the Biases' lawyer, says the family knew nothing of Shapiro's interest in their son. They wanted the best representation they could find and Baltimore did not seem remote to them.

The university accepted Driesell's assertion that he had not steered his star to Fentress and that steering was not the reason for his own half-million-dollar contract with Reebok.

But they did have an opinion on Driesell's cleanup order to Oliver Purnell, his assistant coach, Mingle told Williams during the October 8 session.

According to the university's lawyer, the coach had said, "If there is any pot or coke, clean it out."

"We believe this to be irresponsible behavior, unprofessional conduct, very poor judgment," Mingle said.

Lon Babby, a Williams & Connolly lawyer who had handled the details for the contract negotiation, quickly offered a correction: "Mr. Driesell would say that he did not use those precise words in speaking with Purnell."

In an interview later, Babby said, "If Driesell had had a second chance, he probably wouldn't have repeated that comment, but he certainly hadn't committed a crime. The grand jury didn't find that he had, and the university didn't assert that he had." He said he thought the university was looking for a way to fire the coach without paying him.

Mingle went on to say that Driesell's attention to academics was "anemic." Players had told him that the coach was more interested in eligibility than in academics. Williams scoffed. "The responsibility for academic matters ultimately rests with academics," he said. "Colleges blink at the SATs. Players can't handle the work. They don't want to be embarrassed, so they don't go to class."

Slaughter interrupted: "The tone of the coach is the single most important ingredient in a player's academic success."

Football coach Bobby Ross showed more leadership than Driesell, added Mingle, and took an active interest in his players' academic progress. This was a common observation among athletic department personnel, many of whom thought Driesell had given up.

Williams then said: "There is merit to your ethics issue, and there is merit to your concern about the cleanup order to Coach Purnell. But what you are doing is unjust."

The "ethics issue," Mingle had said, concerned Driesell's shoe contract: Was it ethical for the coach to make money on shoes his players were wearing?

Here, again, the university was searching for grounds to dismiss the coach, Babby says. The concern about coaches and shoe contracts had not come up before. If there were an ethical concern, he wondered, why hadn't it arisen earlier?

As for Williams's comments about the validity of the university's ethics concerns, Babby says, "They were certainly not a fair view of Williams's view of Driesell. These things were said in a settlement context. They were not reflective of any thought that Driesell had done something wrong."

Mingle then proposed a settlement: The university would pay a full year's salary, make a public statement about Driesell's contributions to the university. It would say that he had been unfairly accused by Marshall.

Williams barely waited for Mingle to finish. "That's totally unacceptable," he said. "If you want to get rid of him, you will have to pay him his contract, including consequentials. He wants to stay as coach more than he wants money. Dull may have made a bad bargain. If so, as Lincoln said, you should hug it all the closer. The damage will be far worse if you don't. There is no conduct warranting discharge."

Williams made his intentions clear. "If Driesell is fired in the wake of the Bias tragedy, no one will hire him. A fired coach in the wake of a death is in a death chamber. We'll have to litigate, and we will need to air everything again," he said. "Air everything again" -- the words were chilling. The university wanted to avoid another media pasting at all costs, and Williams apparently knew it.

If the coach were severed from the university, Williams went on, he would become "an economic paraplegic." Thus a proposal of his own -- a face-saving, money-saving compromise. "If we could ride with him for a year, we could work something out. If we kept him as a coach, he could get a job. He couldn't resign. He is an honest guy and simple. He wants to stay." Out of the question, said Williams, was the idea of Driesell stepping down into the position of assistant athletic director. He called it a meaningless job.

Babby echoed the boosters' lament: The university was being hypocritical. "He was doing the same thing then [when the 1984 contract was signed] as he is doing now," Babby said.

"That isn't really correct," Slaughter said. "My major concern is that he is doing things differently now. He has been forced by competition to recruit less qualified athletes. I sense less attention to academic help. I think it isn't going to change a lot." Mingle said the university could not afford an enormous lump-sum payment. And, he warned, the legislature might kill any large settlement.

"I'm not terrorized by that prospect," said Williams, who was not terrorized by any prospect. Referring to his determination to litigate, he said, "The General Assembly is not going to ignore an order of the court." No one mentioned that the legislature, as a good representative of Maryland, was filled with Lefty lovers.

Then, he spoke of Driesell's mood: "He's a wounded bear. He won't accept what you are proposing. He believes he is being treated unfairly. He believes he's twisting in the wind. He's very emotional. He loves his job. He loves being coach."

Try to keep him, Williams urged. It will cost you too much to let him go -- too much money and, perhaps, too much controversy. The university, he said, could place "any restriction it wanted on him." Recalling the restrictions that he himself had tried to impose, Slaughter smiled at Williams's suggestion.

As the meeting ended, Williams said he would advise Driesell that the university was committed to making a change. This, Slaughter thought, was the turning point in the negotiations. The contract gave Driesell all the options, but now the university was saying it wanted those options back. Williams once again announced that he would try to keep his client quiet.

The Regents left the Driesell matter entirely to Slaughter. But its members were increasingly annoyed by the coach's public acts and comments. Regent Frank Gunther of Baltimore said he had had enough of what he called Driesell's "show-and-tell" style -- hiring advisers for appearances, going to graduation in cap and gown. The claim that he was a father to his players rang hollow. Still, Slaughter thought, because the cost would be so high, he would have to build an ironclad consensus for firing Driesell.

Before meeting with Williams, Slaughter had visited Schwait in Baltimore and found no diminution in the Regents chairman's support. Allen Schwait's 16th floor office overlooked Baltimore's resplendent, new Inner Harbor, its World Trade Center, the National Aquarium and Harborplace, the shopping and food pavilions fashioned by developer James Rouse. Slaughter, with a view of the harbor panorama, concentrated on Schwait, who leaned back in his heavy brown rocker to listen.

A tall, raw-boned former lacrosse player who had immersed himself in higher education, Schwait was a partner in one of Maryland's leading law firms, Frank, Bernstein, Conaway & Goldman. His friend, Stephen Sachs, was the state attorney general and also a candidate that year for the Democratic gubernatorial nomination. After June 19, 1986, Schwait saw himself as the employer of a coach who had ordered someone to clean up a crime scene. If tolerating that kind of behavior was the price of big-time college basketball, Schwait wanted out. He was angry. Driesell, he told Slaughter, was not the kind of leader Maryland needed, especially not during a time when it was asking the world to recognize its excellence as a teaching and research institution. How could you justify having someone like that in charge of young men? he wondered.

"What about the cost?" Slaughter asked, probing to see the depth of the commitment. "His ass is gone," Schwait said.

In the middle of the Driesell negotiations, Athletic Director Dull resigned.

Slaughter had decided to fire him if he did not. At a press conference held October 8, the chancellor read a statement of praise and regret, though privately he thought Dull had been a disaster. Dull would remain at the university for one year as Slaughter's special assistant, at a salary of $77,000.

Being athletic director, Dull told the reporters, was like running a relay race: "You run as fast as you can, then you pass the baton to someone else."

Slaughter found Dull to be a sound analyst of problems -- but completely paralyzed when it came to making decisions. During the discussions of the chancellor's task force, Dull concluded that Driesell should go, but he would accept no role in telling him of that decision or explaining to the community of boosters, alumni, and fans.

Dull was an honored son of the university -- at one and the same time an island of enlightenment in the athletic department, and an example of how in-bred the department had become. A champion javelin thrower as an undergraduate at Maryland, he graduated from the university's law school, and came to the Maryland athletic department in 1976 after several years of practicing law. Jim Kehoe, his former track coach, hired him, just as he had hired Driesell. Kehoe also hired Tom Fields to run the Terrapin Club. It was Kehoe's department, and when he retired in 1981, he passed the baton to Dull, who was widely regarded as intelligent and personable.

But he was not the strong manager his mentor and predecessor had been. When Kehoe left, some at Maryland believed Driesell lost his balance wheel. Kehoe could handle him. Dull, they thought, could not.

Slaughter himself noticed that Dull did not attend a single basketball game one year. Dull, it seemed, didn't particularly like his job, which was astonishing to Fields and others. They could not comprehend why anyone would not love it. But Dull did not enjoy cultivating boosters. He told associates he found too many of the players selfish and undisciplined. And he was completely stymied by the need (and inability) to improve Byrd Stadium and Cole Field House. In the spring of 1986, as he was pondering a change, he asked Slaughter to dinner to talk about the future. "I wanted a little career counseling," he said later.

Athletic directors needed tremendous energy and numerous skills, ranging across complex fields -- marketing, advertising, law, educational advising, fund-raising. Nevertheless, it was one of the jobs Terrapin Clubbers liked to say athletes could aspire to, even if, as Governor Mandel had said, they couldn't pass botany.

By outward appearances, Dull was doing well. He had been mentioned as a candidate for the athletic director's position at Arizona State University, Ohio State University, and the University of Southern California. From the outside, he seemed to be confident and in control.

But on the College Park campus and among some of the boosters, his stewardship of the athletic operation and its $9 million annual budget was suspect. The department had no long-term financial plan, according to Vice Chancellor Gilmour and others. The department was fat with hangers-on. Under Dull's loose rein, Gilmour said, the football program quietly ballooned to costs approaching an NFL franchise. The football and basketball coaches got whatever they wanted.

One day in 1985, Dull had gone to see Gilmour. "I think we're going to have about a $400,000 deficit this year," he told him. Gilmour blanched.

"Dick," he said, "we have to discuss this right now."

"Don't get excited," Dull said, "we'll take care of it." Gilmour wanted to take care of it then. He wanted to see a plan.

"They were living from bonus to bonus," said Gilmour. "They were successful in both football and basketball -- going to the NCAA tournament almost every year and getting frequent bowl invitations, all of which brought them hundreds of thousands of dollars at the end of most seasons. That pattern and the generous television contracts that came their way in the early 1980s kept them safe from the perils of having no plan." Gilmour did not intervene.

"It would have taken a lot of energy to get to the bottom of it," he said. "We would have been marching in there as management specialists. And, in fact, the deficit evaporated. They were always able to come out okay," the vice chancellor said. "In retrospect, we should have pushed harder. But we had real emergencies on our hands. The stuff that isn't urgent gets pushed out." Athletic income paid for nothing on the campus, so there was less urgency about what seemed like meddling or at best fine-tuning. And, again, the momentum drove the system comfortably over the rough spots.

It was in that atmosphere of separateness and isolation that Dull renegotiated the final version of Driesell's 1984 contract. Slaughter had seen and approved the basic 10-year contract. When the coach demanded additional pay and benefits, Dull not only handled the negotiations, Slaughter said, but approved the new pact without showing it to him or to the university's lawyers.

Dull's popularity rested in part on his hiring of football coach Ross, an extremely popular choice among the boosters. A former NFL assistant coach, Ross brought to Maryland a pro-style offense that contrasted sharply with his predecessor's off-tackle, no-pass approach. Dull also put academic counseling units in place.

But in his own personal relay race, Dull was matched against superior forces, the foremost being Lefty. Lefty directed Lefty. When Slaughter responded to coaches' appeals for special athletic admissions, he was criticized for allowing Ross and Driesell to go around the athletic director. But Slaughter thought that, in Dull, there was no one to go around.

In 1985, Dull's assistant, Randy Hoffman, worked with Vice Chancellor Kirwan and Admissions Director Linda Clements to develop new academic standards for high school recruits. Hoffman often handled unpleasant jobs like this one, jobs that tended to put limits on the coaches.

"The concept was to go back and see what we had done and get criteria together," Hoffman said, "something the university was comfortable with and the Athletic Department could live with. The university was acting responsibly, finally. Problems on the basketball program had been apparent for some time. But Lefty had never been told that things were going to change. He always got the guys he wanted one way or another."

Regarding the chancellor, he said, "There was nothing malicious in it. He wasn't trying to win national championships. A lot of the athletes were black and Dr. Slaughter became involved in recruitment. He would meet them. And he developed a relationship with them and felt a need to try to assist them."

New admission standards, said Hoffman, were worked out against a stark reality: "The pressure was to win and produce and be solvent -- and to go out and do it again the next year. You had to break even, and to do that you had to have your best athletes playing." So, how stringent could standards be?

Hoffman, Kirwan and Clements finished the new admissions guidelines and passed them on to Dull, who insisted that he would brief Ross and Driesell. But, according to Hoffman, "Ross never got the presentation. Driesell never got it. Ross went out recruiting on the basis of the earlier standards. When it came time to present his new class to admissions, Ross had a bunch of kids who were not admissible. He lost his mind. He wanted to go to the chancellor. I'm in a shouting contest with him. He wanted to take an ad in *The Post*."

Despite the feeling that Dull did not like his job, his forced departure might well have swept through the athletic department like a flash fire. But Driesell said he didn't think the athletic director's departure would affect him at all.

Slaughter came out of the Bias crisis convinced a strong, smart athletic director was indispensable. In fact, ingredients for disaster were: a) big expensive program; b) flamboyant coach; c) weak athletic director; d) inattentive president; and e) powerful boosters. Any one of these factors could be enough to bring a program down.

For his decision to force Driesell out, Slaughter continued to shape and strengthen support. The Regents were with him. But John Toll, president of the state university system, resisted.

Although he assured Slaughter that he supported the decision to let Driesell go, Toll was telling Driesell and Driesell's backers that he supported the coach, Slaughter said.

With Toll well aware that contract-breaking negotiations were under way, Toll and his wife, herself a big Driesell fan, put on what amounted to a testimonial for the coach at their on-campus house; it was held before a football game in late October.

Maryland's state comptroller, Louis Goldstein -- a $3,000-a-year Terrapin Club member and the only man in Maryland more politically busy than Toll -- served as master of ceremonies. The guests included Terrapin Club members who were urging Lefty to hang in there and looking for ways to help him.

Slaughter thought the university's integrity and financial stability -- if not its soul -- were at risk, and here was Toll undermining his effort. There was, he thought, at least as much potential furor inherent in keeping Driesell as there was in firing him. Either way, the cost was extremely high. And, either way, Toll's support was important.

But Toll considered Lefty untouchable. He told Tim Gilmour he thought most legislators and Terp boosters would object if the coach were fired. The university's agenda would become secondary to the fate of the basketball coach -- as if that were not already the case.

Toll insisted that Lefty had run an exemplary program. What other coach, he asked, had produced two Rhodes Scholars, McMillen at Maryland in 1974 and Danny Carrell at Davidson in 1962?

Toll went to Regents Chairman Schwait and urged him to keep Driesell. But Schwait was determined to have change. He had predicted Toll would bow to Lefty and Lefty's claque. He was not surprised to find him making extraordinary appeals on his behalf.

At the game following the Tolls' party for him, Driesell stood at the entrance to the stadium near a series of plaques commemorating Maryland's many football bowl appearances. The marching band swung past and students filed down to their seats while Driesell shook hands, lobbying Terrapin Clubbers and others as they streamed in for the football game. This was the counterattack, the "Cornered Lefty" defense.

Throughout the fall, Lefty assured everyone he would be the coach when the Terps started practice for the 1986-87 season. With Slaughter's acquiescence, and Williams's go-ahead, he was allowed to make one more big public push for his job. He was going to show the world his graduation statistics one more time.

He called a press conference for selected reporters.

"If you know me," he told the reporters, "when I get my back up against a wall, that's when I fight my hardest. I like to be in a corner. Put me in a corner, and I'll get out of it. I always have."

He stood at an easel, whacking it with an orange-tipped pointer, as he laid out the figures. Bias was left out of the averages. "He wouldn't ever need a degree," Driesell said.

But James Bias offered a different view on the value of a degree to a basketball player. "If you don't have an education, and you're a millionaire, you and your money will part quickly. You have to count your own money. You can't have someone else count your money for you," he said. Had Len failed, somehow, to get a pro contract, what would he have had to show for his years at Maryland? The "D" he got in Professor Joyce's black literature course? The cartoons he had drawn of Driesell and the "Divine Dunk"? Counselor Whittemore's confidence he could have been a competent student had he been given a chance?

Prior to his last big push to stay on, Driesell polled his players: Did they want him to remain as coach? They did. Driesell announced the results as if they were an outpouring of unsolicited and heartfelt support, support without coercion.

Leaving no stone unturned, he rallied the players' parents. A contingent of mothers and fathers went to Slaughter's home one evening to plead Driesell's case. The parents had seen the team's academic record, but they liked Lefty and felt they owed him something. The dream, Slaughter thought, had everyone mesmerized. Having watched Driesell escape the corner time after time, Wayne

Curry said, the parents may have been convinced that he would survive again, and if they didn't support him, their sons would pay.

A week later, Dorfman's Task Force on the Academic Achievement of Student Athletes submitted its report. Reporters struggled to pirate a copy, hanging around duplicating machines and draping themselves over Roz Hiebert to cadge an advance look at the document. For the most part, they failed.

The task force made Driesell the clear target, though it did not name him. He had appealed to recruits largely on the basis of the playing time they could expect at Maryland and the publicity they would get in pursuit of their professional basketball aspirations, it suggested.

"For some coaches, there is an implicit set of priorities: athletic performance first, academic performance second and the personal development of their students last, mostly as it has an impact on playing. The athletes are under such pressure that they do not have time to learn about time management and to establish a relationship with counselors or advisors which could make them receptive to self-examination."

What would any of the players, Bias included, have learned had they been more inclined toward self-examination?

Ideally, of course, universities exist to provide an atmosphere in which young minds grow and gain understanding. A student athlete would learn to count his money. A student athlete would stay to hear the words of Gwendolyn Brooks. He evaluated his life. That effort could be a life-and-death matter. Athletes, the task force said, had too little time for any of these pursuits.

"All your time was their time," Veal had said.

The report concluded, as the players concluded, that athletes in big-time programs were different from other students. They needed much more than help in the classroom. They had problems that universities were reluctant to acknowledge, lest the facade of the student-athlete ideal become even more transparent. Athletes, coaches, boosters, and university administrators such as Slaughter knew that athletes often needed conversational and social skills. Their personal well-being and confidence, their readiness to be students, depended on the development of these skills. The player in sweats might have kept his job at Fred Frederick's auto dealership if he had been adequately prepared. Conversational deficits were particularly crippling for young people who were asked by the press and others to have so much poise. Because they had so much less time, they also needed more self-discipline than the average college student. If a student athlete was hundreds of miles away from home, he needed even more care and solicitude.

The magnitude of these personal, academic and social problems was so great that some of the task force members concluded no university could realistically expect to cope with them -- and would attempt to at its peril. The entire big-time athletic enterprise rested, ultimately, on young people who were even more vulnerable than most college students, and Maryland was doing a poor job of addressing their concerns. Later, the National Collegiate Athletic Association's study of minority athletes provided even more support for the task force findings.

"Ultimately the integrity of the athletic program depends on the people who run the university and the Department of Intercollegiate Athletics, especially the coaches," the Dorfman task force report said. "When these individuals emphasize the primacy of academics and acknowledge that revenues and win-loss records are only of secondary importance compared to our primary mission -- education -- then we will be able to maintain our integrity as an academic institution. Otherwise, we will always be on the wrong side of a very troublesome and dangerous situation, fraught with scandal and corruption. At a university, winning is not the only thing."

The final contract-breaking session was held at Edward Bennett Williams's office in Washington. At the session, Slaughter half expected to see Driesell explode into a rage and fly off to the newspapers and the Terrapin Club with a harangue about how mistreated he had been. Well he might have, Babby says.

"The university was hoping he would be indicted," Babby said. "That would have made it easier for them. They were throwing gasoline on the thing. They decided to make Lefty the scapegoat."

At a large conference table, Slaughter and Driesell sat down to hear what the lawyers would propose. The two antagonists said nothing to each other.

Williams again floated the idea that Driesell might remain as coach for one more year. That plan, he said, would save the school some money. It would save face for Driesell. It was not what Slaughter wanted, but he might have accepted it.

But Driesell killed the idea of a transitional year. He knew what a thin remnant of a team remained for the 1986-87 season. Maryland would be inexperienced and under-manned.

Babby says he feared the university would put Driesell in a no-win situation. He would be given the transitional year, but the performance standards would be impossible to meet with such a weakened team. If fired under those circumstances, he would have been without a job, and would have missed the opportunity to get what Babby regarded as fair compensation.

The circumstances left Driesell in an awkward position. He had recruited all these players he was now leaving. He had polled them to see if they wanted him to stay at Maryland -- and, according to him, they did. But now he was saying he wouldn't stay for another year because he couldn't look good with them. If he wasn't wanted, he declared proudly, he would leave. He had proved one thing: He had pull. In one sense, he fired himself. Slaughter says the outcome was what he wanted, but he wishes it had been less expensive. An agreement was reached between Driesell and the university that obligated College Park to pay the coach about $150,000 a year for each of the next five years, a massive sum.

But letting go was more difficult for Driesell than perhaps even he imagined. He refused to sign the agreement, couldn't bring himself to sign. Despite his bluster and concern for money, he was Maryland's coach in his own mind no less than in the collective mind of Maryland fans. His lawyers and friends were urging him to move on, but it was not their life.

"He wouldn't admit that his days at Maryland were over," says Schwait.

"He felt he had been wronged and that, by leaving, the world would think the university was right," Babby said.

Driesell arranged for someone to call the Regents chairman with a final appeal.

"He wants one more shot at you," the intermediary said.

"I'm very reluctant," Schwait said, "but if it would move him toward signing the agreement, I will do it on two conditions. I want him to know I am not a court of appeals. This was Slaughter's decision and the Regents support him, even encouraged him to take it. And second, I want a witness."

Schwait asked Frank de Francis, the race track owner and a member of the Regents, to be that witness. De Francis had a number of qualities Schwait needed. He was personable but tough, very persuasive, and on very good terms with William Donald Schaefer, who had won the Democratic primary and was about to become governor of Maryland. Schaefer was close to several influential boosters at College Park -- men who might ask the new governor to save Driesell -- so Schwait wanted some political insulation. De Francis seemed ideal.

The meeting was scheduled for a weekend day at Laurel Race Track, which is located between Baltimore and Washington. Schwait walked into the club house and at the far end of a huge room, over a sea of empty tables, he saw a small group of people. As he got closer, Schwait was surprised to see two women in the group.

Driesell had come with his wife, Joyce, and one of his daughters. Schwait was taken aback.

"Lefty, why are the women here?" he asked.

Driesell said, "When you ruin my life, you ruin theirs, too."

"This could get a little rough," Schwait said to Mrs. Driesell. "Are you sure you want to stay?"

"Absolutely," she said, according to Schwait's recollection.

Driesell thereupon launched into his presentation on graduation rates and the like, complete with the usual charts.

After a time, Schwait said, "Lefty, we are not going to change our minds. We support John Slaughter. It's over. You should sign the agreement."

Driesell resumed his case, but then De Francis spoke.

"Let me tell you something. You've had a good run at Maryland. You've had some good years and some bad ones. But it's over. It's like a good marriage that's breaking up. We're going to terminate your contract. It's time for you to move on."

"He listened to Frank," Schwait says, and agreed to sign.

According to Gilmour, the money was to come from the general campus treasury, not from the sagging athletic department. The policy of self-support had no flexibility when it came to relieving pressure on players, but it had enough to provide a handsome settlement for a coach.

On the morning of October 29, about 200 reporters and cameramen watched Driesell walk to a bank of microphones set up on the varnished floor of the field house. "Looks like we have a pretty good crowd here," he said as he stepped up. "Maybe we should have charged admission." Then, he announced that his 17-year career at Maryland had ended. He said little else.

With his bald head tilted slightly forward, one arm around his wife, Joyce, and a hand held by one of his daughters, Driesell turned and walked out of the building he had filled so faithfully. The Driesell family, its back turned to Cole, thus walked out of Terrapin basketball history. No V-for-victory signs this time. No cheering, though some reporters wept. One writer called the scene Shakespearean. But it may have been too lacking in scope and size to qualify as classical tragedy. Unlike Lear, or even Macbeth, this man seemed never to recognize how he had contributed to his downfall. Or perhaps he could not admit it. He had labored hard for the sport Americans loved without ever having what *Post* sportswriter John Feinstein called "The Moment," something like the day Jim Valvano's N.C. State team beat Houston for the national championship. Arms wind-milling, Valvano had rushed onto the floor, where he fell into a delirious pile of excited players. He had created the paradigm of the victory swoon.

But October 29, 1986, did provide a Moment of sorts for Driesell and for basketball. It was the Moment of a beleaguered and cashiered coach, a coach whose program had come detached from its traditions and its goals -- torn loose by its own lapses, by drugs, by death, and by scandal. Driesell had a memorable basketball "Moment of the Eighties" -- a moment of personal humiliation and travail visited upon him by the system he served, by fate, and by his own aggressively foreshortened view of life. Poignantly photographed, Driesell's departure was seen repeatedly on television and in local newspapers -- mostly as a story suggesting that he had been a scapegoat. In a sense, he had become, in that moment, even more representative of his sport, grimly, definitely certain of his rectitude.

To the very end, Slaughter worried that Driesell would commit rhetorical kamikaze, dive-bombing into the university. In his journal for that day, a relieved Slaughter wrote: "The Lefthander held a press conference this morning to announce his resignation. He took no questions."

Driesell had said that he still woke up mornings with Bias on his mind. But when a television reporter asked him what he had learned during the travail since then, he put it all in tough-guy, financial terms: "Get yourself a good contract," he said.

Driesell had been carried along by the momentum. He *was* the momentum. And for a time it was a glorious ride. Now he had been elevated to the level of scapegoat. He was beyond reproach, a victim of the ultimate bad call.

At Duke University, Driesell's alma mater, the student newspaper ran an editorial under the headline: "Charles G. Scapegoat." Driesell was taking the fall for Slaughter and the rest of the university, it said. "The University of Maryland is making Driesell a scapegoat for problems it likely never would have addressed if Len Bias were alive.

"John Slaughter, chancellor of Maryland and a leader of the NCAA debate on academic scandal, is as much responsible as Driesell was for success in the gym."

Ira Berkow, *The New York Times* columnist, wrote, "Driesell was only doing his job. His concern was not to get students through their academics. Driesell was hired by the university 17 years ago to win basketball games. He did. He elevated the won-lost record of the University of Maryland -- if not the integrity of the university. . . ."

Even if he had been tied to the university by an ill-conceived agreement, the *Times* commentator suggested, he should have been saved. By this reckoning, Slaughter's actions were compromised by a predecessor's decision to hire Driesell and by his own temporary and incomplete endorsement of the status quo.

"I got letters from people who said Coach Driesell did exactly what he was hired to do and that was fill Cole Field House. I looked at those letters, a whole boxcar full of them," Slaughter said, "and I've thought about that argument. It's made me realize what a terrible thing it is for people to think that a coach's job is to fill the field house. That's giving in to almighty athletics in the worst possible way."

Not even Driesell bought the full field house defense. He knew he was expected to produce graduates. He kept the records. He sold himself as an educator, guaranteeing James and Lonise Bias that their son would graduate. He had to have the graduation numbers for the show-and-tell of recruiting. It was all tied together: If you didn't graduate players, you couldn't recruit, and so on.

Some of Driesell's defenders said Slaughter made him the scapegoat for Bias's death. Slaughter had specifically and vehemently resisted doing that.

"There's nothing Lefty could have done about Lenny Bias, at least certainly nothing he could have done that day," Slaughter said. "Whether or not there was something he could have done three years earlier, that's a reasonable question to ask, a tough question to ask."

It was, of course, the central, most penetrating question. Slaughter asked it of himself again and again that summer of 1986. Was it possible that a different atmosphere might have saved Len Bias in some untraceable way? He did not exonerate himself.

Now, he demanded the coach's authority -- knew he had to have it -- in the campaign to convince athletes that a university has something important to offer, something that literally could save their lives. People still argued that athletics had to be preserved because they built character, but they wanted Driesell because he was outrageous and provocative, a showman. Slaughter concluded that these qualities were not always compatible with being a coach. A choice had to be made.

On the afternoon of Driesell's resignation, Slaughter leaned back a bit in the chair behind his desk and lit a cigar. He was not indulging in a smug, Red Auerbach, we-buried-you victory cigar. He was celebrating survival. Concluding the Driesell episode gave him some satisfaction and the prospect of respite.

"The story is over," he said.

Chapter 11

"Sack Slaughter"

The story was not over, and Slaughter knew it. He had fired a legend.

The reaction to Driesell's departure helps to show why change came so slowly to the big-time revenue sports. The coaches, the players, the university presidents, the writers, and the fund-raisers are all cornered. They are bound together in a whirl of culpability and rationalization.

Coaches are encouraged to be chair-throwing, growling schemers more attuned to the needs of boosters, fans, and their own fortunes than to their teams. The players are too heavily invested in their dreams. (Ray Gillian said white kids in America imagine they can become president -- but plan for something more prosaic. Black kids dream of the NBA, he said, and have no alternative plan.) Boosters are sometimes superannuated adolescents -- with power. Sportswriters and columnists are hypocrites, feasting on victims they have helped to create and unwilling to give anyone a break. Fans are happy with bread and circuses. The university presidents and chancellors are politically neutered, enslaved by the emotion that drives sports and by the real or imagined need for sports revenue.

If a campus is overtaken by a scandal that seemingly threatens the big-time system, the chancellor is disarmed and made laughable as a reformer. He is forever a part of the system's corruption, a person without conscience or courage. He is disqualified from making suggestions for change. Before the scandal, he was an academic who didn't really understand sports. After the fall, he can never establish his bona fides.

Now, Maryland's chancellor was about to replace the legendary Driesell with a high school coach.

Two days after the forced resignation, Slaughter hired Robert Wade, the infamous-at-College Park coach of Baltimore's Dunbar High School. Together, Slaughter and Wade made history. Through Slaughter's appointment, Wade became the ACC's first black coach. In the late 1960s, Maryland had become the first ACC team to have a black player. It had gone on to continue the cycle, hiring the conference's first black chancellor and its first black basketball coach.

Slaughter had contacted Wade two months before, in early September, even as the immediate sports world waited to learn of his decision on Driesell. Ron Shapiro, the Baltimore lawyer and agent, had urged Slaughter to consider Wade if Lefty's job came open. The chancellor and Wade met for lunch in Baltimore.

Slaughter had heard that Wade was a disciplinarian, something he thought Maryland needed desperately. A coach who respected his players as human beings would show his respect by making demands, by having substantial expectations. Slaughter wanted a coach who would be as tough on academics as James Bias had thought Driesell would be when he sent his son to College Park.

Under Wade's leadership, the Poets of Dunbar, named in honor of the black writer, Paul Lawrence Dunbar, were one of the most successful high school basketball teams in the nation with a record of 272-24. During Wade's 11 years at Dunbar, the Poets won nine local conference championships and three national championships; between 1981 and 1985, his team went 119-1.

Wade conducted his own study hall. He enforced manners in the hallways. A reporter visiting the school one day saw Wade grab a player who had been rude to a teacher, walk him back to the scene of the offense, and make him apologize. By 1987, the coach looked more like a former middle guard, a stocky though still agile man, a physical presence who got the attention of his players.

"I thought he was the kind of guy we needed to deal with the players you frequently get in a college program," Slaughter said. "We needed someone in there who could grab hold of that situation immediately and break that team out of the mold it was in."

Wade grew up in Baltimore. He went to Dunbar himself, playing under William F. "Sugar" Cain, who had been his father surrogate. In 1967, after college football at Morgan State University (a black school in Baltimore), he was drafted by the Baltimore Colts. He played for four NFL teams in all, the Pittsburgh Steelers in 1968, the Washington Redskins in 1969, and the Denver Broncos in 1970 and 1971. When a shattered wrist ended his playing career, Wade returned to Dunbar, to succeed Sugar Cain, and to become at least as large a figure in the lives of Baltimore black athletes as his mentor had been.

In Wade, Slaughter had hired someone who knew the city streets, the inner-city schools, and the grind of professional sports. And he was an outsider. Though Baltimore is less than 45 minutes from College Park, Wade was at least another solar system away from its basketball program and the forces that sustained it.

At Maryland, Wade became one of the few black coaches in big-time college basketball, a game dominated by black players. In examining the sports where blacks participated in large numbers at predominantly white colleges -- football, men's and women's basketball, track and baseball -- Richard Lapchick of the Center for Study on Sports in Society found, in 1987, that blacks held about 9 percent of the head coaching jobs and even fewer of the assistant coaching positions. The second figure was more damning; it suggested that blacks were not even on the coaching ladders.

"I've often said that if higher education were graded on what it has done in terms of affirmative action," Slaughter said, "it would get an F."

Sports offered some of the strongest images of racial harmony and progress in American society. People like Harry Edwards, the California sociologist who first compared black American athletes to Roman gladiators, and Slaughter himself, worried that blacks' prominence in professional sports invited the conclusion that they were progressing rapidly throughout society.

Universities, of course, knew the truth. According to the U.S. Department of Education, blacks held 1.56 percent of the 470,673 university faculty positions in 1987. Slaughter had been brought to College Park, in part, to prove that Maryland would not tolerate barriers to education for any minority group. There were too few black students, too few black graduates and too few black faculty members. Slaughter came to Maryland to change that. His task force on student athletes had pointed out that, while many of the revenue sports were populated heavily by black players, there were no black head coaches. Perhaps, the task force suggested, there was something a black coach could bring to a program that would stabilize and support young men, some of them far from home in stressful situations.

Driesell had been hired to win ball games. Slaughter was hired to raise the level of black participation at the student and faculty level. He had done it. And now he was doing it in the athletic department as well. He was doing what he had been hired to do, and while that argument was used to defend Driesell, it would not work as well for Slaughter in the hiring of Wade.

But Slaughter was not simply hiring a coach.

Given the importance of sport in American life, its role in the integration of American society, Slaughter's decision to hire Wade ranked with his own appointment as chancellor at Maryland. He continued the process of bringing blacks into positions denied them by others. His obligation, he thought, was to change thinking, and to do that sometimes required changing people.

When Slaughter was head of the National Science Foundation, he was careful to revise the speaking schedule prepared for him by his aides, who thought he should focus on the name schools. He frequently penciled in dates at the historically black colleges and universities. There he hoped to stimulate more interest in engineering and the sciences. Now at Maryland he could continue the same sort of consciousness-raising, in a field where many more people would notice.

"We must be willing to take risks when the gains can be significant," he had said in his speeches.

Since the firing of Driesell, Slaughter had undergone no metamorphosis of style, no sudden speeding up of his personal decision-making process. Yet he relished the shock value of what he was about to do. On his way to Baltimore, where he would introduce Wade at a press conference, he was exultant. He had not been so happy in months. Sportswriters and boosters had said he was too slow, too methodical, too much the engineer.

Now he would show them some speed.

"He loved the drama of it. He absolutely loved it," says Gilmour. "He was sure he was right. And he loved the speed. As we drove over there, he was asking rhetorically, 'Was that one quick enough for you?' It was a wild turnaround."

The Wade news swept through Dunbar High, across the street corners and practice fields of black East and West Baltimore, and through the 20-story housing project buildings where laundry hangs on the chain link fences lining the balconies. Bob Wade was going to coach at Maryland. "Flaky" was going to College Park. As big and menacing as he was, Wade was a graceful athlete -- like a snowflake, someone had suggested long ago. Now Flaky was going to replace Lefty.

In Baltimore, the possibility that Wade might coach at Maryland was not a dream. It was too remote for dream status. At College Park, black faculty members such as Noel Myricks were elated and incredulous. "I don't know if I would have had the courage," Myricks wrote in a letter thanking the chancellor.

The profound surprise that greeted Wade's appointment showed Slaughter again how little faith the black community had that a black candidate would get a fair shot. After his son's death, James Bias charged that the university was a white institution that actually enjoyed denying degrees to blacks. Jeff Baxter thought the academic advisers, without testing them or determining their wishes and talents, assigned black players to certain classes because they were black and presumably incapable of handling the work. Slaughter himself thought the black players were stymied at Maryland and other universities, purposefully or not, by an over-reliance on SAT scores.

While the Wade news was uplifting the black community, it slamdunked the boosters and the sportswriters. Chancellor Slaughter had spent five months getting rid of Driesell, they said, and now, in less than two days, he had hired a high school coach from Baltimore. A Baltimore newspaper columnist called him "Lightning," a name that had some Amos 'n' Andy overtones. Too fast, too slow. Slaughter couldn't seem to get it right.

"I think the reporters were a little peeved because they hadn't guessed what I was doing," Slaughter said. "They all thought we would name a temporary coach. I thought that was the worst thing in the world I could have done. This thing would have been hanging around my neck for months until I hired a permanent replacement. We just couldn't afford any more time on basketball."

At College Park and among its family of supporters, Wade had been no less than an enemy. For years, he had waged the equivalent of war against Driesell, blocking him from the talent in Baltimore, and, worse, steering players to Georgetown, Clemson, Nevada-Las Vegas, Syracuse, South Carolina, and other programs. Driesell, saying he liked Wade, declined to comment on their disagreements.

At Cole Field House, the announcement of Wade's appointment launched another shock wave, almost as stunning as the death of Len Bias. This man Wade, who had sent his stars to play for John Thompson at Georgetown or to Lefty's ACC rivals, this man who had hurt Maryland over the years, was now going to be its coach.

Terrapin Clubbers reached by the newspapers were outraged.

"I damn near fell out of my seat," said one member. The job of head coach at Maryland was one of the best basketball jobs in the country, and would have attracted many top applicants. If a high school coach were to be hired, said others, it should have been Morgan Wootten, the coach at DeMatha High School. He was a Maryland graduate. His record at DeMatha was at least as good as Wade's and extended over a longer period. But Wootten was not interviewed -- something Slaughter wished later he had done. He hadn't called Wootten, he said, because he had made up his mind. Wootten was a part of the old Terrapin network. Slaughter wanted unmistakable change.

Before he announced Wade's appointment, Slaughter called John Thompson, the black coach at Georgetown -- also no favorite around College Park. He wanted to check references, particularly the stories about Wade's recruiting rules, that had denied Driesell access to Baltimore players. Thompson thought Wade's rules had been reasonable and fair. Easy for him to say, perhaps, since he had done quite well in Baltimore, landing players like Reggie Williams. Slaughter's call to Thompson was particularly galling to the Terrapin clan because their favorites -- Wootten and Driesell -- had feuded with the Georgetown coach for years.

Then Slaughter called Bobby Cremmins, the coach at Georgia Tech. Cremmins considered Wade a fine coach who cared about his players. But Cremmins had another idea. Why didn't Slaughter consider one of Cremmins's assistants for the job? Slaughter thanked him and pushed on to his next call.

George Raveling, the head coach at the University of Southern California, had been an assistant at Maryland under Driesell; he told the chancellor that Wade would be a good choice, particularly given Slaughter's objectives: tightening academic standards and creating an atmosphere of higher expectations. Still, said Raveling, a black Division I coach, he would be interested in the job if Slaughter could fill it on a temporary basis.

UNC's Dean Smith told Slaughter he thought Wade would begin immediately to restore credibility to the Maryland program. He admired Wade's independence, Smith added. And he said Wade's recruiting rules were designed to protect the young men and were not unreasonable.

At first, none of Slaughter's assistants liked the idea of hiring a high school coach. The job was too demanding. The pressure at Maryland would be too intense. But Slaughter was stepping away from his usual deliberate style and hoping that others would buy the idea without coercion. He took Chuck Sturtz, his finance man, to Baltimore to meet Wade. Sturtz, he thought, was impressed. And then he announced his choice.

When the Terrapin Club members heard he had talked with Thompson, there was outrage. Maryland might well play Georgetown at some point. Wouldn't Thompson just love to have a less talented coach opposing him? Thompson could hardly be objective, they charged, since he had landed so many of Wade's best players.

Race was thought to be the motivating factor for Slaughter, but the idea that Thompson would want to see another black coach making it, or that he would have warned a chancellor who was black about taking a chance on a questionable talent, was not mentioned. Even if the two men did not coach against each other, the grumbling went on, they were certain to recruit against each other. On this last point, though, Wade was a prize for Maryland: He would presumably have no peer as a recruiter in Baltimore. Moreover, as much as they cherished the history-making nature of their appointment, Schwait and Slaughter said they were thinking about the Baltimore advantage when they hired him. Winning and money were never far from any decision in big-time college sports, even in the midst of a reform movement.

Almost immediately, Slaughter was accused of racism, of hiring a black coach quickly to forestall the possibility of having to hire a white one.

"I think the way he handled the Lefty thing was terrible," said Fred Frederick, the auto dealer with the Confederate tableau on his wall. "And hiring Wade . . . it appeared to be racist. It really did appear to be racist." Frederick was particularly upset that Slaughter had not spoken to Morgan Wootten. "That was a no-brainer. You can't accuse him of being a mental giant. That's what upset people more than anything else. He could have done the same thing but in a different way. He could've massaged people and gone on. But he up and did it."

Slaughter knew how the club would react, and said he didn't much care. But he may have been unprepared for the ferocity of the response.

"I see you have hired a big ugly nigger as basketball coach," wrote one alumnus who signed his letter, "one in your own image and likeness without even interviewing Mr. Wootten of DeMatha -- Shame on you! And I thought you was a good ole Uncle Tom . . . You were in your chair when all that drug shit was going down -- How come you don't take the fall? It was your responsibility black boy. It happened during your watch. So get your black ass out of that chair and let a decent white boy reestablish order. By the way you and Wade are two of the ugliest niggers I have ever seen. P.S. We need a white ass in your seat."

Slaughter had encountered racial bigotry before in his life. But the vitriol released by his appointment of Wade was chilling.

"If I had been white and I hired a black coach," he said, "I'd have been called a liberal. Because I'm black, I'm a racist."

Both Hotsy Alperstein and Judge Meloy acknowledged that, even before his hiring of Wade, there had been a racial element in the criticism of Slaughter. Meloy said some people did not think a black man could run the university. Alperstein said members of the Terrapin Club elite wanted Driesell to stay because they knew he would find some decent white players. With Driesell, they were sure the Terps would not be an all-black team -- like John Thompson's teams at Georgetown. They were sure Lefty would preserve some balance.

Slaughter found himself in the eye of an emotional hurricane, isolated and targeted now by the aimless forces of irrationality and hatred that seemed to find direction in controversy. At first, he tried to keep it contained in his office. Until late in the fall, he said nothing about the letters -- as if acknowledging their existence would give license to others. "We are not amused by your racist tactics," one writer said. "One night we're going to get you by God." One of his secretaries sent this message into his office with a note attached: "It disturbs me to put this type of letter through, but Tim said you should be aware of it."

The chancellor imagined he could change the hearts of people who propelled this sort of hatred at him, if only he could meet them. He had occasionally done that in his life. So, he invited a few of the letter writers to his office.

One of his correspondents was so grateful to be brought into the university chancellor's presence that his anger subsided almost completely. Slaughter found the man somewhat frightening in appearance and manner, so he was happy to have won him over. Another critic, an advertising executive from Baltimore and a member of the Terrapin Club, seemed to lose the edge of his animosity as well; seemingly, he understood the bigger picture that Slaughter tried to present.

During a conference with members of the editorial board at *The Washington Post*, Slaughter said that no black American believes racism is dead. And he mentioned the mail he had received. When his comments were reported in the press, he got another letter.

"Understand you are complaining about racist mail. Want to see a racist, look in the mirror. Couldn't hire Wootten, wrong color [Wootten is white]. Heeded no advice except Thompson's ..."

Gilmour thought people were looking for the most hurtful thing they could say. He and the chancellor had expected it.

"You go into these things and you know people are going to come after you," he said. "He chose to take this on. He wanted to make it an opportunity. It's just part of the territory. If you're strong, you don't get terribly paranoid about it. You just know those things will happen. They went for what they thought would really hurt him. I think it affected him. He saved a few of those letters. But he's been through so much of that throughout his life, it's not really a way to get to him."

In the midst of all this, as the volume of criticism rose, Slaughter ran into Adrian Branch's father, who shook his hand and told him, "You are either the dumbest nigger I ever met or the most courageous."

At least the football team was playing well.

The Terrapins of 1986 had a national ranking under Bobby Ross. But the coach seemed unusually restless. He spent the fall fretting about his standing at Maryland, and, of course, demanding a vote of confidence -- a statement that he was an exemplary man with an exemplary program, a man the university wished to endorse and to keep as its football coach.

He got an endorsement from the task force. Its report suggested that he was doing relatively well. But it was not enough for Ross. He kept demanding. And he had as many supporters as Driesell.

"If Ross goes," said Maryland State Senate President Mike Miller that fall, "Slaughter is in a world of trouble."

Almost from the day of Bias's death, Ross, like Driesell, complained of being embarrassed. Like Lefty, Ross had harassed the admissions office for special consideration when athletes he coveted fell below the acceptable admissions standards. But as the crisis continued, he complained -- with some justification -- that he didn't know what the rules were and couldn't recruit because he was never sure what level of academic achievement was required.

Ross may have suspected that whatever happened to Dull or Lefty might happen to him. Schwait, for example, found him almost as difficult to tolerate as Driesell. The atmosphere was changing, and Ross knew it. If life had been difficult for a recruiter before, it was going to become more so. "He wanted to be the judge of who could be admitted to Maryland," said Schwait. And he said his judgment, looking at a young man, was admission standard enough, the Regents chairman said with amazement.

Some sportswriters thought Ross was using the turmoil as an excuse to start moving away. Coaches, boosters, and other observers assumed that higher admission standards were inevitable and would keep Maryland teams out of competition for national titles. The adoption of Proposition 48 was said to be robbing teams of speed; the new NCAA rule required players to have a C average in 11 core courses, or a combined score of at least 700 on the SATs.

Ross and other coaches, Slaughter thought, bought into this thinking in a way that held expectations down *and* demeaned athletes. Instead of accepting higher standards and building them into a strength for the program, coaches whined and struggled against them.

But, the boosters thought, surely Ross wouldn't be made to suffer the ills of the basketball program, whatever they were. The boosters didn't want to lose football, too. In the head-rolling atmosphere before the grand jury's report, Slaughter's silence was taken as a vote of no confidence, even when the truth was that the chancellor had not made a decision. Ross's insistent demands for the administration's backing -- raised sympathetically for him by the sports reporters in their stories -- increased the pressure.

Slaughter did not need another prima donna or another crisis. In the summer after Bias died, he wrote to Ross trying to reassure him, telling him that he was proud of his representation of Maryland. The constant public demand for a vote of confidence, Slaughter said, suggested that Ross thought he needed one as much as Driesell did.

"There's no reason for you to put on that shoe," the chancellor said.

Later, though, Ross earned himself a different sort of letter.

In November, during a game against North Carolina at Chapel Hill, there was confusion over how many timeouts had been used by the Tar Heels. The scoreboard showed UNC was out of timeouts, but the official on the field thought one was remaining.

Using the timeout, Carolina got its kicker on the field and won the game with a field goal as the game ended. Immediately, Ross ran looking for the official. TV cameras captured the Maryland coach in hot pursuit, zigzagging through players and fans, gaining on the official. With the chase narrated by an announcer, Ross caught up and clamped his right hand on the official's shoulder. No blows were struck. But they seemed imminent. Once again, Maryland seemed to have a sports figure who had lost control. Instantly, Ross and Slaughter were given another media pummeling. Within days, the chancellor handed Ross a letter of reprimand. The coach had been an exemplary representative of Maryland, but accosting referees was unacceptable, he said.

The Atlantic Coast Conference, supporting the chancellor on this one, suspended Ross for a game. Columnist and Terrapin Club member Robert Novak said the chancellor's reaction was typical of College Park's "pantywaist administrators." Ross's penalty was to be served when the Terps played Clemson University at Baltimore's Memorial Stadium.

The game was a strange, zany spectacle. Neither team had a head coach on the field. A year earlier, several Clemson players had swarmed one of Maryland's defensive backs after the game in South Carolina. For that, Clemson's coach, Dan Ford, was to be suspended during the 1986 game against Maryland. So Ross and Ford, caged lions of the pigskin, paced around in booths above the field as their teams played to a dramatic 13-13 tie.

The game alone was not spectacle enough. At halftime, a small airplane flew over the stadium dragging a banner that said, "SACK SLAUGHTER."

Fred Frederick sat in the stands laughing. People applauded, he said. He thought Slaughter was humiliated. But the chancellor insisted he had been out of his seat at the time, and hadn't seen the airborne attack.

Until then, Slaughter had been content to let the public anger over the Driesell firing play itself out. When he heard what had happened in his absence, Slaughter began to think he had a problem. If people were willing to spend money to embarrass him publicly, maybe there was a real threat. And in fact there was.

A few Terrapin Club members formed a committee to explore ways of deposing him. Former presidents of the club met. Stationery with a Maryland red letterhead was printed. Some members of the club held a rump session to discuss how they might register their unhappiness with Slaughter's stewardship. Jack Heise, the Terrapin Club leader, said some of these men thought they could get Slaughter fired.

"They thought the university should do what they wanted because they gave the money," he said.

According to Hotsy Alperstein, who denied knowing who the movement leaders were, the idea was to urge Maryland's governor-elect, William Donald Schaefer, to fire Slaughter. Schaefer was close to former Governor Mandel. During his campaign, the candidate had been saying that the university was the key to his economic development plan for Maryland, and that sports were an amenity crucial to attracting and retaining business. The role of the Terrapin Club's money, moreover, was only a slight variation of a practice Schaefer had institutionalized in Baltimore: the takeover and subsidization of public functions by private business.

According to Mandel, Schaefer met with the club representatives. "He discussed their problems," he said. "You're talking about big dollars there [club contributions to the university], $2.7 million a year. That's money the state doesn't have to pay out."

Hearing of this activity, Slaughter asked for a meeting of his own with Schaefer. The meeting was arranged by George McGowan, the chief operating officer at Baltimore Gas & Electric Co., who was also a member of the Regents and of the Terrapin Club. A graduate of the engineering school and a former lacrosse player at Maryland, McGowan was a member of the Maryland establishment that had welcomed Slaughter; he had helped make him a member of BG&E's board of directors. As the chief executive officer of a major utility located in Baltimore, McGowan knew Schaefer and the former Baltimore mayor's volcanic moods quite well.

On a cold fall day, the chancellor and John Toll rode to Baltimore. Toll wore a huge Russian fur hat and carried an armload of briefing papers. At the BG&E building, they transferred to McGowan's limousine for the short ride to Schaefer's office.

Spying Toll's baggage, McGowan said, "This meeting is for one purpose only. There's nothing on the agenda but basketball and the way you handled Driesell. It could be tough. He's getting a lot of criticism from the Terrapin Club." Slaughter was grateful for the ground rules. He knew he had to get his own version of events in front of the new governor, a man who made life difficult for people who disagreed with him.

Toll persisted. No, he said, they had to use the opportunity to put important university business in front of the governor-elect. "You don't understand," McGowan said firmly. Toll gave in. And so it was that the governor-elect of Maryland, meeting the chancellor of his state university system's biggest campus for the first time, talked about basketball, a former basketball coach, and nothing else.

Schaefer came into the room wearing one of the grandfatherly cardigan sweaters he favors. His mood, though, was grim.

"I don't like the way you treated Driesell," Schaefer said, according to Slaughter's recollection. "You never told him there were serious problems with his program -- and then you left him in a state of suspended animation when this unfortunate thing happened with Bias."

The chancellor told the governor he had repeatedly warned Driesell that Maryland basketball players had to begin performing in the classroom. During the summer of "suspended animation," he said, he had been following orders from state lawyers and trying to protect the university.

Driesell's lawyer, Edward Bennett Williams, knew exactly what was happening with Lefty from the beginning of the negotiations, Slaughter said. The chancellor said he was not anxious to pay Driesell so handsomely for doing relatively little, and thought that alternative, although unavoidable in the end, was not fair to the taxpayers without a thorough review. With Williams representing Driesell, he said, the Regents had to be concerned about a costly and unpleasant lawsuit. The state's lawyers advised Slaughter that a court battle would be a damaging "nuclear war" -- not the best way to avoid further public relations bruises.

Schaefer well understood the difficulty of bargaining with Williams. As owner of the Baltimore Orioles, Williams had negotiated a stadium lease with Schaefer, when he was still mayor of Baltimore. Williams also had been pressuring the governor-elect to have the state build his club a new stadium, under the implicit threat that he would take the team to another city if it did not.

Schaefer well knew what it was like to be whipsawed by sports and sports figures. He had been humiliated by Robert Irsay, the owner of the Baltimore Colts, who had removed the NFL club from Baltimore and taken them to Indianapolis under cover of darkness. Schaefer had made extraordinary efforts to satisfy Irsay, but to no avail. Whether any of this made a difference -- made him understand Slaughter's travails -- was unclear. But, near the end of the meeting, the subject changed slightly. College Park needed a major public relations effort to recover, Schaefer said. The Bias matter needed to become history.

As the meeting ended, Slaughter handed the governor a book, a glossy, coffee table volume with big pictures of College Park at its best. It was the sort of gesture that Schaefer, himself, liked to make.

"It went a lot better than I thought it would," McGowan told Slaughter as they left the building.

Ten days later, in late November, Slaughter was summoned to appear before the Terrapin Club's board of directors, some of whom were members of the committee that wanted to fire him. Slaughter dutifully responded to the club's summons. Club members were furious, not only over the recent personnel decisions, but over the university's failure to run its athletic department with sufficient attention to its needs as a competitive business.

"The image in the marketplace was that Slaughter had to go," Fred Frederick said later. "He didn't rally the troops. It's got to start with the leaders."

The meeting was held on the campus in the Adult Education Center, a pleasant, rambling building shaded by tall trees. Gilbert DesRoches, Jack Heise's son-in-law and an advertising executive from Baltimore, stood first to deplore the racism that had surfaced. He said he was certain no one in the room that night harbored any racial animosity toward the chancellor, but many were aggrieved by Slaughter's decisions.

The chancellor went through a 90-minute question-and-answer session. When it was over, with Slaughter and Chuck Sturtz, then the acting athletic director, excused, some club members wanted to adjourn to take some private action. But Ralph Frey, the club president that year, said no. Though many Terrapin Club members had been outspokenly critical of Slaughter, the chancellor had an important Terrapin Club ally in Frey, a former member of the Board of Regents and a Slaughter partisan.

"The Terrapin Club's function," he said later, "is to raise money for intercollegiate athletics. Period. We're not to do anything else -- hire or fire, take positions on issues, or send a man to the moon."

Alperstein said it had taken "guts" for Slaughter to appear that night. Others agreed. The pressure on Slaughter began to dissipate after this meeting and the one with Schaefer. Though the club prided itself on being independent from university and athletic department decisions, some members turned in their pins and canceled their ticket subscriptions. But many remained loyal to the school and to the club's director, Tom Fields, and did nothing. Some of those who quit soon thought better of it. Worried about their ACC Tournament tickets, or unwilling to join in further damage to the university, they rejoined.

Schwait, for whom Slaughter worked under state law, said the chancellor was never in any jeopardy with the Regents. The hate mail continued, but there were many messages of praise and encouragement as well.

"Compared to you," wrote former faculty member Ginnie Bourgardez, "Driesell is dross, and the ilk that follow him or berate you are too stupid to see the difference. Don't ever resign. At 75 and a former physical education professor, I know quality when I see it."

"Through your good offices," wrote another professor, "the university has been seen behaving with dignity and according to principle. I thank you for making the university look like a center of enlightenment amid the grim circumstances in which we found ourselves. Although I do not share your expressed regard for Mr. Driesell and have virtually no sympathy for his apparent constituency in the state, I am very proud that he has been treated humanely . . . I feel compelled to express my gratitude for your leadership."

Slaughter emerged from the ordeal having learned something about himself. "I had thicker skin than I thought I had," he said.

But Slaughter had been hurt. Shortly after Driesell was fired, the chancellor shaved his beard, leaving a mustache and only a shadow of the crisis manager's image. He was tired of seeing himself in the newspapers. His friends thought he literally wanted a different identity. He wanted some psychic distance between himself and the basketball-induced turmoil of College Park.

That fall, he gave a talk on leadership to the Bible study class at St. Monica's Parish near College Park.

"God asks each of us, whether we are rich or poor, to accept the condition we find ourselves in and to put our trust in Him," he said. "We must learn to step aside for our egos and let God act through us. I have still not fully learned that lesson. I have learned the humility that comes from facing a tragedy and its resulting consequences."

Before Bias died, the Washington area B'nai B'rith had named Slaughter its "Man of the Year" for 1986. The award was to be presented at a dinner. But suddenly the dinner was canceled. The tickets did not sell. B'nai B'rith officials told Slaughter's assistants that the award would be given to him at some other time. It never was. "It just sort of evaporated. I guess they decided they'd made a mistake. I got the impression that they were embarrassed to give it to me," Slaughter said.

At the same time, honors rolled in for Lefty. He received a certificate of merit from the Maryland House of Delegates and the state Senate. They brought him down to Annapolis and put him in front of both houses, where he was vigorously applauded. Fraternities on the campus honored him, and he was quickly hired to do color commentary on ACC games for the Raycom Sports Network.

And there was a testimonial. No problem with tickets here. More than 400 people crowded into the chandeliered, champagne pink function room at Martin's Crosswinds, a catering hall just outside the Washington Beltway in Prince George's County, not far from College Park. Chief Fastbreaker Emory Harman met everyone at the door wearing his Terrapin red blazer, a white bowler hat, and, of course, a Lefty necktie.

The first speaker was Novak. He spoke as if Terrapin basketball, as they had known it, was finished. Driesell's former players gave him a watch and a video cassette recorder. Wearing a beige ultra-suede jacket, the old Lefthander took a sip of wine each time someone complimented him or criticized the Slaughter administration. The crowd cheered as the coach lifted his glass. He had been keeping his mouth shut, he said, because "They're paying me pretty good. Ed Williams told me, 'You can never get in trouble saying nothing.' Ed's smart. But I'm saying something anyway. You paid $30 a head to be here." He told the Darrell Brown story. Everyone laughed.

And he talked about his new non-coaching job at Maryland as if it were a tremendous joke on the university. "I don't even know what I'm supposed to do," he said. Everyone laughed. He was supposed to be doing something to promote women's basketball, he said. Some of the girls were as good as the boys, he wanted his audience to know. "They've got to pay me for eight years," he went on. "I'm going to collect my money. After eight years, I might think about doing something else. I went to Duke. I'm not too dumb."

When it was over, the crowd walked slowly out of the pink hall, looking slightly disoriented, as if the ACC Tournament had just ended and Maryland had lost the championship game.

The losses continued. At the end of the football season, Ross resigned. He had to leave, he said, to honor his commitment to his players. He had promised them a better stadium, but had been unable to keep the promise. To be faithful to the young men recruited, he reasoned, he was honor-bound to leave.

Maryland now had no athletic director, no football coach, and a controversial new basketball coach. Quickly, Slaughter and the Regents appointed one of Ross's assistants, Joe Krivak, to succeed him. Terrapin Club members were happy with Krivak, but they continued to agitate to get rid of Slaughter.

In his first State of the State address that January, the first formal speech of his governorship, Schaefer gave the Terrapin Club extraordinary prominence. In the speech's final paragraphs, the governor urged a recognition that the club was an important player in the recovery process at Maryland. The Bias matter, he said, should be put in the background, not forgotten entirely, but removed from prominence.

If the governor was trying to get Slaughter's attention, the chancellor says he didn't notice. In his search for a new athletic director, he rejected another Terrapin Club favorite, former Maryland quarterback Jack Scarbath. He chose Lew Perkins, formerly associate AD at the University of Pennsylvania and director of athletics at

Wichita State, one of the most heavily penalized programs in the NCAA before Perkins went in to shut down the football program and otherwise clean house. If there was a message in the appointment of an apparent reformer such as Perkins, Slaughter said, so be it.

Chapter 12

Isolated Incidents

When the State of Maryland went to court against Brian Lee Tribble in May 1987, the nightmare came back.

Bias's friend was charged with possession of cocaine, and possession of cocaine with intent to distribute. Tribble's lawyer, Thomas Morrow, immediately acknowledged that cocaine was present on the night Bias died, but he said it was no big thing on the College Park campus, nothing unusual except that one of the users was a famous basketball player with a million dollar future in the NBA.

Prosecutors referred to Bias during the trial as a "courtesy middleman," someone who supplied cocaine to his friends and teammates at no cost. Famous ballplayers were not only potential customers, it was thought, but potentially good drug dealers; they had so much status among kids who might buy. By its courtesy middleman characterization, the prosecution suggested that Bias himself might have been the supplier of the drug that evening, not the defendant Tribble.

The trial showed why Slaughter had been anxious to avoid a court battle with Driesell: All the pain and embarrassment of the previous summer were replayed. If Bias was a middleman, Tribble's lawyer said, College Park had a lot of them.

Congressman Benjamin L. Cardin, a member of Slaughter's drug task force, observed later that the testimony heard by his panel suggested that illegal drug use was tolerated by lax enforcement and ambiguous policies at practically every level of campus life, from the coaches, to the faculty, to the administration. Those who said Bias's death "could have happened anywhere" were engaging in a foolish and self-deluding rationalization, he said.

Much of what remained of Bias's image as a positive role model was demolished during the trial. Tribble, as presented by his lawyer, was a victim, not only of his own poor judgment but of his friend's fame. Any other alleged offender in similar circumstances, absent the death of a superstar basketball player, would have been dealt with in a way that attracted no attention at all, he said.

As the trial convened for its most conclusive day of testimony -- featuring accounts of the fatal party by Terry Long and David Gregg -- the courtroom filled with television sketch artists, reporters, University of Maryland students, and others. A contractor from Boston on temporary assignment in Maryland leaned against a courtroom wall in his high-top work boots to hear of events that had robbed his Celtics of another great forward, a successor to Larry Bird.

Salome Freeman Howard was a past president of the Charles County chapter of the National Association for the Advancement of Colored People. She attended three of the six days of the trial.

"I was so fond of Bias from seeing him on TV," she said. "I was sort of depressed when he died and angry about the cause of death, that he was using drugs. What made him go that way?" She came for the final arguments wearing a Dallas Cowboys jersey. "My sorrow," she said after the trial, "was that I didn't meet Lefty."

A young woman student at College Park, as gold-bedecked as "Mr. T," came to the trial every day though she had not known Bias. When she had seen him walking to classes on the campus, he seemed so sad. She felt she owed it to him to attend the trial, she said. Jerrod Mustaf, a basketball player and student at DeMatha High School who would go on to play for Maryland and Coach Wade, and his father, Shaar, came to the trial for the educational value. Jerrod, who would leave Maryland after two years to play with the New York Knicks, could barely fold his 6'9" body into one of the varnished oak benches. His knees jammed against the seat back in front of him, he listened impassively as the sullen Long went through his account. Shaar Mustaf said he wanted his son to see what could happen when your fate was decided by others.

Prosecutor Marshall was out of office by now, having been defeated by Alex Williams, so the case was handled by Assistant State's Attorney Robert Bonsib; Bonsib told the jury that Tribble had been the supplier in a "classic" drug conspiracy. On the eve of the trial, Bonsib produced a surprise witness, a 17-year-old street dealer named Terrence Moore, who offered, in considerable detail, a story implicating Tribble in the drug trade. He told of "turning around" $50-packets of cocaine on the street for his supplier, Tribble. If he needed more "product," he testified, he called Tribble using a telephone beeper system. Moore said he had gone to nightclubs where he and Tribble had drunk $125-a-bottle Dom Perignon. He also said he had seen Bias, alone, looking for drugs to buy on Montana Avenue, then an infamous Washington drug market.

To prove that Tribble had supplied cocaine for the June 19 party, Bonsib relied on Gregg's tearful account to Driesell. Lefty himself appeared as a witness, causing a considerable hubbub. Even the judge deferred to him, saying the big coach did not have to be fitted with a lapel microphone as the other witnesses had been. Gregg, Driesell said, told him it was Tribble who supplied the drug. Tribble's lawyer immediately protested this damaging bit of hearsay, which, he charged, had been used deliberately by prosecutors desperate to make their case. Bonsib insisted it was admissible information coming from a kid who was, in effect, speaking with the veracity of "a guy in a confessional." Bonsib's argument prevailed.

According to testimony by both Long and Gregg, Tribble told them he had taken a coffee cup-full of drugs from "the bottom of a stash" and that he would be getting more the next day. If Tribble were not a dealer, Bonsib asked, how did he have access to such large quantities of high-quality, undiluted cocaine? Tribble's car, a Mercedes, and his $675-a-month apartment were cited as further evidence of the defendant's true occupation.

Tribble's lawyer, Thomas Morrow of Baltimore, scoffed at every contention Bonsib made. Gregg and Long, he said, were not credible because they had made a deal with the state. They were testifying with a gun to their heads. Moore, the lawyer said, was even less believable.

He was a defendant in another drug trial where he faced a long jail sentence. If the equivalent of a gun had been used on Gregg and Long, a shotgun had been used on Moore, Morrow said.

The lawyer sought to make the use of cocaine seem normal, at least so far as College Park was concerned. If one were to remove it from the campus, he said, a dump truck would be needed. His client was obviously a scapegoat, he said, the target of a state and a society that needed to convict someone for using a substance it disapproved of and for the embarrassing death of a basketball superstar at a major state university.

"If Len Bias were here today," Morrow said in his opening statement, "I think he would be ashamed of the State of Maryland for making a mockery of the justice system." Maryland would have nothing on Iran or South Africa if Tribble were convicted, he added. He pointed out that the trial was going on during a week when the United States was celebrating the 200th anniversary of the U.S. Constitution -- a hallowed document, he told the predominantly black jury, but a document that had not always protected the rights of minorities.

In his closing argument, he accused Bonsib of ladling out the worst sort of innuendo. "How do you confront this kind of testimony? I might as well have tried to go up there and tack Jell-o to the wall," he said.

The state was after Tribble, Morrow alleged, to divert attention from the University of Maryland.

"'Let's find a nobody. We'll hold him up. We'll divert attention from the University of Maryland, the basketball team. We'll get a whipping boy, someone who drove a car we don't think he should have.' You don't have to be a drug dealer to have a nice car. It's a twisted society we live in when someone is paid more to do a layup than a heart transplant. So we protect them, and go after the nobodies," he declared.

Tribble was acquitted on all charges, including the possession count. The jury apparently agreed with Morrow's contention that the defendant would not have been pursued in an extraordinary manner had the state not been so anxious to convict someone in the Bias case. A conviction on possession would have been somewhat laughable under the circumstances, perhaps, but an acquittal on the charge was a slap in the prosecutorial face.

Blinking into the television lights outside the courtroom, Tribble professed gratitude and renewed faith in the criminal justice system.

A few weeks after the trial, Slaughter presided at a special convention of the NCAA in Dallas on behalf of the Presidents Commission. Thirteen hundred representatives of NCAA member schools gathered at the Loews Anatole Hotel on the outskirts of the city. As the delegates checked in, the lobby floor was covered with souvenir carry bags and suitcases from holiday tournaments -- the Coors Light Tournament, the Peachbasket Festival, the Tipoff Classic, and others.

The Loews Anatole offered splendid isolation for beleaguered presidents who had gathered for a discussion of economizing -- and redefining the role of sports in higher education. One part of the hotel was paved with 39,000 square feet of travertine marble, an expanse nearly as large as a football field, according to the hotel's brochures. There was an inside gazebo of white marble in a sunken foyer where string quartets played for black tie dinner parties. There were 19 restaurants, nine lounges, and 3,000 complimentary parking places.

There was also a $12-million sports center with 16 tennis, racquetball and squash courts and full-size basketball court. Outside the hotel's Chantilly Ballroom, a television reporter stopped Slaughter for an interview. Didn't Slaughter agree? Wasn't it was fitting for the NCAA to be debating the problems of college sports in what might be the cheating capital of the U.S. collegiate sporting world?

Southern Methodist University, located in the northern part of Dallas, was only a few miles from the hotel. Recently banned from NCAA competition for two years for gross cheating (death penalty it was called), SMU had made All-Outlaw in an outlaw conference, becoming the most penalized school in the history of the NCAA. Four other Southwest Conference schools -- the University of Texas, Texas Christian University, Baylor University, and Texas Tech -- were also on probation for various infractions. If history were a reliable guide, SMU would hold the All-Outlaw title for a time and then relinquish it to another, more outrageous offender.

If there were corruption in college athletics, Slaughter told the reporter, it came from a loss of perspective that was not unique to Texas, or Maryland, for that matter.

Embarrassment over SMU's travails or remorse over the death of Len Bias might well have been a force driving the delegates as they considered cost-cutting proposals. Slaughter and the commission hoped that lower costs might decrease pressure to cheat. The presidents wanted to reduce the number of football scholarships from 100 to 95. They proposed reducing the number of assistant coaches. And they wanted to moderate the costs of entertaining recruits. Some schools had recruiting budgets of $200,000 or more. The rules governing such expenditures, solemnly debated and voted on by the delegates (they indicated their yeas and nays by lifting variously colored paddles), were often overwhelmed by rank corruption. Many delegates said openly they had little hope that anything worthwhile would be done in Dallas. Attempts to amend the bulging corpus of NCAA rules were derisively referred to as counting hamburgers.

Remorse and contrition were not among the sentiments displayed in Dallas that week. Homer Rice, athletic director at Georgia Tech, was asked by *The Dallas Morning News* to name the biggest problem faced by college athletics. "I find it difficult to say we have a problem," Rice declared. "We have things that happen, tragedies. But I really think, and this is a bold statement, that programs are better today than they ever have been. We pay attention to graduation rates, athletes' health, welfare, drug and alcohol abuse, gambling abuse. We're on top of all those things now. We have financial constraints, but so do businesses."

"These guys think tragedy and scandal will never happen to them -- or that they won't be caught," countered Lonnie Kliever, a professor of religion at SMU. Or, if the presidents were as aware of the dangers as Slaughter had been, they knew change was imperative -- but they could not act against the mere potential for disaster when all the power, money, and emotion of sports opposed them.

Kliever had headed an SMU task force appointed after that university's scandal. Schools like SMU, Maryland, and Oklahoma, he thought, were mirrors. All had missed opportunities to prevent disaster; all had told themselves they were good enough to ward off the renegades and to resist the pressures.

"We could have blown the whistle on ourselves. We knew the problems and did not come clean. We covered it up," Kliever said.

After the death penalty was imposed on SMU, it had slipped toward chaos. Recruiters from other schools prowled the campus to corral the best of SMU's suddenly disenfranchised players; the governmental structure of Texas, including the governor, who was a member of the Methodist university's governing board, was implicated in the scandal; and SMU's once-energetic and buoyant president, a friend of Slaughter's, resigned in ill health and dropped out of sight.

The first speaker at the Presidents Commission convention was Ira Michael Heyman, chancellor at the University of California at Berkeley. If Homer Rice couldn't think of a problem in collegiate sports, Heyman could.

Heyman asked his colleagues to recognize that the name of the game had changed. "We can no longer just compete with each other," he said. "We have to put on a show for the nation. Being in the entertainment business is expensive. Many of us have to raise large amounts of money to stay competitive and to keep the show going. We all know this and we all know that pressure that to keep the money coming in is what can lead to overemphasis and often to abuse and corruption . . ."

As many as half of the nearly 300 Division I schools were in debt then by amounts averaging almost a half-million dollars. No wonder they were frantic to keep the race going. They were like gamblers hoping that another roll of the dice would turn up the numbers -- the Len Bias-like recruits who would take them to the Final Four.

Heyman later offered an example of the financial pressure felt in his own conference. Since the days of UCLA's John Wooden, the level of competition in the PAC-10 had slipped a notch. It was still excellent, competitive basketball. The fans loved it -- and filled the arenas. But the play, he said, was not at a high enough level to guarantee a television contract.

Heyman was followed by several other university presidents. Kenneth Keller of the University of Minnesota declared somewhat bitterly that reform was a luxury not permitted them. Presidents had to realize that the public knew how corrupt the system had become. And he offered an interesting slant on the integrity issue: Presidents should just acknowledge that they are in the entertainment business and stop intoning the words "student athlete." They knew and the fans knew the exercise was bogus. "It is not realistic to expect people to believe that a freshman student may actually be better off than his or her peers when he is missing 20 percent of his classes," Keller said. "Perhaps," he went on with bitter sarcasm, "we could improve things even more if they missed more classes."

The delegates listened to Keller as if he were slightly crazed.

And they had even less time for Richard Warch, president of Lawrence University in Appleton, Wisconsin, a Division III school -- a place that offered no athletic scholarships and allowed no red shirts, no walk-ons and no revenue-producing sports.

"If television were covering this convention," Warch began, "the cameras would now pan to a fellow with a rainbow Afro holding a sign that read Ecclesiastes 1:9 -- 'What has been is what will be, and what has been done is what will be done; and there is nothing new under the sun.'"

Eschewing pessimism, though, Warch did have something new to suggest -- or was it so old it merely seemed new? Warch suggested that the helping instinct that created athletic scholarships had grown grotesquely beyond its initial purpose.

"We have countenanced the practice of academic institutions 'buying' athletes [with scholarships] and have become outraged only by the excesses and abuses of that practice," he said. Athletes had become an "elite warrior caste to whom much is given and more forgiven."

Then came his proposal: "If sports are to be included in the [educational] program of the college, they should be included as part of the educational expenditure. To finance sports in any other way, that is by revenues, especially those generated beyond the realm of the institution -- is to proclaim that the institution does not value sports enough to pay for them."

He quoted Henry Merritt Wriston, one of his predecessors at Lawrence: "The failure of the colleges to finance sport as education led to gate receipts [and later television and post- season bowl revenues] becoming the dominant factor." People wondered whether the nature of intercollegiate sports had changed from healthy competition to commercialism and to winning for the sake of revenue.

"Once the gate receipts set the key," Wriston said, "the present discord was inevitable. Economic determinism substituted extrinsic rewards for intrinsic values."

Abolish the extrinsic rewards, Warch suggested, by distributing all the bowl or Final Four revenue to all NCAA schools, not just to the winners. His idea was received by the delegates as if it had been presented by the sign holder with rainbow-colored hair.

And then came the other side of the debate, represented by Athletic Director and football Coach Bo Schembechler of the University of Michigan. Wearing his tinted glasses, Schembechler went after the presidents with the skill and intonations of Harold Hill, the "Music Man," poking fun at the pool hall reformers.

"I've never met a president I didn't like," Schembechler began to great laughter. "Big and successful does not mean corrupt, not at all. Revenue producing is not a sin. How could it be a sin when we talk about revenue sharing? You mean it's more important to receive than to give?"

Schembechler was twitting the Presidents Commission by invoking the hypocrisy that infused presidents' offices. Presidents hammered at athletic department folk for being money-grubbers, when the presidents were, too, he said.

"When I went to Michigan, I knew what my mission was," Schembechler said. "I had to fill the stadium. And the legendary Fielding Yost [a former University of Michigan football coach] in all of his wisdom built the damn thing to seat 100,000." Of course these sports were big. The presidents and the alumni and the legislatures made them big consciously -- and then moaned about the excesses that followed.

Schembechler argued that winning was a perfectly reasonable and virtuous objective. "I still think it's important to win," he said. "It's the American way. When we compete in athletics, we compete to win. We don't go out there just to have a good time. I'm not going to spend all that time, ask those youngsters to do all I ask them to do. I want them to have the thrill of victory on Saturday . . . ."

The next day, the delegates addressed the specific cost-cutting proposals. They began with scholarships, the number of which was controlled by the NCAA in its efforts to maintain fairness. Tom Osborne, football coach at Nebraska, said football teams had to have 100 scholarships and could not survive with 95, as proposed by the presidents. Football, he explained, is a developmental sport. One hundred scholarships, he said, were really just 50 or 60. Only 50 or 60 players were ready to play in any given year. The others had arrived at school weighing 220 pounds and needed to be developed -- assigned to work with strength coaches so they would move up to 240 or 260 pounds.

"The guy doesn't know what he's saying," said Slaughter, who had taken a moment to watch the proceedings from the back of the chandeliered meeting room. "We say we're not here to play like the Dallas Cowboys, but we sure act like we are." A system devoted to competition would not be developmental, Slaughter said. Teams would compete with the players who turned out. He and California's Heyman were trying to point out that the system had moved far beyond competition as a goal. SMU's team, Kliever observed, played at the Cowboys' stadium, not on the campus. The symbolism was difficult to miss: SMU recruits could be taken into the locker room to see where Tony Dorsett, then a Dallas running back, hung his shoulder pads.

Osborne and his allies won. Most of the cost-cutting proposals were defeated. Emboldened by the football coaches' success at fending off the cutbacks, basketball coaches successfully moved to restore two scholarships that they had lost the previous January, when the NCAA dropped them from 15 to 13. The presidents were on a slippery slope. Why should basketball suffer when football was spared?

Slaughter voted to restore the two basketball grants. "It was a mistake to change it," he said. If the presidents wanted to bar freshmen from varsity competition, teams needed more players, he said. With 15 scholarship players, a coach could excuse a player who had a lab course that conflicted with practice.

During the special convention, coaches had argued that 13 scholarships meant they might have to "run kids off" -- the practice of pressuring marginal players to leave school to free up a grant for one with more talent. Reform became its own enemy. Agents of change were blocked by those who said their reforms would harm students instead of helping them. Coaches used the rule-breaking renegades in their ranks to keep the sport big. Put pressure on us by making our teams smaller, they said, and some coach will take it out on the players.

The newspapers reported that the Presidents Commission had been drubbed by the coaches. Slaughter was discouraged but philosophical. "A lot more of the Establishment lines up with the Bo Schembechlers than with a bunch of college presidents," he said.

The commission had gone to the self-contained hotel village in Dallas thinking that its previous successes -- the death-sentence legislation, imposed on SMU, for example -- had created momentum for change. Slaughter had suspected going in, though, that the money issues would be the critical tests. The commission was asking the big-time schools to relinquish their big-time advantages. A school with a 100,000-seat football stadium, or a 30,000-seat arena for basketball, undoubtedly would want to keep the proceeds of its investment.

"We were out to take a bite of the biggest apple many of us would ever have to chew -- and most of us weren't ready," he said.

The coaches were out to reassert their control of the games. As they walked along the travertine marbled hallways and beneath the spidery skylights, they talked of regaining prerogatives.

Unlike the coaches, the presidents were not unified. Among them, there were strong differences of opinion on how much emphasis to place on athletics. Presidents disagreed about how sports programs should be paid for, the value of bowl games, and the damage done, if any, by allowing freshmen to play with the varsity. Only 29 percent of Division I presidents thought freshmen should be held out of varsity competition. To justify their position, opponents of banning freshman cited examples of first-year players with perfect 4.0 grade point averages in engineering. What these presidents wanted, Slaughter said, was the money-making prowess of the young men who could contribute as freshmen.

Feeling "outworked and finessed," Slaughter prepared to leave Dallas. Some of his colleagues, including Donna Lopiano, the women's athletic director at the University of Texas, tried to reassure him. Lopiano tracked him down as he and his wife were checking out to tell him not to be discouraged. She thought important issues had been added to the NCAA's agenda -- and would not go away until they were resolved.

SMU's Lonnie Kliever remained pessimistic, though, that university presidents ever could control big-time college sports. The pressures were too great. "To see them as moral giants standing in the breach to steer their own universities, much less intercollegiate athletics, in the direction of bold virtue," Kliever said, "is a little naive."

Slaughter returned to his own incomplete revolution at College Park. He adopted most of the 60 recommendations made by Dean Dorfman's task force, but he blocked the report's most radical recommendation: He would not declare "at-risk freshmen," those arriving with significant deficiencies in math or reading, ineligible for varsity competition. Here was a university chancellor at his most conflicted and compromised. In fact, he thought the Dorfman group had been exactly right in its recommendation, but he couldn't endorse it.

Here again, a good man was trapped in a bad system. Slaughter thought banning at-risk freshmen at Maryland was the same as sending them to the competition. Athletes who did not have the grades simply would not come to Maryland. Only if he were joined by other conference schools was he willing to impose such a rule. On the one side, the Terrapin Club was attacking him for de-emphasizing the program. On the other, Dean Dorfman, joined by the deans of every campus department, were urging him, by confidential letter, to accept their recommendation on freshmen with shaky academic records.

"To subject these students to the pressure and publicity of intercollegiate athletics at the Division I level is irresponsible, and makes us guilty of running an athletic program on the backs of our most poorly prepared students," the letter said. "We cannot in good conscience condone this and must protest. We are not swayed by arguments that all other universities allow this practice and that the University of Maryland could not otherwise recruit good athletes in the face of their competition. Instead, we must realize that the summer of 1986 placed us in a special position, one of potential leadership, and we must rise to the occasion and step in front of the NCAA if necessary. . . . We feel it is time for a unilateral imposition of freshmen ineligibility for our at-risk student athletes."

Slaughter was unmoved. Neither he nor Schwait was willing to deal such a blow to the revenue sports. He would not impede his coaches further in their recruiting. And he chose not to further inflame the boosters and the politicians who wanted Maryland to remain competitive for national championships. Governor Schaefer had made it clear to Schwait and others that he expected nothing less at College Park.

But had Slaughter fallen prey to the same lowered expectations syndrome that he so lamented in others? In the real world, he concluded, parents and players would be lured away from a more challenging environment at Maryland to play for Maryland's opponents. He wanted to raise expectations and he had no doubt that athletes would survive that challenge and even flourish. But expectations had to rise at all universities, not just at Maryland, or Maryland athletics would be hurt. "If a 2.5 grade point average is required to be eligible for basketball," he said, "kids will get a 2.5."

Slaughter said no to his faculty. He had already imposed progress-toward-graduation requirements that were tougher than any other ACC school's, save Duke's. He would go no further on his own. He chose to leave the athletes' counseling unit physically located in the athletic department. There was no greater authority over athletes than their coach, he still thought, and Wade would be committed to having teams that met the new standards. He agreed, however, to campus oversight of the program. It was a major change; the program had been unwatched except by the foxes in the athletic henhouse. To run the new academic assistance program for athletes, he hired Gerald Gurney, an expert in advising athletes who was then at SMU.

Dorfman had asked Slaughter to work for a smaller football program, reducing the number of football scholarships nationwide. If the NCAA resisted, which it did during the Dallas meeting, the report suggested that UM down-size on its own. Among presidents and chancellors, Slaughter continued to work to find support for making freshmen ineligible, and at one point thought he was on the brink of success in the ACC, but the change did not come.

Slaughter did move to limit the number of athletes who could be admitted with less than the level of academic achievement usually required for admission. Under NCAA rules, all athletes had to have at least a combined score of 700 on the SATs and a 2.0 grade point average in 11 core courses. Maryland, the task force recommended, should place an additional limit on the number of athletes whose grades were that low. Slaughter thought this was a start.

Other changes suggested by the Dorfman committee were deferred:

- Containment of each sport within a single semester;
- Post-season play confined to holiday breaks;
- University refusal to participate in sports events during the final exam period unless approved by the Athletic Council;
- Scholarships made available for extended periods to students who left without completing their degrees -- a reform urged by Richard Lapchick and his Center for the Study of Sport in Society. The

university's generosity could be abused, the task force
acknowledged, but taking that risk would provide "a highly useful
tool for the education of our student athlete." Slaughter had
offered an extended scholarship to Jeff Baxter, but without a
change in policy, he had no idea how he would have paid for it.
If Dorfman's recommendation were accepted, a future Baxter
could be more easily taken care of.

All things considered, the university had taken some risks. Good
players might not qualify for admission at College Park now. Another
impediment to the recruiters was the requirement that a student be
accepted by the admissions office before being offered a scholarship;
once again, only Duke made a similar demand.

Almost immediately, boosters began to complain that Maryland's
standards would get in the way of recruiting good players. And
Slaughter's reform-minded critics charged he had missed an
opportunity to make an important statement about academics and
sports.

Slaughter knew what Schwait wanted; he went as far as he
thought the forces at play would allow him, so he was more than a
suicidal witness for decency. But his decisions were still alienating
everyone, reformers and boosters alike.

By moving Lefty out, he had hoped to build a new atmosphere.
Yet, he was increasingly pessimistic that the marginal changes he had
presided over would matter at all or that others would join him in
restoring values in intercollegiate sport. The pressure of schedules,
the intensity of competition, the need for athletic revenue, and the
year-round season seemed likely to overwhelm the changes. The river
of emotion and money had tremendous staying power. The burden of
the reforms fell on the players, who were being asked to perform at
a higher academic level in an atmosphere of undiminished athletic
pressure.

What was needed in Division I, Slaughter concluded, was
something like the Ivy League model: revenue generated by sports
shared within the conference so that teams competed only for
trophies, and so college presidents were not so driven by the bottom
line; scholarships given on the basis of need; bowl appearances
strictly limited or even eliminated; no sport spanning more than one

semester; freshmen ineligible for varsity competition; and practice hours limited.

He thought it rank folly to suggest he could put such a system in place at College Park. What he wanted in the way of reform was beyond his power to provide. The system in which Maryland wanted to play was too big, too complex, and too well-protected.

Chapter 13

Basketball Über Alles

In the spring of 1988, Lefty and the chancellor left College Park together. It was within the same week that Slaughter and Driesell announced their imminent departures from the university. Driesell accepted the head coaching job at James Madison University in Harrisonburg, Virginia. Because his salary at Maryland was $150,000 a year and because JMU was offering him $75,000 a year, Driesell left only when Maryland agreed to pay the $75,000 difference.

The University of Maryland would now pay Lefty to coach at another school. A good contract, indeed.

Schwait ordered Slaughter to make the deal, to cut the university's financial obligation in half. The Regents chairman thought Driesell was an irritant to Wade and a reminder of the past that Maryland was anxious to escape. So did Slaughter. He had called Edward Bennett Williams to say that if Driesell was interfering with Wade's basketball operation, as Slaughter had heard, he had better desist.

Driesell also remained a threat to make embarrassing comments. In the spring of 1987, Driesell made a speech at the University of Rhode Island in Kingston in which he told 100 college and high school coaches that he favored drug testing because "Properly used," said Driesell, cocaine can be a performance-enhancing drug.

"I don't want someone competing against me who's on cocaine. That's an unfair advantage," he said. Proof of his contention, he said, lay in the fact that some of the best players in Atlantic Coast Conference history -- Bias, North Carolina's Walter Davis and Phil Ford, and N.C. State's David Thompson -- had all used cocaine. Lefty was unclear on whether he thought these players were cocaine users in college.

Anthony Daly, a medical and drug-testing consultant for Major League Baseball, called Driesell's comments "unbelievable." Cocaine, he said, tends to reduce endurance and concentration. "People who take it during games are not even sure where they're playing."

Basketball Coach Gary Williams, then at Ohio State, said, "I can't believe Lefty could say cocaine is performance-enhancing. Everyone is torn down by drugs."

Driesell's remarks were astonishing for a coach whose *own* star forward had died of cocaine intoxication. Had cocaine been used to enhance performance on his own team? Had Driesell known of cocaine use by his own players? Had he discussed with his players the drug's "performance-enhancing" qualities? Were his players aware of his views -- as some others in the Maryland community were? Had he given license to its use, however inadvertently?

Driesell presented a horrific inside view of life in big-time college basketball. "Some coaches don't let their players go back to their rooms after the pre-game meal," he said. Coaches worried that players made cocaine a part of their warmup routine, he seemed to be saying. Had he suspected such activities by his own players? If so, what had he done about it?

At Maryland, he said, he brought in ex-addicts and FBI agents to counsel his players: "You've got to be careful about drugs and gambling. The two go together," he said.

Asked if he thought cocaine had influenced the outcome of any game in the ACC, Driesell said, "It wouldn't shock me."

Had any game ever been fixed that he knew of?

"It wouldn't surprise me," he said. "Who would gamblers rather bet on? Tulane and Boston College, or a game in the ACC?"

Driesell called the drug testing program at Maryland "kind of a joke. A kid could be an addict before you got him tested three times," he said. "At least we were doing something." When he was the coach and responsible for the well-being of his players, Driesell never publicly called the program a joke. Slaughter's task force on drugs heard testimony that Driesell occasionally used the testing program as a disciplinary tool, ordering tests when he was unhappy with a player's performance in games, or with their intensity in practice.

Driesell, who had written a paper on drugs when he was in graduate school years earlier, told the coaches gathered in Rhode Island that he thought alcohol was a more serious drug problem than cocaine. When the Chicago Bulls' Michael Jordan accepted an award from the Seagram Company the previous year, he said he was disturbed: "What's a young player supposed to think?" But there was no record of Driesell ever objecting to Budweiser's sponsorship of the Maryland cheerleaders. Nor of Slaughter, either. The chancellor permitted the relationship with Budweiser to continue, though he thought it unhealthy.

Because news organizations reported on Driesell's talk, Slaughter received a new spurt of mail. Several of his correspondents said they were beginning to understand why the chancellor thought he needed a new basketball coach.

When Driesell went to the James Madison campus to accept his new job, a press conference was held in the school's gymnasium, a facility far smaller than Cole Field House, called the Electric Zoo. He walked in to find several hundred students waiting for him in the bleachers. They gave him standing ovations. He flashed the old V-for-victory sign.

James Madison University President Ronald E. Carrier told reporters he was unconcerned about suggestions that Driesell's attention to academics was anemic. Carrier said critics tended to focus on the deficiencies in a man's record, passing over all the good he had done.

After Driesell's second ovation, Carrier grabbed the microphone. "Don't you guys forget who's president of this institution," he said.

John Slaughter was leaving Maryland to become president of Occidental College, a small, wealthy, and prestigious liberal arts institution located in northeastern Los Angeles. His new reputation as an athletic reformer and slayer of coaching legends brought him job inquiries from several prestigious institutions. His willingness to fire a winning coach made him somewhat remarkable among a class of executives who were, generally, without the will or power to act similarly in their own institutions. Slaughter thought this eminence was somewhat undeserved.

"People like Driesell seem bigger than life in the minds of many and when you take them on it's like going to war with Russia," he said. "Actually, these guys are pretty insecure people. You deal with them and you find out they aren't so great."

Because he remained uncomfortable with glory earned by firing someone, Slaughter understated the importance of what he had done. At the very least, he was showing once again the threat posed by big-time winning coaches who filled the field houses.

Considered within the broader context of waning presidential authority and presidential willingness to act, Slaughter's important program reforms and his purging of Driesell were remarkable -- a career-making accomplishment.

But it was not the kind of mark he had intended to make.

He had wanted to be president of an entire university, not just of the football and basketball program. In Division I, though, there was apt to be no choice. Allow these programs to run on a long leash and disaster could easily result.

At Maryland, he had learned some things. He did not wish to stay where he was constantly at odds with the community or with his boss, the governor. He had stayed the course of the crisis. He had made his stand. Now he was ready to leave.

Slaughter's decision surprised and angered some on the College Park campus -- as if he were deserting people after they had stood by him. How could he leave just when state government was saying it would give the campus major, new financial support? What about his goals of a multi-racial, multi-ethnic, multi-generational community? The hurt surprised him. During the previous two years, he had almost forgotten he was still the kind of person that people liked and respected. About 1,700 turned out for a goodbye party in the central mall; there, in his honor, a tree was planted. A plaque at the tree's base marked the dates of his tenure, 1982-1988.

There was one more major reason for his decision: He left to save his career. His was a political job -- and he was losing his political base of support. The Driesell matter had wounded him politically. He and Governor Schaefer continued to disagree on crucial policy matters, including reorganization of higher education in Maryland. Early versions of the governor's plan would have reduced the strength of College Park's chief operating officer -- and eroded further the university's competitive standing for money before the General Assembly in Annapolis. Slaughter resisted. With others, he managed to get the plan changed so that College Park remained the university system's flagship campus, but the reorganization abolished the old Regents. Allen Schwait, who had supported Schaefer's opponent in the primary election, was not reappointed to the new governing board. Ralph Frey was gone from the Terrapin Club. President Toll was well regarded by Schaefer and seemed to be making a comeback.

Slaughter could not have succeeded or survived against Driesell and the boosters without the support and urging of Regents Chairman Schwait -- nor could he have gone further in his reforms without him. Schwait was independent and remarkably willing to support his chancellor. The two men had become a rare team on the field of college sport. Trustees, boards of regents, or governors were often down in the pit with the coaches and the boosters. Of course, Slaughter and Schwait had not done as much as the reform community had wanted. They decided against unilateral action, though the provocation of Bias's death might well have been sufficient to warrant it. They knew the reform side of the college sports debate wanted to see roses growing in Byrd Stadium, so from its perspective, Slaughter and Schwait had protected big-time sports. They had deferred fundamental changes that would have brought immediate change because they were threatening to the program.

Like Toll, the two men did not want the distraction to go on. They wanted to build a strong academic institution, and to avoid an eternal crisis. Slaughter, who was calling the shots said, "play, but play by my rules." He could be faulted for failing to act early enough. He also could be faulted for not knowing the academic status of players he had reason to think were marginal students. But he was extraordinarily resolute when he did act. He took on the full force of the opposition, faced it down and tried to create a more healthy environment. Slaughter and Schwait remained committed to intercollegiate sports and to the idea that individuals could create and run an honest program. After the death of Len Bias, they had started to rebuild the foundation of sports at College Park. Clearly, they came down on the side of fundamental change. For that, they earned the scorn of both sides.

In athletic reform, said Kit Morris, staff director for the Knight Foundation Commission on Intercollegiate Athletics, "No good deed goes unpunished."

Slaughter admitted privately that he was burned out by the crisis. He resented both the distractions from the real work of a university, and the constant challenging of his motives. He could not claim a successful assault on the collective power of the NCAA coaches. But he had sent out the call to his colleagues in the presidents' offices, and the call had gone unanswered. If making life sane and safe for athletes was to be an incremental effort, Slaughter had contributed his increment. Unwilling to be a part of the Division I system as it seemed determined to remain, he was ready for a little unilateral disarmament of his own. He still loved to watch the games, but he knew too well now that vulnerable young men were almost inevitably "ground up" by the pressures.

He had been ground up a bit himself, and he was not alone. Other university presidents told him the happiest day of their year was the day football season ended. In the spring of 1988, before leaving Maryland, he had dinner with Joab Thomas, then president of the University of Alabama. Thomas had hired a Georgia graduate to coach 'Bama football, an action that prompted death threats against Thomas he was still getting a year later. Thomas was afraid to leave his house. The Maryland chancellor saw himself joining Thomas and the ranks of other college presidents who had been run off by big-time college sports.

Each university president was responsible, of course, for his or her own integrity. Those who depended on the NCAA to maintain honest athletic programs were foolish. Those who decided to act on their own risked their careers. Those who asked John Slaughter to risk his presidency, with all its importance to him personally and all its symbolic importance to black Americans, were asking a great deal -- particularly when, at least initially, he thought the sports program could be fixed.

Perhaps he was naive. But he was also a consummate survivor, a black man who had progressed in America with his ideals, standards, and hope for the future intact. His sins may have included an excess of faith that people would do or were doing the right thing.

Critics of presidents seem to think that each president is the architect of his or her athletic program -- responsible for its shape and mission. In fact, few presidents were on hand when the current system was set in motion. Few were there when the big TV money entered the picture, or when the booster money became so essential, not just to impoverished players, but to the programs themselves. Critics seldom realized, too, that state legislatures were ordering university athletic programs to be profit centers, and that this self-support policy was a dark force in the corruption of the big-time system. Power to bring about change drained away in proportion to the need for sports revenue.

Those who wanted presidents or chancellors to take charge of their programs also failed to consider the turnover rate in these positions -- every five years or so a new chief executive officer arrived at most campuses. The successful coaches, such as Driesell, tended to stay much longer. Thus, the balance of power among the presidents, the boosters and the coaches tilted toward the athletic side. A president seldom gained community support equal to what naturally existed for the successful coach. What the president had the power to do, Slaughter said, was to crown the homecoming queen.

It was time for Slaughter to go, and he set about doing so without much regret. He was going back to California, where he had lived for so long before going into government. And he was taking over a smaller institution, where, as he put it, he could get his hands on the gauges and levers.

At Maryland, he calculated, he knew as many as 1,600 of the 38,000 students. At Occidental, there were only 1,600 students. He could know them all. At Occidental, he could walk out of his office, stroll down the hill past the eucalyptus trees, and meet his wife, Bernice, for dinner in the school's small dining hall.

His friends wondered if he would be sufficiently challenged and stimulated at a small school. He thought the challenges would equal or exceed those at Maryland. Soon after he arrived in California, he was made a member of the IBM board of directors, and he began to pursue the civil rights goals he had been forced to set aside at Maryland to deal with athletes and boosters.

In a sense, athletics had robbed College Park of Slaughter's best talents. He was not a master builder or a ram-rodding, tight-ship

administrator. He was a passionate advocate for students and for
diversity -- for equity and quality in higher education. He had been
asked to make College Park a place of harmony and diversity. Sports,
the great engine of school spirit, had plunged him and his university
into a maelstrom. Sports, people said, were a harmless distraction.
But there *were* costs. Slaughter might have been a more prominent
spokesman for civil rights if he had not been coping with athletic
scandals. There were plenty of athletic role models, but not enough
spokesmen for racial equality.

Slaughter had grown at College Park. And he would have another
chance to lead in California and at Occidental, where the school's
trustees wanted to increase enrollment of blacks and Hispanics. Many
of the issues he would face there were no different than the ones at
Maryland, and he seemed anxious to start. Shortly after he arrived,
during a meeting of the university's women alumni, the husband of a
member stood to convey a question; he said he had heard from an
Occidental alumnus, Class of 1926, who was unhappy that a black
man was now the college's president. What could Slaughter say to
reassure him?

"I'm sure you wouldn't have to go too far to find a 1986 graduate
who has the same fears," Slaughter said. "Just tell your friend to be
sure to come back and see us from time to time. I assure you he will
be proud of his college."

A few other alumni withheld their contributions in protest of his
appointment. The chairman of the Occidental Board of Governors,
Donn Miller, a Los Angeles lawyer, assured Slaughter that Occidental
supported him. If people wanted to withdraw their money for reasons
of race, Oxy was better off without it, he said.

In his new job, Slaughter was deluged with speech invitations.
On occasion, he spoke without being asked. One such speech was at
the annual awards dinner of a private organization founded in
response to the Soviet Union's launching of Sputnik and devoted to
encouraging scientific research. Slaughter observed -- even as he
thanked the association for its gift of $20,000 -- that he and his wife
were almost the only blacks in an audience of 800. None of the student
award-winners was black.

He took his message to to the Pacific Association of Collegiate
Registrars and Admissions Officers, urging them to recognize that
the old ways of judging applicants -- by SAT scores, in particular --
were suspect. A study in New York had shown that SATs were only

about 12 percent better than chance at predicting whether a student would succeed in school. High school grades, also inadequate predictors, were 20 percent better than chance. Renewed efforts were needed if people were not ruled out of higher education. To the Pasadena-Foothill Branch of the Los Angeles Urban League, he offered his concerns about the lack of opportunity and the lack of concern for young black and Hispanic children.

He received an award from the Golden State Minority Foundation. In his acceptance speech, Slaughter observed that only 3.6 percent of California's black high school seniors could qualify for admission to the University of California. Black women graduating from college each year were outnumbered two to one by black teenage girls who dropped out of high school. Fewer than 55 percent of minority students finished high school; fewer than 10 percent went to college, and more than half of these went to a community college. Less than 7 percent of blacks who entered a college or university graduated.

". . . Those who choose predominantly white institutions face a level of hatred, prejudice and ignorance comparable to that of the days of Bull Connor, Lester Maddox and Orval Faubus," he said. He based these remarks on persistent reports of racism on college campuses, on such careful studies as the NCAA's survey of black athletes -- and on his personal knowledge of black basketball players who felt isolated and estranged from places they called alma mater.

Slaughter's view on sports as a ladder of opportunity became a casualty of his experience at Maryland. He all but lost hope that a big-time sports program could be attentive to the needs of a student at the same time it was pursuing a place in the Final Four or in the Orange Bowl.

After the Bias crisis, he was willing to live with the possibility that higher academic standards might deny a second chance to some high school graduates who had no demonstrated ability to study and learn. As long as the big sports programs remained devoted to earning money and winning championships, a player would be hard-pressed to use his opportunity for an education; what's more, he believed, the experience could be destructive.

"If you take kids who aren't prepared, who can't make it at your university, they're going to hurt your program in the long run," Slaughter said -- and they are going to hurt themselves as well.

"I've rejected the notion that you're denying opportunity for a person to go to school if you don't give a good player a chance regardless of his grades. I don't believe that anymore. There are a lot of kids who can't get into the University of Maryland who can go to a junior college," he said.

They would be better off there -- and the University of Maryland would be better off without them. His determination to provide opportunity had been used against him by the businessmen of basketball, he felt. The pursuit of championships and money had been masquerading -- even if unintentionally -- as a program of enlightenment and mobility. Instead, basketball had become the goal. "Basketball Über Alles," he called it.

Universities were aiding and abetting the propagation of myth and damaging dreams. "We are sending kids exactly the wrong message," he said. "People say athletics is a way for kids to move out of the ghetto and into society. I think athletics have ruined more kids coming out of the ghetto than they have helped. The problem is that we have not laid in any expectations. If we said people had to have a 2.0 grade point average, they'd have it. If we said 2.5, they'd get that, too. People respond when expectations are made."

For a man such as Slaughter, the crisis that erupted after the death of Len Bias was more than heartbreaking. College sports had become not so much a way out of poverty, or an integrator of universities, or a crasher of racial barriers, but a delusion. The NCAA's statistics on blacks in higher education showed clearly that athletes had a better chance of getting into many universities than other blacks. That was too often hailed as evidence that sports were ennobling -- rather than as proof that aspirations for careers in science or the humanities were not being met. Responsible leaders could no longer think of sports as a door out of privation and discrimination. Sports were too often a trap door.

As soon he walked into Occidental's football stadium, Slaughter learned all he needed to know about Division III sports. There were stands on one side of the field only. Admission was $3, not enough to produce any serious revenue. The arena was built, like the rest of the campus, into the side of a steep hill in the town of Eagle Rock, northeast of downtown Los Angeles.

After the games, players in their uniforms walked up into the stands and into the press box to talk with reporters, or they stood on the field, helmets in hand, talking with their opponents. At Maryland, Slaughter remembered, the team raced off the field immediately as if to begin reviewing film of the game and preparing for the next week's opponent.

After his first few football games, Slaughter wrote an article about the differences between Division III and the big time. "In spite of their lesser physical qualifications, players in Division III are as competitive and have as much heart and desire as any you would find on a team competing for an invitation to the Rose Bowl or the Cotton Bowl," he wrote. "I find it is as much fun to watch them. Almost all of them know that they are in college to get a degree. A chance at a professional contract is a fortuitous by-product and not a goal of their educational program. This is the difference I find to be the most significant."

Reporters and students approached Slaughter immediately with an urgent question. Occidental had a black defensive back that year from Watts, and although black players had occasionally been students at the college, a grapevine theory had developed that Slaughter had come to recruit more black athletes and turn Occidental into a Division I school. Everyone wanted to play in the big time, didn't they?

The questioners acted as if they didn't believe his denials. Slaughter expressed relief that black athletes enrolled at Occidental for what it offered them academically, and not to be used by the college until their years of eligibility were exhausted. He was content with Oxy as a Division III school. The Tigers had won the Southern California Intercollegiate Athletic Conference championship five of the previous six years -- and they won it in Slaughter's first year, too, defeating Whittier, 27 to 10, in the title game. The teams played at Whittier on a cold, mid-November evening. Fans, wearing their black corduroy caps with the Oxy seal on the front, were led by a languorous six-some of cheerleaders carrying large Rudy Valle-era megaphones. The women wore cable knit letter sweaters and pleated skirts. The men were in trousers and long shirts with black and white horizontal stripes.

"They got it. We want it. So take it away," they chanted.

There were no bands and no television cameras. The public address announcer was rather formal. After a Whittier score, he intoned, "Wiley E. Jones the 3rd to kick off . . ." With the conference title came "The Shoes," a pair of bronzed football cleats awarded to the winner of the Occidental-Whittier game every year.

Lefty could have deals with Reebok or Nike or whomever. Slaughter had "The Shoes."

And when the basketball season started, Occidental's new chancellor sat well up in the stands -- with his students.

Chapter 14

Project Survival

Slaughter had one regret about leaving College Park.

He felt he was abandoning Bob Wade, leaving him exposed to the press, to hostile boosters, and to Lew Perkins, the athletic director. The AD and his basketball coach had problems from the beginning. The campus community was generally hostile to the man who had battled with Lefty. And Perkins did not want a situation in which he appeared to be dominated by the basketball coach, as Dull had been by Driesell -- particularly not by a coach who had no other visible support. If a basketball coach needed a constituency, Wade had almost none, except in the chancellor's office. The year after Slaughter left, the relationship between Wade and Perkins deteriorated and became the backdrop for a series of dreary episodes. After all that College Park had been through, after all the agonizing changes, another grinding conflict was about to unfold.

Wade had been ordered to improve his players' academic performance, but he still had to win. And he did little winning in his first ACC season: no conference victories, and only eight overall,

LENNY, LEFTY, AND THE CHANCELLOR

against 16 losses. Few complained. Though some boosters disagreed, the 1986-87 season almost certainly would have been equally disastrous with Driesell.

"Lefty would have found a way to steal a couple," conjectured Cooper Curtice, who seemed happy Wade had been shut out. It justified his belief that Slaughter was a fool to make Wade the coach.

Personnel losses would prove more devastating.

Shortly after the 1986-'87 season ended -- well before Slaughter left for Occidental -- Phil Nevin, the 7-foot center who had been one of Bias's roommates, charged he was being "run off" by Wade. Nevin was said to be a satisfactory student, but he was a player of little promise. Wade told him he would not play much for Maryland. According to Nevin's charge, Wade had threatened to lift his scholarship. Officially, scholarships were renewable yearly, but refusing to renew -- and getting caught at it -- had an unacceptable brutality about it. The unofficial code held that once a scholarship was given, it was not taken back. The risk of a player not panning out had to be borne largely by the coach, lest the exploitation of a young player, who had given up other offers to play elsewhere, proved even harsher.

At the same time, coaches have been known to make players so uncomfortable that they would leave or quit the team. The head man might also find them a mutually agreeable alternative school to which they would transfer. The process was known in the trade as "running a guy off" -- forcing him off the team so the scholarship would be available to a more productive player.

In the Nevin matter, Slaughter intervened. The young man could keep his scholarship. Wade later told *The New York Times* that Nevin initiated the talks, and that he had told the young man he might not make the team. According to Wade, he then asked Nevin if he wanted to transfer to a school where he might play, and Nevin said yes. But before the deal was struck, someone in the athletic department -- reporters said it was Driesell -- leaked the story to the newspapers. Wade and Slaughter took a pasting.

One writer recalled that when Wade was hired, Slaughter had said of him: "He believes in athletes being educated for the sake of being educated." Now, though, the Nevin situation suggested that, at Maryland, "Winning is [still] more important than any trust that must be breached." Depending on whom you believed, Wade had been set up for an embarrassment, or Maryland was slipping back to where it had started.

Sympathetic observers said Wade had "a numbers problem." Players evidently could be cut, dropped, and shipped out more easily, if they were thought of as numbers. Wade had at least 16 players and only 15 scholarships. The problem was doubly vexing because Wade had immediately justified Slaughter's confidence in him by recruiting several talented freshmen; they were among the best to choose Maryland in years.

The first coup was Brian Williams, a smart, 6'10" pivot man from Santa Monica, California. Williams's SAT scores totaled around 1,100. Here was a basketball player who helped to raise the campus-wide SAT average, and who evoked memories of Elmore and McMillen. He said witty things and he was a strong, raw-boned kid who could hardly fail. Wade's future might well have been made secure by Williams alone.

Wade then signed Rudy Archer, a guard from Baltimore. Archer had been playing at a junior college in Western Maryland. He was said to be "one of the best point guards in the country," but, unlike Brian Williams, was, at best, a marginal student. Undeterred, Wade competed for Archer against schools such as UNLV, which flew the young man to Nevada to show him the campus, the gambling strip, Diana Ross, and the show girls. Archer chose Maryland; Clarence "Du" Burns, then mayor of Baltimore, also went to work on Wade's behalf, even going so far as to meet with Archer in City Hall.

Wade was winning, but he had embarked on a treacherous path. When he got the job, Regents Chairman Schwait knew he would be tested soon enough. In Archer, Wade was gambling on a player who, almost by definition, was not up to Maryland's academic demands. As good as he was as a basketball player, Archer would not have had to attend a community college if he had been a satisfactory student.

What happened, though, was not surprising. Despite having access to Baltimore, Wade had to work the same talent pool that every other coach drew from.

When it was learned that Archer would come to Maryland, Slaughter excitedly observed to reporters at an office press conference one afternoon that Archer was a lot like Keith Smart, a guard for Bobby Knight who made the winning shot for Indiana in the 1987 NCAA championship game. Slaughter said later he did not know if Archer was a good gamble academically for Wade or for

Maryland. By then, thoroughly beaten down, the chancellor had withdrawn from decisions about which athletes should or should not be admitted to Maryland.

Archer and Williams made the questions disappear. They produced quickly. Maryland improved from eight wins in Wade's first year to 18 in the second, sixth in the nine-team conference. Maryland and its new coach scored points on the academic side by holding two good performers out of competition during the first semester until their grades improved. "All the Right Moves," *The Washington Post* said in an editorial.

By defeating Georgia Tech in the 1988 ACC Tournament, Maryland also earned an NCAA invitation. Slaughter awaited the outcome of the Tech game with apprehension. "With a $1 million deficit in the athletic department," he said, "whether we get to the tournament or not is a matter of more than casual interest." The Terps, who were one of the 64 teams invited that year, won their first game, but then dropped their round two matchup with Kentucky in a well-played game. Still, they brought home about $400,000. One might have imagined that even if Wade had not reached the tournament, his team's performance would have put him on track to cementing his job. The revenue was an even more compelling argument.

Instead, the new coach seemed to become more vulnerable. He made few friends among the Terrapin Clubbers. Reporters found him abrasive and abusive. And some of his players were not happy. In less than three years, he was almost as cornered as Driesell had been.

The deepest bruises came from the players. Several were unhappy with the amount of playing time they were getting. Some were unhappy with Wade's gruff manner. Hired to impose discipline, he made demands on his players. That made him vulnerable to young men whose talent gave them power -- at least for four years. Boosters such as Maryland Senate President Miller said Wade's problem was an inability to deal successfully with basketball's prima donnas, as if prima donnas had to be pampered, and coaches had to develop or polish their pampering skills.

The first hard blow landed after the 1987-88 season when Brian Williams announced that he was leaving. He cited "philosophical differences" with Wade. The differences were not specified beyond that, though Williams and his mother told reporters he was not developing satisfactorily as a player. Mrs. Williams had complained about this to Slaughter. "Brian's not learning to play in the paint," she had told him. Slaughter wondered how many mothers or fathers even knew what it meant to "play in the paint," the under-the-basket area between the end line and the free-throw line, a zone also called the lane. Those who did know and worried about how their sons were doing in it, thought Slaughter, were in danger of losing perspective.

Williams probably would not have developed faster in another program. Wade's ACC coaching colleagues commiserated with him over Williams's loss, recognizing that if players began to leave their programs at will, no coach could function.

The College Park campus went into shock over Williams's announcement. A rally was held to beseech him to stay. Players and administrators counseled with him. Teyon McCoy, who had been Indiana's "Mr. Basketball," urged his teammate to recognize his obligation to stay and help one of the few big-time black coaches succeed. Williams wavered. But he left. Reports at Maryland suggested he had been "tampered with" -- lured away by a California school. He ended up at Arizona State.

Then Steve Hood, a talented player who felt Wade had not played *him* enough, announced that he, too, would leave. Hood's departure was a double hit. His transfer was to James Madison, where he would play for Driesell. Then, in quick succession, several more players left: One transferred to George Washington University, another was dismissed from the team for undisclosed reasons, and then Archer flunked out. He reportedly was as much a practitioner of flagrant neglect as any of his predecessors.

In Wade's successful second season, Archer had averaged 13 points a game. He had gotten the ball to Williams in the paint often enough to put the team on the road to the Final Four. Archer produced. But his presence subordinated and alienated Teyon McCoy. McCoy, the kind of player Slaughter thought the Maryland team needed, was an all-around performer and good citizen, not a sensational talent but a solid one, a better outside shooter than Archer and a good ball handler who, with improvement, could become one of the league's best by the time he was a senior. McCoy had also been loyal and gritty during the awful first year. At the same time, he had achieved a 3.0 grade point average in his business major. He was the sort of model student athlete that Slaughter had hoped Bias would be, a young man who had the courage to resist the team's no-studying code of behavior. But McCoy was essentially dumped for Archer.

At the beginning of Wade's third year, as the coach was making extraordinary efforts to get Archer back into school, McCoy announced that he would "red-shirt" (sit out a year). He wanted to prepare for business graduate school, he said. Wade did not resist McCoy's decision, though it left him without a competent point guard. If the team had not been so decimated, McCoy's move and Wade's acquiescence might have seemed like signs of a new perspective at Maryland, a decision to put an athlete's educational needs first. But McCoy's decision was interpreted, not as refreshing change, but as another vote of no confidence in Wade. McCoy was saving a year of eligibility, people around the program said, hoping that Wade would be fired. In fact, McCoy's decision made that prospect all the more likely. Suddenly, the coach had nearly no players.

Despite the turmoil, Wade continued to recruit well. His big success of the second year was Jerrod Mustaf, the 6'9" forward from DeMatha High School who had gone with his father to Tribble's trial. Like McCoy and Williams, Mustaf had found a way to impose some of his own will on the process. He and his parents made their way through the blandishments of the recruiting coaches in a way that unsettled the basketball establishment. Shaar Mustaf, Jerrod's father, demanded information about a school's performance as an employer of blacks. Before the college coaches called at his house, he sent them a questionnaire: How many blacks were employed by the university? How many blacks worked in the athletic department? What was the university's graduation rate?

Some coaches were annoyed by this approach, but eight coaches -- from North Carolina, Duke, Georgia Tech, Howard, Maryland, Syracuse, Villanova, and Notre Dame -- came to see Jerrod Mustaf. "It was inspiring to meet them. I can see how a kid would feel like a yo-yo," the player's father said. "They'd go 30-40 minutes straight. They kept telling him how great he was. I had to keep pushing them back to the questions."

Shaar and Jerrod Mustaf were after control and the kind of information that Jeff Baxter and his foundation would have provided. Some thought this was nothing short of meddling. But like Slaughter's decision to force Driesell out, the Mustafs' insistence on a role in the process changed the equation; it made passive participants more active in their own behalf. The Mustafs were taking a less subservient position in a recruiting process that is so heavily weighted toward the coaches as to make even the coaches wince.

Gaining momentum then was the idea of a consumer information bureau for high school athletes shopping for a college. In Congress, Tom McMillen joined New Jersey Senator Bill Bradley in filing legislation that would require schools to provide graduation rates to high school recruits and their families. During bill hearings, McMillen quoted a General Accounting Office study that showed about 110 of 271 universities in big-time college athletics could not manage to graduate a fourth of their basketball players. At two-thirds of the Division I schools, half of them did not graduate. The study covered 1982-1987, years during which Len Bias was a student at Maryland.

The NCAA had problems with the Bradley and McMillen legislation. Yes, it would be good to provide the figures, but there would be some difficulties. The information was hard to prepare and not necessarily public in nature. The concept of "adjusted graduation rates" was introduced, rates like Driesell's that took into account the arrival and departure of players who were transferring, as well as "run offs" and dropouts. Some critics argued that the information was not needed because students and their parents wouldn't take advantage of it anyway.

Sister Mary Alan spoke to this last point of opposition during a congressional hearing. The athletic director at St. Anthony's School in Jersey City, New Jersey, was way ahead of McMillen, Bradley and the NCAA. She carefully screened recruiters, demanding their graduation rates. Duly forewarned over the years, recruiters came to her school prepared to talk about courses of study and the success of players who had been through the school's program. Ninety-five percent of St. Anthony's players who went to college graduated.

While she was at it, the sister took aim at academic requirements for admission and rigid adherence to numerical test scores. Many St. Anthony's athletes, she said, started out with enormous deficits. With help, almost all of them progressed, won admission to colleges and universities, and then graduated. The basketball establishment might well have camped out at St. Anthony's to see how competent students could be made. But no one had time to rebuild the secondary education system of the nation or even to learn how one school was succeeding. Here was an opportunity for basketball to uncover lessons of value beyond the court. But it didn't happen.

On his own, Shaar Mustaf was pursuing a pattern similar to the one outlined by Sister Mary. After Bias's death, when the Maryland team was found to be riddled with failure, critics said parents should have known, should have meddled. Now it was suggested that Mustaf was involved in matters best left to coaches, but he persevered.

At the end of his senior year at DeMatha, Jerrod Mustaf held a press conference to announce the school he would attend. He was introduced by Morgan Wootten, who observed that other DeMatha greats had announced the schools of their choice in the same library. Although the young man was surrounded by books, no one asked him what he planned to study at Maryland. Jerrod said he had chosen College Park because he liked Wade, whom he described as a coach who "wants to help black males succeed in business."

Reporters were anxious to know if the young man thought of himself as "an impact player." He said he hoped he would be. His first impact, some thought, was to send Brian Williams away. The theory was that Wade made commitments to Mustaf: that he would not have to play center, and that he could play guard or forward, and thus face the basket like Magic Johnson and Michael Jordan, two of the game's pre-eminent players. If that were so, if that promise had been made, Williams would be locked into the paint. Was that the philosophical difference between Wade and his young star? Some thought a consideration of that sort might be enough to send a young man off to another school.

Shaar Mustaf was asked how he felt about his son's choice. His answer evoked statements of the Baxters and the Biases before him. "I like having him nearby so I can see him play. Plus," he said, "I'm within fist distance." He knew the Biases had been within fist distance, too. Why did he think it would be different with Jerrod? Shaar Mustaf thought his son could handle his new life.

"I concluded that Len Bias did things he shouldn't have done," Jerrod said. "I knew him. He was still a great person. I had a lot of respect for him. I just think we need more positive role models. I think I'm ready for that responsibility."

Wade began his third year at Maryland by announcing that Terrapin practices would be closed to the press. He was retreating deeply into the corner. There was a report in *The New York Post* that Perkins was preparing to dump him and that he had a replacement in mind. Perkins made a weak denial.

From California, Slaughter called Peter O'Malley, who had been named to replace Schwait as chairman of a newly reconstituted Board of Regents. O'Malley went publicly to Wade's assistance. He said he regarded Wade's five-year contract as a sacred document and expected Maryland to honor it. Perkins then seemed to move closer to a vote of confidence for his basketball coach.

But the season was a disaster. Its talent having fled, Wade's team was again shut out in the ACC. The previous year, he had taken a good but inexperienced team to the second round of the NCAA tournament, but reporters said now that Wade was slow with the Xs and Os, a bad coach. All the talk turned to how much longer Wade could hang on.

The season's dramatic high point came, once again, at the ACC Tournament. In the first game, Wade's team miraculously beat N.C. State and Jim Valvano by a big margin. Valvano, whose program was under fire for grade tampering and other improprieties, went crazy on the sidelines. The Terps were in one of those can't-miss zones, and State, a far better club, was at the other end of the performance spectrum. In the style of Lefty, Wade had stolen one, pulled off the kind of upset that sometimes salvaged a season and extended a career. But it was too late for Wade. As the players savored their victory, Wade collapsed in the locker room. A heart attack was suspected, but doctors said the problem was acute dehydration caused by profuse perspiring during the game. He did not return to tournament play. His team returned to earth, and lost its next game. A columnist wrote that Wade probably wasn't on the bench for his last coaching game in the majors.

Shortly after the tournament, the Archer factor came back to wound Wade one final time. The coach was accused of giving Archer rides from Baltimore to classes at the University of Maryland campus. By flunking out, Archer had become once again a "recruitable athlete" under NCAA rules, and, therefore could not be helped in any way by a recruiting coach. But Wade had already recruited Archer; he might not have thought what he was doing amounted to recruiting. Or, if it did, how could anyone object? But Wade had violated a specific rule. The NCAA came to College Park to investigate.

Of Wade's misjudgments, the Archer situation was the most understandable and the most self-defeating. He had ignored Slaughter's conclusion that players who can't make it at the college level are time bombs. The old Terrapin Clubber Jack Heise had observed the same thing: How a team's chemistry was affected by each recruit, how that recruit measured up to the program's traditions and standards, were judgments of critical importance, not just for the moment but for years to come. Those warnings were there for Wade, but they had to be balanced, if recognized at all, against more intrusive and unavoidable laws:

Fill the field house.

Go to the NCAA tournament.

The future is now.

The NCAA inquiry added other possible offenses to the bill of particulars. Wade was accused of passing out sweat suits and T-shirts to recruits, of promising to send videotapes of games to a player's mother, of paying a $232 bill for Archer, and of allowing players to accumulate frequent flier bonuses. The latter was a violation of rules written by NCAA delegates who met in hotels like the Loews Anatole and spent thousands of dollars of their universities' money in a single weekend.

While all these alleged infractions were being investigated, Maryland's black legislators tried to help. Prince George's County Delegate Sylvania (Skip) Woods went to see Perkins about Wade. He said Perkins told him: "Just before you came in here, I was talking with a Terrapin Club guy who said, 'Here's a $10,000 check. Get rid of Wade and I'll sign it.'"

The money pressure was palpable. Bruce Bereano, the highest-paid lobbyist in Annapolis, a friend and business associate of former Governor Mandel and a major political fund-raiser, had been enlisted to raise money for Byrd Stadium and Cole Field House. Bereano said fund raising had been brought almost to a standstill. Boosters were declining to give money until Wade was dismissed. For a man like Perkins, who had a deficit to erase and a need for major improvements in his stadium and field house, Wade had become a distinct financial drag.

Fearful and mistrustful of everyone by now, Wade denied providing the rides to Archer or even knowing about them. In fact, he knew of them. Few, however, thought that offense important in itself. The idea that a coach would be hauled up on charges for taking a player to class seemed, at one level at least, the ultimate spoof of basketball mania. Instead, the issue became Wade's veracity. Newspapers said piously that he had violated the morality clause in his contract; the sportswriters concluded that Wade had lied about the rides for Archer. And if that were the case, they said, surely he had to go. (He was not filling the field house or giving the press many good quotes, either.) What he should have done, the columnists said, was admit his mistake and call the rule stupid. But Wade may have lacked confidence that such a gambit would work for him.

Thus began the Wade Watch.

As with Lefty before him, reporters said Wade might go quietly -- for a price. Finally, the university paid him a $120,000 severance fee; with that transaction, the Wade years swiftly came to an end. Maryland became the only university in the nation to have two former basketball coaches on the payroll, one of whom was coaching at another school, and the other who was entirely out of coaching.

Wade's demise was Slaughter's fault, the columnists wrote. Wade was the wrong man for the job. No high school coach had ever made the transition to a school like Maryland, they said. If Slaughter were determined to hire a black coach, he had to hire a Jackie Robinson. Otherwise, it was said, Slaughter had dealt a setback to blacks. The country apparently had not gotten to the point where a black coach could succeed or fail in his profession without indicting the entire black community.

Slaughter thought Wade had failed because of the coach's own shortcomings, but also because the university community never accepted him, never supported him, and found it easy to get rid of him once Slaughter himself had left. "You can't divorce the fact that there was a black coach put in by a black chancellor, someone who many people, from the beginning, felt had no business there. It's just the whole ambiance -- and not just at Maryland. It's part of the national mood," he said.

No one made much of the fact that the team, under Wade, had a higher grade-point average than in any other recent year. It took a committee of black faculty members to get that information into the newspapers: Two of Wade's players made the honor roll -- including Tony Massenburg, the player who was suspended for cheating in the immediate aftermath of Bias's death. All three seniors were graduating, one of them on time, one by the end of summer school, and the other by the end of the 1989 fall semester.

Driesell sent out a letter on James Madison stationery announcing the academic achievements of his JMU team -- and taking credit for the success of the Maryland players that he had recruited while still at College Park. The real credit for the improved classroom performance under Wade had to be given to the academic advising unit put in place by Slaughter. But if it was true that a coach's attitude was the most important ingredient in the recipe for an athlete's academic success, Wade had to get some credit, too. He got none.

Wade had proved the truth of something Dick Dull had told Dorfman's task force months earlier: "I know that if I graduated everybody and didn't win, I'd lose my job." After three years as coach, Wade was fired because of the belief he had lied -- but also because he was not good with reporters, not as well versed in the arcanum of NCAA rules as he should have been, and not loved by the boosters. Terrapin Clubber Mandel said athletes don't have to pass botany, suggesting that athletic ability is enough to survive in life. But Wade's experience made clear that a modern coach's arsenal of skills had to reach far beyond the game.

Slaughter did not second-guess himself or Kirwan, who, as his successor at Maryland, made the decision to let Wade go. Kirwan thought Wade had been well supported at Maryland, but what he had in mind by support was a new locker room provided at Wade's request and an extra coach. Wade never felt that he had what Herman Veal had wanted -- a feeling that he was a part of the campus and of the wider athletic community.

As new president at College Park, Kirwan had gotten an immediate introduction to the pervasive pressure of money in college sports. When Lew Perkins came to Maryland, the athletic director built himself a house for about $390,000 -- $90,000 more than he had budgeted. The $90,000 difference was made up by nine unidentified individuals recruited by Terrapin Clubber Heise. These benefactors simply chipped in the monthly cost of covering the extra $90,000, said Heise, who insisted that there was no quid pro quo, no accompanying pressure on Perkins to do the club's bidding -- to fire Wade, for example. If people looked at the arrangement and concluded that Wade was doomed because his boss was in hock to people who wanted him fired, they were just wrong, Heise said. A few people wanted to help Perkins, nothing more. He declined to identify the men who were paying Perkins's mortgage.

Compounding his difficulties, Perkins had not reported the house or the $90,000 gift on the financial disclosure form required of all state employees. Had he lied about his assets? Had he violated the morality clause of *his* contract? An oversight, Perkins said. No quid pro quo. No undue influence. Perkins agreed finally to make other arrangements for his mortgage. Wade, of course, had departed College Park by then. Whatever pressure had been exerted on Perkins, if any, by his indebtedness to Heise was lost in the shadows of the field house.

Kirwan called the Perkins/Terrapin Club arrangement inappropriate and unacceptable. Slaughter and Schwait denied any knowledge of a side deal between Perkins and the boosters. Both condemned it as inevitably compromising the athletic director's objectivity. But no sanctions were ordered, and Perkins survived without immediate damage.

Within a month, Maryland had a new coach, Gary Williams, then the head man at Ohio State. Williams left the players he had so earnestly recruited to play for him at OSU with regret, no doubt. Yet his departure was another of those silent brutalities, breaches of faith that have become an accepted part of college basketball. Williams brought with him a reputation for winning *and* graduating his players. And he was an old boy at Maryland, a Terrapin grad who played on the pre-Driesell-era teams. He would earn an estimated $300,000 a year, including radio and television deals and other aspects of his package.

And what about the man at the center of Wade's dismissal -- Rudy Archer, "one of the best point guards" in America two years earlier? Archer had rejected UNLV and others for Maryland. Despite all the academic furor at College Park when he chose to go there, Archer had arrived seemingly unaware of the situation he was entering. He had been frank to tell reporters that his goal was to play in the NBA. He was a victim of his own lack of academic focus and effort. In the struggle between his coach and his coach's enemies, Archer ultimately had been forgotten. No one thought to go back and check on his status.

As for Wade, he had been angry with Driesell for years because one of Wade's Baltimore players, Ernest Graham, had not graduated from Maryland. People assumed that Wade's only interest in taking

Archer to class was one more year of Terrapin basketball eligibility. And even if Wade had been trying to help Archer earn a degree -- and only a fool would buy that idea, right? -- he could not say so, because he had denied giving him the rides to class.

Archer needed Jeff Baxter's post-eligibility perspective. He needed Shaar Mustaf's guidance. He needed Teyon McCoy's attention to the future. He needed Tony Massenburg's change of direction. He needed help. But with Wade gone, the university made no effort to get Archer to class. As if fearful that some lasting stain would attach to the university by associating with a young man who had helped to bring $400,000 home from the NCAAs, College Park officials were now anxious to assert he was not a student there.

Archer went back to Baltimore that summer. He played basketball in a league called Project Survival. Rich irony colored this devastating epoch. Delving into the treasure trove of Baltimore high school players he had barred to Lefty, Wade picked a kid who helped to bring him down.

Maryland's basketball fraternity thought Wade's violations would bring only mild NCAA sanctions. Senate President Miller said Perkins assured him Maryland was safe. The focus remained on the possible penalties, not on the deeds that had prompted them. When university President Kirwan volunteered to accept certain sanctions in advance, the gesture seemed unnecessary because the infractions had been so widely minimized and discounted.

But there was, at College Park, some whistling past the graveyard. The NCAA hit Maryland hard. Its investigators certified what almost everyone associated with Maryland basketball knew by then: Wade or his assistants had driven Rudy Archer to class. The coach had given T-shirts and sweat suits to recruits. He had paid a $232 bill for Archer, and sent him $40 while he was still a student at Allegany Community College. Players had sold complimentary tickets. Recruits had bought clothing at a discount -- inconsequential gifts for some, but violations that the NCAA could prove.

Also among the NCAA charges was an allegation that the university had failed to exercise "institutional control" -- had failed to properly guide and control the basketball program. This charge was widely interpreted to mean that Maryland had failed to instruct Wade, a high school coach who may not have known the NCAA rule book as well as a man with college coaching experience.

The finding had historical resonance -- and irony. Driesell had been fired at great risk to the institution, as part of a deliberate attempt to regain institutional control. There was clearly a lack of institutional control when Driesell ran the program. Even his defenders said so. The athletic department was a separate entity then, operating as if its stewards had little desire or need to cooperate with the campus administration. The failure of that relationship was, in a sense, the failure of college sports at Maryland over the years, a failure that led to athletes getting little education and to Driesell's determination to act as if there were no other authority on the campus. That effort was nullified by the problems that developed or came to light under Wade.

Maryland's defenders wanted to look at the Wade penalties as the bitter legacy of a misguided chancellor. But the infractions for which the school was punished were part of a history. Driesell and the boosters were as much a part of the complimentary ticket-selling practice as Wade, who had inherited the practice along with his office and desk chair. What had occurred under Wade, when seen in the context of earlier years at College Park, may have suggested to the NCAA and others that Maryland had not really come to terms with the need to properly administer its program.

"During at least one season," the NCAA said, "members of the basketball team provided complimentary admission to regular-season away games for members of the university's athletic booster club. It was not established that the student-athletes who provided complimentary admissions to boosters received compensation for these complimentary admissions. The former men's head basketball coach, former members of the men's basketball staff, and a car dealer who represented the institution's athletic interests -- all provided a variety of improper benefits to a young man who had been a member of the university's basketball team, but who had left the university and enrolled in a junior college."

The infractions committee also found extensive violations of recruiting rules, many of them patterns. And it found that a petty cash account in the athletic department was so loosely controlled that one employee "withdrew large amounts of cash for athletically-related expenses without having to provide a timely reconciliation of the advances with evidence justifying that the withdrawals were used for proper expenses."

Because of these violations, the Terps were banned by the NCAA from tournament competition, including the ACC Tournament, for two years. Tight limits were placed on recruiting for at least one year. They would not be permitted to participate in post-season tournaments or to play on television for one year. And more than $400,000 from the NCAA tournament of 1988 had to be returned -- because Maryland players had sold their complimentary tickets to the ACC Tournament that year.

The total loss of television revenue, according to an outraged and defensive President Kirwan, was $3 million. He promised an appeal. Maryland had received no consideration for its cooperation with the NCAA during the investigation, he complained. The appeal was denied.

Maryland's defenders paid little attention to the confession by former Maryland player and coach Jeff Adkins that players at College Park sold their complimentary tickets to the ACC Tournament as a rite of spring. Driesell said he knew nothing about the selling of tournament tickets -- though Adkins told the NCAA the practice went back at least to 1981, when Lefty was the head man. Terrapin Club member Cooper Curtice said he remembered buying tickets from players.

"You knew when you had players' tickets," he said, "because you were sitting in a section with people who were obviously cheering for their sons."

Had the NCAA wished to be particularly harsh, it might have required repayment of revenues received during each of the years in which ticket-selling players had helped Maryland bring back money from the NCAA tournaments. If this was a form of NCAA leniency, though, no one in College Park recognized it as such. And no one stopped to acknowledge that the 1988 infractions were, as Adkins had observed, a way of life at Maryland. The school kept saying it had never been penalized by the NCAA, but it had clearly broken NCAA rules without being caught.

The penalties were compared with those handed to Kentucky, a school whose history of ignoring the rules was surely worse than the violations that Maryland had committed. As in the days after Bias's death, the friends of College Park wanted to minimize their culpability. Marylanders found consolation in declaring themselves similar to, but different from, the rest of the NCAA-sanctioned programs. Certainly not corrupt. More like unlucky.

President Kirwan looked back on the episode with bitter incredulity. The university had been told it would face censure for minor lapses in control of its program. But when the findings were released, the issue of institutional control had mushroomed into a federal case, a thoroughgoing indictment of central administration. In letters from the NCAA, Kirwan said, the scope of the investigation had been carefully limited in this regard and, as a result, the university did not address it as fully as it would have otherwise. Kirwan found himself suddenly sympathetic with the complaints of UNLV's beleaguered Jerry Tarkanian and others; they claim the NCAA operates a kangaroo court that offers no semblance of due process.

Nevertheless, the NCAA's finding of insufficient administrative control paralleled some of the criticisms made by the Maryland General Assembly's Legislative Black Caucus, which had accused the College Park administration of allowing Wade to sink in a sea of mistrust and suspicion. A lack of sophistication about rules was, perhaps, the least of it. Indications that Wade needed help came early with the "firing" of Phil Nevin. There had been loud warnings: The recruiting of Archer, thought to be a poor student, headed the list. How could a basketball program emerge from the Bias crisis and continue to recruit players with inferior academic qualifications? From the beginning, Perkins and Wade had difficulty communicating. Their differences were aggravated by Wade's surly reclusiveness, and by rumors, passed on sympathetically in the newspapers, that Perkins would not be happy until he had hired his own basketball coach.

Many continued to hold Slaughter responsible for the damage. To them, college basketball was like rocket science. High school coaches couldn't succeed and, according to the theory, shouldn't be brought into a difficult college coaching position. Sportswriter John Feinstein called Slaughter's hiring of Wade "incredibly irresponsible."

But Slaughter wanted a black basketball coach at Maryland. Wade had a reputation for providing discipline, something Slaughter thought Maryland had lacked under Driesell. Wade was a Marylander. He had access to a pool of basketball talent. He seemed like a good risk, and was never going to get a shot without someone like Slaughter making the decision. The chancellor had tried to act in a wider context, as if basketball's social objectives really could go beyond the players. Was the game a vehicle for social progress as it claimed to be? When would it be the right moment for an ACC school to hire a black coach? When would all the pieces be in place? If John Slaughter had not acted, who would?

The hiring of Wade could *not* have happened everywhere. But a failure such as his surely could have and did. As Maryland's penalties were being announced, N.C. State's Valvano was on his way out for running a program swamped in allegations of grade tampering, point shaving, illegal payments to players, and a host of other sins. Like Driesell, Coach V was a character, a colorful personality who made a lot of money -- the kind of personality always tolerated, even coveted in the big-time game. Like Driesell, Valvano had always been able to defuse potential disasters with a deft quote, a big smile. His parting was mourned, whereas Wade's was a case of "good riddance." He didn't even have a newspaper nickname.

But Wade *had* made the big-time. Joining Valvano, Driesell, and even Maryland's new coach, Gary Williams, he became a victim of the basketball business. Driesell had been banished to the mountains of Virginia, where he worried that his reputation had been smeared. Williams had adhered to the coaching ethic of recruiting players and then abandoning them when a good opportunity arose; now, he was at the helm of a team that could not play for the high stakes. He left Ohio State apparently believing that the NCAA sanctions against Maryland would be mild. Now he faced two years in basketball purgatory. His best players -- Jerrod Mustaf, Teyon McCoy, Walt Williams -- might leave to showcase their skills at schools where television appearances were still permitted, paid for, and watched by NBA scouts. Universities, after all, were just showcases.

Williams had been hit with something that might be called the Frieder effect: As coaches moved around in search of more money and fame, they sometimes walked out of good situations into bad ones. Bill Frieder had left the University of Michigan just before the start of the 1989 NCAA tournament. Athletic Director Bo Schembechler had learned that Frieder was thinking of moving to another school. He would have stayed for the NCAA tournament, but Bo immediately sent him out the door. Under his former assistant, Frieder's team won what every player and coach wants more than anything else, a national championship. At times, the system consumed those who loved and defended it.

What the NCAA imposed on Maryland in the late winter of 1990 took absolutely no notice of the extraordinary institutional control applied in the wake of Len Bias's death. Slaughter's anguished effort to reconnect the university with its athletic department went completely unrecognized. When the NCAA imposed its penalties, the advances made in the classroom under Wade, and the new regime instituted by Slaughter were not even mentioned -- making the university's efforts seem less important than infractions involving sweat suits and a few hundred dollars. Slaughter's insistence on self-examination and self-criticism, done at the risk of his job and over the objections of sports lovers at Maryland, went unnoted.

State legislators were publicly silent about the NCAA sanctions -- but Governor Schaefer condemned the university; facing a $4 million deficit, Kirwan had suggested that some non-revenue sports might have to be dropped. If Maryland wanted to be big-time, Schaefer observed, it would have to keep its athletic program big-time. He suggested a more vigorous private fund-raising drive. There would be no new state aid, he said. The non-revenue sports contributed nothing to basketball's troubles, but they were vulnerable to big budget cuts. The lesson was there to be learned again: The value of intercollegiate competition could only be sustained if football and basketball were profitable.

When it came to Wade's departure, only Slaughter grieved. He felt Wade's isolation and alienation. Almost no one, the former chancellor thought, had wanted Wade to succeed. He knew Wade had shortcomings. He knew his own departure had made Wade's fall more likely. But surely he was a victim of the game that professed more commitment to brotherhood and opportunity than it delivered.

Chapter 15

Linchpin

After Len Bias's death, the belief that the demands of athletics could be kept in balance with those of education became a guiding principle of big-time college basketball at Maryland. As Lonise Bias had hoped, her family's tragedy led to important improvements in the lives of others.

From the crisis over academic values, Maryland emerged as a leader in the national examination of why black students with good SAT scores fared so poorly in college as compared with white students who had the same scores. The Dorfman student-athlete panel was surprised to discover that black students in general, not just black *athletes*, were having difficulty at the University of Maryland.

John Slaughter's critics had suggested that the chancellor was lavishing time on a few black basketball players in distress. But Dorfman's group had learned that athletes were simply the most prominent among the black students suffering at College Park. In time, the Dorfman findings would place Maryland in the forefront of the national drive to improve the quality of campus life for all

African-American students. The complaints of basketball players, regarded as among the worst students, turned out to be complaints of the entire campus and of campuses across the country. Perhaps, if the education ideal of the boosters had been in focus, the academic problems of athletes would have led much earlier to the realization that the needs of all students were going unmet. Instead, the complaints were submerged by the effort to keep athletes "on track" to graduate and by the assumption that athletes, particularly those who are black, were hopeless as students.

In the years immediately after Bias's death, College Park became a high priority of state government. Millions of dollars were pumped into the university treasury as the State and Governor Schaefer sought distinction for its flagship campus.

College Park's physical landscape was improved. A refurbished mall with a fountain and reflecting pools now stretches from the McKeldin Library to the main administration building. Fresh paint was in evidence all over the sprawling complex.

The university's bad luck continued when a recession hit just in time to block implementation of the new financial initiative promised by state government. A commitment was made to resume the higher spending level when the economy recovers, but by the fall of 1991, the College Park campus had suffered cuts of $40 million -- 15 to 20 percent of its state budget.

All the news was not bad, however. After Bias's death, there was a general decline in booster contributions and a drop in booster membership -- from 3,700 to 3,200 in 1990. Yet, the university reported that endowments increased from $17.1 million in 1987 to $50 million in 1990. Even in a time of athletic scandal, private gifts and contributions increased 41 percent -- more evidence that university giving is not dependent on athletic success.

The university's undergraduate population, once its major claim to fame, was pared down from 38,000 to 27,000, as academic standards rose and the university became more selective. At the same time, the quest for quality and diversity has continued. The percentage of full-time black students in 1989 was 15.8 percent -- more than double the 7.4 percent in 1979. Even as admission standards ascended and competition for places in the freshman class intensified, the number of African-American students increased.

The General Studies program was dropped. John Toll, who retired in 1990, said unconvincingly that the Bias crisis had nothing to do with that decision. Whatever the cause, James Bias and Dervey Lomax applauded. "You could put your General Studies diploma on the wall in the bathroom, and if you ran out of paper, you could use that," Mr. Bias said with much bitterness.

Many of the rule changes urged upon the athletic department by the Dorfman task force were not only adopted by the Administration, but remained in place. Several good basketball players were lost to the new procedures and standards. What that meant, said Dorfman, was that the University of Maryland had redefined itself during its crisis: It had become a school, first and foremost. The athletic department was running a huge financial deficit -- several million dollars -- and, yet, it was turning down kids who could bounce the ball and fill the field house.

Influential Marylanders worried that too much balance had come to College Park.

At a meeting of the university's Board of Regents in the summer of 1991, Regent Earle Palmer Brown said the "conventional wisdom" among Maryland sports enthusiasts was that College Park had handicapped its coaches with the new academic standards. The playing field, he said, was not level because Maryland was insisting that an athlete be approved by the admissions department before being offered an athletic scholarship. Only Duke in the ACC had requirements as stringent as those adopted at College Park under John Slaughter.

Did the new rules put Maryland at a disadvantage? Brown asked President Kirwan during the meeting.

The president acknowledged that they did. But he thought Maryland was acting in the best interests of young people -- moving ahead of the reformers.

"I don't think we're alone," Kirwan said.

As the Carnegie Foundation for the Advancement of Teaching had done in its celebrated 1929 study, the independent Knight Foundation Commission On Intercollegiate Athletics, in a 1991 report, called upon university presidents to take charge of their athletic programs. "You are the linchpin of the reform movement," advised the commission, in a report called "Keeping Faith with the Student Athlete." Offered were some beginning guidelines, a template for examining athletic decisions and concerns.

Other Knight Commission recommendations for university presidents included:

- University trustees should explicitly endorse and reaffirm presidential authority in matters of athletic governance
- Presidents should control athletic conferences.
- Presidents should control the NCAA.
- Presidents should control their institutions' involvement with television.
- High school students should be ineligible for a reimbursed recruiting visit to a campus until the admissions office says they have reasonable promise of being admitted.
- A university should be allowed to spend general funds -- not just funds generated by the teams -- to pay for athletics: "There is an inherent contradiction in insisting on the one hand that athletics are an important part of the university while arguing, on the other, that spending institutional funds for them is somehow improper."

Contradiction or not, the use of general campus funds for athletics would require immensely difficult negotiations with legislatures and faculties -- both of which would be suspicious of these moves. Legislatures would worry about charges they were subsidizing athletics at the expense of education. Faculty would be certain this was true. Someone would have to have enough courage to make the case: the case that forcing athletes to make money is wrong and harmful to both student and university.

With the reform foundation so arduously built by Slaughter and Schwait, Maryland was standing where many universities were headed, Kirwan insisted. But Maryland Senate President Mike Miller disagreed.

Miller wanted the new admissions requirements repealed.

"Maryland fans are entitled to the best scholar athletes we can recruit on the playing fields and courts," he argued. "We need to be able to admit students, as [basketball coach] John Thompson does at Georgetown, with SATs of 400 and 450."

Like other universities, Georgetown has been accused of admitting players who can't read. Georgetown has denied the charges, but the suspicion incited Maryland boosters to push their own school in a similar direction. Stories circulated about players being rejected at Maryland and then being accepted at Virginia, Rutgers, or Syracuse. Pressure to eliminate the standards increased.

Miller asked President Kirwan to relax the rules and to admit basketball players who had been rejected by the admissions department. The new coach, Gary Williams, was threatening to leave.

Boosters, too, were frustrated, convinced that the Maryland coach was recruiting with "both hands tied behind his back." The drop in Terrapin Club membership appeared to be partly caused by concern that the university was allowing itself to be defeated on the recruiting fields.

Miller conceded that football coach Joe Krivak, despite the higher standards, had been able to bring a half-dozen highly skilled players to College Park for the 1991 season. Kirwan somewhat gleefully observed that Maryland's football team had beaten the highly ranked Virginia team in 1990. Just lucky, Miller seemed to think.

The Senate president's entreaties put extreme pressure on Kirwan, and clarified the issue as never before. The coaches wanted to recruit players whose academic skills were not good enough for the admissions director. One of these prospects was said to have a seventh-grade reading level -- "an overstatement" of the young man's abilities, said Kirwan, who had seen the player's high school records and test scores.

Kirwan turned Miller down. One of the university's most loyal and powerful alumni, Miller represented the same county where College Park was located. As a legislative leader, he had helped the university achieve the priority status in the state budget it had pursued so desperately. In 1988, Miller prodded the legislature toward a higher education program that would have sent an additional $100 million to College Park. It had been Miller who provided borrowing authority and a matching state grant to pay for major improvements at Cole Field House and at Byrd Stadium.

Now, in the time-honored ways of sports and politics, he wanted a couple of basketball players and Kirwan was saying no. Miller said he thought Kirwan was a "gentle soul" and a bit "naive." Slaughter had heard the same complaint.

"Mike is a devoted alum," Kirwan said. "I think he's very proud of what he's done for his alma mater. I listen to what he has to say, but in the end I have to make certain decisions. We do what is the right thing for the university, and I think Mike respects that."

H.L. Mencken wrote that university presidents were "far too politic a class of men to take any really effective steps against an enterprise that brings in such large sums of money."

Kirwan thought it was now impolitic not balancing sports with academics -- perhaps more dangerous than ignoring senate presidents and boosters.

The pressure, unrelenting on the linchpins of reform, also came from academic quarters. Peter Wolfe, a professor of mathematics, charged the university with a continuing refusal to demonstrate how big-time athletics could be justified as a part of campus life. The hypocrisy of earning money on the backs of the players and paying huge salaries to coaches could not be defended, he argued. A man who had season tickets to Orioles games, who played basketball at lunch, and who had always regretted the absence of football at his high school, Wolfe found himself ashamed to be a fan of Terrapin sports. He urged a debate beginning with these questions: Should College Park have an intercollegiate athletic program? Why? What does it contribute to university life and to the mission of a university? What would be the costs? Who would pay? Did the State agree with Senate President Miller that Maryland should recruit players with 450 SATs?

What was needed along with debate, President Kirwan thought, was an end to self-support.

"The way to reform," he said, "is to decrease financial pressure, and there should be some form of subsidy if it's important to the State to have these teams. The alternative leads to a flawed system. The money pressure that leads to cheating has to be dealt with in some way."

The Knight Commission had suggested the lifting of bans on the use of general university funds, this as a way of reducing the pressure for profit.

President Richard Warch of Lawrence University, a Division III school, had told Slaughter's Presidents Commission: "To finance sports in any other way -- by revenues, especially those generated beyond the realm of the institution -- is to proclaim that the institution does not value sports enough to pay for them."

Since Warch had spoken, the problem increasingly was cost. More and more schools, including Maryland, could not make enough to cover the cost of 22 intercollegiate sports. Terrapin Clubber Heise said increasing tuition rates had made it impossible for the club to meet the scholarship bill in the years since Bias's death. So the pressure on the athletic departments was increasing.

In Annapolis, where the decree of self-support had been issued, Senate President Miller said he was unconvinced the policy should be abandoned -- but for another reason. "It would be subsidizing mediocrity," he said. By that he meant mediocre sports programs, not mediocre students. "When Lefty Driesell and Bobby Ross were at Maryland, no one talked about this sort of subsidy," Miller said. They filled the field house. Miller agreed that the pressures created in sports often led to abuses. At the same time, he said, good performances on the field would eliminate the need for state involvement.

The money pressure was unrelenting. Few Division 1A programs made money -- an average of $39,000 a year for those that were profitable. More than half faced troubling deficits, such as the $3 million to $4 million shortfall at College Park. The pressure to perform well on the athletic fields seemed to be increasing, with relief in sight only for those schools lucky enough to end up in a premium TV market.

Maryland did get a break in this area. The Atlantic Coast Conference's Committee on Infractions limited Maryland's financial penalty to the loss of TV revenue resulting from its shortened season. Maryland didn't lose its full share of the television money; it was not penalized by the Raycom Sports Network, which broadcasts ACC games. Raycom recouped its losses by substituting other games for Maryland games. The conference and Raycom thus saved Maryland as much as a $1 million, Kirwan said.

And, on the horizon loomed a real windfall -- the fall 1991 addition of Florida State University to the ACC.

The name of the game here was viewing audience: An additional 500,000 Florida homes would be added to the TV market, a 60 percent increase over the 900,000 already in the ACC fold. If the revenue went up accordingly, the additional payoff for each school in the ACC could be significant. Maryland had a 10-year plan for retiring its athletic department debt. Now, though, Kirwan talked of digging out much sooner.

The prospect was both tempting and troubling. Maryland, Kirwan said, did not spend as much money for football as FSU. Would it now be forced to increase the football budget? What about travel time for the athletes? Wasn't there some commitment to follow the NCAA and the Knight Commission in their advocacy of reduced costs? How did expansion of the ACC fit in with that goal?

As much as Kirwan was leery of the Florida State deal, he did not object vociferously or at length. Slaughter had said several years earlier, "We can't do stupid things. We need the gate receipts." Kirwan was under even more financial pressure than his predecessor had been.

When the 1991 football season opened, Maryland showed off Byrd Stadium's $10 million face-lift, made possible by Senate President Miller and the state legislature. The five-story facility included a new press box and 412 luxury seats for Terps fans who paid $10,000 to reserve one for 10 years. Meeting rooms, kitchens, and a presidential reception room were among the new amenities.

Kirwan, who feared that money was the corrupting force of intercollegiate sports, would be expected to meet with wealthy benefactors, impressing upon them how generous donations support the character-building glory of the gridiron. His concerns about the loss of independence associated with this sort of activity had to be suppressed, along with his concerns about the ACC's expansion.

Maryland's thoughtful new president and its new reform-minded athletic director, Andy Geiger, who had been hired to replace Lew Perkins, seemed to be acting in philosophic concert. Yet, despite their commitment to fairness and decency, they remained in danger of getting stuck on the same old treadmill, racing desperately for the bucks. A new stadium was needed to keep coaches, to recruit players who were shopping for a showcase commensurate with their talents, to retire its debts and, of course, to draw the fans. All that was costly.

The key to restoring balance in intercollegiate sports, the Knight Commission had said -- echoing John Slaughter -- was to control costs and establish a new culture at every level.

"You have to have a thousand individuals attempting to do the right thing every day, people who say, 'I'm not going to tolerate this. I'm going to work to achieve something,'" said Kit Morris, staff director for the Knight Commission.

Athletic departments, he said, needed committed leaders like Geiger. Critics and supporters alike said Geiger wanted to do it right at Maryland, that he had deliberately put himself into one of the most trying situations in intercollegiate athletics.

At Stanford, Geiger had enjoyed the prospect of having one or two championship teams almost every year. He worked for a well-respected, well-endowed institution. But, his friends say, he wanted to achieve something in an environment where the revenue and the high-quality athletes were not guaranteed.

"He wants to look back and say, 'I went into a tough situation and made some good things happen,'" said Morris.

At College Park, Geiger found a devastated program racked by both recurrent controversy and bankruptcy.

As much of a force as the Terrapin Club had been in the athletic department, Geiger was surprised to find "no reinvestment, financial or philosophical." For one thing, so much revolved around the core group at the Terrapin Club. What was needed was even more boosters, 10,000 if possible, he said. For another thing, the university and the state, under the flamboyant leadership of Ross and Lefty, had been content to let the athletic department run along on its own. The teams challenged for national titles and made lots of money.

But even in the good times, sports at Maryland had lost their way. Scandal had stripped the sports program to the bare bone and the university had never come to terms with its plight.

In the absence of a debate, Geiger was willing to offer his own answers.

An oarsman at Syracuse University during his undergraduate years, Geiger loved the idea of "college athletics" -- "sports as a metaphor for life." He thought athletes, if allowed to be more than stereotypical jocks, were interesting people with something to offer the campus. But athletes themselves had to begin recognizing the value of education. "We need to get kids a little more interested in the smorgasbord available to them on the campus," he said, using the term more favorably than Slaughter had.

Maryland now would recruit players with some real hope of doing well as students, he said.

"Our job is not to win basketball games separate from other considerations. It's alright to win. But our program has to fit into the university's envelope. The university has every right to say what that envelope should look like and how big it should be."

When basketball Coach Gary Williams had sought recruits with marginal SATs, Geiger said no.

"When I did that, [Williams] went ballistic," Geiger said. "He called everyone he knew." For the athletic director, the release of information about these recruits and the pressure Williams applied on him led to a moment of truth.

"If I had backed him on that one, I would have been finished on this campus. One of the reasons I came here was to keep the athletic department from fouling its own nest."

Williams's frantic phone calls resulted in a meeting in President Kirwan's office. Influential boosters with high-level Annapolis connections assembled to hear Geiger review the qualifications of the players that Williams had recruited.

"I said, 'Here are the risks we took and here are the ones we didn't take,'" Geiger explained. "These guys were stunned to see the low level of qualifications. They went right out and called the power centers in Annapolis and said we were doing the right thing."

Geiger is convinced that beyond the daily decision-making, there is no magic bullet for reform.

Eighty percent of the problems that crop up in athletics, he said, arise from "bringing in totally unqualified students for athletic reasons. If all the kids were graduating with degrees, you could win a lot of arguments. At the same time, when you see a marginal kid, you can't be sure the right answer is no. We ought to take risks. But the risk has to be an informed risk. We're providing opportunity for people who will fail if we don't make smart choices. You talk about psychologically castrating young black males! I think we've done a lot of that in sports.

"It can't be all bread and circuses," he said. "We ought not to be involved in intercollegiate athletics unless we benefit the participants."

In spite of all the pain and embarrassment associated with the business of college sports, universities and their presidents were still trapped. They were obliged under state policy and by booster emotion to stay in the entertainment business. The dilemma expressed by Dick Dull had not been solved: Geiger had more support for a saner program, but still had to avoid the temptation to make financial decisions in an academic environment. The choices were grinding. Young lives were at stake. And the unrepentant power centers pounded on him to win and make money.

"It isn't ever going to be fixed totally," Geiger said. "It's going to be no more perfect that any other enterprise that has the ambiguity of human involvement."

Geiger's strength and determination gave Kirwan optimism about the direction and integrity of his athletic program.

"You never can be completely confident," he said, again echoing Slaughter's words. "But I believe that in the national context we're ahead of most other places in implementing reforms." The criticisms he faced were to be expected, he added. Tension between reformers and boosters was unavoidable, part of the American landscape.

Soon after completing the Knight Commission's report, Staff Director Kit Morris saw a film about the Normandy invasion; it suggested an analogy to him. The 1944 invasion plans had been dashed by high seas and a million unforeseen events. Utter chaos prevailed. Soldiers were caught in a murderous rain of artillery. The officer corps was decimated. Only individual heroism earned the beachhead.

Morris thought balancing intercollegiate athletics and academics *could* occur. But, in ways not unlike World War II battles, the effort would continue to leave "wounded and dying on the beach."

Chapter 16

Full Circle

Len Bias made a celebrity of Brian Tribble.

Tribble, the alleged drug merchant, emerged from the trial and a year of newspaper headlines with name recognition and a somewhat mysterious aura. He hired an agent and considered writing a book, going into business with his mother, or returning to the university for his degree. At one point, he hosted a series of parties at a Washington nightclub; couples came to pose for photographs with the man who had been with Len Bias during the last minutes of his life, the man who had escaped all the assembled power of the law. It was a final endorsement for the Terrapin star who had brought Lefty Driesell his only ACC Tournament victory.

Unfortunately for Tribble, police, following up on long-lingering rumors of his return to the cocaine trade, arrested him again in July of 1990. The police trap for him was near the hotel where the jury in the cocaine trial of Washington Mayor Marion Barry was being sequestered. Tribble eluded police there, but was later taken into custody.

Facing what his lawyer, Tom Morrow, called "substantial government evidence," Tribble, then 27, pled guilty to a charge of conspiring to buy a kilogram of cocaine for delivery to an accomplice.

Morrow insisted his client was a victim.

"As long as an individual can make as much money in one hour selling cocaine as he can in a month of hard work, drugs will be a deadly attraction," the attorney said.

The U.S. Attorney had a different view. "People who distribute drugs are victims only of their own greed," said Breckinridge Wilcox.

Brian Lee Tribble went to jail on a 10-year sentence.

Morrow could not keep the Jell-o on the wall this time.

In the springtime after the basketball season, Lonise Bias still half-expected to hear the front door slamming, the keys landing on a table, and the voice of her superstar son, her baby. Kidnapped and ransomed by basketball, he would be given back to her at the end of another season. When Lenny didn't come home that first spring, her expectation, ingrained by repetition, caught Mrs. Bias cruelly unaware. It rose in her heart with a rush and then crashed against reality.

"You feel his spirit, but you wish you could see him," she explained. Her memories, often harsh and hurtful, were vivid.

Once, when brother Jay Bias was dressing for a high school dance, his sister, Michelle, tried to imagine how Len would have teased his younger brother.

Though he would have been impressed with Jay's appearance, "He would have made a joke of it," Michelle told her mother. He would have called his brother "Nessa," a name he had invented for Jay. He would have said, "Look at Nessa. Look how pretty he is." The big brother teasing would have led to the usual playful boxing in the small kitchen. "Maaaa," Jay would complain. "Let him alone," their mother would have instructed her older son.

After Lenny's death, the other three Bias offspring never said they were too sad or too grief-stricken to go on with their lives. "They give and give and give," Mrs. Bias said of her remaining children.

And so did she, taking a message of pride and self-esteem into high schools across the country. As she introduced herself, she often anticipated the tough questions that she knew would come.

"Where were you when your son died? Why couldn't you save your own son? Who died and left you in charge?" she always asked at the beginning of her talks about drugs, abortion, alienation. The questions were not actually accusations. In the cruel context of drugs and relationships between parents and children, understanding and empathy erased accusations.

Mrs. Bias insisted that no one had conclusively proved to her that Len had voluntarily used drugs. It was entirely possible, she thought, that someone had poisoned him, slipping the cocaine into a Coke or a beer. At the same time, she was quick to say, "There are no perfect children. There are no perfect families in this world."

The final explanation, she insisted, was fate. "God took something beautiful, raised it up, and when everyone could see it, took it away. Len died of cocaine. He died of drugs," she would say.

Her son's life and death provided another important lesson, she said: Trying to please everyone is a mistake. "The greatest love of all," she told young people at New Britain High School in Connecticut, "is the love you have for yourself. But how can you know who you are if you are always following someone else? Anyone can march to another man's tune, but who are you?"

In her school visits all over the country, she also advised students to "choose your friends carefully. Keep your dignity. If you don't have dignity, you have given it away." She might well have been talking to her son. And she seemed to wonder if *he* had ever really seen and accepted the beauty in himself.

During her talks, Mrs. Bias listened to the problems of strangers, and offered them sympathy, but she also reminded them that life is tough, far tougher than they could know. "Tough," she would say, "is having to bury your baby on national TV." Yet, she remained serene.

People whispered that her husband was critical of the university because he had missed out on a fortune. Mrs. Bias dealt with that head-on. "People said, 'Oh, you're going to have this or that. Len was going to do so much for you,'" Mrs. Bias recalled.

It just wasn't so. "My husband and I, we never had that on our hearts. Whatever Len got, we didn't expect to get. He worked hard for it. It was his. I would never allow myself to think about a lot of wealth."

To her young listeners, she spoke of life's fragility, and the urgency of coming to terms with that. "Get a new mind about drugs, about self-esteem, and loving your parents and making them love you," she said.

"Parents need to be taught," she continued. "If we don't make time, come and pull us by the collar." The message was clear: You never knew when something could happen. "I never thought I would see my son stretched out on a slab in a hospital morgue," Lonise Bias said.

For some, Mrs. Bias seemed too strong. "Something's missing in that family," a Prince George's County high school principal said. "How can a mother not cry?"

She had cried, of course, but she did little crying in public.

"Black Americans of my generation," said the writer Maya Angelou, "didn't look kindly on public mourning except during or immediately after funerals. We were expected by others and by ourselves to lighten the burden by smiling, to deflect new assaults by laughter. Hadn't it worked for us for centuries? Hadn't it?"

In the days after his brother's death, Jay Bias had gone on playing basketball, and was frequently compared to Lenny; Jay was a better player, though not as physically dominant as Len had been at his age, coaches were saying. Jay was brave, the writers said, because he went on playing in spite of the pain. Basketball was therapy, solace: Dribble the pain away, jump-shoot the pain, slamdunk it. Just what Lenny would have wanted.

But basketball was not always a refuge. During games against Northwestern High School, Jay's opponents taunted him with jokes about his brother. How are flowers and Len Bias alike? You pick 'em and two days later they die.

At the end of his junior year, Jay and his teammates played in Cole Field House for the Maryland high school championship, according to Mrs. Bias. "Everyone would have understood if he hadn't wanted to play," she told her young audiences, "but Jay Bias went out and scored 28 points. Every day, you must go out and score."

Jay sometimes insisted that he was not trying to be like his famous brother -- and, yet, of course, he must have been on some level. For some reason, he followed his brother's wayward lead off the court, too.

Jay was seen occasionally with Brian Tribble.

Bob Wagner and others said Tribble drove Jay to school. How the two met, why Jay would have risked such a relationship, was no more fathomable than his brother's ventures into cocaine. Was there some dark compulsion to travel down every road taken by his brother? The relationship had no immediate negative effect that anyone could see -- except to raise urgent questions about Jay's judgment, his safety, and the supervision he was getting from his coaches and parents.

At the end of Jay's senior year, the parade of coaches resumed at the Bias household. Jay was among the 20 best high school players in the nation, according to *Street & Smith*, the basketball magazine. As a senior, on a team that slipped overall, he averaged almost 33 points a game.

At 6'7" and 190 pounds, Jay continued to show skills that compared favorably with his brother's. *Cumberland [Maryland] Times* sportswriter Mike Burke said it was chilling to see Jay Bias move down the court, stop on a dime, and then soar in born-ready style so eerily reminiscent of his older brother. Offered scholarships at several colleges and universities, Jay was considered a Proposition 48 player. Because he had not scored higher than 700 on his SATs or averaged at least a C in 11 core courses, Jay would not be eligible to play as a freshman year -- but he could get a scholarship for a year, during which he could make up whatever academic deficiencies he had. (Many schools are loath to accept a player under these NCAA conditions; it marks them as institutions willing to take grossly under-qualified players.)

Jay bypassed these conditional scholarship offers to enroll at Allegany Community College near Cumberland in Western Maryland. He chose ACC, as it is called, because it was far from the dangerous climes of urban Washington, and because several of his friends from Northwestern High had gone there.

He might well have prospered at ACC. But he had a bit of an attitude problem, according to Mike Burke. He would occasionally remind people he was Len Bias's brother, as if that relationship gave him license to offer basketball views with an arrogance that players and coaches alike resented. He lasted a year at ACC. According to Burke, at the end of Jay's freshman year, the coach told him and his parents he would not tolerate Jay another year unless it was understood who called the shots. The sides parted on friendly terms, but Jay did not return to school. Instead, he worked at a Washington television station and later at a city hotel. Friends said he was attempting to improve his academic standing before enrolling, he hoped, at American University.

But then, in November 1990, James Stanley "Jay" Bias was murdered in a parking lot at a shopping mall.

His death was more difficult to believe than his famous brother's. The nation wondered how such misfortune could have visited the same family twice. John Slaughter heard about it on a radio news show and, shaken once again, called from California to find out what had happened.

Jay and a young woman friend had gone into a mall jewelry store in Prince George's County to buy a ring. The sales clerk's husband, who was standing by, accused Jay of flirting with his wife. Jay ignored challenges to a fight, but the man became incensed and followed Jay and his friend outside the store and into the parking lot. After Jay entered a car, the man drove up behind it and fired four shots, two of which struck Jay Bias in the back. He died on the way to the hospital.

James Bias said he found some consolation in knowing that his son mentioned each member of his family by name as he was rushed to Leland Memorial Hospital, where Len had died more than four years before.

"Jay is all right. He's not here, but he's all right," his father said during a press conference at his home.

Now the Bias family had a second campaign to wage.

"I'm going to do all in my power to act against the flow of guns and get other citizens involved," Mr. Bias said. "These are young children dying. I'm not talking about Jay alone. I've seen it over and over and over. You've all seen it every morning in the papers . . . a bad attitude and a gun have taken another life."

Reporters asked if he would consider moving to a place where violence was less likely.

"I don't think there is any such place," James Bias answered.

If such a place does exist, perhaps it is in the mountains of Southwestern Virginia.

There, fully ensconced at James Madison University, Lefty Driesell took his teams to the National Invitational Tournament his first two years, and continued to decline interviews about his tenure at College Park. He took Harrisonburg, Virginia, more or less by storm, wisely avoiding any prediction that JMU would become the UCLA of the Shenandoah. Nevertheless, the inevitable bumper stickers soon proudly announced, "JMU and Lefty, too!"

JMU's president, Ronald Carrier, who had urged students in the Electric Zoo to remember he was still the school's president, said booster enthusiasm spiked upward with Lefty's arrival, and then leveled off a bit. But a surge, particularly in recruiting and in overall profile, was precisely what President Carrier had in mind when hiring Driesell. If the old persona and the old shtick had lapsed into liabilities at College Park, they could still work magic for JMU.

"I hired him because we're out of range for the Washington and Richmond media. Lefty gave us media attention. We were getting killed recruiting," Carrier explained. The president's approach to Driesell-coached basketball is nothing less than daily micro-management. It is a degree of oversight many say was never focused on Driesell in his former, more or less untouchable, incarnation at College Park.

What Carrier wants from Lefty, though, is the same thing Maryland wanted: athletic respect and annual trips to the NCAA tournament. "We have goals for every program," the president said. "In basketball, a goal is to get into the NCAA, because it's a fun experience."

Like John Slaughter, Carrier has been making a small place for himself in the athletic reform movement. Carrier is a longtime official in the Southern Association of Colleges and Schools (SACS), the regional organization that certifies educational credentials for about 800 southern schools. The region includes Southern Methodist University, North Carolina State University, the University of Georgia, and the University of Florida, big-time schools where sports have proved acutely embarrassing. Because a college that loses its accreditation can lose its federal financial aid, the association wields financial power that could give athletic reform important impetus.

Carrier, chairman of a SACS subcommittee urging a careful monitoring of athletics, has said that one infraction will not cost a school its certification; but the new oversight, he has added, will give more power to university presidents who need it if they are to restore balance on their campuses.

· "JMU coaches report to the presidents and to no outside influence," he insisted. At JMU, athletics are supported by student fees of $500 per student per year. Financial support of the athletic program, he said, must be "an integral part of the system, part of the mission and doctrine that guides us.

"We're not going to operate on other people's money. We don't depend on outside money. We don't have to make money in the marketplace, and we don't intend to have that. When you do, it reduces your control." At JMU, he said, basketball and football are not regarded as revenue sports. Boosters contribute $1.5 million to the athletic department's $7 million annual budget -- not enough to make them overly influential, he said.

If the students object to the fee, they can go elsewhere, he suggested. When they choose JMU in the first place, the fees are there for all to see. "It's part of our program. If they want to complain, fine, but it's an education decision we have made," the JMU president said. An educational decision! "We don't have to be beholden to any group. Presidents get in trouble when they have 110,000 seats to fill. Money starts to drive the thing."

So far, the Carrier assertion is that he is accomplishing some of the social goals claimed for sports. "We had a kid out of Washington who, if it wasn't for JMU, would be dead. He'd have gone back on the streets," he said. Now, he's progressing toward a degree, and may join JMU graduates Charles Haley, who has a big contract with the San Francisco 49ers; Gary Clark, the Washington Redskins wide receiver; Scott Norwood, the Buffalo Bills place kicker; and Steve Hood, the former Maryland player who graduated last year and eventually landed with the NBA's Sacramento Kings. "If you can keep athletics in balance," Carrier said, "it can be a tremendous opportunity for everyone."

Whatever changes are made by Carrier, Slaughter, and others in authority, the coaches will continue to face tough choices and tricky judgment calls.

Driesell recalled a JMU recruiting trip to a junior college where he spotted a talented player he knew little about.

"Hey coach," Lefty said to his host, "that kid gonna graduate?"

"Oh, yeah," the other coach replied. "When you're talking to that kid, you'll think you're talking to Bill Bradley." Problem was, the kid had never been to high school. He'd been in a gang, and had never studied at all.

"We got him here," the coach said, "and he made the second best score on the graduate equivalency degree (GED) in the history of this state." Driesell did not say if would recruit the young man or not --

but the temptation was clearly there. The coach's life, the life of the striving competitor, was getting no easier. Was Driesell looking at opportunity or disaster?

When asked in 1986 what he had learned from the Len Bias death and all the events that followed, Driesell's response, "get yourself a good contract," hardly ranked among the most thoughtful. Asked the same question four years later, he either lacked new insights, or declined to offer them.

"Life goes on. I have a great family and a great job. Life goes on."

Clearly, though, the nightmare lingers: "I still can't believe Leonard is dead," he said. "I went to his grave the other day. There's not even a tombstone there. I loved Leonard. He was a great kid."

In his appointment of Bob Wade, John Slaughter had tried to merge social development with basketball, but Wade brought further disaster. The enterprise was often too big and complex to serve anything but its own tightly focused goals. There were times, Slaughter thought, when the uplifting joy of sports was hard to find. There was too much scrambling for profit, too much heartbreak, too much back-stabbing. Young men were risking their lives in the long and the short run, and no one was intervening effectively to say, "Enough."

Slaughter remembered a night at Cole Field House in 1988, two years after Bias's death. He was sitting at his spot behind the large R for Maryland at the north end of the court, arms on the red-felt table cloth. Lew Perkins was sitting next to him. Suddenly he thought of Len Bias, as he often did.

"When are we going to hang Lenny's number?" he asked the athletic director.

Perkins looked at him with surprise.

"We already did," he answered.

Slaughter turned to his right to look up into the field house rafters. A Maryland jersey with the name BIAS and the number 34 beneath it hung there with the numbers of Elmore, McMillen, Lucas, and others whose records and performances had inspired Bias when he was still a high school kid selling ice cream and popcorn in the concession stands. Fearing controversy, Perkins had hung the jersey without ceremony. There were no photographs taken, no reminiscences exchanged, no newspaper stories written recounting the glorious Bias career. Nor had James and Lonise Bias been invited to see their son honored. There were no students, no John Slaughter, no Lefty, no admiring teammates.

No one at all to shout: "LEN-NEE, LEN-NEE, LEN-NEE."

Len Bias's Career Statistics at University of Maryland

Year	Games Played	Field Goals Made/Attempted	Percentage
1982-83	30	86/180	.478
1983-84	32	211/372	.567
1984-85	37	274/519	.530
1985-86	32	267/491	.544
TOTALS	131	83/1562	.536

Year	Free Throws Made/Attempted	Percentage	Assists	Blocked Shots
1982-83	42/66	.636	22	16
1983-84	66/86	.767	48	24
1984-85	153/197	.777	65	33
1985-86	209/242	.864	33	27
TOTALS	470/591	.795	168	87

Year	Steals	Personal Fouls/ Fouled Out	Rebounds Average	Points/ Average
1982-83	10	55/1	125/4.2	217/7.2
1983-84	13	81/3	145/4.5	488/15.3
1984-85	34	106/2	251/6.8	701/18.9
1985-86	27	90/2	224/7	743/23.2
TOTALS	84	332/8	745/5.7	2149/16.4

Appendix B

Chronology of Events

1986

- *June 19, 1986* -- Len Bias dies less than 48 hours after being drafted by the Boston Celtics.
- *June 23, 1986* -- Bias funeral is held in the campus chapel; a memorial service is conducted at Cole Field House at which the Rev. Jesse Jackson speaks.
- *June 24, 1986* -- State medical examiner says Bias died of "cocaine intoxication."
- *June 26, 1986* -- University of Maryland releases figures showing fewer than one-third of basketball team members were graduating.
- *June 27, 1986* -- Don Rogers, Cleveland Browns defensive back, dies of a cocaine overdose the night before his wedding.
- *June 30, 1986* -- Chancellor John Slaughter names task forces on drugs and the academic lives of athletes.
- *July 1, 1986* -- Grand jury begins to hear testimony on Bias death; newspaper publishes story about a Board of Regents report asserting that UM athletes were adequately educated.

- *July 3, 1986* -- Slaughter says that UM failed its athletes.
- *July 4, 1986* -- Freshman basketball player Tony Massenberg is declared ineligible after cheating allegation.
- *July 6-9, 1986* -- The *Washington Post* runs series on UM sports.
- *July 10, 1986* -- Questions raised about how cocaine was used at the last Bias party; possibility of free-basing suggested.
- *July 15, 1986* -- Terry Long and David Gregg subpoenaed by grand jury.
- *July 18, 1986* -- Allegations reported of consistent drug abuse among basketball team members.
- *July 21, 1986* -- State's Attorney Arthur "Bud" Marshall suggests point shaving may have taken place at UM.
- *July 24, 1986* -- Players Gregg and Long are indicted.
- *July 26, 1986* -- Brian Tribble, suspected of supplying the fatal drug to Bias, seeks refuge in Baltimore.
- *July 27, 1986* -- UM Athletic Director Dick Dull tells academic task force members that university coaches lack an academic philosophy.
- *July 29, 1986* -- Players Gregg and Long are suspended for the 1986-87 season.
- *August 13, 1986* -- Chancellor Slaughter postpones the season's start, and cancels two games and a holiday tournament.
- *August 17, 1986* -- James and Lonise Bias, Len's parents, testify before UM task force.
- *August 20, 1986* -- Coach Lefty Driesell; Driesell's lawyer, Edward Bennett Williams; and Chancellor Slaughter testify before grand jury.
- *August 26, 1986* -- Grand jury decides not to indict Driesell.
- *August 27, 1986* -- James Bias says in newspaper interview that the university failed to protect his son.
- *August 28, 1986* -- Slaughter says that James Bias's charges from day before deserve to be investigated.
- *September 5, 1986* -- Slaughter, Driesell, and Williams begin negotiating on Driesell's contract.
- *September 9, 1986* -- State's Attorney Marshall, lead prosecutor in the Bias case, is defeated for re-election.
- *September 25, 1986* -- Slaughter asks former UM provost Francis Staerk to investigate Driesell's contract.
- *October 1, 1986* -- Driesell mounts public effort to retain his coaching position.
- *October 2, 1986* -- Task force on student athletes releases report critical of coaches who, it says, put winning above all else.
- *October 7, 1986* -- Athletic director Dick Dull resigns; announcement made by Slaughter the next day.

- *October 9, 1986* -- A "Lefty Watch" begins in earnest; $3 million buyout of his contract reported to be under consideration.
- *October 15, 1986* -- Driesell polls the team to see if members want him to stay as coach.
- *October 16, 1986* -- Long and Gregg testify before grand jury.
- *October 17, 1986* -- Resolution of contract discussions near, Driesell's lawyer (Williams) says.
- *October 20, 1986* -- Criminal charges against Long and Gregg are dropped.
- *October 21, 1986* -- Slaughter endorses the task force recommendations.
- *October 25, 1986* -- Driesell says the Board of Regents refuses to meet with him; Regents Chairman Allen Schwait later relents, and personally meets with the coach.
- *October 28, 1986* -- Driesell resigns as coach; Slaughter says he will resign as chancellor only if Regents ask him to.
- *November 2, 1986* -- Slaughter names Bob Wade, coach of Dunbar High School in Baltimore, to replace Driesell.
- *December 2, 1986* -- Football Coach Bobby Ross resigns.

1987

- *January 12, 1987* -- Governor Schaefer defends Terrapin Club during State of the State Address.
- *February 24, 1987* -- Brian Williams, one of the most exciting basketball prospects at Maryland since Tom McMillen, is recruited by Wade; Rudy Archer, a promising guard, later signs, too.
- *March 2, 1987* -- Driesell gets award from the Maryland State Legislature.
- *March 6, 1987* -- Wade concludes his first season as coach (his team loses every ACC game, as expected). Governor Schaefer tells Regents Chairman Schwait he's unhappy because the team's not winning enough.
- *May 6, 1987* -- Wade is charged with attempting to "fire" Phil Nevin. Slaughter intervenes, saving Nevin's scholarship; Nevin transfers to Millersville.
- *May 7, 1987* -- New university policy on illegal drug use is announced.
- *May 8, 1987* -- Reformer Lew Perkins is hired as new UM athletic director.

1988

- *March 11, 1988* -- With Athletic Department facing $3 million deficit, Wade team concludes good season (his second), goes to NCAA championship tournament, and wins one game -- and quarter million dollar payday.

- *April 3, 1988* -- Slaughter resigns to become president of Occidental College in California; Driesell leaves to coach at James Madison University in Virginia.
- *September 5, 1988* -- Rudy Archer is suspended for poor grades.

1989

- *February 15, 1989* -- Tony Massenburg, once mired in academic trouble at Maryland, is saluted as member of ACC Athletic Directors' Honor Roll for achieving a 3.0 grade point average. Teyon McCoy is also honored.
- *February 20, 1989* -- Wade is accused of improperly providing rides to Archer; NCAA investigates.
- *May 28, 1989* -- Wade, charged with covering up and lying about his involvement in Archer matter, resigns. The deal: a $120,000 buyout, $5,000 in moving expenses, and a promise by the boosters to buy his $375,000 house at market value.
- *June 13, 1989* -- Maryland grad Gary Williams leaves Ohio State University to take the Maryland basketball coaching job, worth an estimated $400,000 a year.
- *August 4, 1989* -- NCAA says Maryland committed 18 separate violations of NCAA rules, including improper financial payments, improper gifts, assisting a recruitable athlete (Archer), and major lapses in "institutional control." College Park is banned from tournament play for two years and from television for one year.

1990

- *July 10, 1990* -- Lew Perkins leaves to take athletic director's post at the University of Connecticut.
- *August 10, 1990* -- NCAA rejects Maryland's appeal of penalties imposed; sanctions predicted to cost UM $3 million.
- *September 7, 1990* -- Andy Geiger, Stanford AD, hired by Maryland to replace Perkins.

1991

- *April 26, 1991* -- Athletic Director Geiger supports Admissions Director Clements' decision to reject three academically substandard basketball players seeking admission. At showdown later in the university president's office, boosters agree that the three players in question should have been rejected.
- *June 19, 1991* -- President Kirwan feels pressure from Regents; at about the same time, he rebuffs urging of Maryland Senate President Miller to roll back academic standards.

Notes

This book is based on more than 150 interviews with persons knowledgeable about the athletic program at the University of Maryland; on newspaper accounts of the problems at College Park; on official university documents; and on other materials. For the most part, the reader will find in the text itself the names of pertinent sources, as well as the sources for referred-to materials, studies, information, and opinions. When additional information seemed useful, or where a point appeared worthy of amplification, I have provided chapter by chapter end notes.

The following people were interviewed for *Lenny, Lefty, and the Chancellor*: Mark Hyman, Baltimore *Sun* reporter; Amy Goldstein, *Washington Post* reporter; Milton Kent, Baltimore *Evening Sun* reporter; Molly Dunham, *Evening Sun* reporter; John Hawkins, *Washington Times* reporter; Lon Babby, lawyer, Williams & Connolly; Linda Clements, University of Maryland Admissions Director; Carolyn Branch, mother of Adrian Branch, University of Maryland player; Charles G. Driesell, James Madison University basketball coach, and former University of Maryland coach; John B. Slaughter, former chancellor of the University of Maryland, College Park, and now president of Occidental College in Los Angeles, CA.; Arthur Marshall, former Prince George's County (Maryland) state's attorney; Jay Robert Dorfman, Dean of Students, and chairman of University of Maryland task force on student athletes;

Christopher Fordham, former chancellor, University of North Carolina; Steve Hale, former player, UNC; Alex Isherwood, former University of Maryland marketing department employee; and Randy Hoffman, former Maryland assistant athletic director.

Also: Alan Goldstein, the Prince George's County lawyer who represented players Terry Long and David Gregg; Ronald Shapiro, Baltimore lawyer; Kurt L. Schmoke, mayor of Baltimore, and member of task force on drug policy, University of Maryland; Allen B. Schwait, former chairman, University of Maryland Board of Regents; Frank A. Gunther, Jr., University of Maryland Board of Regents; Ben Unkl, student member, University of Maryland Board of Regents; Roz Hiebert, public relations director, University of Maryland; Aubrey Williams, University of Maryland anthropology professor; Barbara Bergmann, president, American Association of University Professors; Professor Peter Wolfe, University of Maryland mathematics professor; Phil Nevin, former University of Maryland basketball player; Jeff Baxter, former University of Maryland basketball player; Herman Veal, former University of Maryland basketball player; Dervey Lomax, friend to University of Maryland basketball, and former mayor of College Park, Maryland.

Also: Fred Frederick, auto dealer and member of the Terrapin Booster Club; Tommy Marcos, restaurant owner and member of the Terrapin Club; Marvin Mandel, former governor of Maryland and member of the Terrapin Club; Candy DiPietro, Terrapin Club member; Mike Anderson, Terrapin Club member; Bonnie Shields, Maryland graduate and fan; Andy Geiger, University of Maryland athletic director; Kit Morris, staff director, Knight Commission; Randy Hoffman, former assistant athletic director, University of Maryland; Richard (Dick) Dull, former athletic director, University of Maryland; Robert (Bob) Novak, columnist and member, Terrapin Club; Pam Harris, former aide to John B. Slaughter; Tim Gilmour, assistant to the president at Georgia Tech, and former Maryland vice chancellor under UM Chancellor John Slaughter; Jan McKay, president of Mills College, and former UM vice chancellor; William E. Kirwan, president, University of Maryland; Charles (Chuck) Sturtz, financial officer and former acting athletic director at College Park; and Delegate Timothy Maloney, Maryland House of Delegates.

Also: Delegate James Rosapepe, Maryland House of Delegates; Sylvania "Skip" Woods, former member, Maryland House of Delegates; John Toll, former president, University of Maryland; David Simon, Baltimore *Sun* reporter and former *Diamondback* reporter; Sterling Parker, AAU coach; Rob Correia, *Providence (R.I.) Journal* reporter; Thomas Morrow, lawyer for Brian Tribble; Melody Simmons, *Evening Sun* reporter; Lonise Bias, Len Bias's mother; James Bias, Len Bias's father; Wayne Curry, Bias family lawyer; Wilson H. Elkins, president emeritus, University of Maryland; Ray Gillian, University of Maryland vice chancellor; Professor Lonnie Kliever, Southern Methodist University faculty representative to the NCAA; Lee Madkins, Len Bias's recreation coach; Professor Joyce Joyce, English Department, University of Maryland; Denton L. Watson, author, *Lion in the Lobby*, a biography of civil rights leader Clarence

D. Mitchell, Jr.; Richard D. Lapchick, director, Center for the Study of Sport in Society; Judge Sam Meloy, Terrapin Club member; and Dr. Patricia Florestano, aide to Dr. John Toll, former university president.

Also: Rep. Steny P. Hoyer, congressman from Maryland's Fifth District; Rep. Benjamin L. Cardin, congressman from Maryland's Third District; Rep. Tom McMillen, congressman from Maryland's Fourth District; Emory Harman, head of the Fastbreaker booster club at the University of Maryland; Jack Heise, banker and longtime Terrapin Club member; Tom Fields, former chief fundraiser at the club; Ralph Bennett, former Faculty Senate president and architecture professor at the University of Maryland; Professor George Callcott, author of the University of Maryland history; Len Elmore, former University of Maryland player; Senator Thomas V. "Mike" Miller, Jr., president of the Maryland Senate; Shaar Mustaf, father of Jerrod Mustaf, former University of Maryland player and now a member of the NBA's Utah Jazz; Morgan Wootten, coach at Demotha High School; John L. Moylan, principal, Demotha High School; Jim Valvano, coach at NC State; Louis L. Goldstein, comptroller of Maryland; Hotsy Alperstein, furniture dealer and Terrapin Club member; Millard Baublitz, one of Dean Dorfman's star physics student; Protagoris Cutchis, another of Dean Dorfman's physics students.

Also: Sam Schoenbaum, head of the University of Maryland Renaissance Center; Ronald Carrier, president, James Madison University; Harry R. Hughes, former governor of Maryland; Ralph Frey, former Terrapin Club president and member of the Board of Regents; Ira Bloch, a UM professor of textiles, and member of a faculty committee studying the General Studies program; Katie Theus, UM journalism department; Dr. Dennis Smyth, former assistant medical examiner in Maryland; and Mike Burke, reporter, *The Cumberland Times*.

Maryland Governor William Donald Schaefer did not consent to an interview, but verified the accuracy of the book's portions relating to him.

Chapter 1, Dreams

Page 2 -- Within the outline of Bias's dream as he recounted it to reporters, I have taken the liberty of guessing how he must have felt when he thought he had over-slept the draft.

Page 2 -- Accounts of Bias's experiences during and after the 1986 NBA draft are drawn from newspaper accounts and from official NBA film. Larry Donald's comments, quoted in the text, were made during the draft.

Page 6 -- The projected earnings for Fentress's firm and his arrangements with Len Bias are drawn from an article by Bill Brubaker in *The Washington Post*. Court documents filed by Fentress in a suit brought by the Biases say the firm was to receive 20 percent of Bias's fees from Reebok. In connection with the dormitory room in which Bias's fatal cocaine party took place, Fentress said he advised having the room cleaned because he thought it should be presentable when the inevitable television cameras arrived. Fentress declined the author's repeated requests for an interview.

Page 13 -- Accounts of the fatal drug party are drawn largely from testimony given during the trial of Brian Tribble on cocaine charges.

Page 14 -- A tape of the 911 call was played at the trial.

Chapter 2, Crisis

Page 23 -- According to Vice Chancellor Tim Gilmour, who was present at the time, Maggie Bridwell, head of the campus health service, reported directly to Chancellor Slaughter on Bias's health record. From her review, she discounted the chance Bias had had a heart attack.

Page 28 -- Sometimes, when he walked into his office in the morning, Slaughter thought that former chancellor Byrd might have been taken aback at the turn history had taken -- that a black man had become chancellor of *his* university.

Page 30 -- The study on the athletic program was done for the university's Board of Regents and, while pointing out areas that needed improvement, it left the overseers confident they had a solid program.

Chapter 3, A Rose

Page 32 -- Driesell's prowess as a recruiter was legend, but he did not succeed with Malone, who wanted to be the first high school player to skip college and go directly to the professional game.

Page 37 -- At a memorial service for Len Bias, Presidential Candidate Jesse L. Jackson spoke about the threat of drugs in the black community. But Jackson also had views about the status of black athletes at American universities. During a meeting with black legislators in Maryland shortly after Bias died, Mr. Jackson offered a pithy assessment. People were fond of observing that athletes should be grateful for the scholarships they received. Commenting on the millions of dollars earned by athletes for their alma maters, Jackson said, "Our young men have the universities on scholarship."

Page 39 -- Prince George's County autopsy #86-999 says Bias probably consumed five grams of cocaine -- 3 to 6 times a fatal dose.

Page 39 -- Five years after Bias's death, after Los Angeles Lakers star Magic Johnson announced he had the AIDS virus, other National Basketball Association players saw something of a master plan. Johnson had declared his determination to be an educator on the threat of AIDS. His friends suggested

God needed a charismatic and strong individual to take on such a gargantuan chore.

Page 41 -- Congressional Quarterly said Bias's death provided irresistible leverage for passage of major drug-fighting legislation.

Page 46 -- There is no evidence to suggest an attempt by the university to hide Bias's academic status.

Page 48 -- The political connections and acumen of John Toll, the university president, may have headed off even more of a circus atmosphere at College Park in the days immediately after Bias's death. He says he convinced a number of legislators to allow the university time and space to deal with its problems internally. In fact, there were no legislative hearings, though some observers at the time attributed this forbearance to political calculations: Few wanted to risk the appearance of interfering in a volatile crisis involving sports, race, money and a major state institution -- the university.

Page 49 -- University of Maryland mathematics professor Peter Wolfe said Maryland is just a helpless partner of the National Collegiate Athletic Association, itself a cartel that exploits young men and women, many of them poor and black. If players were paid at an hourly rate derived from the monetary value of their scholarships, "they would do just as well delivering pizzas."

Page 49 -- Not everyone thought athletes were exploited by universities -- not by a longshot. In a 1990 study called "Light and Shadows on College Athletes," Clifford Adelman, a researcher at the U.S. Department of Education, concluded that the charge is false. Based on the economic status of athletes and others who graduated in 1972, Mr. Adelman found that "at age 32, ex-varsity football and basketball players had the highest rate of home ownership and the lowest rate of unemployment of all groups, along with earnings 10 percent above the mean for all former four-year college students." Given the fact that many of these athletes grew up in relative poverty, Adelman says the study's findings are even more striking. Those arguing the other side of the issue, however, say that the exploitation became most evident in the late 1970s and 1980s, when fewer athletes graduated and many who did graduate earned degrees of questionable value.

Page 56 -- Alan Goldstein, Long and Gregg's lawyer, and one of the most respected members of the Prince George's County bar, died in the summer of 1990.

Page 58 -- In his study of how athletes fare in life after college, Clifford Adelman, a researcher at the U.S. Department of Education, observes: ". . . No research grant ever brought to a university the national visibility that a Final Four or bowl appearance does, though how much such appearances have to do with the fundamental reasons colleges and universities were established in this country . . . is a mystery."

Page 58 -- Bob Bodell, president of the UM Basketball Alumni Association, wrote a letter defending his old coach (Driesell) on July 11, 1986, and suggesting that youth was to blame for Bias's death. "It is youth that is heady, addictable to the rush of attention, winning, press and potential pro contracts. The degree of vulnerability to this aspect of college basketball cannot be predicted. It depends on the mystery of what makes a person an individual. Perhaps we all played a part in that with Len Bias, and with every other young athlete who dares to be great in our eyes."

Chapter 4, Role Model

Page 61 -- In an interview with Ray Gandolf, an ABC-TV sports reporter and weekend sports anchor, NBA star Bernard King tried to offer his own definition of role model. Gandolf, citing King's recovery from alcoholism and serious knee injury, said he surely was such a role model. King said he didn't think so. Educators and engineers were the role models, he said. Gandolf, seemingly not getting King's meaning, suggested the star was just being modest. Perhaps, but Gandolf was making a point as well. What accounted for this role model mania? Was it another way of making sports more than mere games, more than mere entertainment? If the program were populated by role models, perhaps it was all right to make so much money from it.

Page 65 -- Observations about the attitudes of black Topekans in the early 1950s appeared in Simple Justice, Richard Kluger, Alfred A. Knopf, 1976.

Page 67 -- Employment and occupational statistics for blacks in Topeka in the early 1950s are taken from Simple Justice.

Page 70 -- The university learned later, partly as a result of the inquiry begun after Bias's death, that black students encountered substantial difficulties at College Park and did not fare as well as white classmates who had entered with comparable SATs.

Page 77 -- Clarence Mitchell, as a black reporter, covered the lynching of George Atwood. Atwood had been accused of attacking a white woman. A mob broke into the jail, seized him, and announced their plans for his fate. Mitchell arrived the day after Atwood was fatally beaten. The body had been burned and left outside, where Mitchell saw it. The mob wanted what they had done well-advertised. With Clarence Mitchell, they succeeded in a way they had not intended. Then and there, Mitchell became a civil rights activist -- a man later credited with helping to pass one of the landmark civil rights laws of the century, the Voting Rights Act of 1964. (Mr. Mitchell's life is chronicled by Denton L. Watson's Lion In the Lobby: Clarence Mitchell Jr.'s Struggle for the Passage of Civil Rights Laws, William Morrow, 1990.)

Page 77 -- In 1935, as a lawyer for the NAACP, Thurgood Marshall won admittance to the University of Maryland Law School for Donald Gaines Murray, a 22-year-old Marylander who had graduated from Amherst College. Officials in Maryland were suggesting that Murray might just as easily have gone to the law school at Howard in Washington, D.C.. Marshall himself had gone there. The counter-argument, however, prevailed. Since Murray wanted to practice law in Maryland, he thought it wise to study in Maryland. Of the university's opposition to Murray, H.L. Mencken wrote: "What the Regents really fear is that if the courts order Mr. Murray admitted to the law school, other negroes will appear for admission to the so-called college of arts."

Chapter 5, All World

Page 91 -- UM academic counselor Wendy Whittemore saw her view of athletes' academic aspirations confirmed by a 1989 NCAA study of black athletes. It found that black athletes generally came to college in search of an education that would lead to business careers. When pushed on their aspirations, only 7 percent of black athletes at predominantly white schools said they expected to play professionally. The study also found a considerable gap between players' objectives -- for graduation or for professional life -- and their academic standing. Thirty nine percent of those who said a degree was important to them had grade point averages of 1.99 or less -- below the level needed to graduate.

Page 94 -- The skit depicting the harried life of the college basketball player was performed by UM players Keith Gatlin and Len Bias; it was recited for Sally Jenkins of *The Washington Post*, who recorded it in one of her stories for the newspaper.

Page 95 -- Some might want to argue that the UCLA of the East was coached by Mike Krzyzewski at Duke University, rather than Dean Smith at UNC.

Page 100 -- After his years as a college basketball player, UNC's Steve Hale enrolled in medical school at Chapel Hill. Like Tom McMillen, Hale had his life-after-basketball carefully planned while still in college.

Chapter 6, Filling the Field House

Page 112 -- Bob Neall, whom Tom McMillen defeated for Congress in 1986, was elected executive of Anne Arundel County in 1990.

Page 123 -- Admissions Director Linda Clements said she was as impressed as Mrs. Branch was by Driesell's charm. Clements, who occasionally visited at the coach's home, thought of him as "Old Papa Driesell." At the same time, she thought he and other coaches just didn't understand the judgments made by admissions directors like herself. For them, she said, a student with a relatively low grade point average sometimes was a better prospect. The ultimate decision-maker, however, was Clements, and she stood by her decisions, no matter how much the coach protested. "The yelling never changed my decisions," she said. In a few cases, said Clements, Chancellor Slaughter overruled her. Later, she said, "I think he wishes he hadn't done it. He's such a decent man and a man who did so many good, courageous things."

Page 130 -- Vice-Chancellor Tim Gilmour says the central administration was unable then to track the academic progress of athletes. "Before the crisis, unless the athletic department tracked them, they weren't tracked," said Gilmour. In some cases, he said, athletes were allowed to drop courses they were failing at any time during the semester -- and then to sign up for independent study courses. This maneuver sometimes involved the further step of getting an incomplete in a course -- usually on the theory that some paper had not been finished. Since a failing grade meant no grade points, the freedom to drop a course at any time was a grade point average (GPA) saver of the first order.

Page 131 -- The idea that admitting sub-standard students was endemic, that every school was playing the angles, became the underlying self-justification for continuing business as usual.

Page 131 -- In 1987, Driesell declined to be interviewed for this book, citing a pending contract to write his own book, and a wish to save his stories and insights for then. But he agreed to entertain questions at a later time if research for my book raised questions. Calling in 1988 with such questions, I told him many of the people I had talked to were very complimentary of him, but that some were critical.

"You put their names in your book," he told me over the phone, "and I'll sue their ass. And if you don't put their names in the book, I'll sue your ass."

In 1990, I tried to reach Driesell through his lawyer, Lon Babby, who told me he thought it would be a good idea to have Driesell's side told. But both he and the coach were concerned about having the Bias tragedy dredged up again. I heard nothing further from either. In the summer of 1991, I made another attempt to reach Driesell, again through Babby. Babby said he would present the coach with a series of questions if I would provide them in writing. I did so and, I am happy to say, Driesell agreed to respond to many of them in a telephone interview.

Chapter 7, Low Point

Page 133 -- Those who yearned for better PR for the university were missing Schwait's point: He thought good PR would mean bad long-term outcomes, decisions made for short term gains in the public arena. "The Regents wanted a slow recovery and re-structuring," Gilmour says. "The only thing that would get us out, and get us out the way we wanted to be out, was the long haul."

Page 138 -- In the chancellor's office, the pressure was intense. Tim Gilmour, Slaughter's closest aide, thought his boss might have to resign. And later, he said, Slaughter took positions which all but invited boosters and politicians to seek his resignation. Within the university councils -- the vice chancellors and the Regents primarily -- Slaughter's willingness to risk firing gave confidence to those who were working with him, according to Gilmour.

Page 139 -- If Driesell's tantrums actually included spitting, no one but UM Professor Aubrey Williams mentioned it to the author.

Page 140-141 -- Slaughter dismissed suggestions that efforts to put more minority students on the College Park campus would undermine the overall quality of education there. Such suggestions were false and dangerous, Slaughter thought, a major impediment to increasing minority enrollment.

Page 149 -- In an interview with the author, former UNC Chancellor Christopher Fordham, one of Slaughter's friends and confidants, credited Slaughter with doing a solid job under enormous pressure. Neither Fordham nor any other president of an ACC university publicly praised or supported their Maryland colleague during the Bias crisis.

Chapter 8, Joining the Lynch Mob

Page 160 -- Wayne Curry, the Bias family lawyer, says Bias had scrapbooks with letters from elected officials urging him to attend the University of Maryland.

Page 161 -- Booster Bob Novak gave his views on the Maryland situation in a January 1987 phone interview.

Page 164 -- Former U.S. Senator Joseph Tydings told the Elmore story during a banquet for Driesell at Martin's Eastwind.

Page 165 -- On National Football League teams in 1990, blacks constituted 74 percent of the players, 18.5 percent of the head coaches (five of 27), and 0 percent of the team owners. *Source:* Center for the Study of Sport in Society.

Page 169-170 -- Boosters considered themselves especially qualified to opine on Maryland athletics if they had attended the Queen's Game in 1957. By that measure, I am also qualified, having been there as a University of North Carolina freshman. I remember game conditions as splendid, if a bit overcast. Because my mother is Canadian by birth, I had some vague feeling I should be suitably awed by the royal presence. I upheld my inherited responsibility.

Page 173 -- I was unable to determine the precise origin of the self-support concept. Though some think of it as state law, it is, instead, a policy matter whose utility is political *and* financial.

Page 174 -- University officials would like to have a fail-safe fund for those years when big-time teams don't measure up in the marketplace. Pressure on coaches, players and administrators would be relieved. At the same time, administrators would not welcome the loss of budget autonomy, which exempts the university from the close scrutiny of state fiscal advisers. If a $1 million or $2 million athletic fund were provided annually, Delegate Tim Maloney said, the state would want to know how the money was to be spent. And if the university permitted that sort of oversight, it might set a precedent for examination of other university accounts -- a loss, in other words, of the cherished autonomy. Sadly, the matter is moot, according to Maloney. Maryland's current financial condition is so dire that the legislature would not even consider changing the policy of self- support. "Not in a hundred years," he said. (*See next note for details.*)

Page 175 -- The prospects for relief from the policy of self-support grew more remote as state budgets fell deeply into debt in the 1990s. By the end of 1991, Maryland had cut its spending by more than $1 billion, and faced cuts of $700 million during the next fiscal year. Unfortunately, the cost of big-time college football and basketball is not regarded as a legitimate expense -- despite the proof that the lunch is not free.

Chapter 9, Outcasts

Page 179 -- To promote the basketball team, UM athletic department marketers needed such stars as Len Bias. One year, they used the massive Tony Massenberg, whom they referred to as a battleship; Walt Williams appeared a later year wearing a magician's outfit, underscoring his nickname, "The Wizard."

Page 185 -- According to Professor Ira Bloch, a UM professor of textile marketing, there were real problems with the General Studies major, even after efforts were made to rectify them. "We learned over time that there wasn't a lot of faculty oversight of this program. The counselors were overworked. In textiles, my department, we required a year of chemistry. Some textile majors would shift over into General Studies to avoid the chemistry requirement, and they would then advertise themselves as textile marketing majors." Also, Bloch said, because the program's requirements were "fuzzy," and, because counseling was poor, students were allowed to spend a lot of time in lower division courses.

Page 187 -- On their face, something was curious about Driesell's UM graduation figures: his players were arriving at College Park with extremely low SATs, and yet he claimed they graduated at twice the rate of the university proper, where students' SAT scores were, on average, hundreds of points above those of his athletes.

Page 187 -- Driesell claimed that his UM program was "solid" and "beautiful," though over its last ten years an increasing number of players did not graduate. Included among the non-graduates were Len Bias and Tom Jones, a senior in 1986 who later enrolled in summer school and in fall classes in an attempt to graduate.

Page 188 -- Discussing the academic standing of his players one day, UM Coach Lefty Driesell told *The Washington Post*: "Some of them, their writing is -- I don't even know how they got out of high school, tell you the truth."

Page 192-193 -- The comparison of overall minority enrollment in Division I universities and enrollment of minority athletes at those same institutions comes from Report #3 by the Center for the Study of Athletics, American Institute for Research, Palo Alto, California. The suggestion of minority athlete exploitation seems to be bolstered by this statistical comparison, which shows relatively low levels of minority enrollment, versus high levels of minority *athlete* enrollment. Minority athletes were recruited so much more assiduously and resourcefully than other minority students, it seems, because their athletic skills would help the coaches fill the arenas.

Page 192 -- "It takes virtually a heroic performance by a black athlete to graduate," says Richard Lapchick, head of the Center for the Study of Sport in Society. "They come into an alien atmosphere onto a predominantly white campus that has only 7 percent black students, and less than 1.6 percent black faculty ... Race and academics are the central issues in college sports today."

Page 193 -- Sister Mary Alan, Athletic Director at St. Anthony's High School in Jersey City, New Jersey, testified before a congressional committee (House Subcommittee on Education and Labor). She was also interviewed by the author. No one came to study her methods.

Page 194 -- Concerns about the human development of UM student-athletes were expressed in a letter written by UM academic advisor Larry Roper and quoted in *The Washington Post*.

Page 195 -- Vice Chancellor Ray Gillian's view that a "negative atmosphere" surrounded Maryland basketball was shared by various other observers.

Page 196 -- Chancellor Slaughter, whose high school advisers tried to steer him to vocational school, saw his life reflected in the lives of the athletes. In Darrell Brown, a forward on the earliest of Driesell teams, he saw a very close image of his own origins. Teachers had tried to push the chancellor into trade school, though he had said he wanted to be an electrical engineer. Slaughter escaped the forces of authority. Darrell Brown did not.

"I went to a predominantly black high school where the counselors felt that a person, especially a black youth, had more chance of making it with his hands than his mind," Slaughter told the *Washington Post*. "So they kind of gear you towards shops and things of that sort. Let me give you an example of what I took: I had auto shop, wood shop, and electric shop one year."

Page 197 -- UM basketball player Jeff Baxter wasn't fully accepting of assertions from Coach Driesell that he cared about his academic performance. A 1989 NCAA study found that only 31 percent of college athletes thought that their coaches sincerely encouraged academic achievement. Black athletes were the most skeptical.

Chapter 10, A Good Contract

Page 204 -- On paper and in advance, the chancellor mapped out his conversation with Driesell's lawyer, Edward Bennett Williams.

Page 205 -- Driesell's fringe benefits (what Williams referred to as "consequentials") were listed and totalled by the university as it tried to calculate the cost of removing Driesell from his job.

Page 205 -- Professor Barbara Bergmann, president of the American Association of University Professors, believes the money and other financial demands of the big-time coaches -- the domes, the weight rooms, school-guaranteed radio and TV packages, houses, and shoe contracts -- were a major reason for the commercialization of the university game. In response, the AAUP has adopted its own set of proposals to reform college athletics.

Page 208 --Many of those interviewed for this book were struck by Driesell's interest in making money, an interest as undisguised as his interest in winning basketball games. Ron Shapiro, the sports agent and lawyer in Baltimore, says he told Driesell he could not represent him unless he was available for unpaid community service assignments. Driesell, he said, balked. Milton Kent, then a student at the University of Maryland, wanted Driesell to appear on a campus radio show. The coach refused, saying he didn't want to do anything that "might take money out of my own pocket."

Page 214 -- UM President John Toll calculated what the political costs would be of ousting Driesell, and found them to be too high; those calculations were related to the author by Vice Chancellor Tim Gilmour.

Page 216 -- Big-time college athletes might find it difficult to use their university in the time-honored way -- for contemplation and self-discovery. Universities could erode their reason for being -- some said their soul -- by allowing money-making in the name of competition to deny their best efforts for any student.

Page 217 -- If Driesell had been more contrite about the alleged deficiencies in his program, he might well have put the university under greater pressure to retain him as coach. Being Lefty, though, meant never having to apologize.

Chapter 11, "Sack Slaughter"

Page 224 -- Billy Jones and Julius "Pete" Johnson became the first black players at Maryland and in the ACC when they joined the Terps' 1965 basketball team.

Page 225 -- Harry Edwards is the noted sociologist from the University of California at Berkeley, author of *The Struggle That Must Be* (Macmillan, 1980) and one of the first scholars to not only see the problems of big-time sports, but to demand solutions.

Page 225 -- In 290 big-time college basketball programs in 1987, blacks constituted 65 percent of the players, and 10 percent of the coaches. In football, they represented 55 percent of the players, and 0 percent of the coaches (two of 290). In all of Division I, there were four black athletic directors. Only a few majority white campuses, like Maryland, were headed by a black president or chancellor.

Page 225 -- Over the years, Maryland had several assistant coaches who were black, including George Raveling (the 1970s) and Oliver Purnell (during Driesell's long run as head coach). Raveling later became head coach at the University of Southern California (USC).

Chapter 12, Isolated Incidents

Page 246 -- During the summer of 1987, Georgia Tech Athletic Director Homer Rice observed appropriately that universities are more aware than ever of athletes' well-being. Just how concerned they should be was presented scientifically two years later in a study commissioned by the NCAA. The study found that football and basketball players spent an average of 28 hours a week on sports, 11 hours preparing for classes, and 12 hours in classes. Athletes missed an average of two classes per week during the season of their sport. Even out of season, athletes spent 18 hours a week practicing and working out.

Page 255 -- University of Maryland Professor Peter Wolfe thought the intercollegiate game continued in spite of all its problems because it served the financial empires built by coaches and athletic directors, who have controlled the NCAA. Wolfe urges professionalization, allowing players to wear the school colors but exempting them from the embarrassment of having to attend class. The AAUP's Barbara Bergmann agrees with this prescription. John Slaughter rejected the idea of "hired Hessians" roaring up and down the field. He thought that idea gave in to the forces that would keep black kids out of the classroom. He wanted to keep struggling to restore values, to downsize and to reclaim the games in all their ideal splendor. At the same time, he regarded the current state of affairs as shameful.

Chapter 13, Basketball Über Alles

Page 261 -- University of Alabama President Joab Thomas, pilloried and threatened for hiring a non-Alabaman to coach football, later became president of Penn State.

Page 262 -- In the spring of 1991, following the videotaped beating of Rodney King, and the national furor over it, Los Angeles Mayor Tom Bradley appointed Slaughter, then president of Occidental College, to a commission examining practices in the police department. "What I experienced when I first saw the videotape," said Slaughter, "was a feeling of horror and grief, followed by a protracted period of hopelessness from witnessing the ugliness and brutality." Slaughter eagerly accepted the Bradley appointment as an opportunity "to do something more than curse the circumstances that would allow a person to be so brutalized."

Page 263 -- The distracting power of sports -- sports as narcotic in national life -- is a subject that may deserve more attention. The thought of sport as a risk-free preoccupation is probably outdated. Unlike Walter Mitty, we seem to have risen from the rocking chair with a fantasy implant. Researcher Clifford Adelman, of the U.S. Department of Education, says, "It is a sign of our cultural values that the question of whether college athletes actually graduate is of greater concern in national policy than whether college students study any college-level math after high school (only half do), whether business administration majors study any international affairs or foreign languages (not much), or whether engineering majors have demonstrated proficiency in English sufficient to communicate with clients (they have not)." Mathematicians, business people, and engineers have a far greater impact on the quality of life in our nation than athletes do, Adelman says.

Chapter 14, Project Survival

Page 277 -- One of lobbyist Bruce Bereano's clients donated $50,000 to the university's business school. The school athletic department was allowed to count this contribution toward the $5 million in matching funds the school needed to raise for improvements at Byrd Stadium. Bereano says his client didn't want to give directly to athletics lest it appear to be favoring Maryland over other ACC schools.

Page 279 -- Bob Wade's three-year tenure as head coach at College Park was doomed from the start, according to the sportswriters. They may have been right, but not for the reasons they seemed to have in mind. Wade *could* recruit. He recruited a talented big man, something Driesell hadn't done for years. And his teams did well enough when he had talent; he did as well as Lefty under those circumstances. The problem was he seemed to drive away his best talent. Several

Wade players suggested that the coach didn't respect them. Slaughter had forced Driesell out because he thought Lefty didn't respect the young men. Irony suffused virtually every aspect of the UM basketball story.

Page 280 -- UM Athletic Director Lew Perkins said that the university and Chancellor Slaughter knew in advance of his financial arrangement with the boosters (they made full monthly payments on $90,000 of his mortgage), and that college lawyers had approved it. Slaughter insisted that he knew nothing of the deal.

Page 281 -- After being forced out at Maryland, Bob Wade was thought to be in line for the vacant head basketball job at Morgan State, his alma mater and a predominantly black institution in Baltimore. He was not selected, perhaps because of the sanctions that would be inherited by any school hiring him within five years. Instead, he took a job with the City of Baltimore's recreation department.

Chapter 15, Linchpin

Page 288 -- The 200-foot-long water fountain at the College Park campus is the centerpiece of a $3 million investment in the central mall's appearance since Bias's death. In addition, an $18 million College of Business and Management and School of Public Affairs building was under construction, as were three new administration buildings: a $13.6 million Animal Sciences Building; the $10 million A.V. Williams building for electrical engineering, astronomy and automation research; and a $9.7 million physical sciences laboratory.

Page 288 -- While defenders of intercollegiate sports argued that they provide an entry point for benefactors who otherwise would take no interest in universities, others said the involvement of sports could hinder fundraising efforts. Barbara R. Bergmann, 1991 president of the American Association of University Professors, says a professional UM fundraiser became visibly upset when she asked him about the relationship of sports and university giving. More would-be givers were deterred than encouraged, said the fundraiser.

Page 289 -- According to UM President William E. Kirwan, Maryland's higher admission standards for athletes, as well as tougher, meaningful progress-toward-graduation requirements, in time, will make it more competitive in its quest for good athletes. In the fall of 1990, solid students were successfully recruited by both the football and basketball coaches, despite boosters' moaning that the higher standards hurt the recruiting process. The boosters remained skeptical, but Kirwan says Maryland has become a leader. And, indeed, the NCAA is scheduled to adopt progress-toward-graduation rules in January 1992 similar to those in effect at College Park.

Chapter 16, Full Circle

Page 301 -- Maya Angelou's comments are from her book, *All God's Children Need Traveling Shoes*, 1987, Vintage Books.

Page 301 -- Information related to Jay Bias's association with Brian Tribble comes from *Cumberland Times* sportswriter Mike Burke, who told the author he heard about it from Bob Wagner, who was high school basketball coach of both Bias brothers.

Index

About the Author

C. Fraser Smith has covered Maryland politics for the Baltimore *Sun* since 1983.

During his 28-year career as a reporter, including stints with the *Jersey Journal* and the *Providence Journal*, he has received AP, Sigma Delta Chi, UPI, and other journalism awards. In 1969, he used an American Political Science Association Public Affairs Fellowship to spend a year in graduate study at Yale University.

Smith has freelanced for a wide range of magazines, such as *Sports Illustrated*, *Change Magazine*, the *Rhode Islander,* the *Sunday Sun Magazine*, and *Regardie's*.

In Maryland, he is best known for an eight-part, 22-article Baltimore *Sun* series in 1980 on what he termed Baltimore's "shadow government" -- a little-known development bank that helped finance Baltimore's renaissance.

Smith played high school basketball, college football, and college track and field (the latter two at the University of North Carolina, where he earned his undergraduate degree).

He lives with his family in Baltimore.